GRAND STAND 5

Design for Trade Fair Stands

FRAME PUBLISHERS

CONTENT

Apparel

Architectural Products

Consumer Products

Electronics

Interior Products

Lighting

Materials

Mobility

Services

Shoes & Accessories

Telecom

APPA

APPAREL

FALKE
Keggenhoff | Partner

1 A glossy dark inner world contrasted strikingly with the radiant white exterior.

2 The eye-catching mysterious white structure aroused visitors' curiosities as to what lay inside.

3 The textured, interconnected surface of the structure resembled a cubist painting.

2

TRADE FAIR **ISPO**
WHERE **Munich, Germany**
WHEN **July 2011**
DESIGNER **Keggenhoff I Partner**
STAND CONSTRUCTOR
Innenausbau Biermann
CLIENT **Falke**
MARKET SECTOR **Socks and bodywear**
TOTAL FLOOR AREA **200 m²**
PHOTOGRAPHER **Constantin Meyer**

3

Ergonomics is at the core of Falke's sportswear named the ESS Collection (Ergonomic Sport System), which focuses on the idea of clothing that adapts to human physical processes. At the 2011 ISPO sports exhibition, Keggenhoff I Partner was briefed by the global knitting company to design a visual stand that reflected this approach. Abstract notions of structure, movements, connections and physicality of the human body formed conceptual starting points of the design, a striking stacked white structure that enveloped the entire presentation. Aptly entitled 'House of Cards' the stand presented itself as an interconnected modular installation. Vertical HPL panels of differing heights balanced delicately on top of each other in varying configurations. A beautiful play of light and shadow resulted from the structure's angled planes and slotted connections; unfolding across the stand its surface resembled a white cubist painting. Cleverly engineered to be self-supporting, the structure stretched at some points to seven metres high. The closed exterior gave little indication of what awaited inside, interrupted only by two controlled openings. A glimpse of a row of mannequins positioned strategically inside the main entrance triggered visitors' curiosities to enter. Once inside a black contrasting world was revealed. This dark realm intensified the vibrant colours of the collection's products; dramatic reflections in the dark floor added depth and a contrasting glossiness. Dark visuals on the walls depicted images of athletes in motion. The linear layout of the interior echoed the stand's aesthetic where three long rows of displays for socks formed the focal point. Mannequins were positioned inside the niches of the inner face of the white structure, the high faceted surface forming a stunning backdrop in this dynamic presentation. ⮕

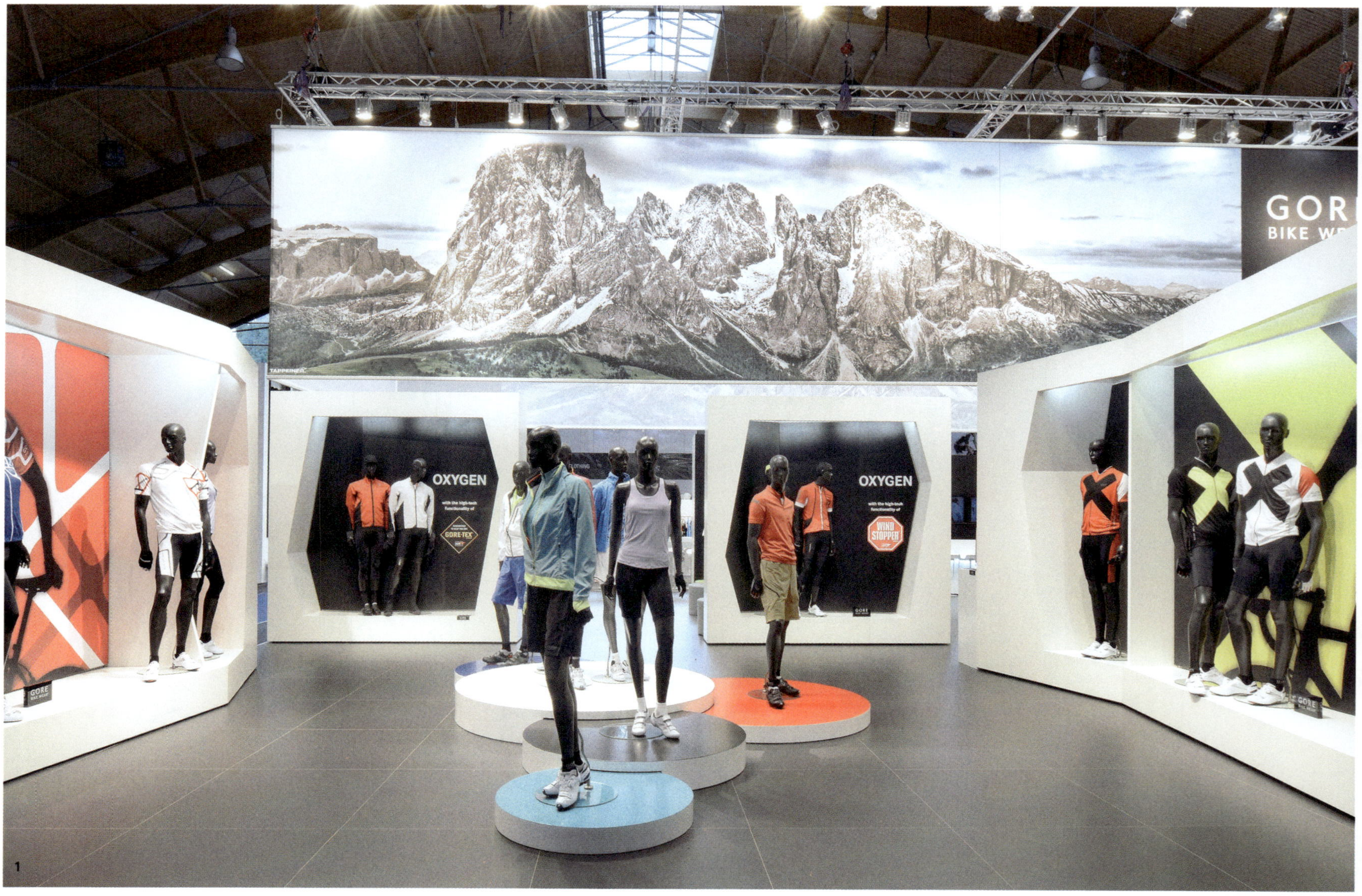
OXYGEN
OXYGEN
1

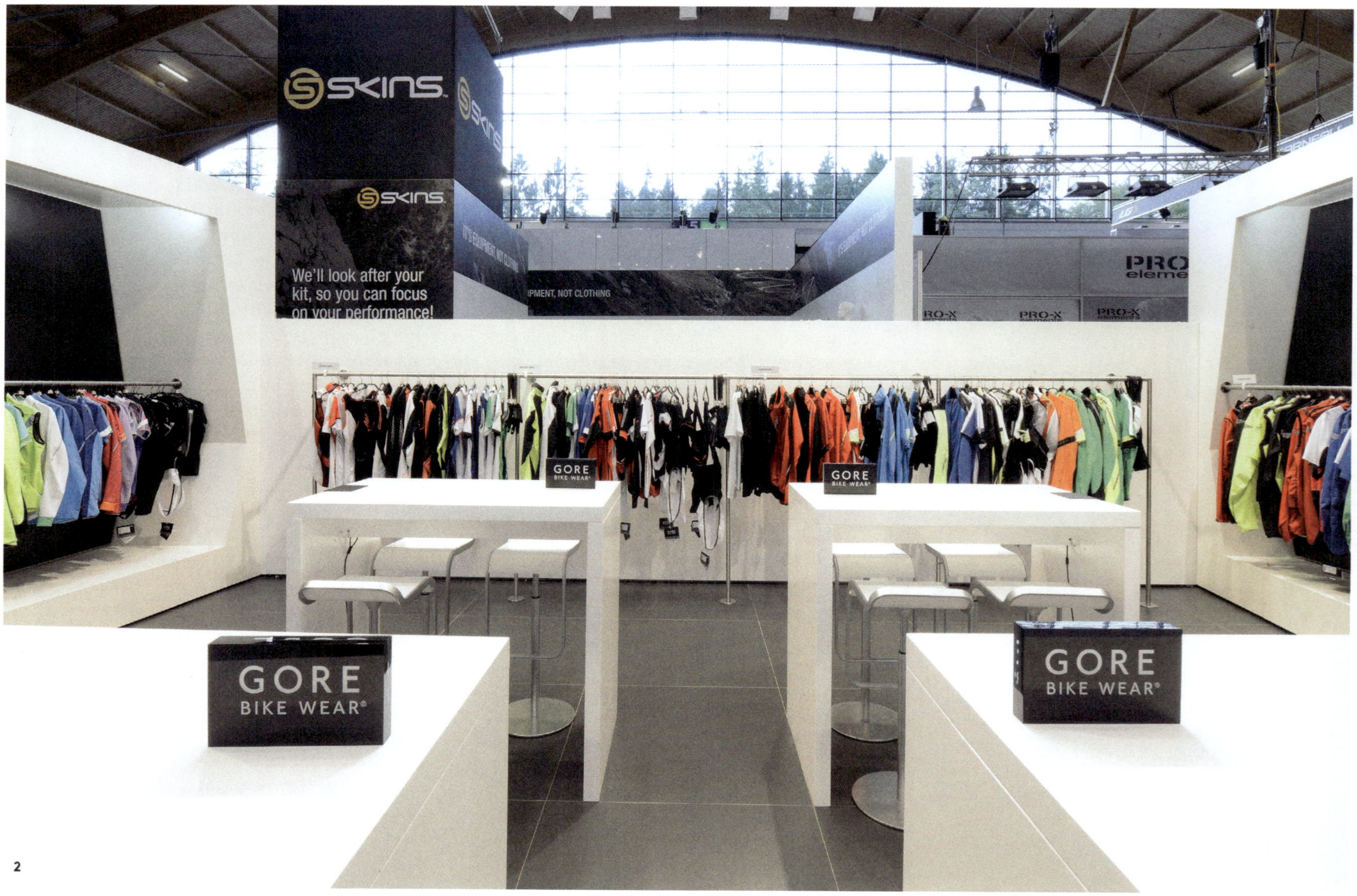
skins.
skins.
We'll look after your kit, so you can focus on your performance!
GORE BIKE WEAR
GORE BIKE WEAR
GORE BIKE WEAR®
GORE BIKE WEAR®
2

GORE
Arno Design

1 The colours of the clothing matched the showcases to ensure a coherent presentation.

2 A calm white background was the ideal basis for presenting the colourful garments.

3 Clusters of circular seating provided informal meeting areas.

3

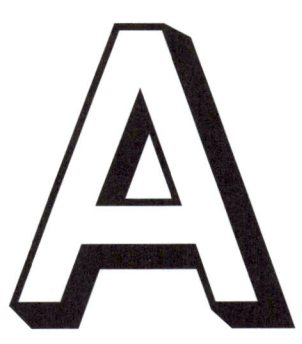

An impressive suspended mountainscape set the scene for Gore's presentation of bike wear at Eurobike, a leading trade fair for the cycling industry. Arno Design was entrusted with the task of designing the stand to clearly showcase new product lines for the 'Road' and 'Mountain'. The largely open stand was organised into three distinct areas. One side hosted the product presentation area, a sales showroom was situated at the opposite end of the stand and an open forum was positioned centrally. Four product families were showcased that year: Road Ambitious, Road Performance, Mountainbike Ambitious and Mountainbike Performance. On the exterior of the booth, oversized illuminated photographs depicted mountain bikers biking on mountainous terrain, showing the apparel in action. The open, central forum welcomed visitors onto the stand. A palette of black and white dominated the space in line with the company's corporate colours. High showcases in black and white were used for presenting products and doubled as partitions to structure the space. The irregular angles of the niches lent the displays a dynamic quality, their angular quality perfectly echoing Gore's corporate identity. To accentuate the products, the main clothing colours such as yellow, red and green were applied to the backdrops of the showcases. Contrasting with the angular showcases were circular felt seats and pedestals in sporty colours. In the showroom, the minimal white interior provided a calm background for displaying the brand's vibrant collection of bike wear. Here the showcases were extended to create more privacy in the space. Black floors ensured continuity through the space. ⚊

TRADE FAIR **Eurobike**
WHERE **Friedrichshafen, Germany**
WHEN **August 2014**
DESIGNER **Arno Design**
STAND CONSTRUCTOR **Arno Design**
CLIENT **Gore**
MARKET SECTOR **Sportswear**
TOTAL FLOOR AREA **280 m²**
PHOTOGRAPHER **Frank Kotzerke**

KHUJO
Werkstatt65

1 The Khujo House symbolised the home away from home for the company's founder.

2 The stand's bold black architecture distinguished Khujo's presence at Bread & Butter.

2

While fairgoers are accustomed to receiving cool goodies at fairs, those who visited Khujo's bold presentation at Bread & Butter in 2014 received a gift they'll never forget: a tattoo. Welcome to the Khujo House. During the event visitors were invited to – if they dared – get a permanent memento of their visit at the stand's pop-up tattoo parlour. This touch of edginess paired with a raw, industrial aesthetic and a hint of the American West definitely made the stand the talk of the show. Perfection through imperfection and eye on detail are the label's main design principles, coupled with a focus on materials and forms that tell a strong story. Werkstatt65's design clearly encapsulated these core values. An archetypal American timber barn formed the basis of the stand; painted black inside and out, its strong architecture distinctly stood out. While the structure enclosed a separate realm within the hall to host the presentation, its design and construction were kept more open to maintain contact with its surroundings. Two large openings punctured the facade. One was intersected with the white profile of a house that formed the entrance. The other accommodated a shop window where visitors could see the tattoo artist in action. The atmospheric interior comprised different rooms used to present the collections; here robust materials and thoughtful detailing featured prominently. Glass-and-steel windows evoked interiors of industrial warehouses and workshops. Steel was also used to construct the greenhouse that served as the bar – and social hub – which was accompanied with a ceramic-and-timber counter. Wide timber floorboards added a warm, rustic feel. Design classics and vintage pieces furnished the lounge area in the shop window. Vintage workshop benches were transformed into showcases that displayed the clothing almost as pieces of art. ⟶

TRADE FAIR **Bread & Butter**
WHERE **Berlin, Germany**
WHEN **July 2014**
DESIGNER **Werkstatt65**
STAND CONSTRUCTOR **Werkstatt65**
CLIENT **Khujo**
MARKET SECTOR **Clothing**
TOTAL FLOOR AREA **300 m²**
PHOTOGRAPHER **Inga Powilleit**

3 A well-detailed glasshouse bar was the life of the party on the stand.

4 The stand's design perfectly captured the essence of the brand, especially the focus on detail.

5/6 A restrained palette of robust and honest materials complemented the label's ethos and aesthetic.

4

5

A RAW, INDUSTRIAL AESTHETIC CROSSED WITH A HINT OF THE AMERICAN WEST

6

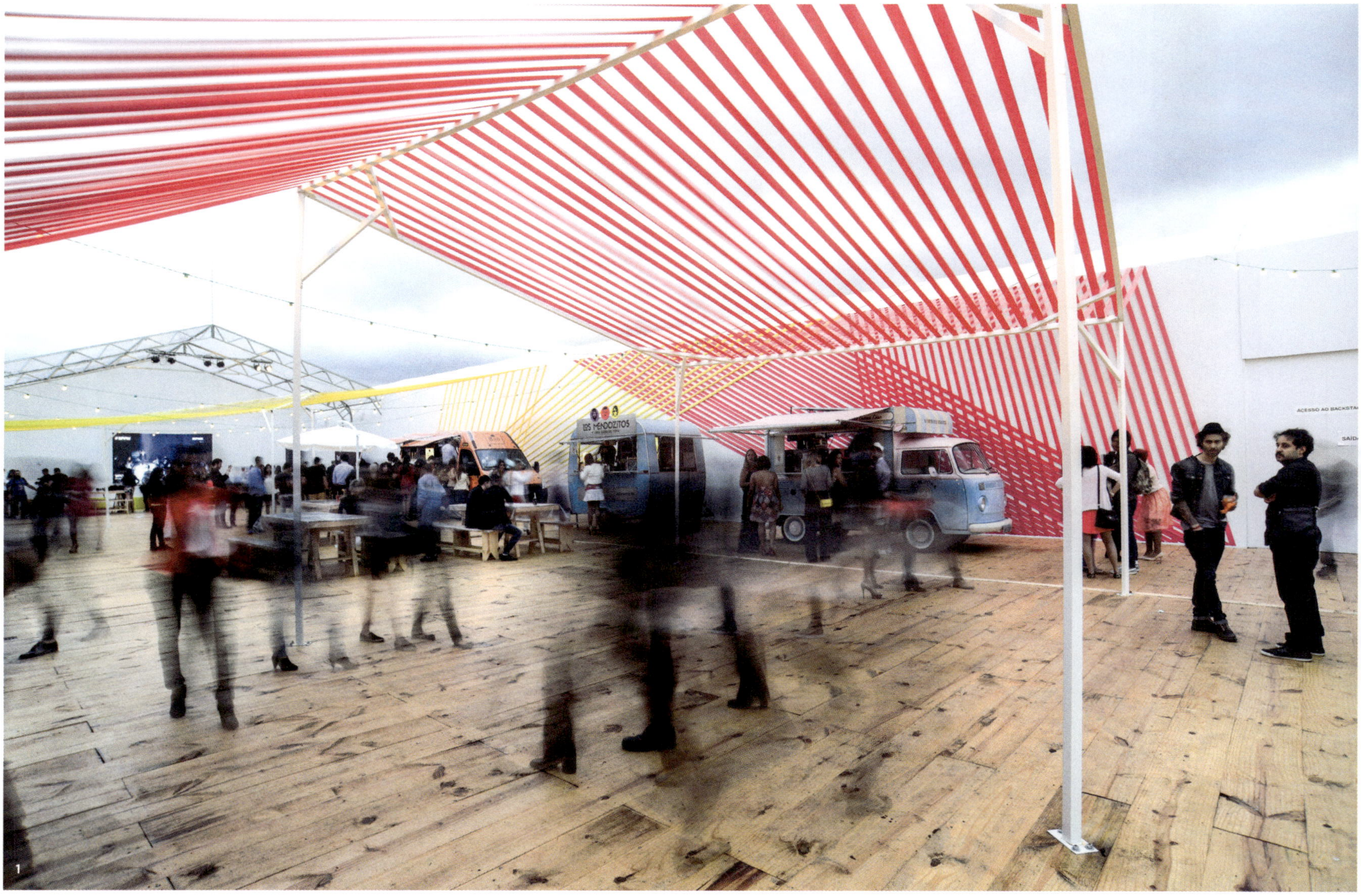

1

2

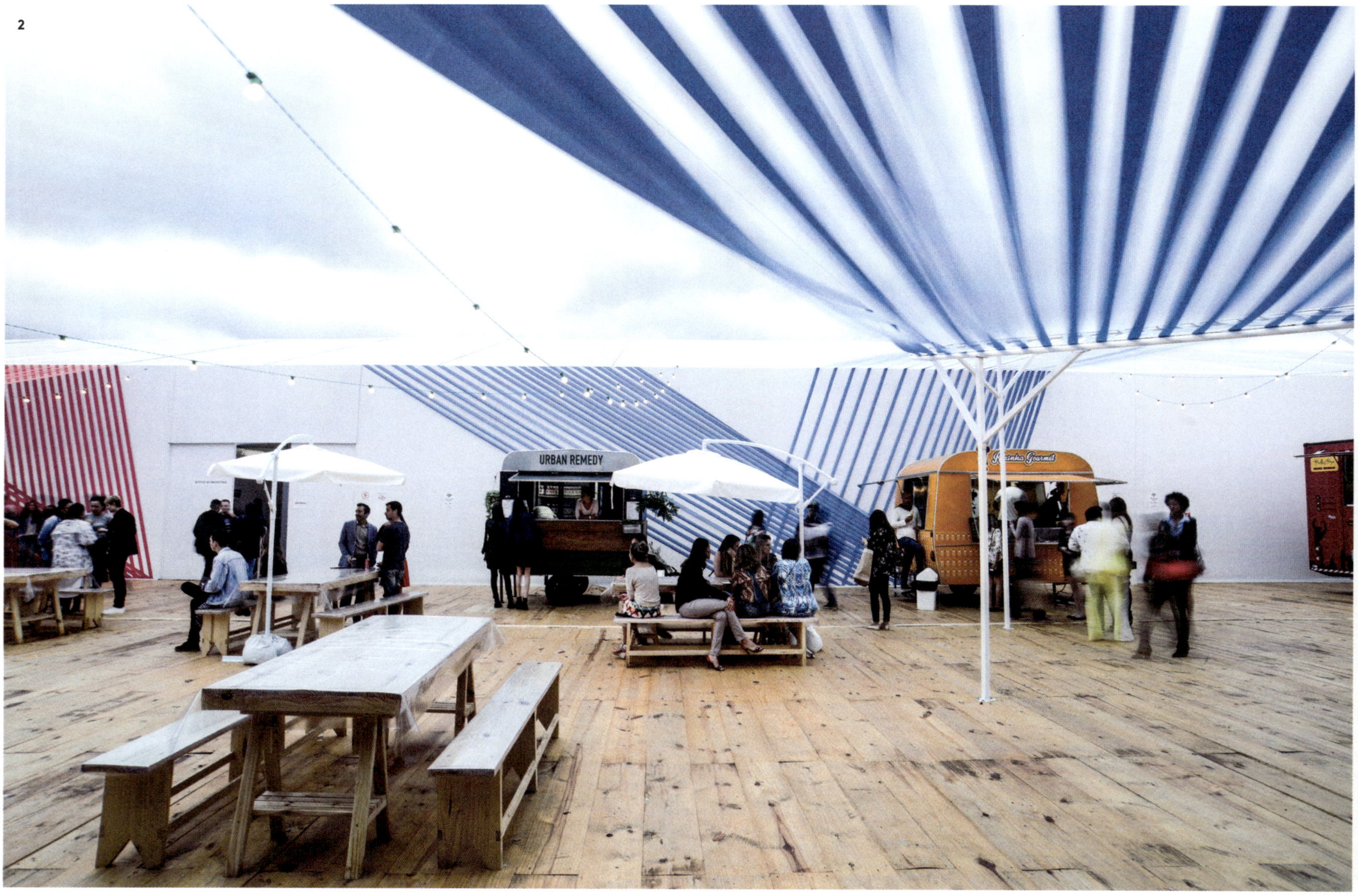

LUMINOSIDADE
Atelier Marko Brajovic

1/2 The festive courtyard formed the social hub of the event.

3 The multicoloured elastic stripes expressed both the tension and connection of geometries.

TRADE FAIR **São Paulo Fashion Week**
WHERE **São Paulo, Brazil**
WHEN **November 2014**
DESIGNER **Atelier Marko Brajovic**
STAND CONSTRUCTOR **Fresh**
CLIENT **Luminosidade**
MARKET SECTOR **Fashion**
TOTAL FLOOR AREA **10,000 m²**
PHOTOGRAPHERS **Atelier Marko Brajovic and Agencia Fotosite**

3

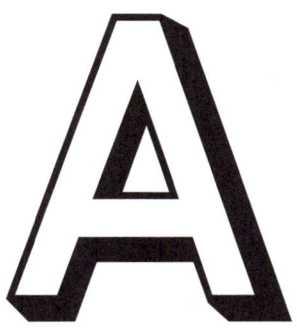

Atelier Marko Brajovic was commissioned by Luminosidade, creators of São Paulo Fashion Week (SPFW), to infuse an element of art into the set of the summer edition of the event. The initial research began with the first modern experimentations at the intersection of costume design, art and performance. The inspiration for the concept derived from Oskar Schlemmer's avant-garde ballet entitled Triadisches Ballett (Triadic Ballet) that dates from the Bauhaus. Ideas of choreographed geometry and the stylised movements of actors explored in the ballet were translated by Atelier Marko Brajovic into a dynamic, colourful design. The identity of this edition was characterised by CMYK stripes made from thick elastic bands that took over the festival architecture and outdoor space. The stripes began at the SPFW logo on the front of the main tent and travelled across the exterior walls, generating a sense of movement across the structure. On the way the stripes popped out to mark the main entrance. From the highway, the tent structure appeared as an unusual, colourful object. The main component of the project focused on the open courtyard space that connected all the different functions of the structure and formed the social hub of the event. In this central patio, the stripes bounced off all surfaces to both create tension and connection of the elastic geometries across the space. Spanned across the courtyard, the stripes functioned like pergolas that provided shelter and created a sense of intimacy. Plywood furniture and floors added a casual feel. The colourful intervention lent a distinctive visual identity and an artistic and festive atmosphere to the event. ▭

RICH & ROYAL
Blocher Blocher Shops

1 A palette of black, grey, metal and gold characterised the design.

2 The concrete bar formed the meeting hub of the space.

3 The outer walls were composed from black scaffolding connected with gold-coloured joints.

2

Glamour met Rock at Rich & Royal's presentation at Bread and Butter 2014. Led by this theme Blocher Blocher Shops developed an eye-catching exhibition stand that encapsulated the essence of the womenswear brand. In true rock style glamour, a palette of black, grey and gold dominated the design. The interplay of open and closed surfaces added a sense of liveliness to the space. Placed centrally a monolithic concrete bar formed the focal point of the space, surrounded on the concrete floor by ornamental tiles that resembled a rich tapestry carpet. Suspended overhead was a 3D metal sculpture whose form was translated from the company's logo. Two curved mirrors on the ceiling reflected distorted views of the stand. The open outer sides of the stand were occupied by towering scaffold-like shelves of black steel with gold-coloured brass connections, the bling of the connections alluding to the glamour factor of the brand. Apparel was hung from the lower scaffolds while mannequins and black utility trunks (often used by musicians on tour) filled with lush plants took over the upper sections. Stage spotlights, inspired by rock concerts, highlighted the fashion in a dramatic light. With the texture of oversized lacework full height metal screens with a laser-cut pattern inspired by the company logo created a striking backdrop for two of the walls. The rear wall was covered in a traditional panelled wall that integrated several display niches. Painted in a rough finish, the solid wall provided a calm contrast to the dynamic space and functioned to anchor the presentation. The stand not only made a lasting impression on visitors but also gave a sneak peek of the label's new store concept. ⟶

TRADE FAIR **Bread & Butter**
WHERE **Berlin, Germany**
WHEN **July 2014**
DESIGNER **Blocher Blocher Shops**
STAND CONSTRUCTOR **kubix**
CLIENT **Rich & Royal**
MARKET SECTOR **Womenswear**
TOTAL FLOOR AREA **150 m²**
PHOTOGRAPHER **Joachim Grothus for Blocher Blocher Shops**

APPAREL

GRAND STAND 5

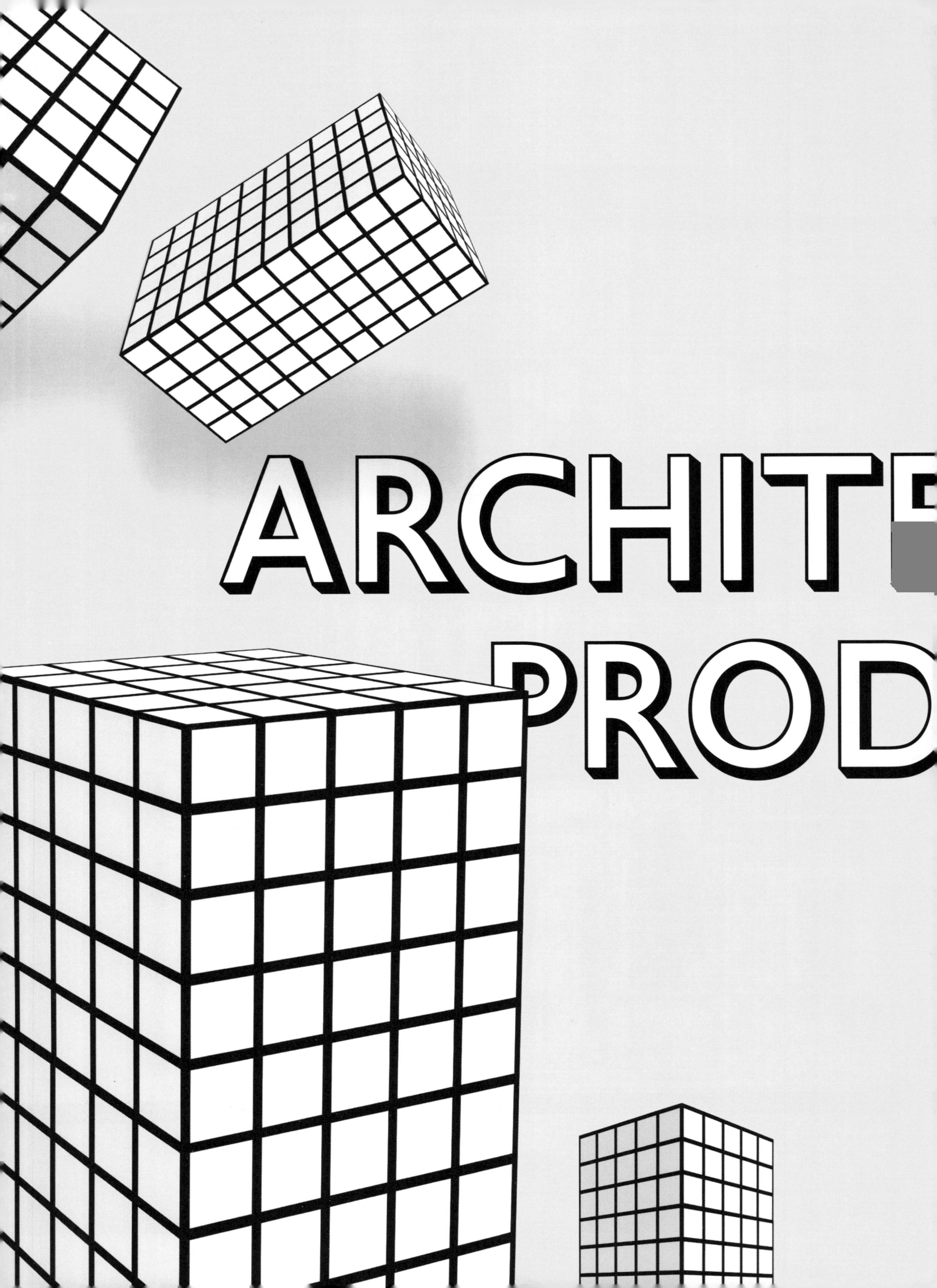

ARCHITE
PROD

BURKHARDT LEITNER CONTRUCTIV

Ippolito Fleitz Group

1 A cloud of speech bubbles featuring quotes from friends, colleagues and partners greeted visitors at the entrance.

2 Burkhardt Leitner's minimalist modular architecture systems were the focal point of the stand.

2

Burkhardt Leitner's stand at EuroShop 2014 showcased creative ways of employing its modular architecture systems. This year, the company's core strengths – precision, innovation and modularity – took centre stage. Adopting the motto, 'In Love with Detail' designers Ippolito Fleitz Group framed surprising new ways of employing the company's functional, minimalist system architecture to appeal to new and existing audiences.

The square stand was composed of different cubes, structures and objects, each constructed from a different Burkhardt Leitner system. With its architectural focus, the stand appeared as a mini illuminated cityscape. Black and white dominated the design, punctuated by bright bursts of colour, lush plants and

mirroring. Different stretched fabrics and lighting were playfully paired with each system to create special effects. Stretched across a high framework, the mysterious dark outer skin paired transparent gauze with a textured viscose inner lining. It created a uniform, eye-catching exterior to bring together the presentation.

An opening in the outer skin marked with a perpendicular mirrored wall formed a distinct main entry point. From here, visitors proceeded under the speech bubbles towards a reception counter. Its printed glass front listed design awards won by Burkhardt Leitner; a colourful six-metre-high modular wall formed the backdrop behind. Two protruding volumes showcased two different systems. A bright white box was wrapped in transparent white gauze to reveal the structure underneath. Inside, the rainforest of tropical plants provided a green oasis within the bustle of the fair. With walls of dark wood and dark finishes, a second volume presented one of the company's mobile space systems in a high-end

manner. A third glazed volume displayed a collection of mementos designed by the company's founder for his employees over the years, honouring the occasion of his seventieth birthday. A long patterned counter served as the social heart of the stand. ⇒

TRADE FAIR **EuroShop**
WHERE **Düsseldorf, Germany**
WHEN **February 2014**
DESIGNER **Ippolito Fleitz Group**
STAND CONSTRUCTOR **Format Atelier fur Messe+Design**
CLIENT **Burkhardt Leitner constructiv**
MARKET SECTOR **Modular architecture system**
TOTAL FLOOR AREA **182 m²**
PHOTOGRAPHER **Zooey Braun**

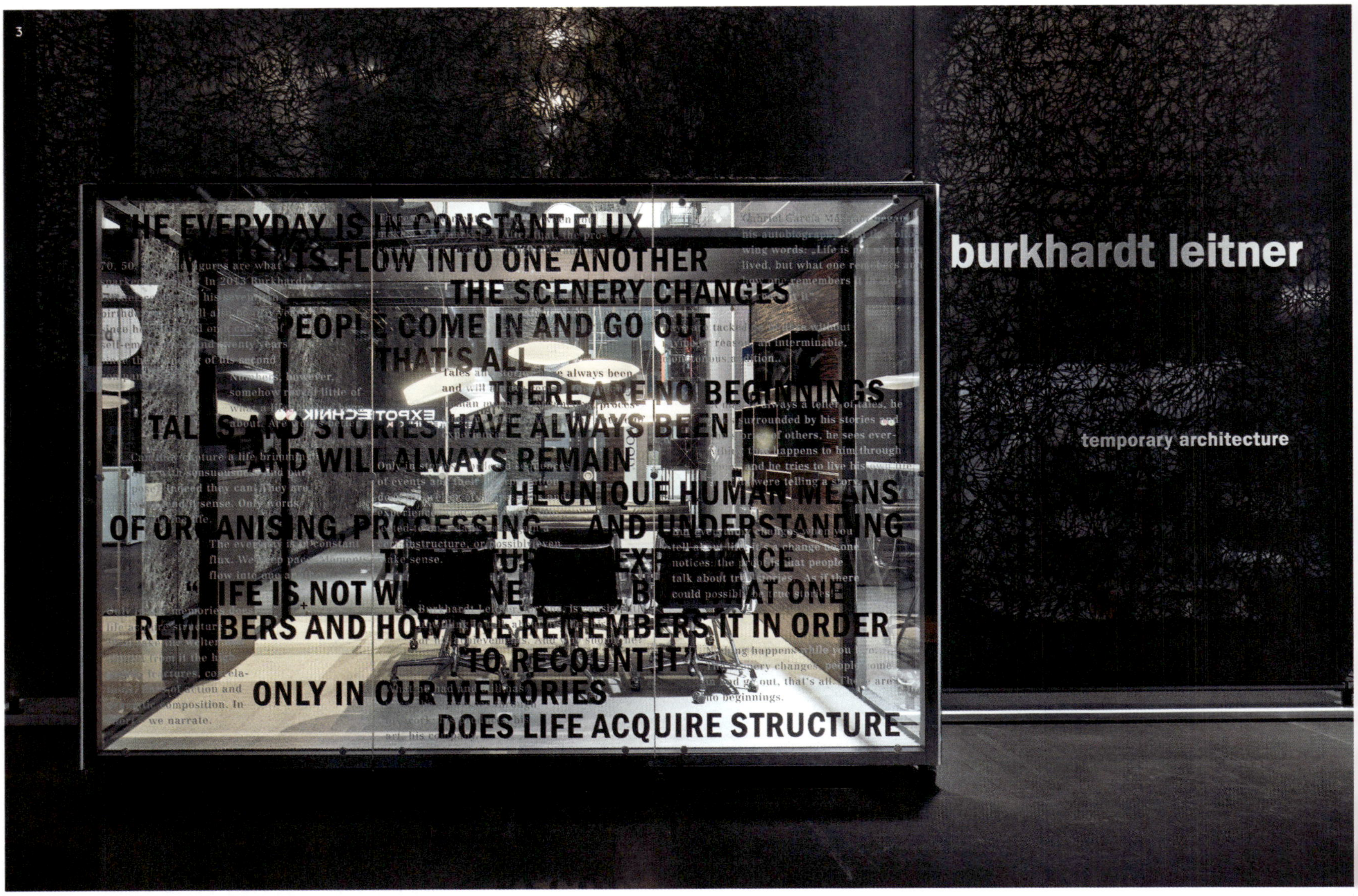
THE SCENERY CHANGES
THAT'S ALL
ONLY IN OUR MEMORIES
DOES LIFE ACQUIRE STRUCTURE
burkhardt leitner
temporary architecture
3

4

5

6

3/4 The volume presenting the mobile space system pops out of the stand.

5 Dark wood in the enclosed mobile space volume suggests warmth and luxury.

6 A six-metre-high framework behind the counter featured colourful new rotating wall elements.

THE DESIGN ADOPTS THE MOTTO: 'IN LOVE WITH DETAIL'

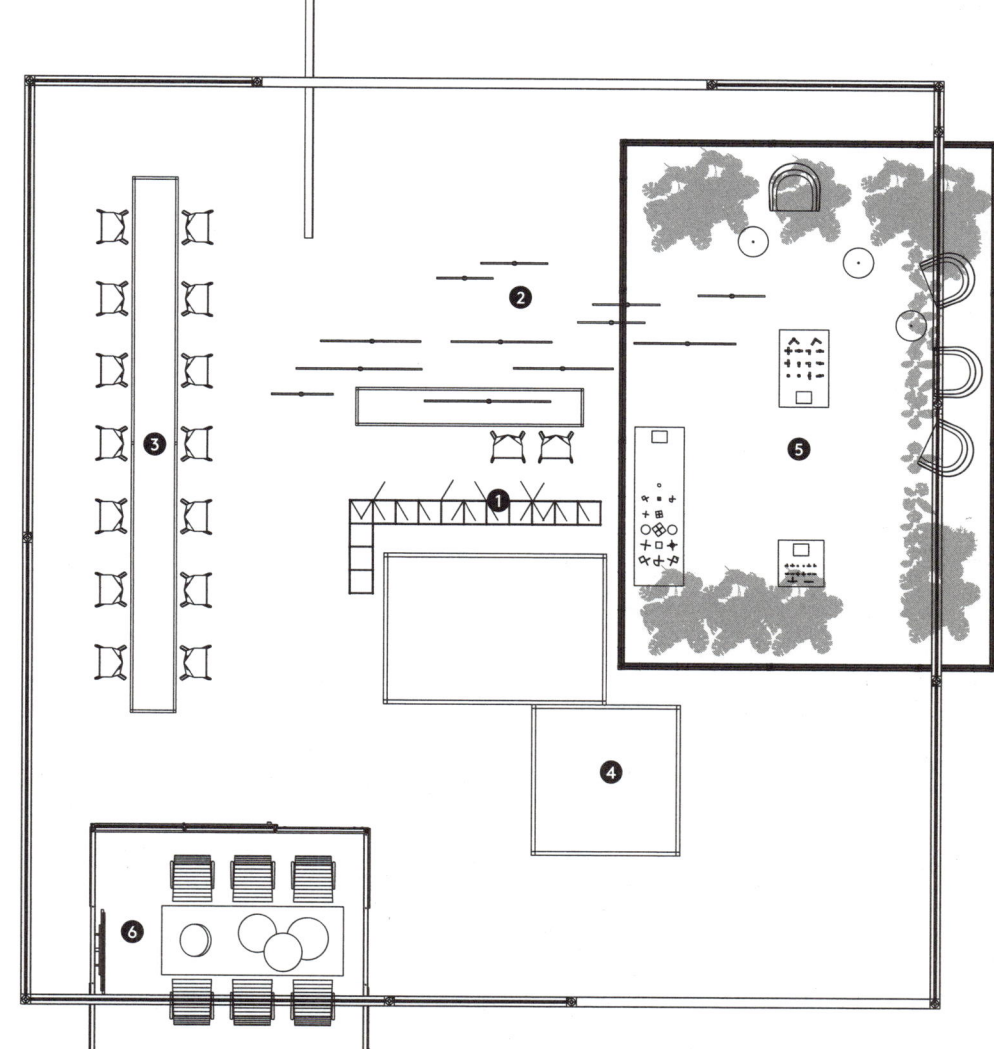

FLOOR PLAN

01 Reception area
02 Speech bubble cloud
03 Communication area
04 Homage tower
05 Glasshouse
06 Ottobox presentation

ARCHITECTURAL PRODUCTS GRAND STAND 5

EDUARD KRONENBERG

BachmannKern & Partner

1/2 The playful composition of frames resulted in a dynamic layering of space.

3 Showcases incorporated into the work table displayed the connectors as loose elements.

2

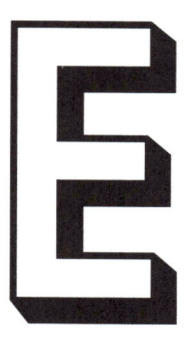

Eduard Kronenberg's focus lies in steel connectors and system solutions for the glass industry. Its appearance at Glasstec, the international trade fair for glass production, processing and products, was represented by an expressive design that encapsulated the company's modern spirit and professional expertise. In its design, BachmannKern & Partner focused on communication, sales presentation and innovation, central themes of this exhibition. An oversized cut-out of the company's logo formed the principal element of the space, giving immediate brand presence and arousing visitors' curiosities. The simple palette of white and red – the corporate colour – applied in block colour contributed a smart, contemporary look that perfectly reflected the brand's identity. Huge white frames positioned on the perimeter of the stand seemed to unfold from the logo. These slanted frames were used to creatively showcase the metal connectors which were installed on the inner faces of the frames, like in a window. Intersecting each other, the frames lent the space a playful dynamic, and also captured views into and outside the booth. The compact interior was kept open to provide space for mingling and interaction, focusing on a central work table with integrated product showcases. Visitors could also engage with staff at the long white information counter marked with a high red backdrop with the logo in white. Besides the frames and table, full-sized windows embedded in the back wall could be pulled out to show the products in practice. Echoing the palette, red and white lounge furniture invited visitors to take a break. Unexpected and contemporary, the stand elevated the connectors to a new level, turning a utilitarian product into a playful prop. ▬

TRADE FAIR **Glasstec**
WHERE **Düsseldorf, Germany**
WHEN **October 2014**
DESIGNER **BachmannKern & Partner**
STAND CONSTRUCTOR **Manuel de la Rosa**
CLIENT **Eduard Kronenberg**
MARKET SECTOR **Glass**
TOTAL FLOOR AREA **104 m²**
PHOTOGRAPHER **Frank Dora (photoprop)**

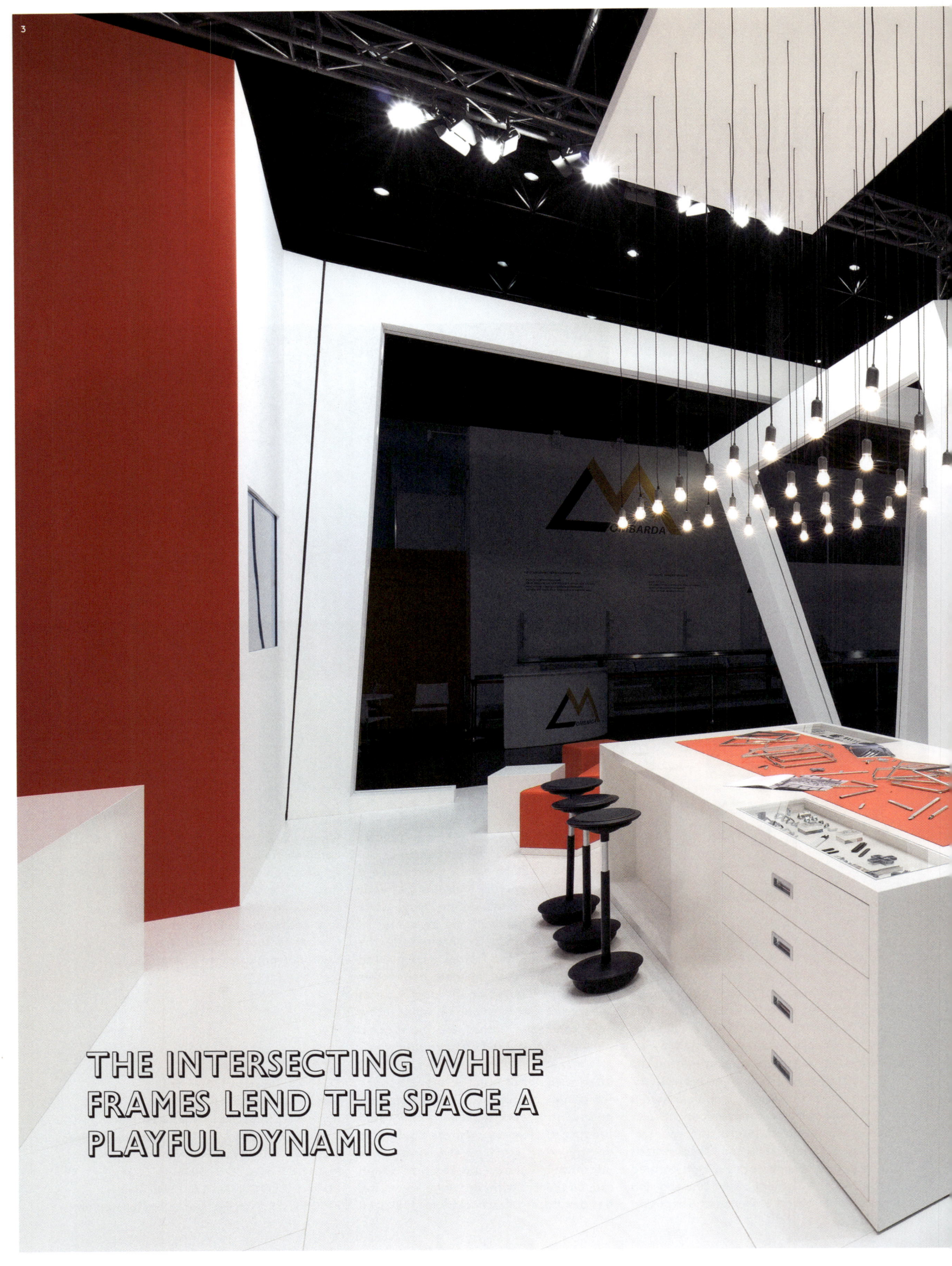

THE INTERSECTING WHITE
FRAMES LEND THE SPACE A
PLAYFUL DYNAMIC

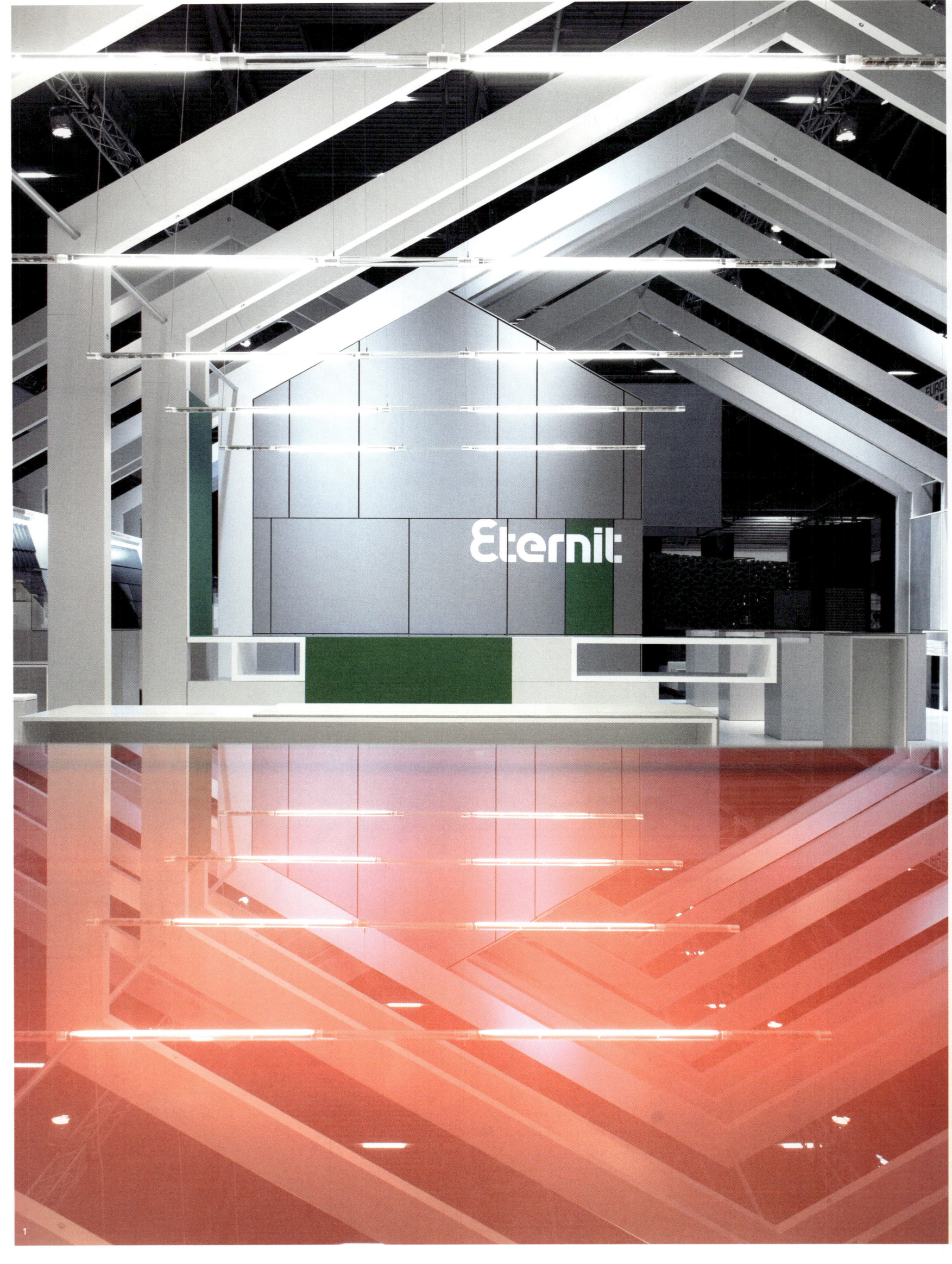

ETERNIT

Astrid Bornheim

1 The stand was designed with a strong sense of three-dimensionality.

2 The irregular spacings framed the stand and surroundings in a playful way.

TRADE FAIR **Bau**
WHERE **Munich, Germany**
WHEN **January 2015**
DESIGNER **Astrid Bornheim Architektur**
STAND CONSTRUCTOR **Zeissig**
CLIENT **Eternit**
MARKET SECTOR **Building materials**
TOTAL FLOOR AREA **385 m²**
PHOTOGRAPHER **David Franck**

Eternit is a leading German producer of fibre cement building materials for roofing and facades. At Bau, an international trade fair for architecture, materials and systems, Eternit sought a sustainable and reusable stand that clearly communicated its position as a leading producer of energy-efficient building skins. This task was entrusted to architect Astrid Bornheim who deconstructed the archetypal house to present the products in an unexpected way.

The stand was composed of exposed frames lined in a staggered arrangement to form a long shed-like building, which intersects with a second parallel large shed. The random spacings of frames created an irregular rhythm in the structure that made a strong visual impact, and enabled varying possibilities to exhibit the products. In this way materials and systems solutions were integrated into different parts of the structure, which showcased them in a surprising way. Approximately 100 products were on show ranging from individual exhibits to entire building shells made of fibre cement. An array of greys and white formed the basis colour palette with accents of red and green representing the company's corporate colours. The architectonic furniture complemented the overall aesthetic of the stand. Regarding construction, great effort was taken to minimize material use and maximise recycling and reduce waste. Only reusable or easily recyclable materials were used including wood, glass and fibre cement. The stand can be adapted to different contexts for upcoming presentations through altering the composition of the frame sequences and spaces. Furthermore the structure was designed to be easily assembled, disassembled and transported, further fulfilling the client's ambitions. ⇒

2

THE DECONSTRUCTED HOUSE PRESENTS THE PRODUCTS IN AN UNEXPECTED WAY

3 Vistas and views shifted continuously as visitors moved through the space.

4 A smaller house was incorporated into the main structure.

5 Wall systems were cleverly integrated into the frame as displays.

3

4

ASTRID BORNHEIM   ETERNIT

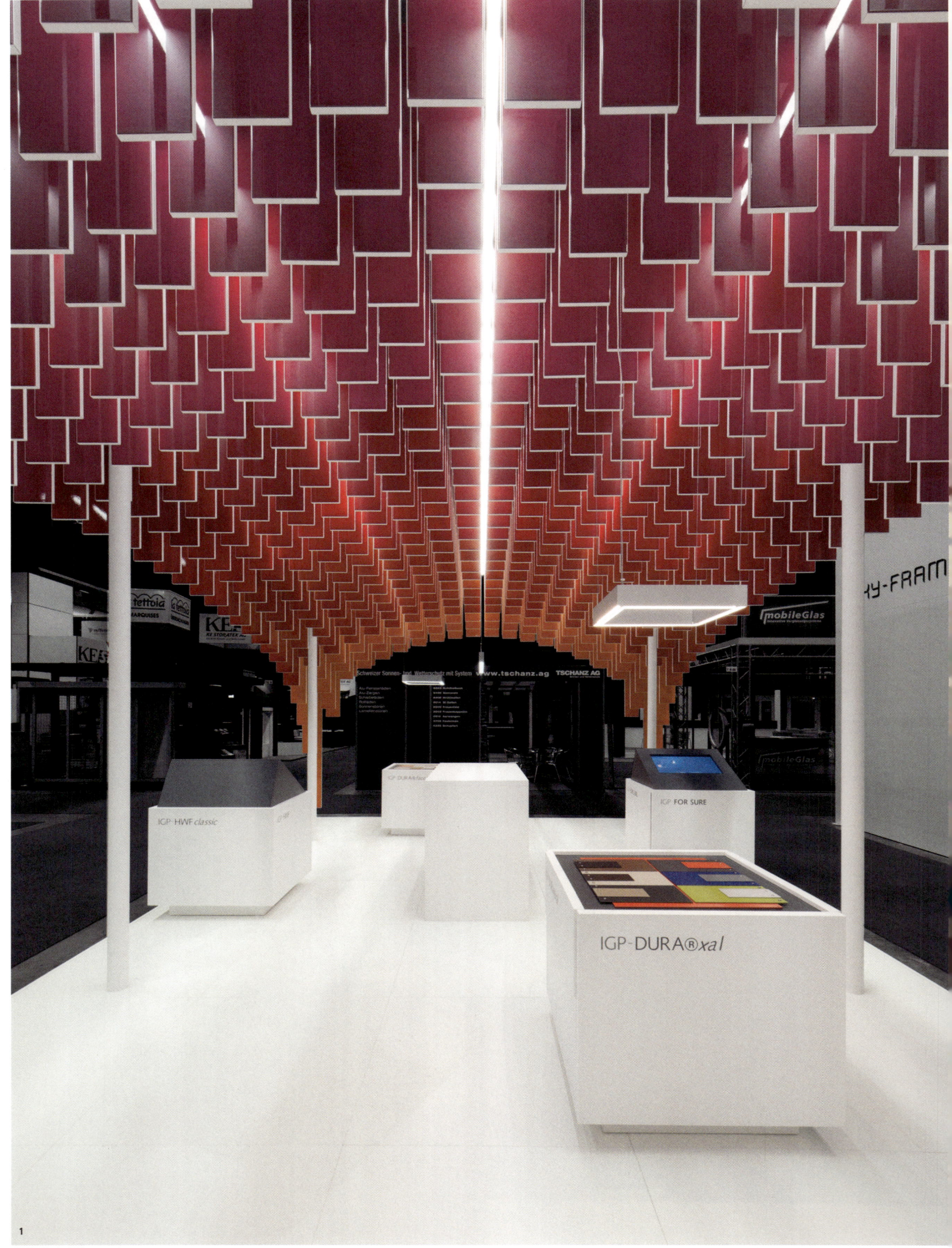

IGP PULVERTECHNIK

Space4

1 The reverse side of the white aluminium fins were adorned with a shifting composition of crimsons and pinks.

2 The stand was a haven of peace and quiet within the hustle and bustle of the trade fair.

2

At first glance, IGP Pulvertechnik's completely white stand at Swissbau 2014 appeared rather understated for a manufacturer of powder coatings. Architecturally, the curved structure composed of slim suspended vertical fins was a definite eye-catcher at this biennial event in Basel dedicated to construction, energy and architecture. However, the all-white space had a big surprise in store when visitors turned around: the fins were coloured on the reverse side showcasing a riot of crimsons and oranges. The white setting was perfect for reflecting these rich colours, which bathed the entire stand in soft, coloured light. This effect came courtesy of two IGP products. More than 800 hollow aluminium profiles were powder coated with extra white matte lacquer on both sides. On top of that, one side was applied with coloured transparent gloss finish. The combination of both layers resulted in a beautiful depth of colour resembling ceramic glaze. In addition, the ceiling's construction also contributed a unique spatial effect. Varying lengths of hollow profiles were composed to create a dome-like structure. Internally this architecture contributed an intimate and inviting atmosphere to the space, particularly in combination with the warm glow of the ceiling. Additionally the structure was cleverly designed as a system whereby the number and composition of the fins can be adapted to varying spatial requirements. The custom-made powder coated display furniture elements were also designed in line with the stand concept. Visitors were invited to take a closer look and discover the product samples integrated into the furniture and explore the content of the multimedia tables. ⚊

TRADE FAIR **Swissbau**
WHERE **Basel, Switzerland**
WHEN **January 2014**
DESIGNER **Space4**
STAND CONSTRUCTOR **Raumbüro**
CLIENT **IGP Pulvertechnik**
MARKET SECTOR **Powder coating system**
TOTAL FLOOR AREA **50 m²**
PHOTOGRAPHER **Roland Schweizer**

ARCHITECTURAL PRODUCTS   GRAND STAND 5

INFINITYCONST.
Studio Dega

1 Its mysterious glow lent the stand an otherworldly appearance.

2 The unusual biomorphic structure functioned as an eye-catcher to entice people onto the stand.

3 The curved surface had a height of 6 metres and ceiling area of 16 x 9 metres.

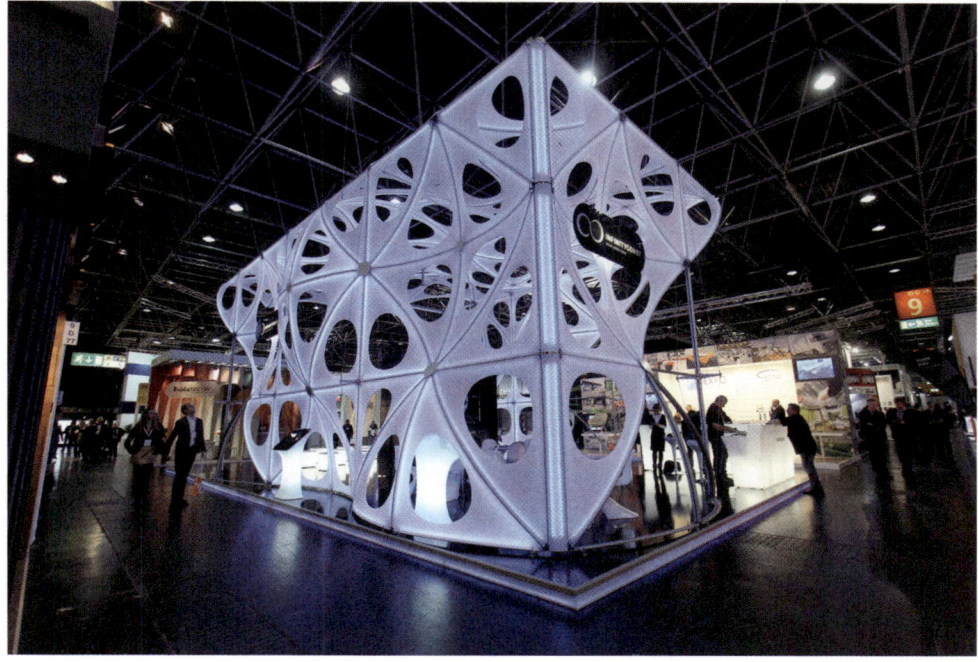

2

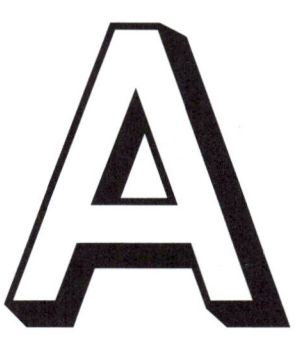

At EuroShop 2014 visitors encountered an intriguing, glowing amorphous structure called Infiniticonst. Designed by Studio Dega, the structure was actually a modular exhibition system that formed the entire stand itself. With its curvilinear form that resembled a butterfly the stand seemed more a living organism than a fair booth, especially when it changed colours. The structure was constructed from a self-supporting aluminium framework covered in tensile fabric. Openings in the fabric created a dynamic interplay between openness and enclosure. Throughout the day, the structure transformed dramatically in a show of colour and light, shifting from blue to green, purple and red. Once inside the stand, visitors felt almost cocooned in light and colour. The lighting design comprised a programmed system of LEDs that were cleverly attached to the structure using magnets. Central to the space was the interactive presentation area occupied by glowing white cubes. Here visitors gathered to participate in workshops or have casual meetings. A large multi-touch screen display was also located here. Using a computer program, visitors could design their own curved construction and then take a virtual tour inside it. The other end of the stand hosted the reception counter, its illuminated form matching the stand. Reflections of the structure and furniture in the glossy black laminate floor added to the dramatic atmosphere. An LED strip around the elevated base of the stand created an illuminated pedestal, its colour programmed with the main structure. Like insects to light, visitors were immediately drawn to the radiant stand that definitely lit up the show. ⬠

TRADE FAIR **EuroShop**
WHERE **Düsseldorf, Germany**
WHEN **February 2014**
DESIGNER **Studio Dega**
STAND CONSTRUCTOR **Studio Dega**
CLIENT **Studio Dega**
MARKET SECTOR **Modular exhibition system**
TOTAL FLOOR AREA **144 m²**
PHOTOGRAPHER **Boris Demin**

KALE ITALIA

Paolo Cesaretti

TRADE FAIR **Cersaie**
WHERE **Bologna, Italy**
WHEN **September 2014**
DESIGNER **Paolo Cesaretti**
STAND CONSTRUCTOR **La Bottega**
CLIENT **Kale Italia**
MARKET SECTOR **Tiling**
TOTAL FLOOR AREA **700 m²**
PHOTOGRAPHERS **Lorenzo Pennati
and Stefano Stagni**

1 The display of the Edilgres hi-end collections played with the sculptural quality of the materials.

2 The intriguing textured and illuminated facade united the presentation.

C

Cersaie 2014 marked the official international launch of Kale Italia, a new subsidiary of the Kale Group, a leading manufacturer in the European ceramic market. The new venture brings together five different brands from the group and operates across all market segments. In charge of the stand concept – and also visual communication – was architect Paolo Cesaretti who wanted to capture the fresh energy of the new brand in the design. A dynamic outer skin formed the principal element of the stand, literally and figuratively uniting the five brands into a singular entity. Composed of thousands of vertical MDF blocks, the skin wrapped around the entire space, appearing simultaneously enclosed yet open, digital and analogue, solid and transparent. Staggered arrangements of back-lit panels illuminated sections of the facade to bring it to life. The interior was planned as a series of open fluid spaces around a central spine. The spine incorporated services such as the reception, business lounge, meeting rooms, private offices and storage rooms. A simple circular route guided visitors through the exhibition areas. Two types of displays were created to distinguish differing product segments. Slim black wireframe volumes housed stylish interior scenarios furnished with accessories and shifting compositions of ceramic surfaces – these displays were dedicated to residential applications. Larger displays composed of wall-sized surfaces of ceramics installed on plywood panels and elevated platforms focused on products for more technical contexts. The Edilgres hi-end collections received their own presentation area designed as a landscape of sculptural surfaces organized around two chandelier-like installations fashioned from hundreds of workshop lamps. With a strong identity, the design presented the new brand in a coherent way, helping to pave a promising way forward for Kale Italia. ⸻

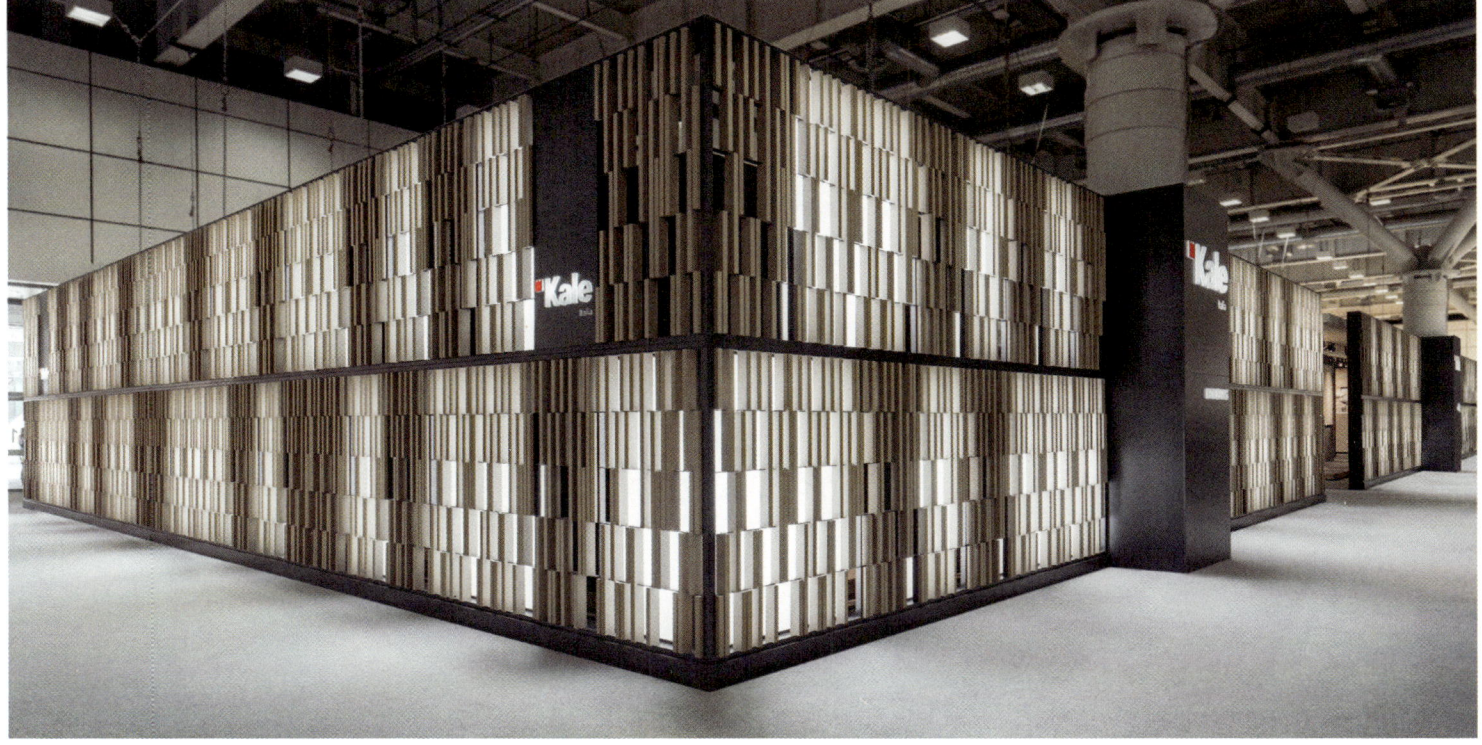

2

A DYNAMIC OUTER SKIN UNITES THE FIVE BRANDS INTO A SINGULAR ENTITY

3 Wireframe presentations contributed a sense of space and openness on the stand.

4 Each wireframe had a different atmosphere and identity.

5 Wall-like displays of ceramics showcased products for technical applications.

6 Elastic ropes were used to create the filtering screen of the lounge.

KÖNIG

atelier 522

1 A strong, black background set the stage for the expanding white grid.

2 The framework showcased the functionalities of the shop fitting system in a dynamic way.

White cubes were the unmistakeable feature of König's stand at EuroShop 2014. This year, the presentation had to focus entirely on König's brand new modular shop fitting system that was to be launched at the show. The system was designed by atelier 522, and König also commissioned the interdisciplinary designers to create their stand. With their system in mind, atelier 522 responded with a holistic concept that puts the spotlight entirely on the product.

The idea behind König's new shop system is simple: stylish cubes. atelier 522 used this as the building block – literally and figuratively – for König's entire presentation. Besides the actual stand design at EuroShop, the cubes found their way into all of König's identity regarding the exhibition, from the invitations to the overall communication design.

The main feature of the design was a white framework of cubes that expanded from the corner of the stand. Composed of stacked white cubes, the framework was structured in a staggered way, with some sections almost reaching the ceiling. Interplaying open and enclosed modules, this grid showcased the possibilities of the display system that could also be combined with different materials. The stand's black walls and floor provided the perfect stage for the sculptural white installation. On the walls cubic white graphics mirrored the form of white grid. Even the central bar counter made from medium density fibreboard took its cue from the modular theme. By showcasing just one single idea to create a bold, memorable stand, atelier 522's design ticked all the right boxes. ⎯

TRADE FAIR **EuroShop**
WHERE **Düsseldorf, Germany**
WHEN **February 2014**
DESIGNER **atelier 522**
STAND CONSTRUCTOR **König**
CLIENT **König**
MARKET SECTOR **Modular display systems**
TOTAL FLOOR AREA **54 m²**
PHOTOGRAPHER **Courtesy of atelier 522**

2

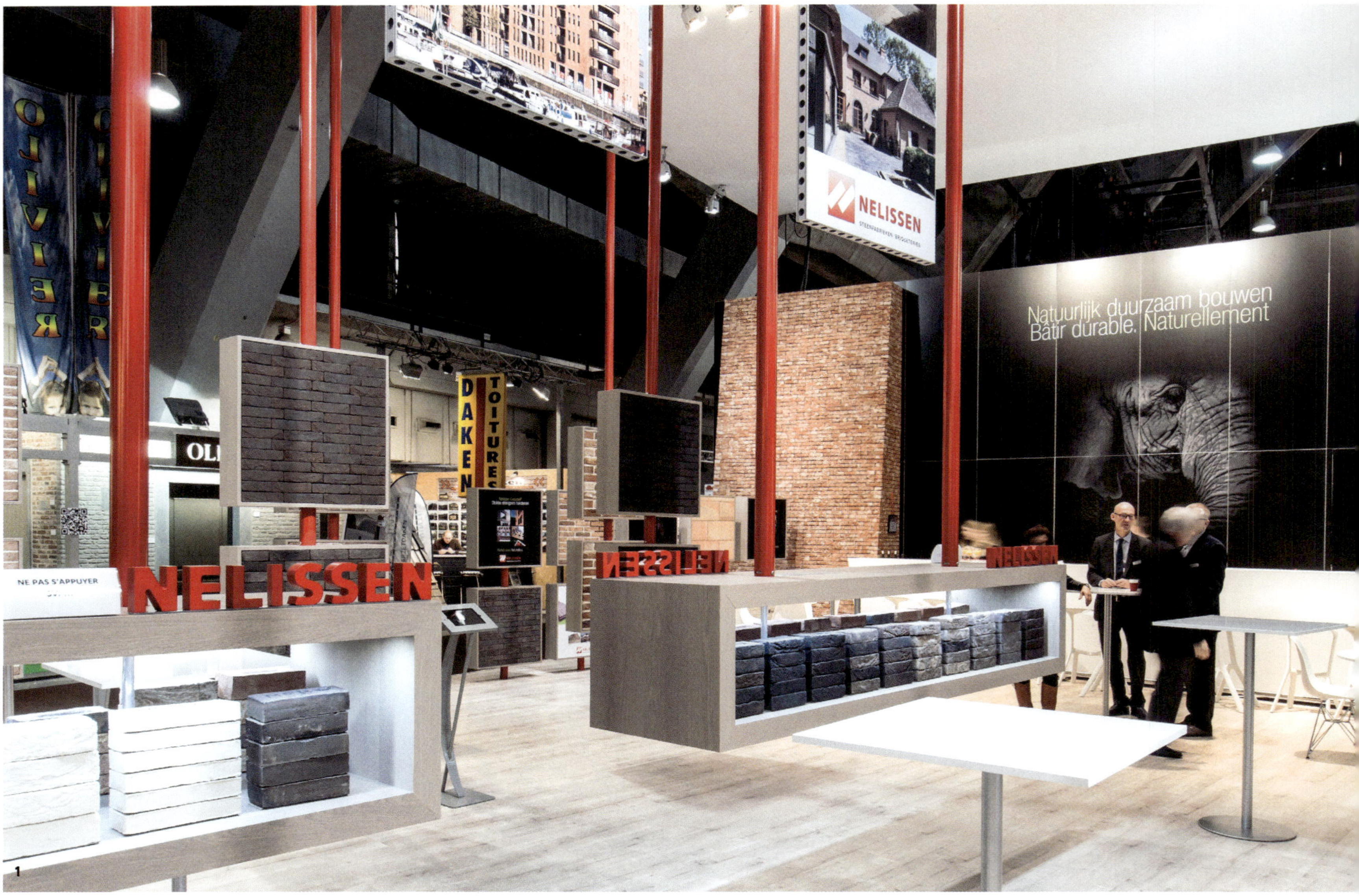
NELISSEN
NE PAS S'APPUYER
Natuurlijk duurzaam bouwen
Bâtir durable. Naturellement
1

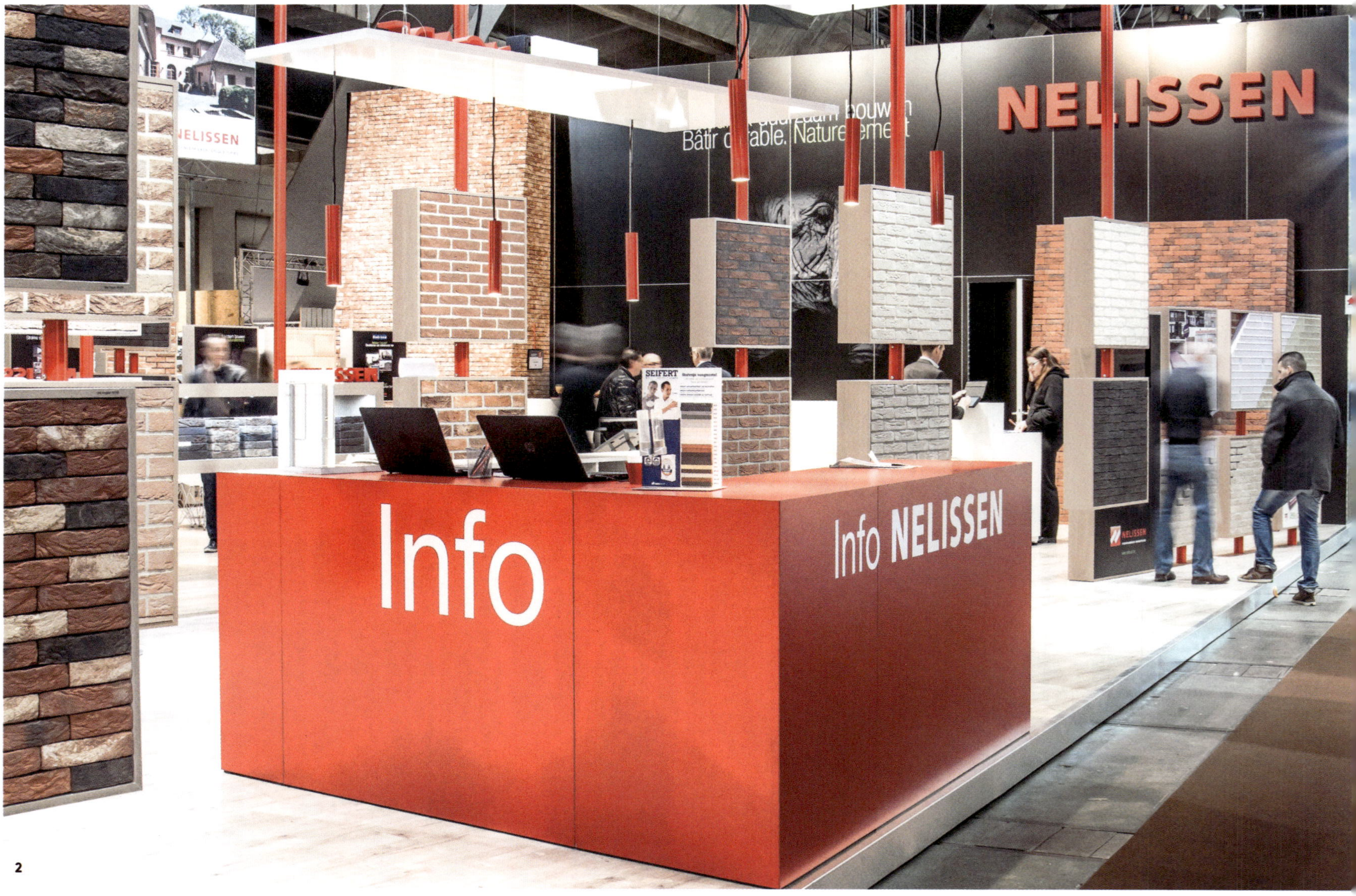
NELISSEN
Info
Info NELISSEN
SEIFERT
2

NELISSEN BRICKS

Ontwerpbureau Jan

1 Echoing the main concept, open shelves were also suspended from the ceiling.

2 Branded in Nelissen's corporate colour, the red information booth welcomed visitors onto the stand.

3 The suspended panels, together with the floating ceiling, promoted a wonderful flow of space on the stand.

3

What if the bricks could float? This concept of lightness is not normally equated with something as heavy as bricks. But it was exactly this impossibility that challenged Ontwerpbureau Jan for the design of Nelissen Bricks' stand at Batibouw – the construction and renovation fair – in Brussels. The client requested a stand that proposed a radical change to past presentations and wanted to avoid constructing heavy walls in the space. It should also be able to accommodate the company's full range of bricks and have a light look and feel.

The result was a vibrant, unexpected design that shone the spotlight on bricks in a completely new way. Framed panels of bricks were suspended from the stand in a light, airy space defined by a floating white ceiling and timber platform. Pairs of brick panels appeared almost like portraits hung artfully in the open space – this also functioned to structure the presentation. Each portrait featured a different type of brick, which was mounted onto a steel frame, and then encased in wood. The diagonal alignment of panels across the space and strategic spotlighting intensified the presentation's dynamic feel. Thin steel tubes in red, the company's corporate colour, were used to hang the panels from the ceiling, and a detailed system of 40 hoists kept the whole installation afloat – no easy feat for a structure weighing over 12 tonnes.

Open rectangular shelves containing the brick library were also suspended in line with the concept. High and open on all sides, the stand exuded an inviting atmosphere that enticed curious visitors into the space, perfectly complemented the warm quality of the material and clearly showed that bricks can indeed float. Mission accomplished. ⇐

TRADE FAIR **Batibouw**
WHERE **Brussels, Belgium**
WHEN **Feb-March 2014**
DESIGNER **Ontwerpbureau Jan**
STAND CONSTRUCTOR
Ontwerpbureau Jan
CLIENT **Nelissen Bricks**
MARKET SECTOR **Bricks**
TOTAL FLOOR AREA **276 m²**
PHOTOGRAPHER **Bert Oerlemans**

NEU: ClickTex
NEW: ClickTex

> Der erste textile Boden zum Klicken
> In zwei Top-Qualitäten
> Außergewöhnliche Dielenoptiken
> Freies Kombinieren von Farben
und Designs

> The first textile floor for clicking
together
> In two top qualities
> Unusual plank looks
> Colours and designs can be
freely combined

Vinyl

Parkett
Engineered wood flooring

Individualität ist eine Einstellung
Holz mit allen Sinnen erleben

Individuality is an attitude. Experience
wood with all the senses

PARADOR

D'art Design Gruppe

2

P

Parador is a flooring manufacturer renowned for its high-end solid wood, laminate and parquet floors. At Domotex, the international trade fair for floor coverings, in 2014 Parador made a strong impression with a dynamic brand sculpture designed by D'art Design Gruppe. Over 121 innovations were on show this year. The design continued the idea of lifting the flooring to visitors' eye levels, first presented at the previous Domotex show. However this year, the flooring was completely transformed into a huge piece of architecture.

A rectilinear steel structure wrapped in sheer black gauze formed the basis of the stand. This became a screen that defined the perimeters of the stand as well as provided a filter to the external surroundings. At the core of the space was The Paragraph, a dynamic spatial gesture that symbolized the company's strengths. The form folded and unfolded, and twisted and intersected itself through the space. As it transformed out of the floors to become walls and ceilings this created a series of architectural structures that were used to display the products. In this way, visitors were able to easily touch the products, which enhanced the experience of their materiality. Of course, people could also walk on the flooring.

A special highlight at this presentation was the launch of Click-Tex, the world's first carpet floorboard. Coloured carpet boards were arranged in a gradated pattern of pixels that shifted colour from black to yellows and white, beautifully showcasing the product's possibilities. The design of the stand successfully elevated flooring onto another level – literally and figuratively – to bring people closer to the product. ⌐

TRADE FAIR **Domotex**
WHERE **Hannover, Germany**
WHEN **January 2014**
DESIGNER **D'art Design Gruppe**
STAND CONSTRUCTOR **Viva Messe- und Ausstellungsbau**
CLIENT **Parador**
MARKET SECTOR **Flooring**
TOTAL FLOOR AREA **600 m²**
PHOTOGRAPHER **Lukas Palik**

1 The structures changed appearance depending on the angle of the viewer.

2 Yellow carpet floorboards welcomed visitors onto the stand.

3 Angular bar furniture reflected the dynamic architecture of the stand.

3

POLYTAN
jürgensarchitekten

1 An installation of suspended sports jerseys showed the clubs that train on Polytan flooring.

2 The open design of the compact stand enabled better visual impact and more exhibition space.

2

Polytan's dynamic stand at the bi-annual FSB fair for amenity areas, sports, pool facilities in 2013 was impossible to miss. For its presentation that year, the international sports flooring producer wanted to communicate not only technical capabilities of the product but also demonstrate its creative potential to a more design-orientated audience. Designed by jürgensarchitekten, the stand takes the company's products to new heights. A strong visual statement was immediately made by using synthetic turf in violet as the basis of the stand, instead of the classic green. The vibrantly coloured surface curved up the wall to define the back of the stand, which was topped with a white rectangular volume emblazoned with the company's logo. White lane markings activated the surfaces, suggesting a sports field as well as running track. Custom-designed white furniture – by Stadtnomaden – displayed the wide variety of products in surprising ways. Surfaces were integrated onto table surfaces and special drawers showcased more materials. Display tables also doubled as bar tables. High-backed sofas served as private meeting spaces. Instead of creating enclosed meeting rooms, this solution saved space to allow more product exhibition area and helped maintain openness on the compact 150 m² stand. Two small service rooms were discretely concealed in the wall block. Visible from afar, a suspended installation of colourful jerseys was a highlight, proudly representing the sports clubs that train on Polytan flooring. The lighting was done by Neumann & Müller. The stand's colourful, optimistic and eye-catching design conveyed the company's forward-thinking approach and definitely got visitors excited about new possibilities of sports flooring. ⁃

TRADE FAIR **FSB**
WHERE **Cologne, Germany**
WHEN **October 2013**
DESIGNER **jürgensarchitekten**
STAND CONSTRUCTOR **Display International**
CLIENT **Polytan**
MARKET SECTOR **Flooring**
TOTAL FLOOR AREA **150 m²**
PHOTOGRAPHER **Andreas Keller Fotografie**

3

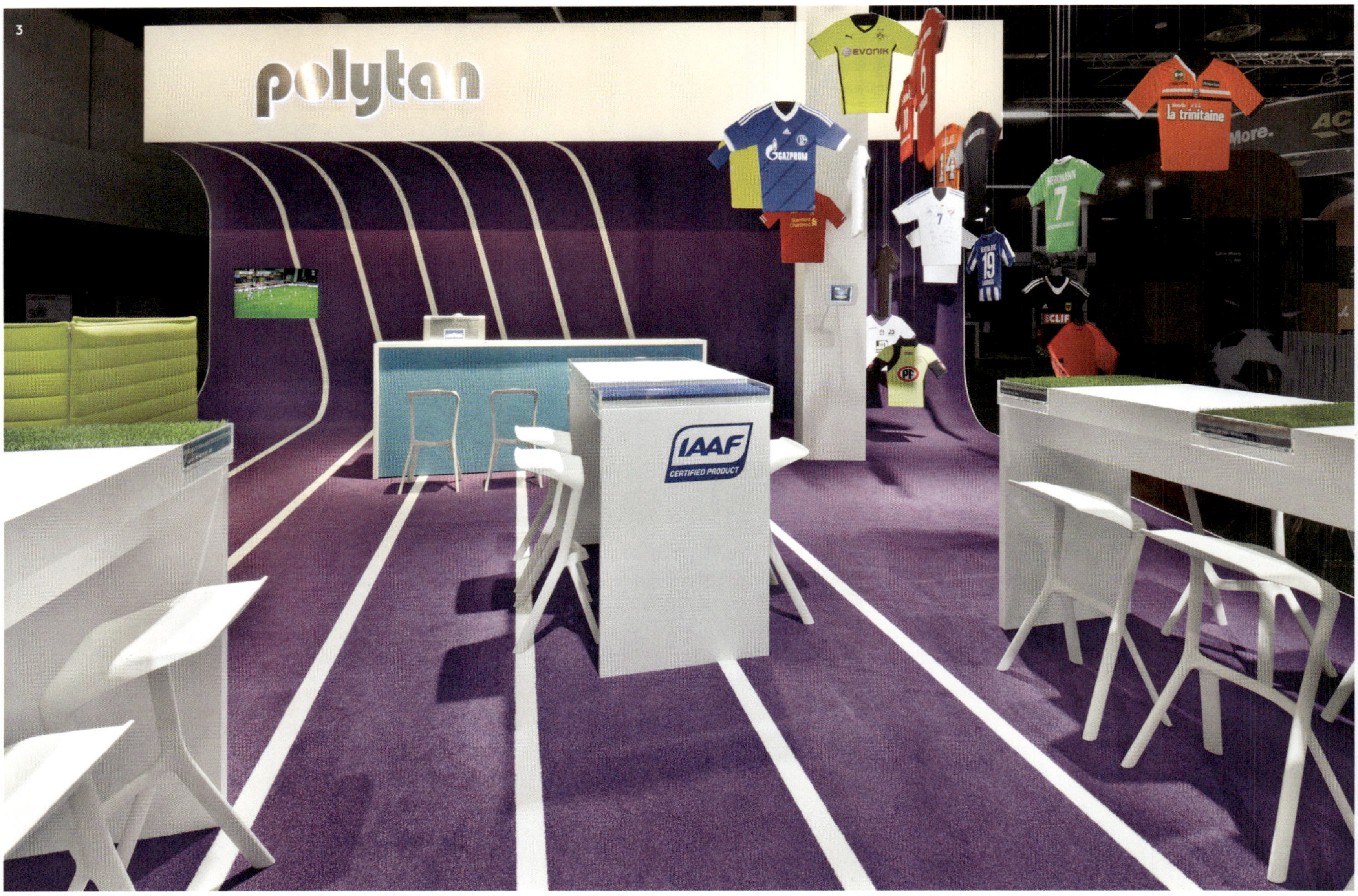

4

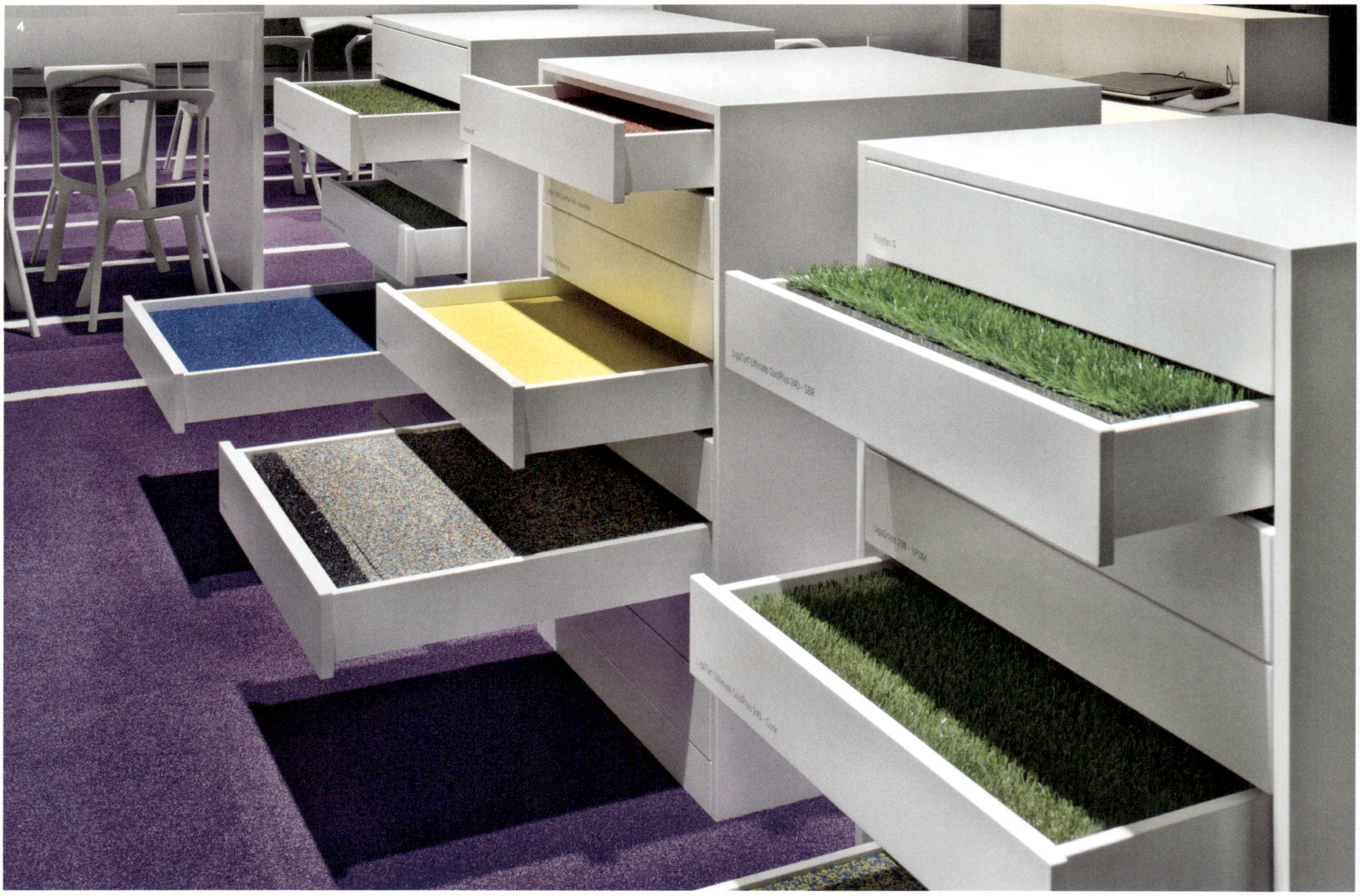

3 White furniture and white lines complemented the colourful space.

4 Visitors could open the display cubes to discover the materials inside.

SECTION

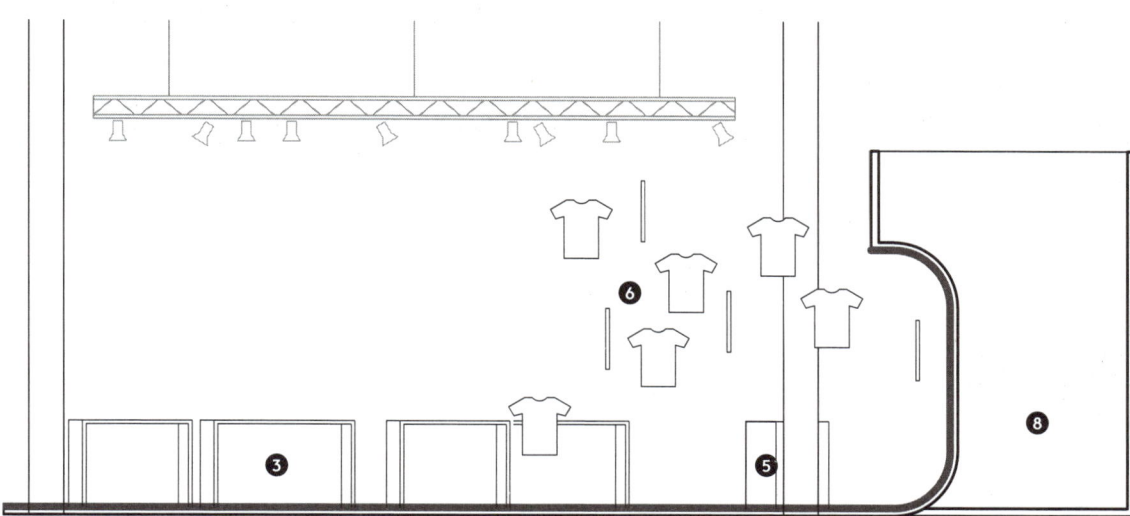

WALL RENDERINGS

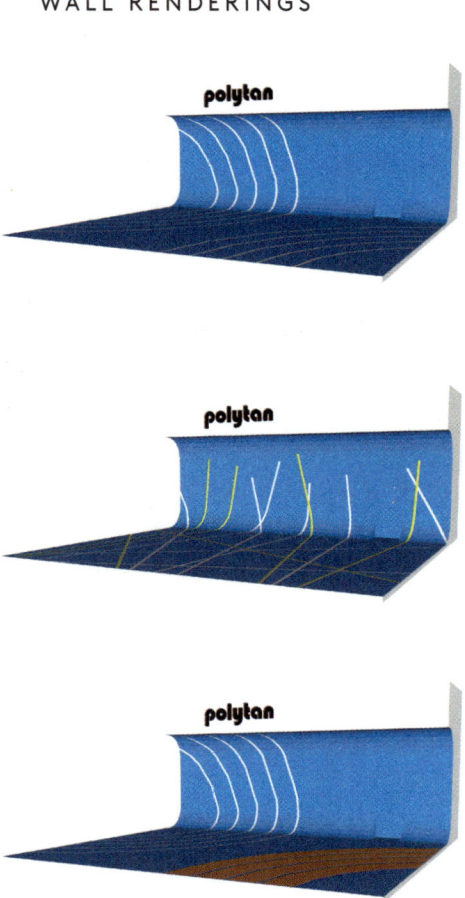

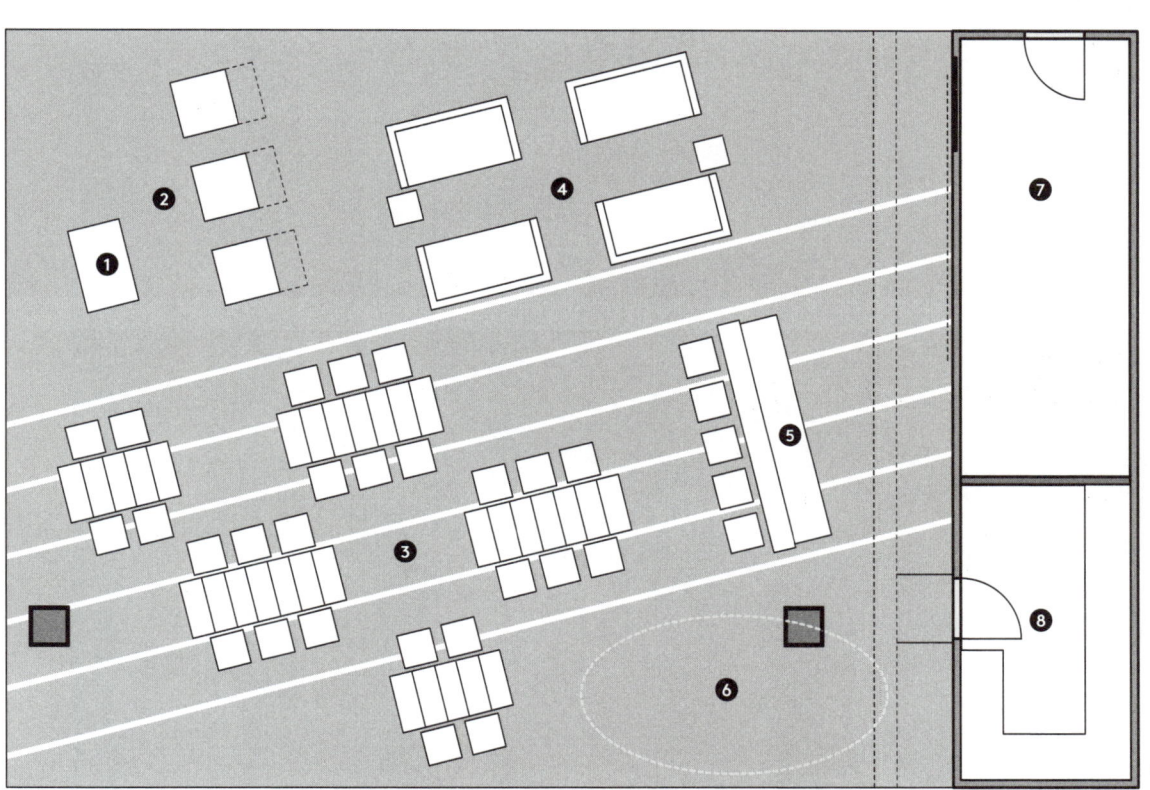

FLOOR PLAN

01 Information desk
02 Display cubes
03 Sample desks
04 High-back sofas
05 Cocktail bar
06 Mobile t-shirt sculpture
07 Storage
08 Catering

THE STAND TAKES SPORTS FLOORING TO NEW HEIGHTS

1

2

Roto
Energieeffizienz
Komfort
Design
Geschwindigkeit
Trends

ROTO
atelier 522

1 Roto's stand appeared as a dynamic white domestic landscape.

2 atelier 522 were also responsible for the design of the displays and graphics.

3 Red wall accents echoed Roto's corporate identity.

3

'People without humour are just like houses without windows': With this quote from the Austrian writer Ernst Ferstl in mind, atelier 522 set out to create a stand for Roto that literally laughed out loud at fensterbau/fontale 2014 in Nürnberg. This bi-annual trade fair showcases the latest innovations in the window, door and facade construction sector. For Roto, a leading manufacturing company specialising in door and window technologies, atelier 522 developed a holistic concept that invited visitors to explore Roto's latest innovations in a familiar yet abstract environment.

The design played with the form of an archetypical house. On the stand a series of small white houses were grouped around a larger open house that formed a prominent corner entry point. Roto's products were exhibited almost like artworks on the walls of each house. Sections of open facade on the exterior and interior of the stand invited visitors to meander between houses and wander around at their own pace. White floors between the white houses enabled continuous surfaces where the roofs, walls and floors morphed fluidly into each other. Sections of freestanding red partitions provided bold red accents that perfectly reflected Roto's corporate identity. The stand also accommodated a catering area and conference room.

With its team of interior architects, product designers and communication designers on board the project, atelier 522 designed not only the booth, but also ensured an overall coherence to the visual presentation. In this way, they also designed the display systems and key visuals, plus one of the new door handles on show. With its dynamic white domestic landscape, Roto's stand was a definite crowd pleaser during fensterbau/fontale. ⇒

TRADE FAIR **fensterbau/frontale**
WHERE **Nürnberg, Germany**
WHEN **March 2014**
DESIGNER **atelier 522**
STAND CONSTRUCTOR **Stagegroup**
CLIENT **Roto**
MARKET SECTOR **Door and window technology**
TOTAL FLOOR AREA **1064 m²**
PHOTOGRAPHER **Behrendt & Rausch**

ARCHITECTURAL PRODUCTS GRAND STAND 5

ROYAL CERAMICA

Paolo Cesaretti

1 Furniture in the lounge and meeting area were custom designed for the presentation.

2 Visitors felt like they were transported to a charming middle-eastern courtyard.

2

Paolo Cesaretti's long-term design collaboration with the middle-eastern ceramics manufacturer Royal Ceramica is characterised by a subtle balance between eastern and western elements. In line with this approach, the design for Royal Ceramica's stand at Cersaie 2013 celebrated the best of both worlds, in particular focusing on the private/public courtyard. Layered spaces gradually unfolded to reveal the presentation. The stand was encapsulated by mysterious timber walls with a bleach finish. Perforated with a honeycomb pattern, the walls allowed controlled glimpses of the interior, which triggered visitors' curiosities to enter. Once inside visitors encountered a second layer of screens composed of hexagonal segments of latticed partitions. The shifting directions of timber battens resulted in a dynamic wall surface. At the heart of the space was the central courtyard that housed the main presentation. Here 19 marble-like blocks of different sizes and heights were arranged in careful compositions and positioned centrally on floating platforms. This landscape of volumes gave the impression of a serene sculpture garden. Surrounding the public courtyard were the private lounge area and meeting space, both furnished with custom-designed furniture. Throughout the space light was used to create a beautiful play of shadows together with the patterns of the screens, much like sunlight shining through an outdoor courtyard.

A palette of warm materials like oak and colours such as beige and dark maroon complemented the stone, further contributing an intimate atmosphere. The visual overlapping of the inner hexagonal screens with the outer facade continued the layering effect, lending the whole interior a sense of vibrancy. ⸺

TRADE FAIR **Cersaie**
WHERE **Bologna, Italy**
WHEN **September 2013**
DESIGNER **Paolo Cesaretti**
STAND CONSTRUCTOR **Olgiati**
CLIENT **Royal Ceramica**
MARKET SECTOR **Tiling**
TOTAL FLOOR AREA **250 m²**
PHOTOGRAPHERS **Marco Marchetta, Stefano Stagni and Lorenzo Pennati**

3

LAYERED SPACES GRADUALLY UNFOLD TO REVEAL THE PRESENTATION

3 The carefully composed display of floating platforms resembled a sculpture garden.

4 The patterns of the outer screen and inner partitions complemented each other beautifully. vibrancy in the space.

5 The visual layering of screens added a sense of vibrancy in the space.

SCHATTDECOR

Kohlhaas

1 Varying wood finishes were combined to create a warm, welcoming atmosphere in the communication area.

2 The structure wrapped around the stand to create a mysterious front.

2

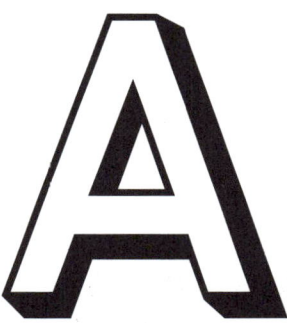

At the 2015 edition of Interzum, the fair for furniture production and interior design, Schattdecor took a reflective approach with its message, 'The deep longing for authenticity and self-fulfilment'. Specialising in surfaces and décor printing, the company wanted to show a clear focus on the future, both in relation to new trends and in celebration of its 30th anniversary. The main theme communicated the importance of individuality today, where consumers are now able to select products that reflect a truer expression of their personalities. A series of dynamic parametric forms dominated the stand. The angled planes of the forms shifted to define open and enclosed zones to accommodate different functions. Product presentations were contained inside the closed forms while the communication area with café and bar was hosted in the open sections. Made from printed décor paper, the dark surfaces of the main structures contributed a mysterious yet luxurious feel to the space. Visitors were guided through a route structured into three trends, each of which was accompanied by a complementary décor that unveiled the company's latest offerings. 'Casual Black' showcased rich, dark materials and finishes in a classic yet bold ambience. 'Cultural Spirit' explored the opening up of cultural boundaries, and brought together furnishing ideas from all over the world to create a feeling of eclecticism and individuality. Simplicity and authenticity were integral to the theme 'Freestyle Clarity' where a minimal palette of black, white and light materials set a restrained tone. With an inviting atmosphere thanks to the plentiful use of warm wood finishes, the communication area formed the social hub of the presentation. ⇒

TRADE FAIR **Interzum**
WHERE **Cologne, Germany**
WHEN **May 2015**
DESIGNER **Kohlhaas Messebau**
STAND CONSTRUCTOR **Kohlhaas Messebau**
CLIENT **Schattdecor**
MARKET SECTOR **Décor paper**
TOTAL FLOOR AREA **700 m²**
PHOTOGRAPHER **Fotodesign Schiemann**

3

3 'Cultural Spirit' took inspiration from all corners of the globe.

4 Rich, luxurious finishes were highlighted in 'Casual Black'.

5 The space appeared different from every angle depending on the location of the viewer.

6 'Freestyle Clarity' conveyed lightness and simplicity.

INDIVIDUALITY, AUTHENTICITY AND PERSONALITY ARE KEY THEMES OF THE PRESENTATION

4

5

SIMONSWERK
gambit marketing & communication

1 The colourful, textured central wall feature contrasted strikingly with the slick black stand.

2 The eye-catching design of the stand gave a big presence to a small product.

3 Visitors were encouraged to interact with the display, almost becoming part of the exhibition themselves.

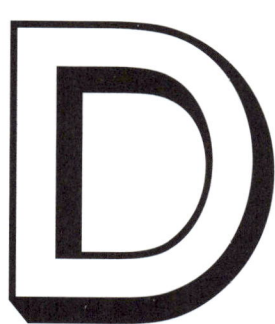

Door hinges enable the opening and closing of doors and thus facilitate 'Movement in Space'. This poetic idea was adopted by Simonswerk, the manufacturer of hinges and hinge systems, for its presence at Bau, the trade fair for architecture, materials and systems. Design by gambit, the slick black stand immediately made a strong visual impact. A series of rectilinear forms dominated the space, positioned to clearly structure the presentation. The perimeter of mesh screens mounted above stand strongly defined the boundaries of the stand. A wall of doors that measured 6.5-metres-long by 3.4-metres-high formed the central feature, immediately attracting people's attentions from afar. The striking wall was composed from a series of slim doors made of different materials including timber, concrete and leather. In this way, the presentation concept allowed the products to be showcased in the context in which they are actually used. Visitors were invited to interact with the wall by opening the doors, touching the materials and examining the hinge systems. This display was accompanied by a huge back wall made of entirely compartments containing removable samples and product information. Glass showcases were also integrated into the tables, creating another layer to display products. On this stand, the products were displayed in surprising ways that transformed them from being humble utilitarian objects into precious artefacts. ⚊

TRADE FAIR **Bau**
WHERE **Munich, Germany**
WHEN **January 2013**
DESIGNER **gambit marketing & communication**
STAND ARCHITECT **Planwerk**
CLIENT **Simonswerk**
MARKET SECTOR **Hinge systems**
TOTAL FLOOR AREA **140 m²**
PHOTOGRAPHER **Bernadette Grimmenstein**

TURKISHCERAMICS

vPPR

2

TRADE FAIR **100% Design**
WHERE **London, United Kingdom**
WHEN **September 2014**
DESIGNER **vPPR Architects**
STAND CONSTRUCTOR **setWorks**
CLIENT **Turkishceramics**
MARKET SECTOR **Tiles and sanitaryware**
TOTAL FLOOR AREA **81 m²**
PHOTOGRAPHER **Benedict Johnson Photography**

1 A calm atmosphere pervaded the stand.

2 The pavillion was composed of a four-metre-high geodesic dome covered in mesh and real foam.

3 White Turkish ceramics on display.

T

The Foam Dome was a special installation designed by vPPR Architects for the Kitchen and Bathroom Hub at 100% Design. Sponsored by Turkishceramics, the installation focused on the idea of cleanliness, referencing the luxurious experience of a spa and recalling traditions of the Turkish bath culture. A sculptural white geodesic dome, with a diameter of nearly eight metres, formed the main feature of the installation, its structure inspired by the structure of bath bubbles. Suspended centrally in the space, the dome was constructed from strong lightweight plastic piping covered by mesh and real foam, which was produced by a foam machine installed at the top of the structure. The resultant skin constantly transformed throughout the week as the foam expanded, shrunk and floated onto the stand. In combination with light, the glistening foam produced an intriguing surface effect that aroused people's curiosities and created a dream-like atmosphere. Visitors couldn't resist playing with the foam. Below the layout of the presentation mirrored the dome's circular form, and featured Turkish ceramic products from tiles and basins to a circular bathtub – with a diameter of 160 cm – designed by Ross Lovegrove. Products were displayed in white to maintain a serene atmosphere on the stand. Piles of plush white towels and white chairs invited visitors to chill out, relax and immerse themselves in the giant cloud of foam. ⇒

3

WICONA

Atelier Seitz

TRADE FAIR **Bau**
WHERE **Munich, Germany**
WHEN **January 2015**
DESIGNER **Atelier Seitz**
STAND CONSTRUCTOR **Atelier Seitz**
CLIENT **Wicona**
MARKET SECTOR **Aluminium profiles**
TOTAL FLOOR AREA **648 m²**
PHOTOGRAPHER **Olaf Schiemann**

2

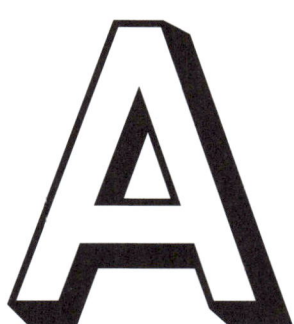

At Bau, the biennial trade fair for architecture, materials and systems held in Munich, fairgoers took a trip to 'Wicona City' to view Wicona's aluminum profile systems for facades, windows and doors. Designed by Atelier Seitz the bold 648 m² stand was unmissable, immediately attracting the attention of visitors. Wicona's corporate colour red was featured as the dominant colour on the stand to give the brand a strong presence. In contrast the interior was kept predominantly white to create a quiet atmosphere to display the products. This calmness is complemented by the simple, minimal architecture and screening elements such as walls and the ceiling banner that shielded the stand from the bustle of the fair. Appearing as a mini cityscape a series of bold red volumes were positioned to create an outer boundary wall and also partitions on the stand. The design of the interior took inspiration from a streetscape, where the grey floor lined with road markings, street lights and pedestrian crossings conveyed a vibrant atmosphere. White freestanding rectangular elements incorporated the product displays, which were organised into blocks. These blocks together with the meeting rooms, sidewalk café and cloakroom were connected by a network of roads. In this way, the roads were not only a visual feature but functioned to guide visitors through the presentation. Set against the background of a vast blue sky Wicona's stand shone brightly during the fair. ⟹

3

1 The minimal architecture paired well with the red and white colour palette to create a striking streetscape.

2 Products displays were organised into blocks connected by roads.

3 The company's corporate identity was visibly showcased on the stand.

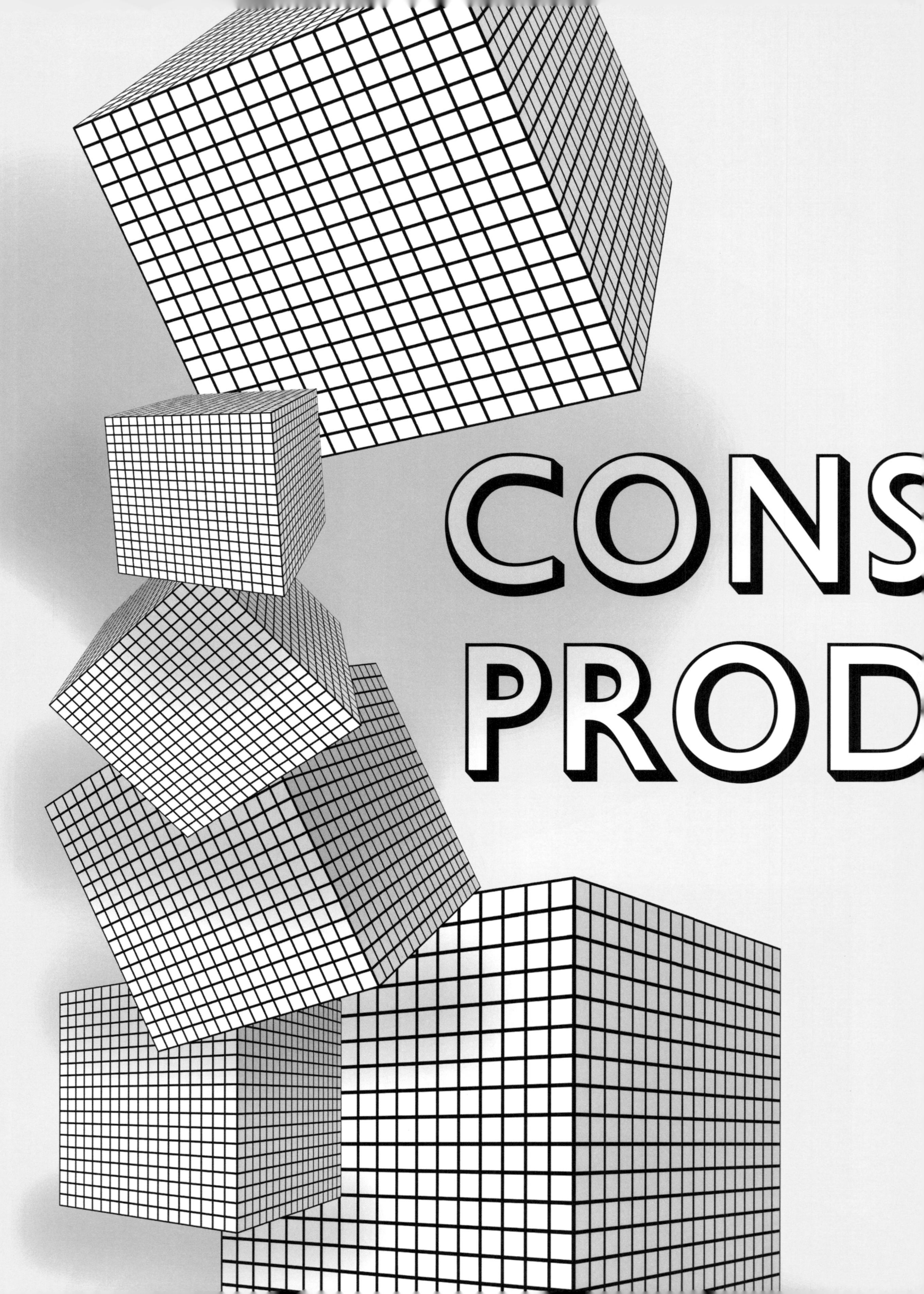

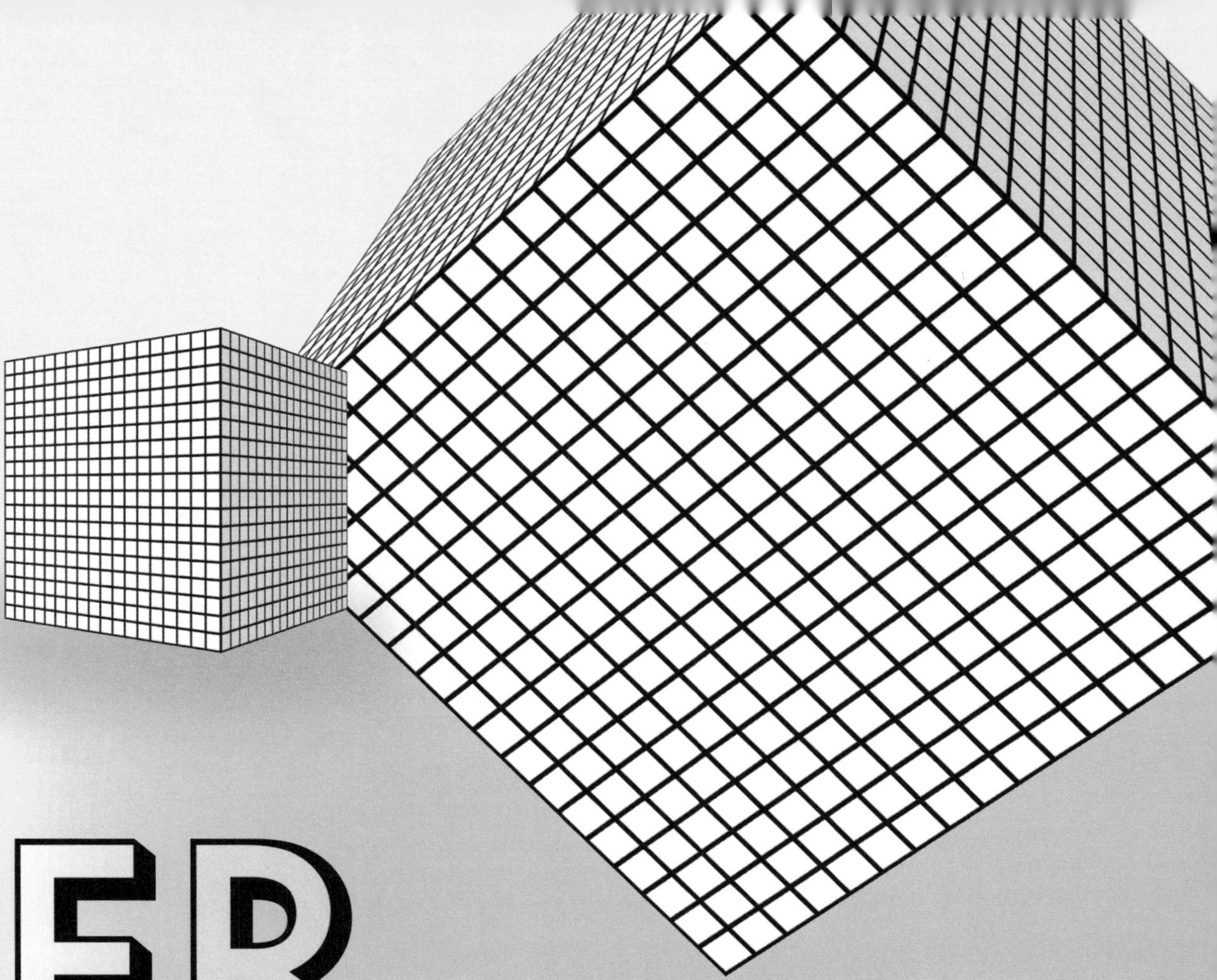

UMER

UCTS

CONSUMER PRODUCTS GRAND STAND 5

AFA
studiomfd

TRADE FAIR **Interpack**
WHERE **Düsseldorf, Germany**
WHEN **May 2014**
DESIGNER **studiomfd**
STAND CONSTRUCTOR **Fiction Factory Amsterdam**
CLIENT **Afa Dispensing Group**
MARKET SECTOR **Dispensing technologies**
TOTAL FLOOR AREA **90 m²**
PHOTOGRAPHER **Johannes Van Assem**

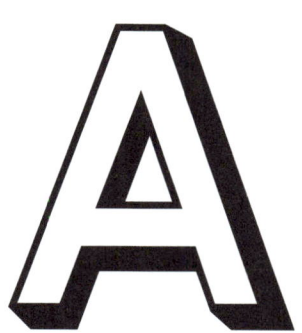

Afa is a leading innovator and global supplier of dispensing technology for all types of liquids. For the 2014 edition of Interpack, the international trade fair for processes and packaging, studiomfd was commissioned for the second consecutive year to design a striking stand to display Afa's latest dispensing innovations.

Afa works from the laws of physics to develop state-of-the-art dispensing products designed to be mainly hand operated. In line with Afa's approach, studiomfd decided to put the laws of physics to use for the design of the stand. Here, a fluid aluminium sculpture unfolded through the spacious and minimal stand to create maximum visual impact. A giant roll of aluminum was modeled, on location, and suspended into a giant curling wave using a crane, numerous cables as well as much pressure, tension and gravity itself. The undulating wave represented liquids that form the starting point for Afa's innovative techniques, while at the same time, symbolized the rush of continuing innovation, development and production. The silver colour suggested the shimmer of light bouncing off water, emphasized by strategically placed lighting. Amid the bustle of the fair the wave swayed gently, subtly reflecting people's moving silhouettes. White high-gloss HPL walls and white spray-painted MDF floors provided a stylish, minimal background.

The new products were displayed around the curl, balanced on slim vertical white spikes that emerged from the stand. Four sprayers were each set in a fitting design that corresponded to its function: a mirror (Personal Care), cat collar (Pet Care), plant (Plant Care) and cloud (Air Care). A white semi-circular partition displayed the various brands that use Afa's trigger sprays and zoned off a private meeting room. The expressive, organic sculpture worked a treat to trigger visitors to become acquainted with Afa's new products. ⇒

1 The suspended sinuous form created a dynamic play of space.

2 With a stunning metallic sculpture and minimal aesthetic, the stand was a definite crowd-pleaser.

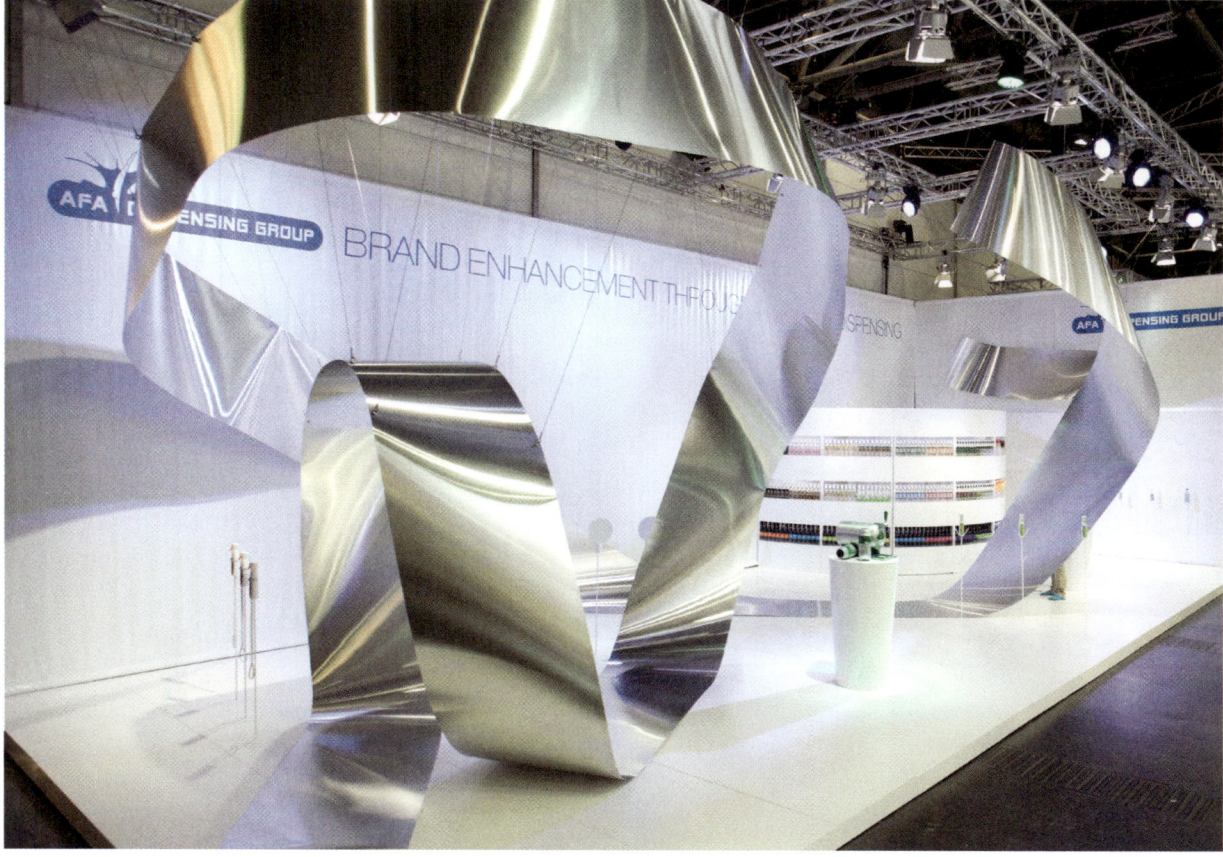

2

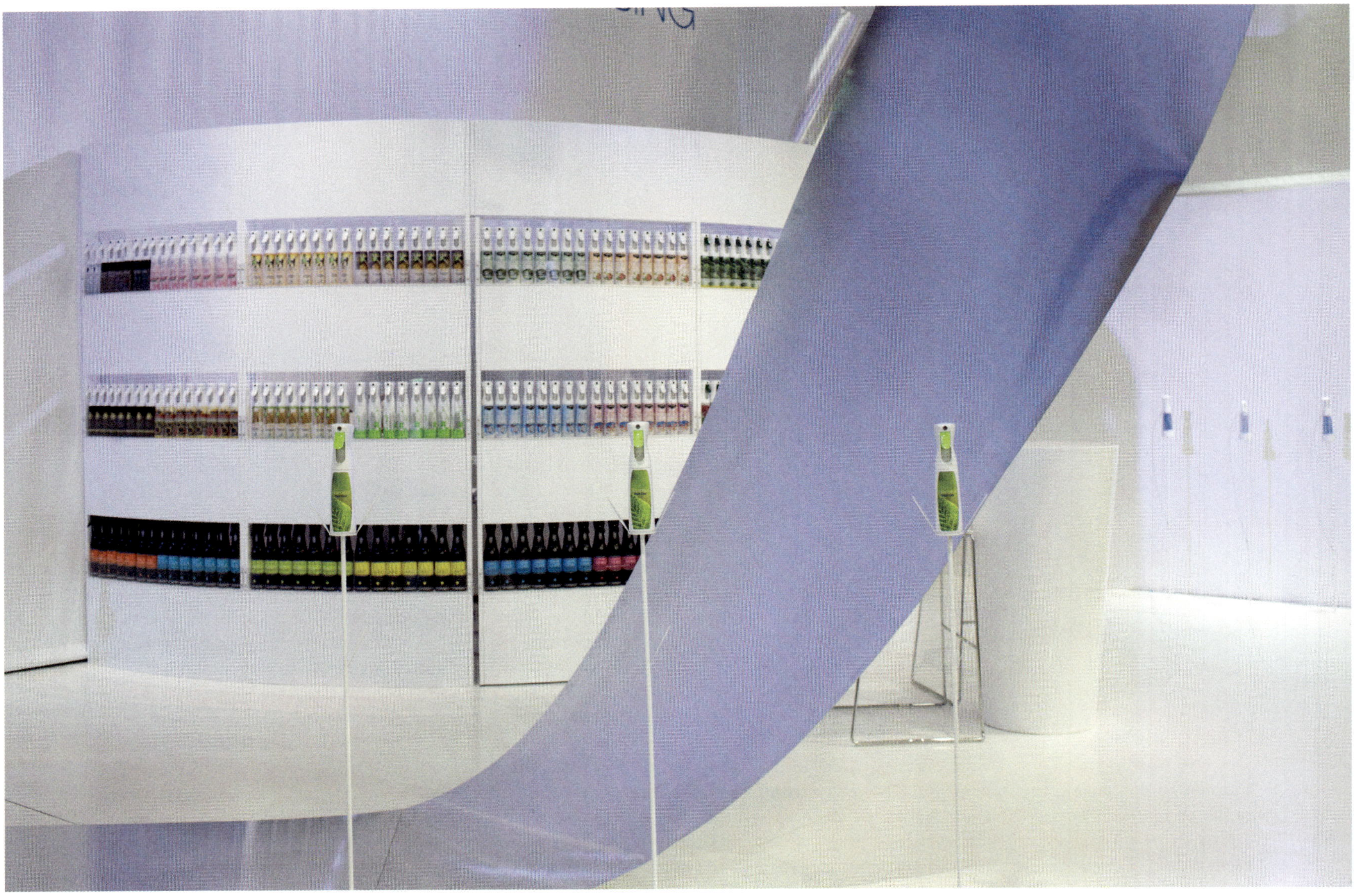

3

THE EXPRESSIVE
WAVE
REPRESENTS
LIQUIDS THAT
FORM THE
BASIS OF AFA'S
INNOVATIONS

3 A display on the curved wall demonstrated applications for Afa's trigger sprays.

4 Display for personal care.

RENDERING

DISPENSER DISPLAYS

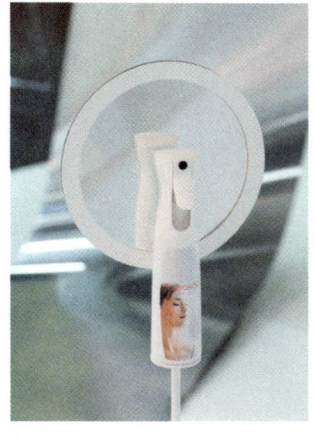

4

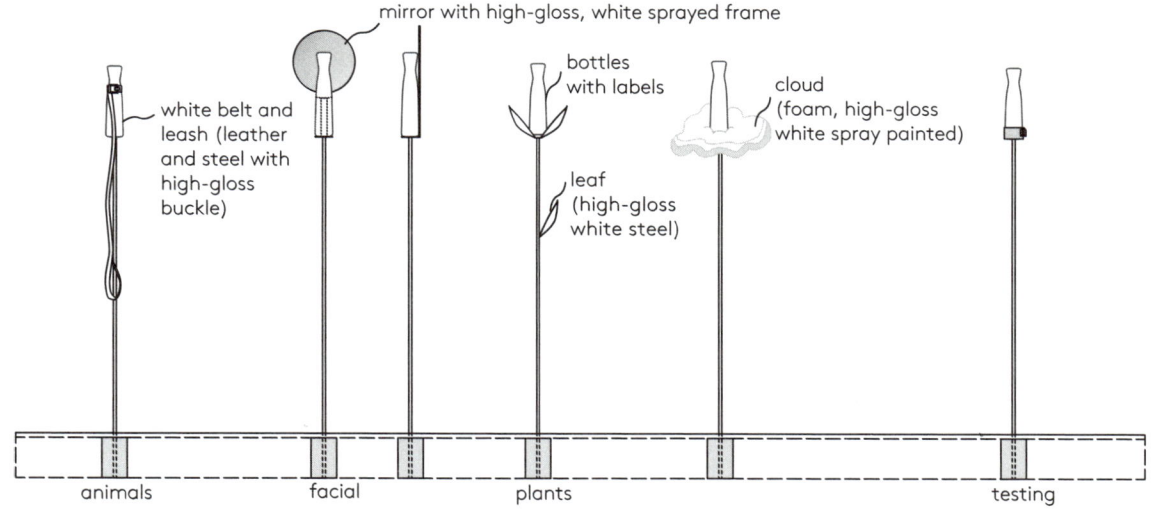

mirror with high-gloss, white sprayed frame

white belt and leash (leather and steel with high-gloss buckle)

bottles with labels

cloud (foam, high-gloss white spray painted)

leaf (high-gloss white steel)

animals   facial   plants   testing

MEETING ROOM

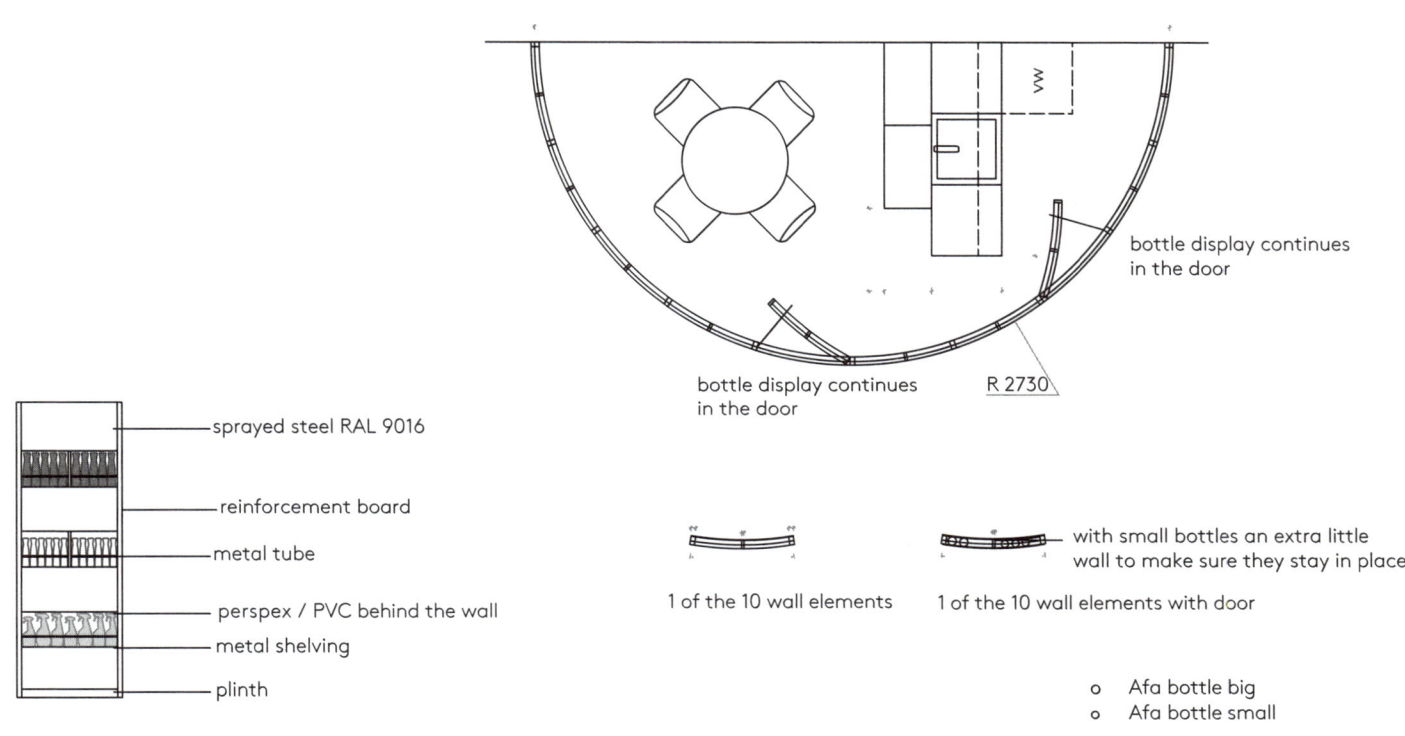

bottle display continues in the door

bottle display continues in the door

R 2730

sprayed steel RAL 9016

reinforcement board

metal tube

perspex / PVC behind the wall

metal shelving

plinth

1 of the 10 wall elements

with small bottles an extra little wall to make sure they stay in place

1 of the 10 wall elements with door

o   Afa bottle big
o   Afa bottle small

FLOOR PLAN

01 Meeting room
02 Testing area
03 Air fresheners
04 Water spray
05 Plant care
06 Pet spray
07 Beer tap

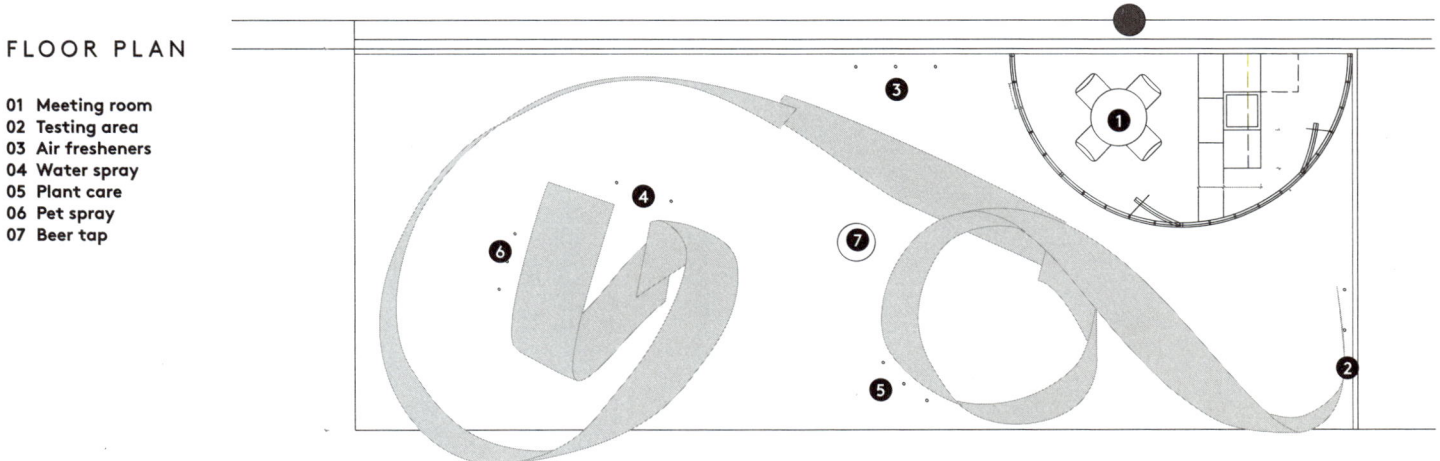

1

CURAPROX
MIND THE GAP!
CURAPROX
PREVENTION ONE
CURAPROX
CURAPROX ultra soft 5460

2

RAPROX
PREVENTION ONE
CURAPROX ultra soft 5460

CURAPROX

simple

1 Bright colours immersed visitors in the brand experience.

2 The company's trademark colours were proudly on show especially in the product displays and photography.

3 Open wide: each washstand was beautifully crafted with a basin, mirror, integrated lighting and an ornate stand.

TRADE FAIR **International Dental Show**
WHERE **Cologne, Germany**
WHEN **February 2015**
DESIGNER **simple**
STAND CONSTRUCTOR **simple**
CLIENT **Curaprox**
MARKET SECTOR **Dental care**
TOTAL FLOOR AREA **80 m²**
PHOTOGRAPHER **Annika Feuss**

3

Bright colours are not normally associated with dental hygiene, however, Curaprox used this to its advantage to create a stand that clearly stood out at the 2015 International Dental Show. In contrast to the pristine white look of most stands, Curaprox's booth was a celebration of colour and photography. This perfectly reflected the Swiss brand's brand identity – with its trademark colourful toothbrushes – and contemporary lifestyle approach to dental hygiene. Designed by simple, the stand comprised two sections separated by an aisle. One side catered to the German-speaking markets (Germany, Austria and Switzerland) and the other was dedicated to the international market. Large illuminated walls adorned with product and campaign photos, graphic patterns, vibrant colours and the company logo formed the framework of the stand. Strongly featured in the backdrop of oversized photography were the brand's iconic toothbrushes with their expressive colour combinations and bold form. Coloured floor coverings structured the area into zones according to product groups and themes. Five dainty washstands with basins and mirrors invited visitors to try out various products, and freestanding showcases artfully displayed other collections. As a playful detail, the entire range of inter-dental toothbrushes was presented on a spinning wheel of fortune. The rainbow colours of the iconic Curaprox toothbrushes were exhibited in compartments fashioned from sliding double-walled polycarbonate panels. Suspended inflatable foam clouds marked the stand from a distance. The combination of strong artwork, vivid colours and playful furnishings resulted in a surprising, sensory experience; dental hygiene has never looked more appealing. ⬤

DURABLE HUNKE & JOCHHEIM

Ueberholz

1 An architectural framework provided a solid, neutral backdrop for the stand.

2 Each module measured 24 m².

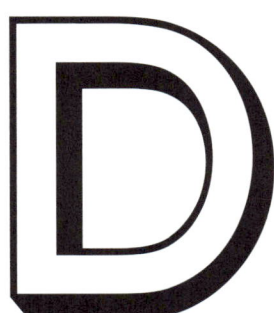

2

Durable Hunke & Jochheim, a producer of office equipment and accessories, placed Ueberholz in charge of its booth at Paperworld 2015. The company wanted a stand that could be easily and economically reused for upcoming events. The structure should be easy to assemble and disassemble, with a different appearance from conventional system stands. The design should enable a large number of small products to be exhibited in different ways, and be adaptable depending on the varying contexts of each trade fair. In this case, the presentation took place at Paperworld, the annual international trade fair for paper, office supplies and stationery products held in Frankfurt. The stand is divided into two sections. Durable Hunke & Jochheim occupied the larger stand while its sister label Pagna was located across the corridor. Ueberholz's concept utilised an architectural framework to first establish a solid, neutral foundation that was designed not to detract from the product. An aluminium post-and-beam construction facilitated a modular setup for maximum flexibility to accommodate changing exhibitions, and aesthetically, suggested more an architectural building facade instead of a booth stand system. Product groups were exhibited between the modules in individual zones. Across the corridor, Pagna's colourful and homely space reflected its retro office accessories on display. LED spotlights with different colour temperatures were used to differentiate the zones, and meetings areas were characterised by warmer lighting. Oversized images showed the products in use, making a visual link to the working world of the company's clients. Lighting and graphics were designed to be easily adapted according to the different needs of each presentation, as was the zoning of the meeting areas. ⚊

TRADE FAIR **Paperworld**
WHERE **Frankfurt, Germany**
WHEN **January 2015**
DESIGNER **Ueberholz**
STAND CONSTRUCTOR **Ueberholz**
CLIENT **Durable Hunke & Jochheim**
MARKET SECTOR **Office supplies**
TOTAL FLOOR AREA **240 m²**
PHOTOGRAPHER **Alexander Schwarz**

3

3 Across the corridor, the stand took on a homely atmosphere.

4 The retro lounge offered a comfortable, warm space to take a rest.

5 Products were exhibited in different zones dictated by the modules.

A FRAMED CONSTRUCTION ENABLES A FLEXIBLE MODULAR SETUP

4

5

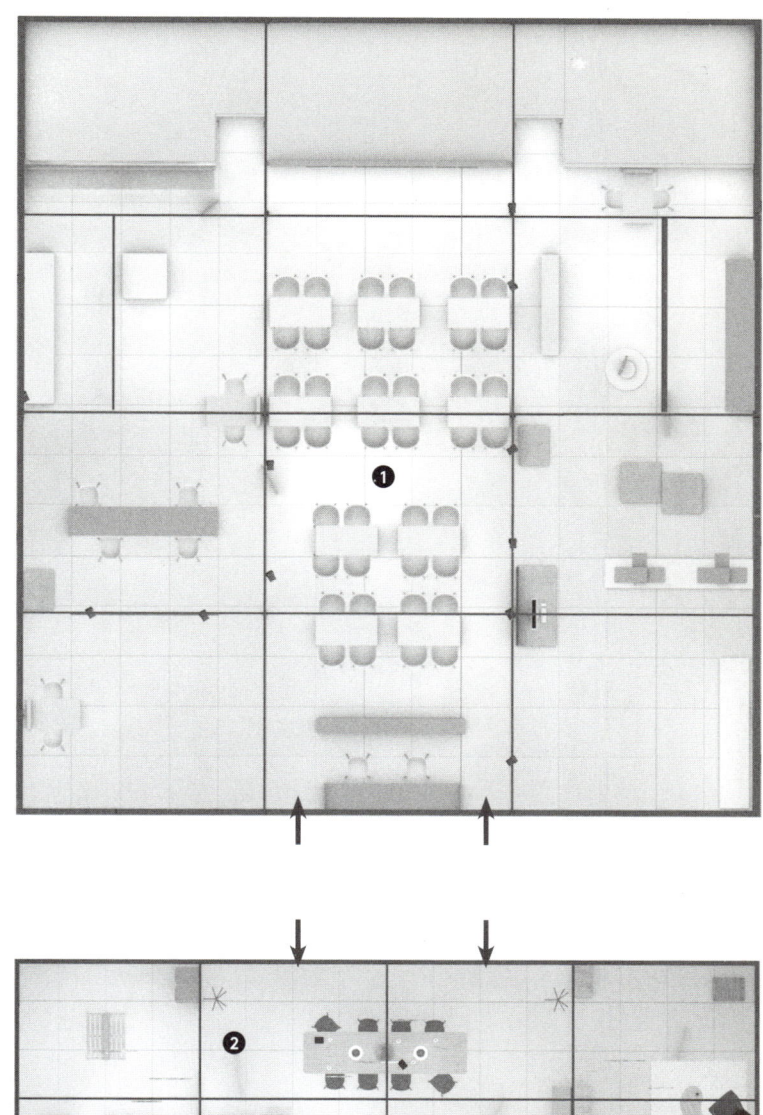

FLOOR PLAN

01 Durable Hunke & Jochheim
02 Pagna

KUHN RIKON
Uniplan

TRADE FAIR **Ambiente**
WHERE **Frankfurt, Germany**
WHEN **February 2014**
DESIGNER **Uniplan**
STAND CONSTRUCTOR **Uniplan**
CLIENT **Kuhn Rikon**
MARKET SECTOR **Kitchenware**
TOTAL FLOOR AREA **130 m²**
PHOTOGRAPHER **Stefan Schilling**

1 A red ladder complemented the white interior, a nod to the Swiss national colours.

2 Its spacious layout, warm materials and bright products lent the stand an inviting feel.

3 The cube units displayed the products in a structured format.

2

3

D

Designed by Uniplan, Kuhn Rikon's inviting stand at Ambiente 2014 perfectly reflected the brand's modern Swiss identity. The brief was to create a presentation for the company's kitchenware that made visitors feel at home and showcased each product as a unique tool. The stand should also feature an element of playfulness and not feel static. Prominently located on a corner, the stand immediately caught visitors' attentions with the flying cubes and bright products on display. Cubes, literally and figuratively, formed the building blocks of the design. Each cube featured a different product, which gave each item its own individual stage. On the perimeter of the space were themed islands consisting of cubes stacked onto horizontal L-shaped wooden bases. Here, visitors were invited to interact more closely with the products. At the ends of the benches, white cubes launched upwards to join other cubes overhead, appearing as if they were flying out of their wooden transport crates. Visible from afar, the suspended boxes functioned as eye-catchers and animated the space. At the back, a high wall of cubes extended the full height of the stand, with a central section also fashioned from wood in line with the themed islands. In front of the back wall, a long test station provided the opportunity for visitors to use the products. A central seating area hosted informal meetings. The use of a simple base palette of white and wood accentuated the vibrant colours of the kitchenware, giving them maximum visual presence. The cubes interplayed the balance between modern minimal design with traditional materials and craftsmanship, showing the best sides of Swiss design. ⏤

PROJECT KYO-TO
Little

1 The simple finishing and detailing of the textile divider avoids detracting attention from the presentation.

2 Minimal, serene and graceful: Project Kyo-To's stand translated Japanese traditions into a new light.

3 Images on the outer faces of the pedestals featured details of the products displayed.

2

3

P

Project Kyo-to brings together 20 artisans in a unique initiative that connects traditional techniques from Kyoto with the future. For four years in a row now, the 20 new craft products realised are launched to a global audience at the Tokyo International Gift Show. In 2014 Saori Miwa from Little was once again in charge of designing the stand. The idea was to create an atmosphere of 'Kyoto-ness' in Tokyo and communicate Kyoto's transition into the future. In line with the concept of Project Kyo-to, Japanese heritage formed the starting point. The idea was to wrap the space with the precious craft objects on display and then unveil them to the world. This gesture derived from Furoshiki, a traditional Japanese wrapping cloth used to carry gifts, objects, clothes or other goods. A suspended translucent white fabric formed the primary element of the space. Hung at the top of the stand across the front and curving around the side, it created a calm border that demarcated interior from exterior. This feature also took inspiration from Noren, delicate Japanese curtain dividers hung in doorways to mark transitions between spaces or on walls or windows. Spotlighting was used to illuminate the divider in a dramatic way, beautifully accentuating the textile's texture and transparency. Products from the 20 exhibitors were displayed on simple white rectangular pedestals, each item allocated an equal amount of space. Prints on the sides of the volumes depicted detailed textures of the products. Orientated along the stand, the row of pedestals also functioned as an information counter. Dark flooring intensified the lightness of the delicate space, which successfully evoked the charm and grace of Kyoto. ⸺

TRADE FAIR **Tokyo International Gift Show**
WHERE **Tokyo, Japan**
WHEN **February 2014**
DESIGNER **Little**
STAND CONSTRUCTOR **D-9**
CLIENT **Kyoto Chamber of Commerce and Industry**
PRODUCER **Sachio Hihara**
MARKET SECTOR **Craft products**
TOTAL FLOOR AREA **72 m²**
PHOTOGRAPHER **Kenta Hasegawa**

CONSUMER PRODUCTS

GRAND STAND 5

SODASTREAM
Barzilai Exhibition Experts

1 The capsule installation was set against a bright and fun background with vibrant visuals.

2 Varying themed areas summoned visitors to engage with the brand in different ways.

2

SodaStream is the world's largest manufacturer of home carbonation systems. For its presentation at the International Housewares fair, the company approached Barzilai, with whom they have successfully collaborated before this scope. The client envisioned a space that effectively communicated the brand's new messaging, 'stylish rebel', in line with key themes of 'fun', 'health', 'freshness' and 'engagement', while reflecting the company's core values.

Focusing on maximising the visitor experience, the designers sought to demonstrate how simple, convenient and fun it is to create your own soda beverage

at home. The challenge was to bring these elements into play, while infusing the right amount of colour to convey the soda variety. Two main strategies were applied to fulfil the design aims: the use of wood panelling, white walls, and modern furniture evoke a contemporary home environment, while rebellious, vivid colours reflected the brand identity and syrup range.

The stand was divided into separate areas with themed partitions to create well-defined presentation spaces. The new carbonation system, 'The Source', was presented on white pedestals in a dedicated space while the existing collection was nestled into a wooden wall. Two separate demonstration bars invited visitors to engage with the products. Three access points controlled the flow of traffic through the stand. To present the brand's soda variety was a colourful mobile, featuring 367 suspended capsules.

High-definition background visuals and bright packaging further emphasized the burst of fruit flavours. The 'Cage of Global Shame' was a provocative installation consisting of 56 metal cells filled with plastic soda bottles, demonstrating the issue of environmental waste associated with conventional soda drinks.

The overall result was a highly aesthetic, young-spirited and vibrant space that inspired visitor interaction and brand engagement. ▬

TRADE FAIR **International Housewares**
WHERE **Chicago, United States**
WHEN **March 2013**
DESIGNER **Barzilai Exhibition Experts**
STAND CONSTRUCTOR **Expo Veres**
CLIENT **SodaStream**
MARKET SECTOR **Home carbonation systems**
TOTAL FLOOR AREA **325 m²**
PHOTOGRAPHER **Arthur Mueller**

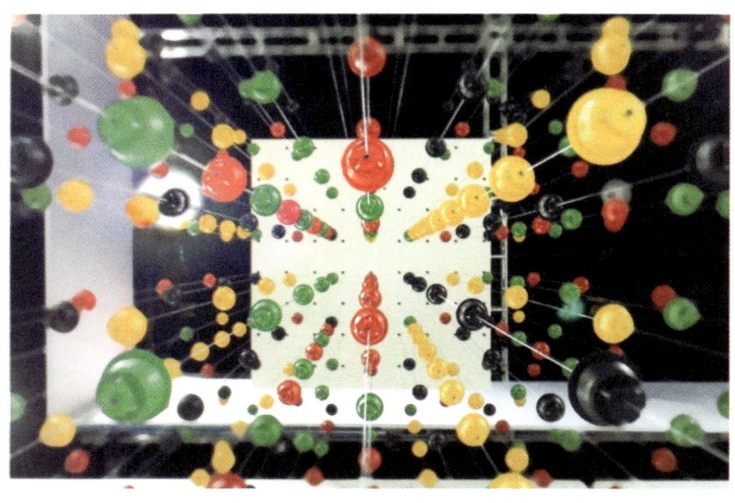

3

REBELLIOUS, VIVID COLOURS REFLECT THE BRAND IDENTITY AND FRUIT FLAVOURS

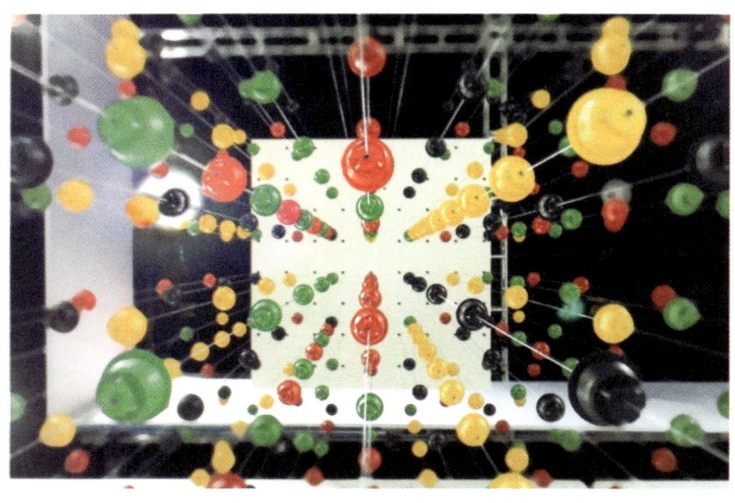

4

5

RENDERINGS

3 The wall of the informal meeting area featured the outline of a modern kitchen.

4 For the feature installation, 367 capsules were strung on metal wires suspended from the ceiling.

5 The back wall features the complete product range and syrup variety.

FLOOR PLAN

01 Source area
02 Frontal bar
03 Media wall
04 Open meeting area
05 Caps display
06 Partnership display
07 Bottles cage
08 Back bar
09 Syrups wall
10 Machines display
11 Meeting room
12 USA merchandise
13 Storage

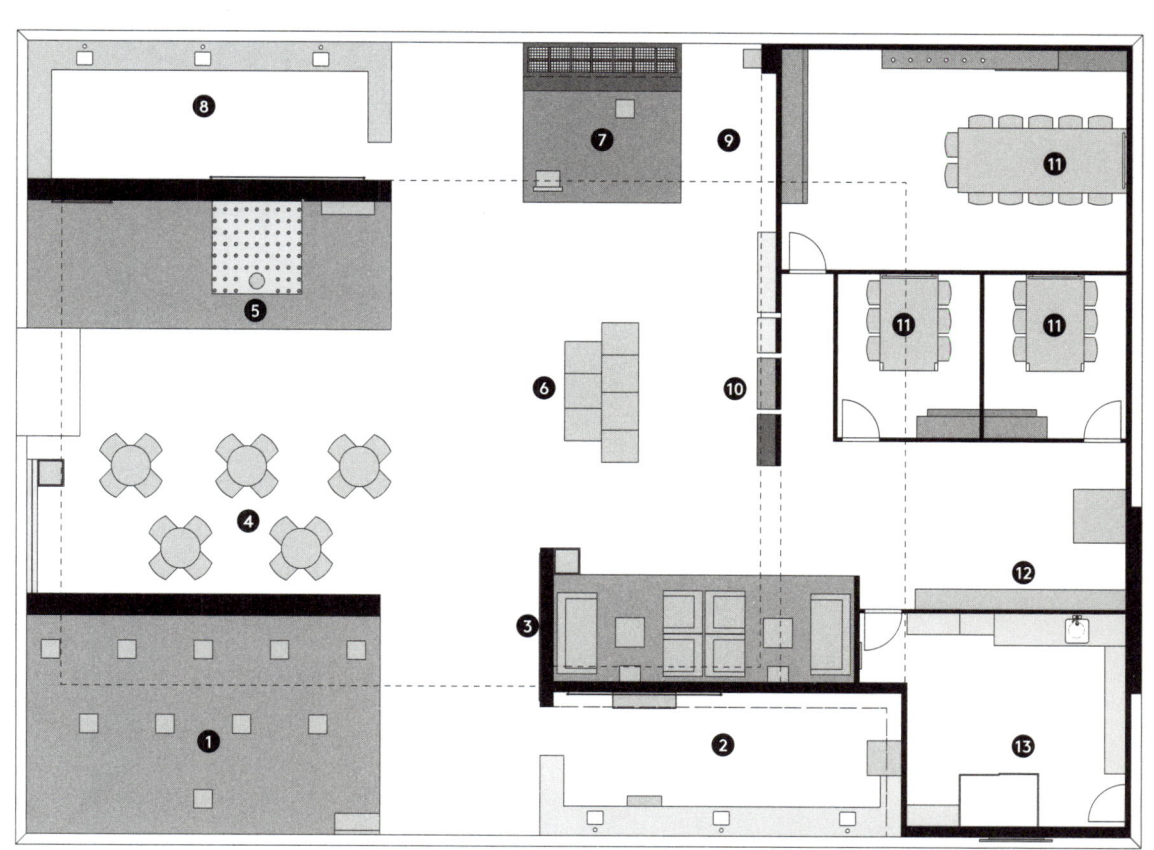

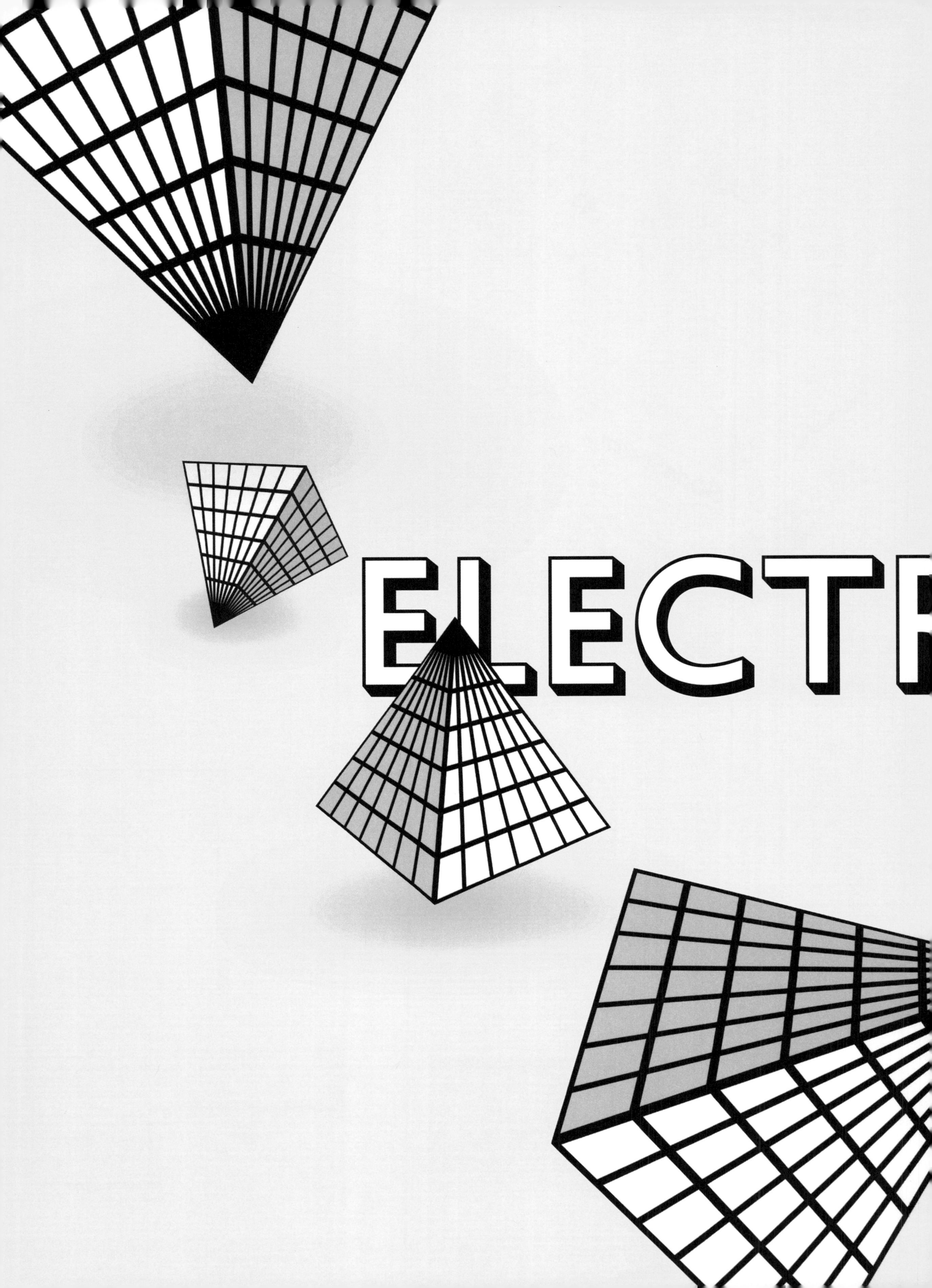

ELECTR

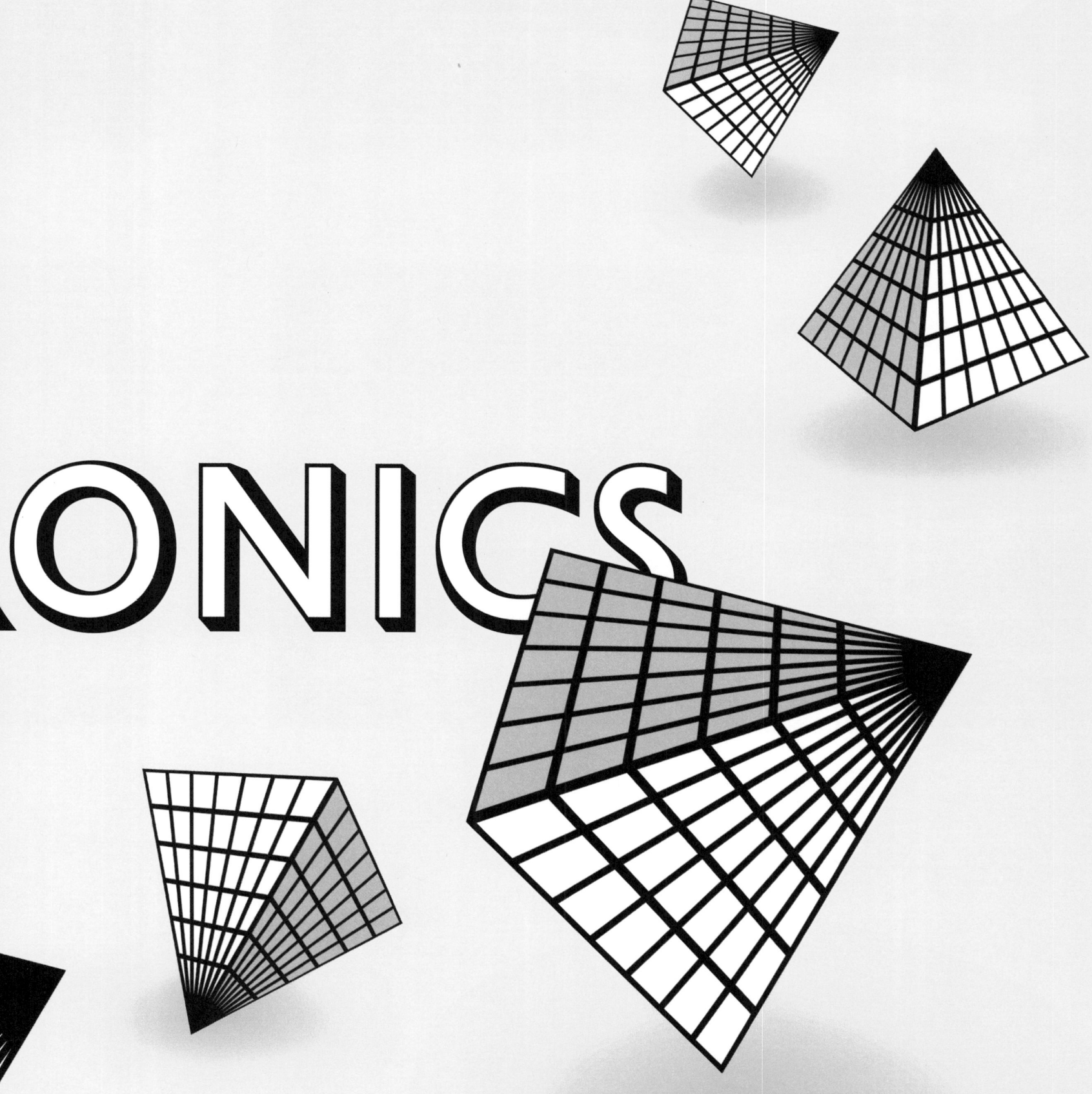

ELECTRONICS GRAND STAND 5

BEKO

eins:33

1 A lush vertical garden with vegetable plants and herbs was a feast for the eyes.

2 A central courtyard formed the focal point of the stand where platform seating area built under real pine trees invited visitors to take a break from the busy fair.

2

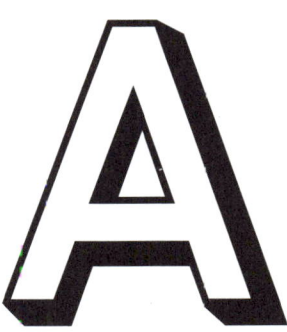

A friendly green urban campus awaited fair visitors at Beko's presentation at IFA in 2014. For its fourth presentation at this consumer electronics and home appliances fair, Beko wanted its stand to express the company's innovative and responsible approach, global relevance and close relationship with the consumer. The focus should remain on important themes relevant to today's consumers, namely sustainability and wellbeing. With this in mind eins:33 conceived an inviting design inspired by urban gardens,

in particular the High Line in New York, that transported fairgoers into a green oasis. The nearly stand was transformed into a buzzing urban landscape dotted with different architectural structures. Walking through the vast space visitors discovered a roof landscape with beehives, a vertical garden with flowers and vegetables and a live cooking station. Centrally located was a courtyard-like recreation area with felt-covered decks and platform seating which was ideal for guests to take a break from the busy fair. Three pine trees and the sounds of twittering birds added a sense of nature and atmosphere of relaxation. Complementing these natural areas were surrounding product presentation sections that had a more technical appearance to highlight functionality and

environmental performance. Different materials were used on the floors to define the various exhibition sections, resulting in a dynamic floorscape. The spacious layout of the stand facilitated a good flow of traffic through the space and ensured the presentations were well visible. ⊐

TRADE FAIR **IFA**
WHERE **Berlin, Germany**
WHEN **September 2014**
DESIGNER **eins:33**
STAND CONSTRUCTOR **Raumtechnik, Messebau & Event Services**
CLIENT **Beko**
MARKET SECTOR **Household appliances**
TOTAL FLOOR AREA **1740 m²**
PHOTOGRAPHER **Felix Nürmberger**

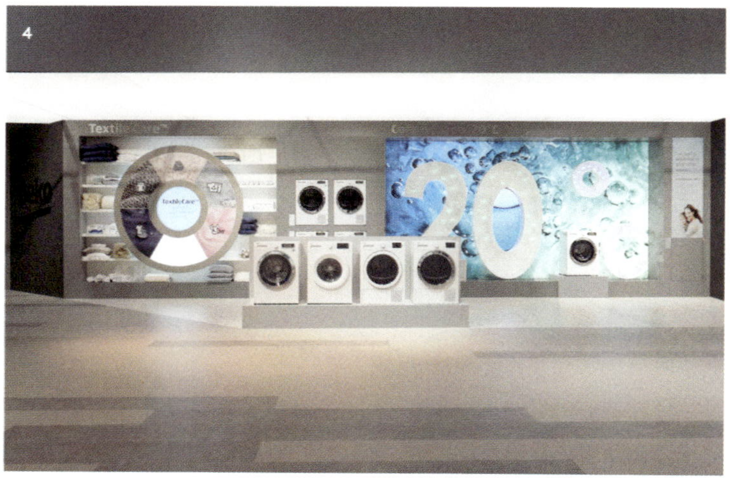

3 Designed like an inviting roof terrace, the informal meeting area was surrounded by beehives and colourful flowers.

4 Product presentation areas focused on functionality and environmental performance.

5 The awards showcase presented the accolades awarded to Beko's designs.

6 A sculptural installation of wine glasses accompanied the dishwasher display.

AN INVITING GREEN CAMPUS AWAITS FAIRGOERS AT BEKO'S STAND

THE BUZZING URBAN LANDSCAPE IS DOTTED WITH ARCHITECTURAL STRUCTURES

RENDERINGS

SECTIONS

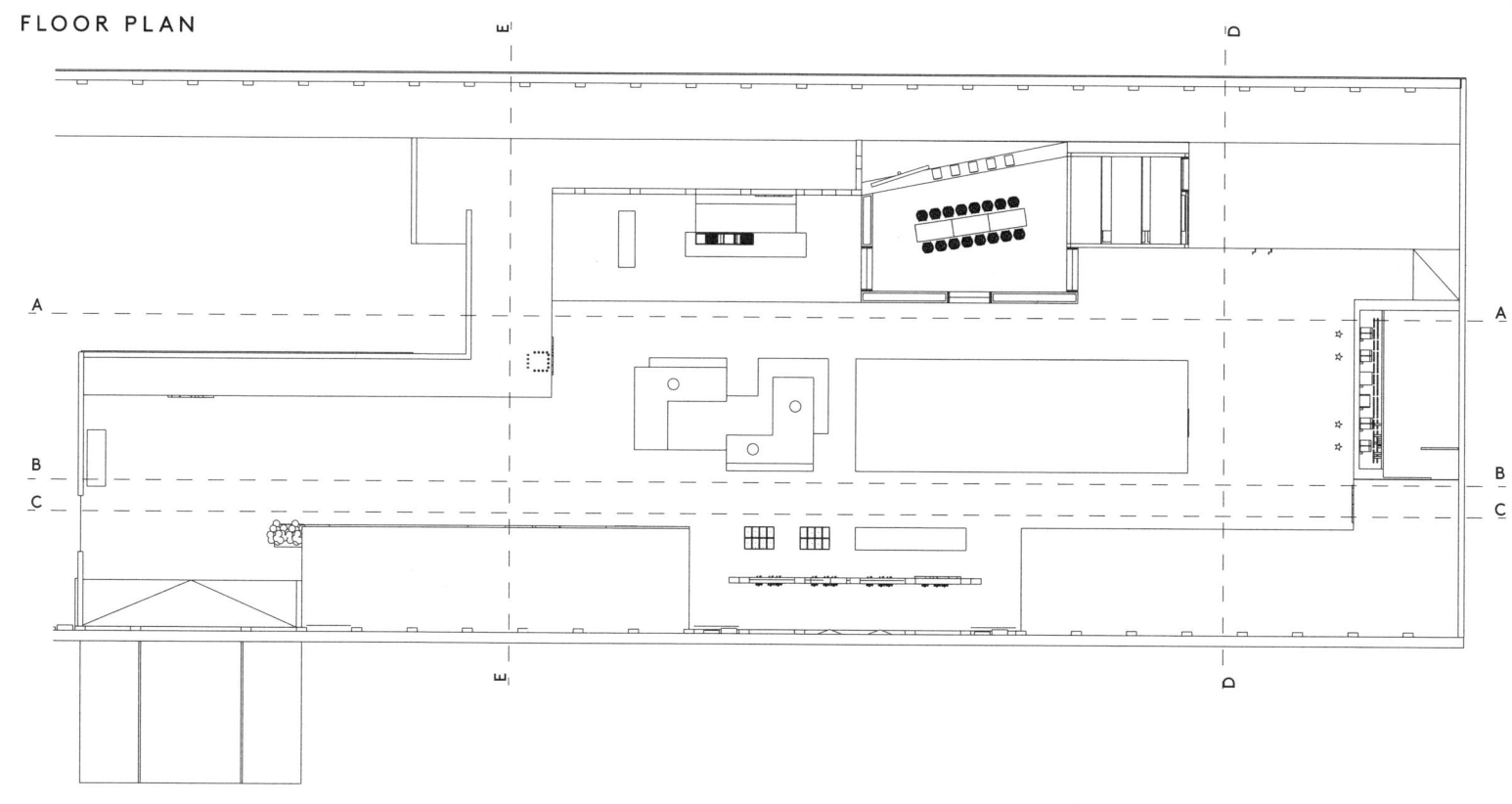

Section AA

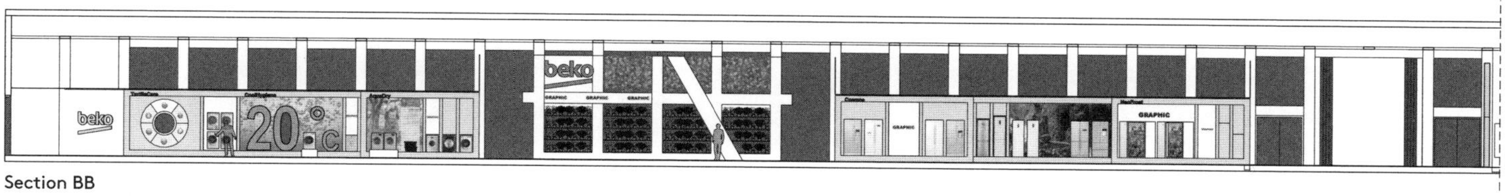

Section BB

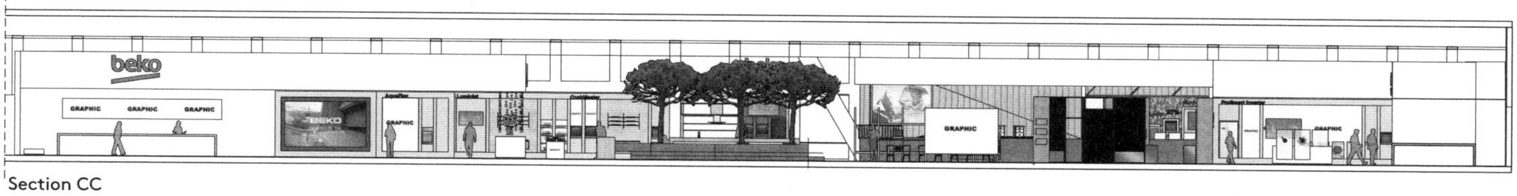

Section CC

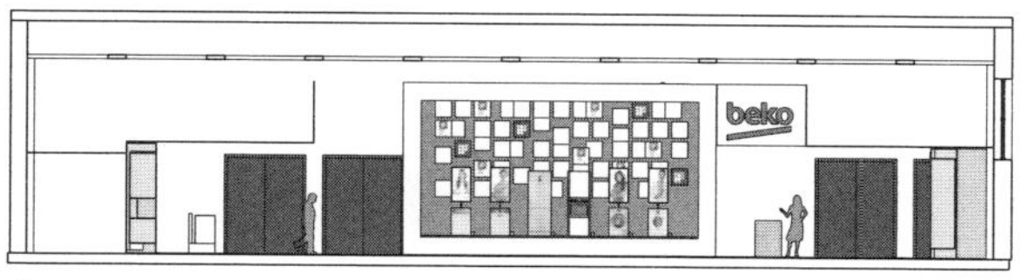

Section DD

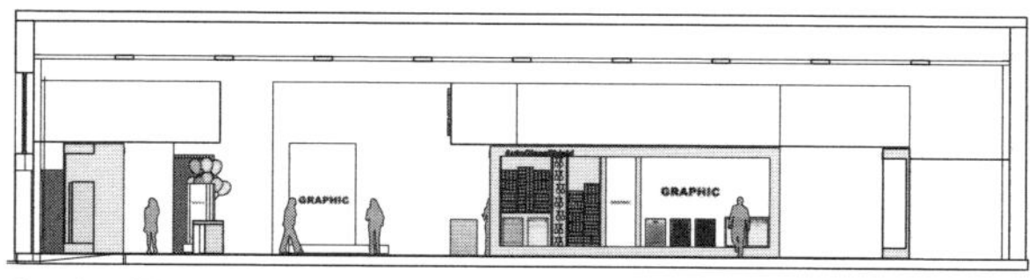

Section EE

FLOOR PLAN

FREOR

a01

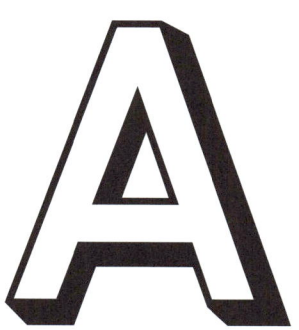

a01 architektai were tasked with designing the presentation for the fridge and freezer producer Freor at EuroShop 2014. Fittingly, the design of the double storey stand focused on the concept of frost/freeze. A series of inverted triangular metal fins formed the principal element of the stand, appearing almost as oversized icicles. These 7.3-metre-high fins divided the stand into a grid of 3 x 5, each square measuring 3 x 3 metres. The fins were orientated in varying directions to establish a dynamic spatial grid internally and demarcate the boundaries of the stand externally.

Inverting the triangles on the ground floor created more floor space for exhibiting Freor's products and for the movement of visitors. Designed without any enclosed walls, the ground floor had an open and inviting atmosphere. The space felt more enclosed as the triangles started to widen towards the ceiling, which perfectly suited the private function of the upper spaces used for meetings, receiving guests or just chilling out. Zigzagging through the stand, the upper floor had a triangular geometry that reflected the overall theme. The use of white united the design in line with frost/freeze.

In contrast with the coolness of the stand, a warm element was introduced in the form of an angular copper reception counter. Composed from copper-finished HPL (high pressure laminates) board, the counter looked like a skilfully folded origami object. Copper also referred to the copper tubes used for circulating the freezing agent in fridges and freezers. The theatrical combination of ice and light also found its way into the design, where each fin was uplit with a spotlight for dramatic effect and perforations in the steel created a beautiful texture in the fins, especially when viewed with light from behind. ▬

TRADE FAIR **EuroShop**
WHERE **Düsseldorf, Germany**
WHEN **February 2014**
DESIGNER **a01 architektai**
STAND CONSTRUCTOR **Freor**
CLIENT **Freor**
MARKET SECTOR **Refrigeration equipment**
TOTAL FLOOR AREA **217 m²**
PHOTOGRAPHER **Courtesy of a01 architektai**

1 Its striking triangular composition made the Freor booth well recognisable from afar.

2 a01's design for the Freor stand celebrated the idea of frost/freeze.

3 Perforations in the metal fins lent a sense of texture and depth.

GROUND FLOOR

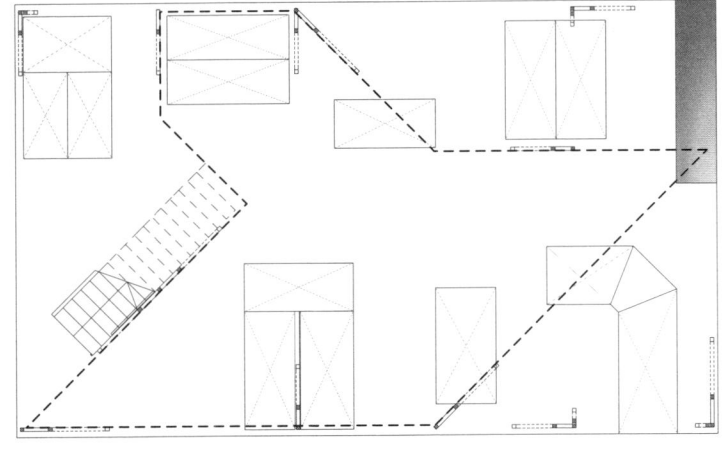

FIRST FLOOR

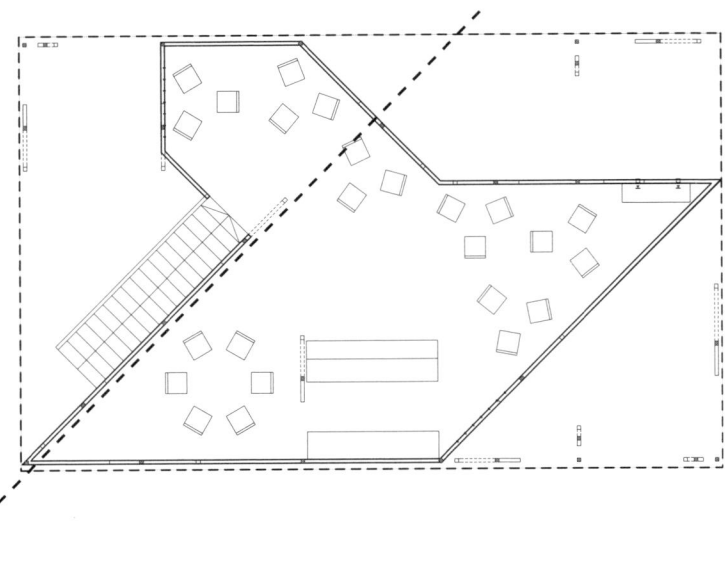

Section

INVERTED TRIANGULAR METAL FINS APPEAR ALMOST AS OVERSIZED ICICLES

SECTION

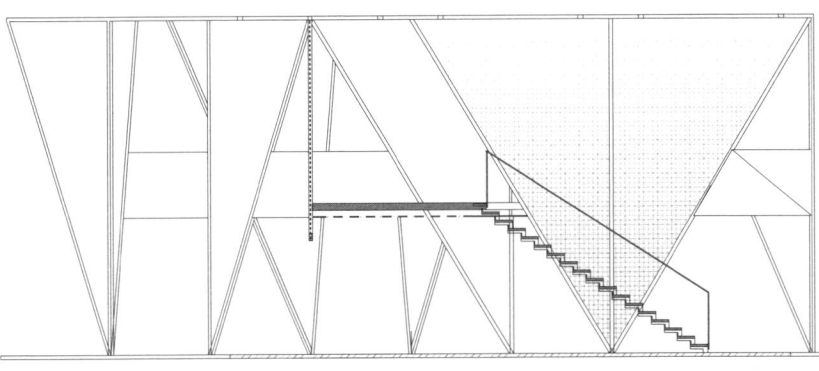

3D PERSPECTIVE RECEPTION TABLE

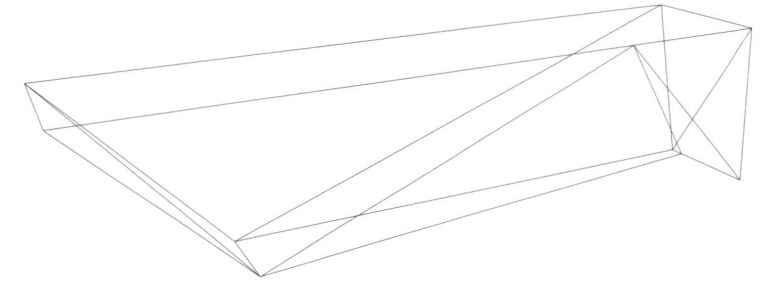

FRONT ELEVATION

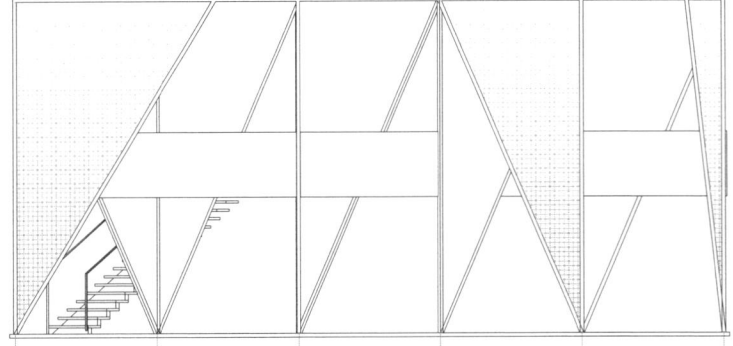

SIDE ELEVATION

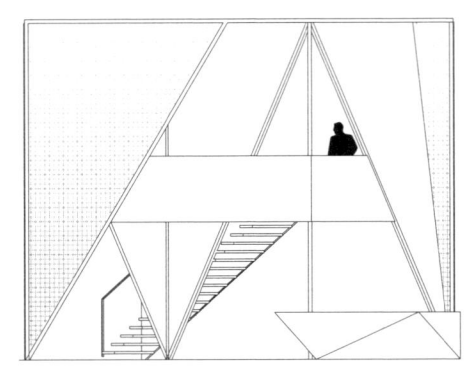

4 The copper bar provided a warm contrast to the coolness of the stand.

FUJITSU
Walbert-Schmitz

1 Designed as the event's communication hub, the imaginary hyper-connected city brought together participants at the Fujitsu Forum.

2 Dynamic facades were constructed from backlit textiles.

3 Participants could meet and chat at various social spaces or watch the lectures from seating areas.

3

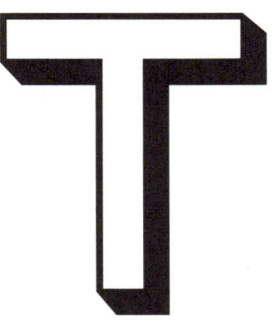

The Fujitsu Forum is Fujitsu's largest IT event in Europe held annually at the International Conference Center in Munich. The event brings together diverse parties including companies, partners and institutions to users and presents the latest in ICT trends, new ideas and intelligent opinions. Keynotes and breakout sessions form the core of the programme. The theme for 2014's event explored 'Human Centric Innovation', relating to the idea of global technology and Fujitsu's vision of the continuous pursuit of innovation as the driving force behind business objectives. Walbert-Schmitz was responsible for designing the setting of the main public space which formed the communication of the event. A starting point was the campaign image that featured a stunning nightscape of blurred city lights. The concept of a hyper-connected city was developed to visualise the idea of global technology and guide visitors into Fujitsu's world. The designers imagined a futuristic and abstract city in which visitors had the opportunity to meet, interact and exchange new ideas within their business field. In the entrance hall illuminated high-rises with different styles of architecture set the stage. Their vibrant facades were fashioned from backlit textile stretched over different shaped frames. Changing facade lighting and projections alluded to the movements of a connected city. An angled urban plan positioned the tall buildings to create dynamic in-between spaces used for various functions. Open gathering areas provided plentiful space for people to meet and large viewing sections with screens enabled participants to watch the keynotes. Fujitsu's innovations were also showcased throughout in various exhibition areas. Furthermore the venue's gates, passages and staircases were concealed as much as possible (without compromising safety and security) to create a realistic, atmospheric setting that truly immersed visitors in Fujitsu's realm. ⇒

TRADE FAIR **Fujitsu Forum**
WHERE **Munich, Germany**
WHEN **November 2014**
DESIGNER **Walbert-Schmitz**
STAND CONSTRUCTOR **Walbert-Schmitz**
CLIENT **Fujitsu Technology Solutions**
MARKET SECTOR **Computing**
TOTAL FLOOR AREA **1000 m²**
PHOTOGRAPHER **Andrè Loessel**

GRUNDIG
D'art Design Gruppe

TRADE FAIR **IFA**
WHERE **Berlin, Germany**
WHEN **September 2014**
DESIGNER **D'art Design Gruppe**
STAND CONSTRUCTOR **Visage
Messe- und Ausstellungsbau**
CLIENT **Grundig Intermedia**
MARKET SECTOR **Consumer electronics**
TOTAL FLOOR AREA **890 m²**
PHOTOGRAPHER **Lukas Palik**

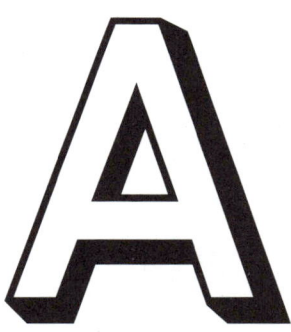

A mysterious nocturnal landscape marked the seventh successful collaboration between D'art Design Gruppe and Grundig at IFA, the leading trade show for consumer electronics. For its 2014 presentation Grundig showcased its latest home entertainment collection, with a special spotlight on TVs.

On the stand, visitors were transported into the depths of night. Amidst a completely blacked-out environment, dark cubes were stacked and framed in luminescent bands of pale blue light. The blue lines moved fluidly through the dramatic dark backdrop, lending the space depth and dynamism. The eight-metre-high installation had a distinctly urban quality, with high screens resembling billboards. Housed in and around the cubes were presentations of seven different product areas, which were indicated by illuminated oversized icons and text that were designed not to detract from the main attraction: the TVs. Consequently, products from the ultra-high definition series occupied most of the stand. Here, screens were artfully displayed and floated like mobile paintings in a gallery-like space. Two highlight presentations of curved TVs were complemented by a suspended circular light installation, whose form was echoed in the illuminated lines in the floor. Fashion and technology met on an illuminated catwalk with a half-hourly fashion show presented in collaboration with fashion label HolyGhost. Large LED walls broadcasted the show into the whole exhibition area. Hair care products were showcased in the styling studio adjacent to the exhibition area, its dark atmosphere reflecting the mood of the stand. After having their hair professionally styled, visitors could capture their new look in a photo booth with a Polaroid camera. It wasn't all dark: with a sunny yellow interior that contrasted with the dark night, the sound box exhibited the latest in compact audio products. ▬

1 The mystery of darkness and neon light enticed fairgoers onto the Grundig stand.

2 Illuminated frames focused all eyes on the screens.

2

4

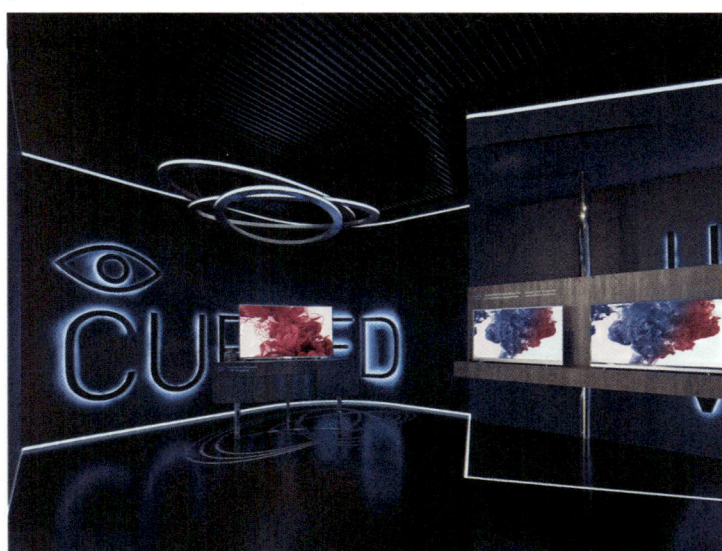

5

6

3 Fashion took the spotlight on the illuminated catwalk and screen above.

3 Fashion took the spotlight on the illuminated catwalk and screen above.

4 The popular gaming box formed one of seven product areas.

5 The image quality of the TVs was enhanced by the extreme darkness of the stand.

6 An oversized screen that broadcast the fashion shows appeared as a beacon.

VISITORS ARE TRANSPORTED INTO THE DEPTHS OF NIGHT

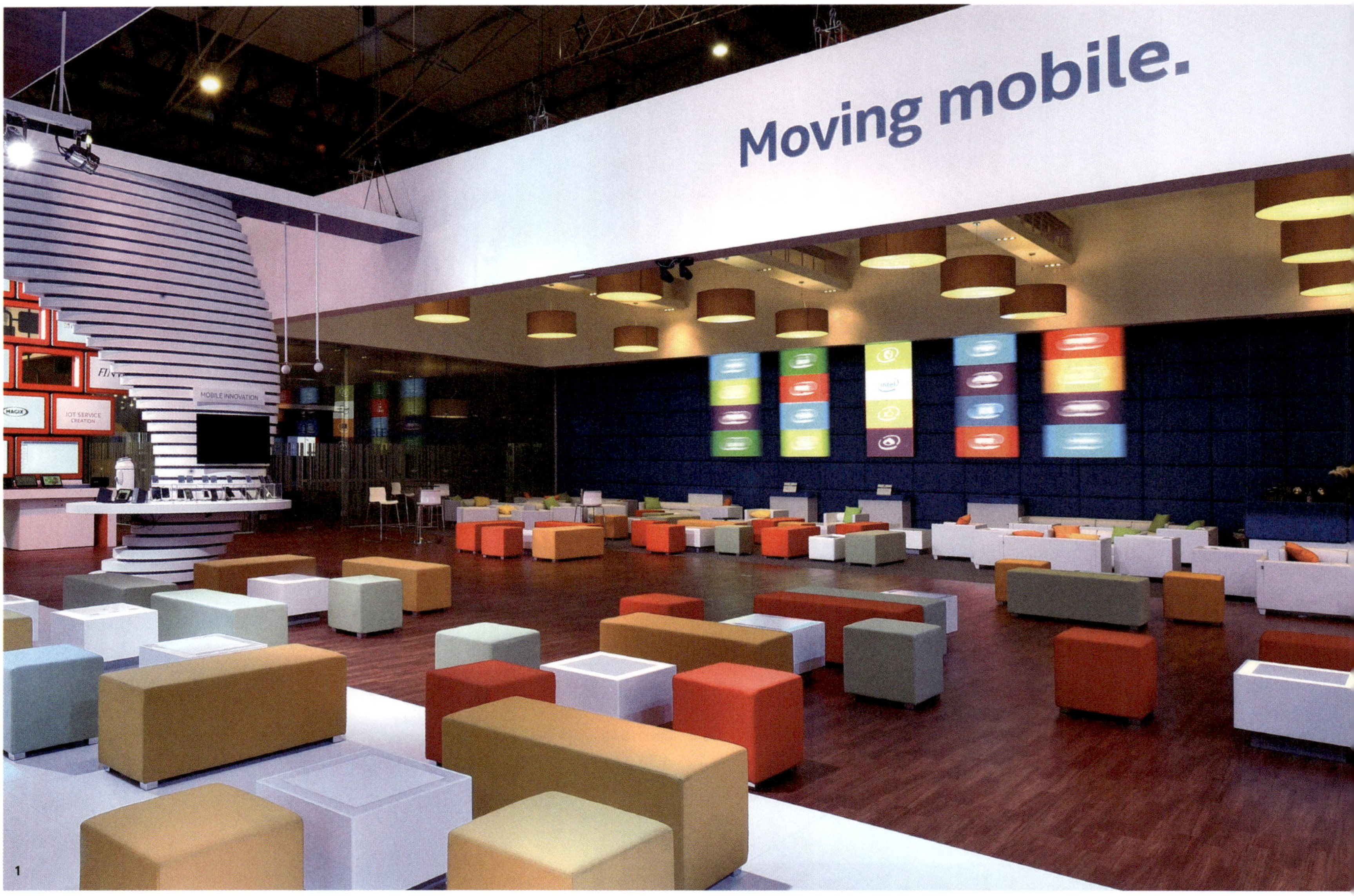
Moving mobile.
1

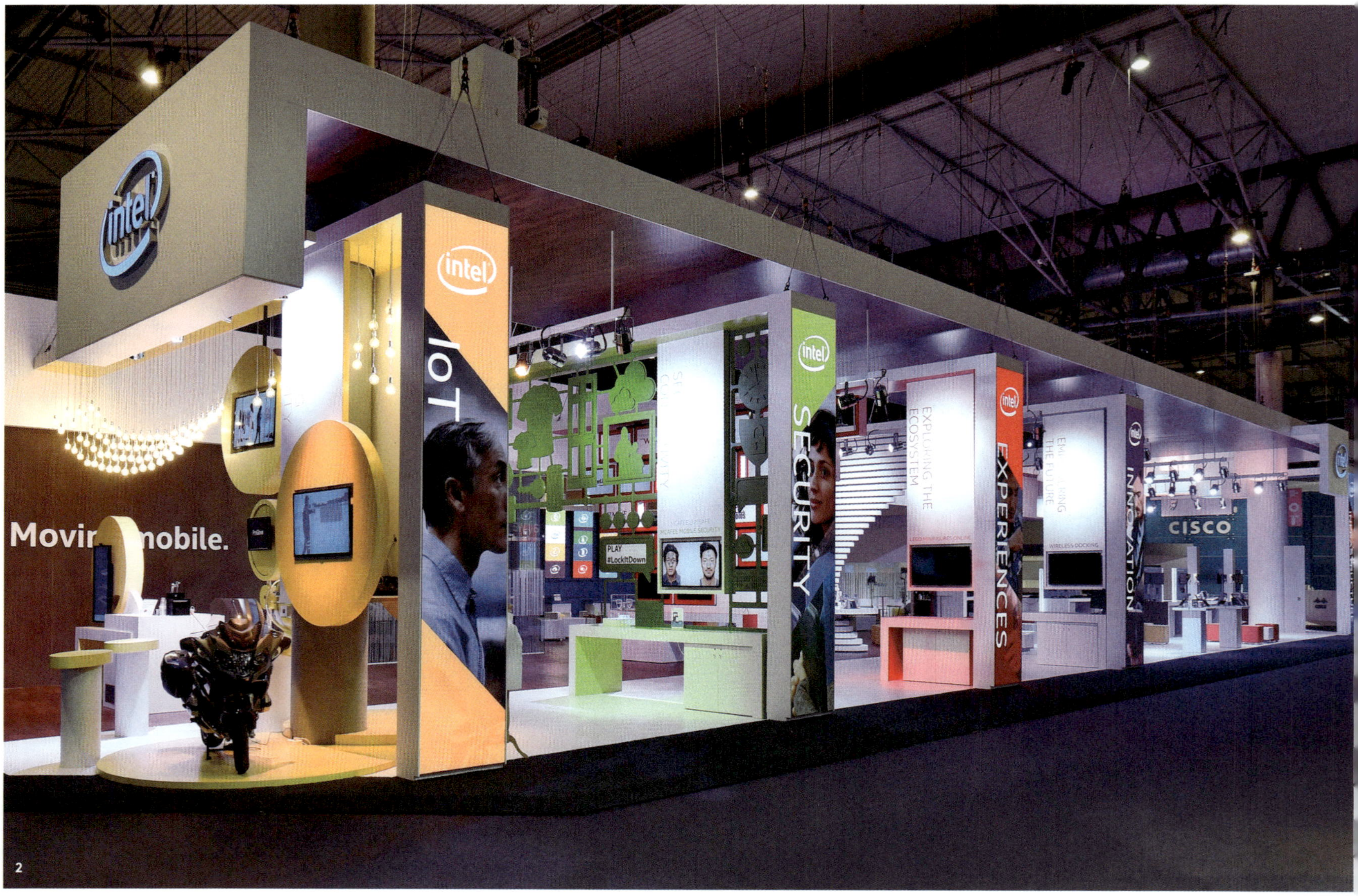
intel
IoT
SECURITY
EXPLORING THE ECOSYSTEM
EXPERIENCES
INNOVATION
CISCO
2

INTEL
2LK Design

1 The colourful modular lounge furniture echoed the vibrance of the stand.

2 The experiential gateways and themes were identified by distinguishing colours.

3 Digital and tangible exhibits complemented each other in the presentation to encourage maximum visitor engagement.

3

For the 2015 edition of the annual Mobile World Congress (MWC), Intel commissioned 2LK Design to develop a stand that would significantly raise its profile in the mobile market. Every design decision was focused around three main aims: raising visibility, increasing desirability and reinforcing brand credibility.

The strategy was to create an immersive and participatory environment to encourage maximum hands-on engagement with the high profile audience on the show floor. Prominent experiential 'gateways' placed at the front of the booth attracted visitors onto the stand. Using a distinguishing style and colour, each gateway highlighted different applications of Intel technology under key themes.

Designed to facilitate interaction and promote participation, the gateways became active spaces to inform, inspire and delight. Visitors were encouraged to touch and explore the products on display. A conscious effort was made to profile next generation technologies; experimental prototypes were exhibited below a 30 m² suspended cloud sculpture and Intel wearable technology demonstrated in real-world scenarios.

Informative digital content was designed alongside the physical structure ensuring an integrated brand expression, including a giant kinetic LED screen. Conceived to perform multiple functions the Tech Lounge was pivotal to the stand. This flexible space evolved throughout the day acting as a public hospitality lounge and demo space, hosting cocktail parties, interviews, competitions, video blogging sessions and staff briefings. Lightweight modular furniture allowed the space to be easily reconfigured to accommodate these changing functions. Theatrical lighting and changing content on the huge kinetic video wall helped to transform the space. ⚊

TRADE FAIR **Mobile World Congress**
WHERE **Barcelona, Spain**
WHEN **March 2015**
DESIGNER **2LK Design**
STAND CONSTRUCTOR **Level Exhibitions**
CLIENT **Intel Corporation**
MARKET SECTOR **Computers**
TOTAL FLOOR AREA **1800 m²**
PHOTOGRAPHER **Steve Eastell**

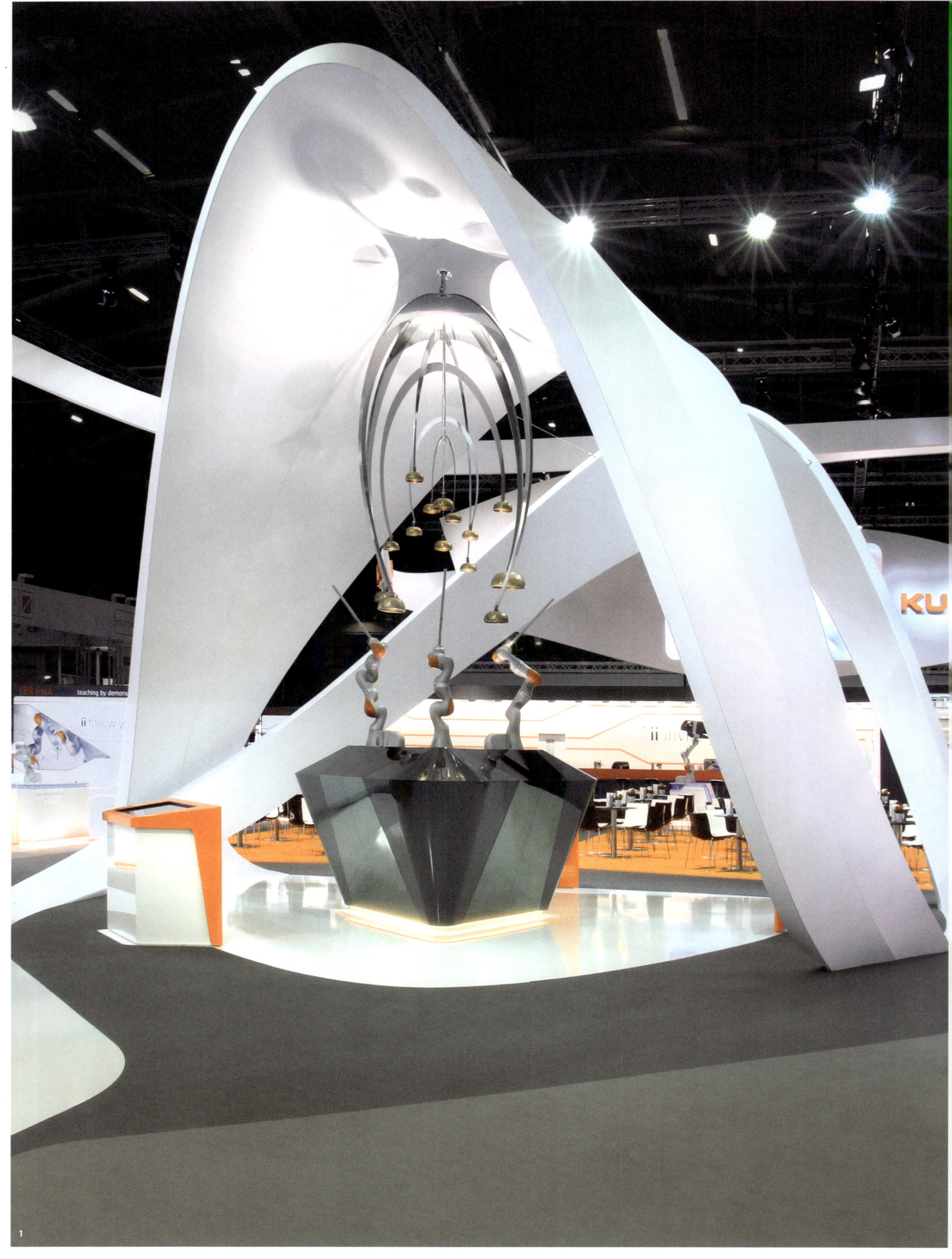

KUKA
Benz & Ziegler

1 The sculptural quality of the pavilion and installation presented the new robots in an eye-catching way.

2 Strongly branded with Kuka's corporate identity, the information counter welcomed visitors onto the stand.

2

Kuka is a leading manufacturer of robotics systems and automation technology. Automatica, the international trade fair for robotics forms a core element of Kuka's global brand communication as it sets the tone for subsequent shows to come. For its presentation at Automatica 2014, Kuka wanted to celebrate the launch of a major innovation in sensitive robotics: the LBR iiwa, the first sensitive lightweight robot suitable for industrial applications. These intelligent robots are equipped with sensors to detect human contact or movement, which enables very close interaction between humans and robots.

Thanks to this, protective barriers become obsolete, opening up new possibilities for processes and applications previously off-limits for robots. Under the project lead of Weiskind Werbeagentur, Benz & Ziegler took inspiration from this new sense of freedom, openness and flexibility to develop the architecture for the stand.

A main challenge posed the question of how to generate a big presence for a relatively small product. The freedom of movement by sensitive robotics is used as a metaphorical starting point translating the freeform movements into a series of large expressive sculptural forms that wound through the stand. A sinuous white pavilion was positioned centrally to showcase the robots in motion. In a series of sweeping, choreographed moves, the robots automatically avoided the suspended moving chimes, demonstrating their reactive ability. The fluidity of the lines continued in the suspended ribbons that curved around the stand's boundaries above. Framing

the edges were 12 interactive themed booths that represented capabilities of the robots applied in actual working scenarios. The spacious bar and lounge formed the communication hub of the stand. The use of Kuka's corporate colour orange throughout made a strong visual impact. With its slick presentation inspired entirely by the product, Kuka succeeded in creating a strong brand presence at Automatica. ⸺

TRADE FAIR **Automatica**
WHERE **Munich, Germany**
WHEN **June 2014**
DESIGNER **Benz & Ziegler**
STAND CONSTRUCTOR **Zeeh Design**
CLIENT **Kuka Robotics**
MARKET SECTOR **Robotics**
TOTAL FLOOR AREA **880 m²**
PHOTOGRAPHER **Fine Result**

3 Themed booths featured custom-designed furniture with Corian counters and lacquered sides.

4 Sketches illustrating the sculptural forms running through the stand.

5 Sketch of the robot presentation.

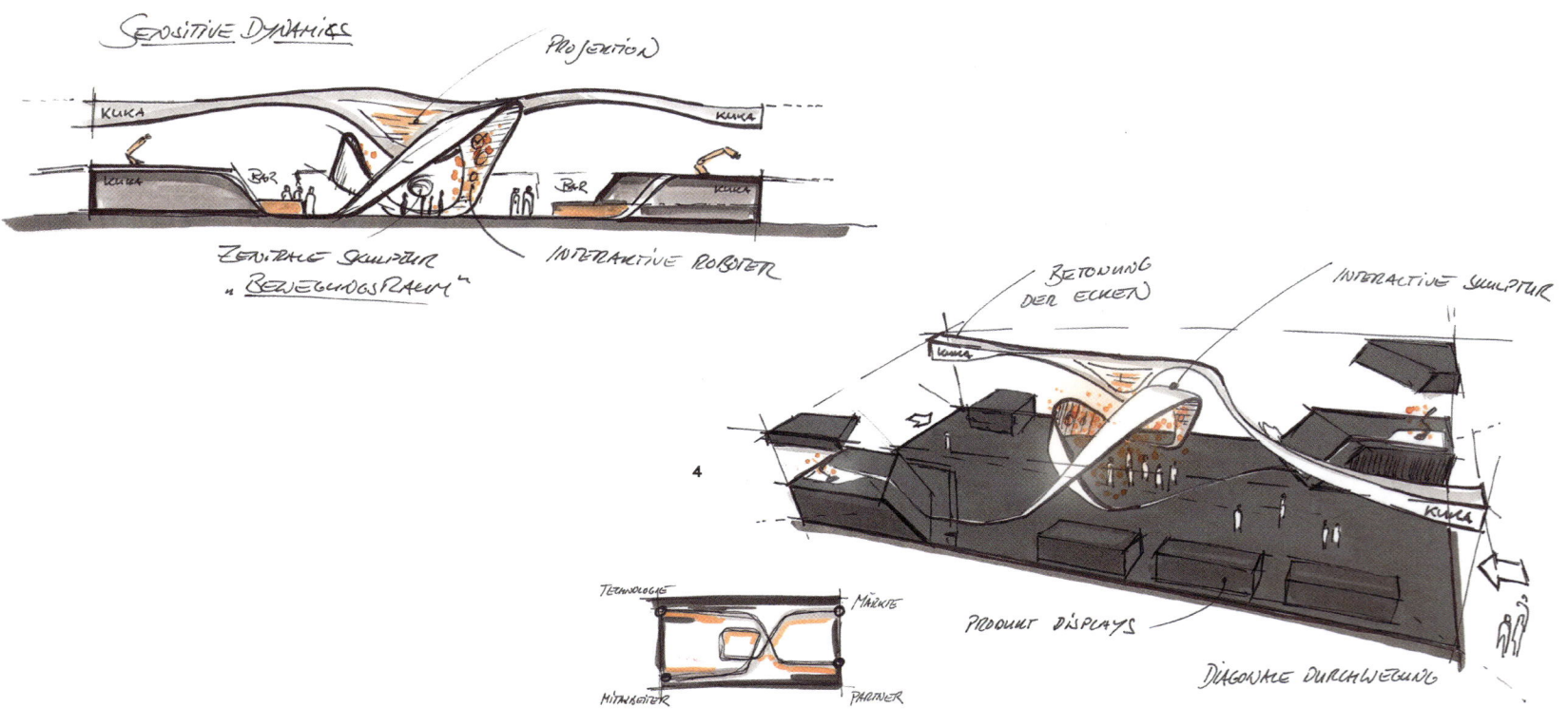

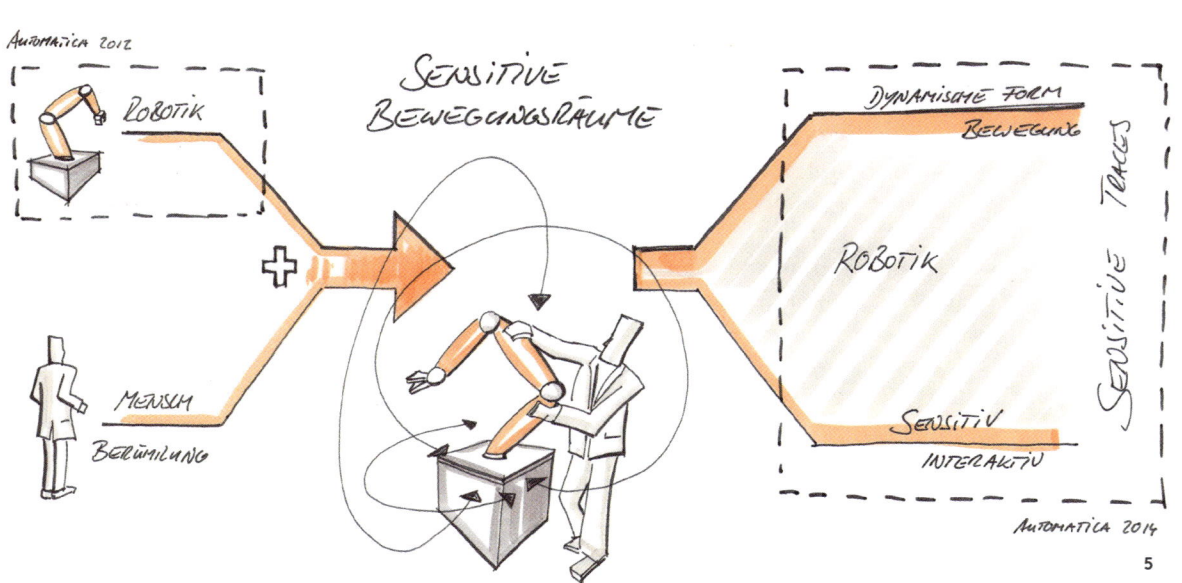

FLOOR PLAN

01 Sensitive highlight
02 Info
03 Interactive exhibition
04 Lounge
05 Bar
06 Back of house

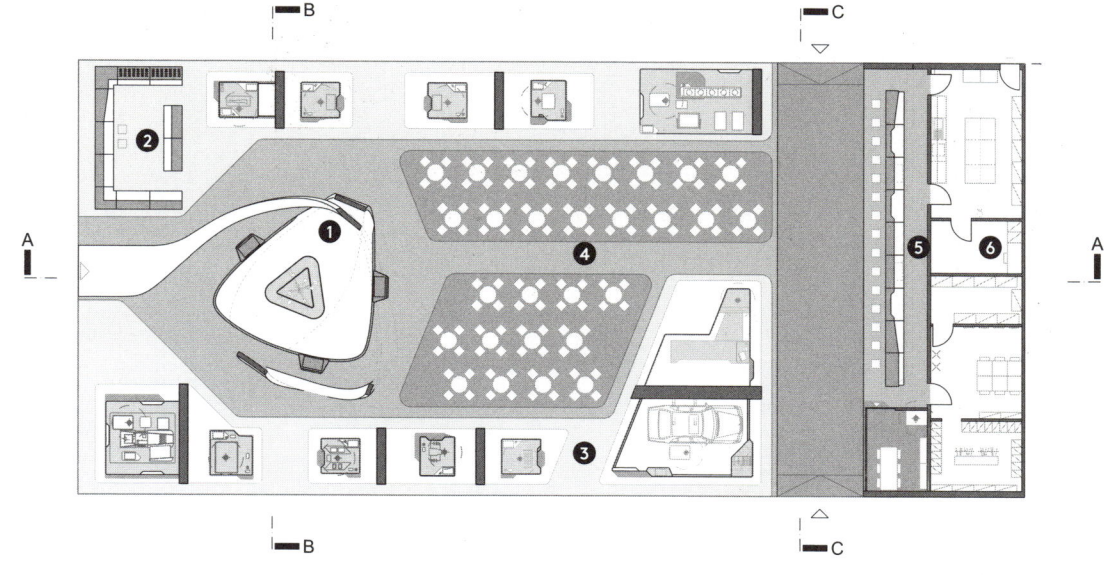

THE DESIGN TRANSLATES FREEFORM MOVEMENTS OF SENSITIVE ROBOTS INTO EXPRESSIVE STRUCTURES

ELEVATION

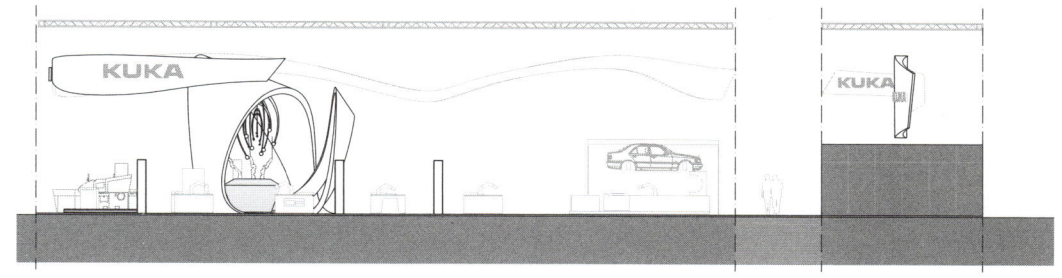

SECTION AA

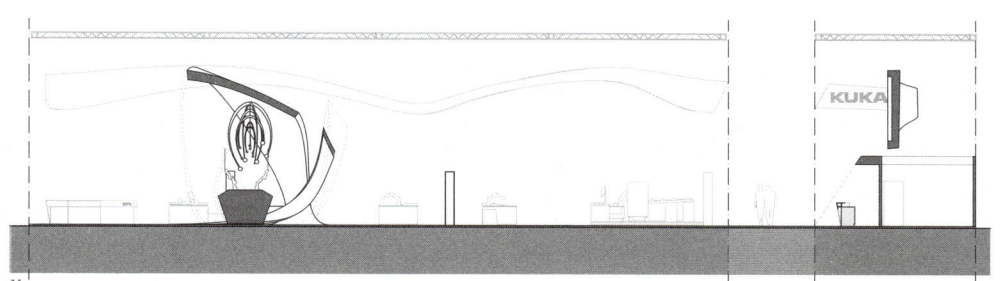

RENDERINGS

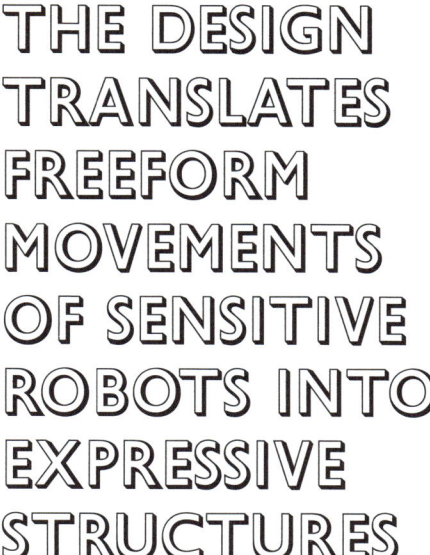

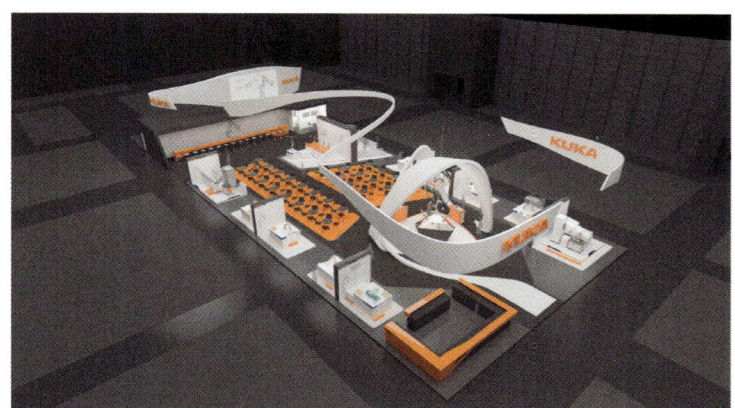

SECTION BB

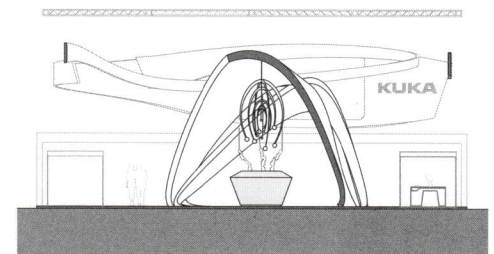

SECTION CC

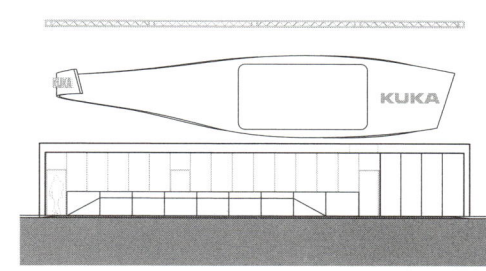

1

PlayStation
GUITAR HERO LIVE

WELCOME TO THE FUTURE OF PLAY
PlayStation
HORIZON ZERO DAWN
INFINITY

2

PLAYSTATION
Walbert-Schmitz

1 The PlayStation stage functioned as the pulsating hub of the stand hosting cosplay, live play and dance acts and interviews.

2 'The Flow' provided visual and brand coherence to PlayStation's presentation that had to unite ten different gaming realms.

3/4 Detail of the Tearaway Unfolded area.

3

4

V

Visitors definitely felt like kids in a candy store when they discovered there were ten different gaming worlds showcased on the PlayStation stand at gamescom 2015. Each world had its own dedicated area on the stand, with a different environment that reflected the theme of the game. Tearaway Unfolded featured windy, colourful surrounds; Horizon Zero Dawn transported visitors to a lush post-apocalyptic landscape; and Until Dawn was set in a dark, chilling atmosphere in an abandoned house in the forest. The main challenge for the designers at Walbert-Schmitz was to unite these individual worlds and simultaneously give prominence to the PlayStation brand. Completely branded in the Playstation identity, 'The Flow' ensured maximum visibility of the brand. Suspended high above 'The Flow' snaked along the edges of the space – measuring a total of 250-metres in length – encouraging visitors to move freely through the worlds below. Complete branded in the PlayStation identity, 'The Flow' ensured maximum visible for the brand. This was complemented by the central PlayStation stage which functioned as the focal point on the stand and viewed into all gaming areas. Animated with projections in combination with sound and lighting, the stage set a thrilling atmosphere for the presentation. Blue carpet on the floors served as a connecting element between the exhibitions, further strengthening the brand's presence. A final challenge for the designers was to address the lengthy queuing process. Points of entertainment like photo booths for cosplay enthusiasts, original gaming tokens, seating areas and the latest videos were placed along the queuing areas to soften the wait. The PlayStation stand functioned as a tangible interface for visitors from all over the world to meet and connect without digital boundaries, and battle it out over their favourite games. ▬

TRADE FAIR **gamescom**
WHERE **Cologne, Germany**
WHEN **August 2015**
DESIGNER **Walbert-Schmitz**
STAND CONSTRUCTOR **Walbert-Schmitz**
CLIENT **Sony Computer Entertainment Deutschland**
MARKET SECTOR **Gaming**
TOTAL FLOOR AREA **3600 m²**
PHOTOGRAPHER **Schiemann Fotodesign**

SIEMENS

Schmidhuber and KMS Blackspace

1 A solid curtain of rain reacted to visitors' movements to communicate the motion control technology at work.

2 Spanning 3600 m² Siemens' impressive stand immediately stood out at IFA.

2

S

Siemens' vast stand at IFA took visitors on an experiential brand journey. For the third consecutive year, Siemens commissioned Schmidhuber and KMS Blackspace to design its presentation. The resulting architectural concept 'Space Lab' embodied Siemens' future-thinking approach. Walls, floors and ceilings were seamlessly joined together to form a white polygonal frame that acted as a physical link between different themed areas. Like an oversized origami form, the stand folded and unfolded across the L-shaped space. Four distinct presentation islands placed the focus on feature themes and products, each island distinguished by a different material, colour and lighting design. Irregular-shaped niches in the walls functioned as product showcases. At the heart of the space was the new iQ700 oven series presented under the theme of 'Speed'. Here three ovens were incorporated into a 35 m² LED screen as part of a virtual film, making them the star attraction on the stand. The presentation of the 'iSensoric' technology used in next generation appliances integrated a solid curtain of rain that reacted to visitors' movements. This interactive feature was a visual representation of the sensitive motion control technology at work. The theme of 'Experience Passion' was dedicated to the new EQ.6 coffee machine. Coffee was clearly central here, with a sculptural relief wall fashioned from 1500 espresso cups and a 3D sculpture of a coffee cup suspended above the space. The 'Home Connect' area showed how networked appliances from a brand family could be controlled using a smartphone app. Visitors were invited to use an interactive wheel to follow a virtual character through a normal day to experience how this technology would work in real life. Through its innovative and interactive design Siemens' product presentation platform became an immersive brand world. ⚊

TRADE FAIR **IFA**
WHERE **Berlin, Germany**
WHEN **September 2014**
DESIGNERS **Schmidhuber and KMS Blackspace**
STAND CONSTRUCTOR **Metron**
CLIENT **BSH Hausgeräte**
MARKET SECTOR **Home Appliances**
TOTAL FLOOR AREA **3600 m²**
PHOTOGRAPHER **Jörg Hempel Photodesign**

Intelligent
Heater inside

Senso Flow System

Maximales Aroma durch ideale Brühtemperatur:
Intelligent Heater inside.

Ideal brewing temperature for maximum aroma:
Intelligent Heater inside.

Das weltweit einzigartige sensoFlow System von Siemens garantiert den vollen Espressogenuss dank stets idealer und konstanter Brühtemperatur.

The only system of its kind in the world, the sensoFlow System from Siemens guarantees maximum coffee indulgence every time, thanks to its ideal, constant brewing temperature.

Experience p
For a life less ordin

3

LIKE AN OVERSIZED
ORIGAMI FORM, THE
FUTURISTIC STAND FOLDS
AND UNFOLDS ACROSS
THE L-SHAPED SPACE

4

3 The coffee presentation was distinguished by using warm timber finishes.

4 The stand's open and spacious design facilitated a good flow of visitors through the space.

5 In the 'Connectivity' presentation high resolution LED panels mounted behind smoky glass enhanced the 3D quality of the imagery.

6 An LED screen integrated with three real ovens as part of a virtual film formed a major highlight.

5

6

SOFTWARE

Schmidhuber

TRADE FAIR **CeBIT**
WHERE **Hannover, Germany**
WHEN **March 2015**
DESIGNER **Schmidhuber**
STAND CONSTRUCTOR **Messebau Tünnissen**
CLIENT **Software**
MARKET SECTOR **IT and telecommunications**
TOTAL FLOOR AREA **950 m²**
PHOTOGRAPHER **Jörg Hempel Photodesign**

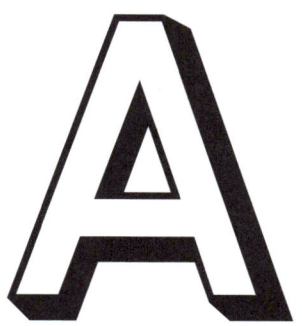

At the 2015 edition of CeBIT, Software focused attention on its new Digital Business Platform that enables the company to offer its customers customised digitisation solutions. In charge of designing the stand was Schmidhuber who coined the slogan 'Stand out in the Digital World' to create a meeting point between people and data: a digital campus. As an interactive intersection between the physical and virtual worlds, the campus connected and unified the varying software components to communicate the business platform concept. The design language was informed by the platform's logo, a rotated square with two diagonally opposite rounded corners. This motif was applied across the whole stand from the facade to signage, lending coherence to the presentation. Large cutouts of the logo pierced the exterior to create openings onto the stand. Internal partitions were also perforated with these cutouts, resulting in playful screens. Central to the presentation was the Partner Park. Distinguished in black this section featured interactive showcases exhibited on black island counters. Behind this was a huge Digital Gate, a large-format screen that provided a prominent backdrop for the presentation. Surrounding the centre were Workspaces grouped into clear themes, each distinguished by a different colour. With their design inspired by the modern workplace, the Workspaces demonstrated the modularity of the Software product components that together make up the Digital Business Platform. Mirrored spheres in different sizes floated above, reflecting the product world below. Behind the screen was an enclosed section that hosted a lounge and café area, private meeting rooms, offices and service spaces. Thanks to its multifaceted design Software's stand clearly stood out at CeBIT. ⏤

1 With its interactive format, the Partner Park formed the heart of the presentation.

2 Software wanted a stand that stood out at CeBIT, the biggest IT trade fair in the world.

2

A DIGITAL CAMPUS THAT PROVIDES AN INTERACTIVE MEETING POINT BETWEEN PEOPLE AND DATA

3 Informal meetings could be held in the lounge and café located behind the Digital Gate.

4 'Stand out in the Digital World' was the slogan used to design the stand.

5/6 Workspaces were positioned on the periphery of the stand, each one demonstrating a different element of the Digital Business Platform.

SONY
Schmidhuber

1 A meandering product journey and expansive streamlined screen defined the Sony stand.

2 The base of the screen transformed seamlessly to become walls and product displays.

3 Wood was used to contrast warmly with the glossy white interior and create an element of tangibility.

'One Sony - The best of Sony for the best of you': Sony's briefing to Schmidhuber for the design of its stand at IFA 2014 had to fulfil two goals. The first was to create the experience of a holistic Sony world. Simultaneously the stand should also communicate the company's new brand strategy that unites the three sub-brands of Devices, Content and Services. The idea of 'One Sony Experience' incorporates the best technology from every department into each device. Using the design concept of 'Hightech meets Experience' the stand also made a connection between the digital and physical worlds. Two main features dominated the design. 'The Winding Road' comprised a meandering product journey that structured the route through the presentation. Individual product areas connected seamlessly to adjoining activity zones and showed the close interplay between gadgets and appliances. Enveloping visitors completely was a mega elevated screen that measured 10-metres-high and 100-metres-long. It wowed the audience with changing visuals that used 14 million pixels projected from 56 projectors. As the enormous curved screen intersected the winding product path, the presentations alternated between both sides of the screen. The base of the screen lifted and descended to define openings, walls and displays resulting in a dynamic streamlined form. Tangibility was an important theme to emphasise the devices, which represented the physical world of technology. This idea was suggested by the focus on tactile, high quality materials to complement the predominantly sleek white interior; wood was used to clad the base of the screen, for the floors and display furniture. The patterns of all the wood finishes were aligned in one direction along the length of the stand, creating coherence in the design and communicating a strong, clear path for Sony's new identity. ⁓

TRADE FAIR **IFA**
WHERE **Berlin, Germany**
WHEN **September 2014**
DESIGNER **Schmidhuber**
STAND CONSTRUCTOR **Display International**
CLIENT **Sony**
MARKET SECTOR **Consumer electronics**
TOTAL FLOOR AREA **4000 m²**
PHOTOGRAPHER **Olaf Becker**

THE WORLD OF
PC INNOVATION

ULTRA HD

...ATION OF TOSHIBA

...EDDED STORAGE SOLUTIONS

...OUCH EXPERIENCE

> DATA STORAGE SOLUTIONS

> WINDOW...

TOSHIBA
Leading Innovation >>>

ULTRA HD

Windows 8.1

TOSHIBA

Uniplan

TRADE FAIR **IFA**
WHERE **Berlin, Germany**
WHEN **September 2013**
DESIGNER **Uniplan**
STAND CONSTRUCTOR **Uniplan**
CLIENT **Toshiba**
MARKET SECTOR **Consumer electronics**
TOTAL FLOOR AREA **2000 m²**
PHOTOGRAPHER **Victor S. Brigola**

1 The islands featuring the TVs, tablets and PCs were a big hit with fairgoers.

2 Functionally and aesthetically, circular display tables worked best for product engagement.

2

Uniplan was commissioned to conceptualise, design and construct Toshiba's presentation at IFA, the trade show for consumer electronics and home appliances. The brief was to create an innovative and eye-catching stage for the new innovations, which reflected the company's ambitions in a unique way. The result took visitors out of the dark through its mysterious and luminous surrounds. Uniplan's concept placed maximum focus on the products through interplaying darkness with light. Visitors were intuitively drawn to the illuminated displays in the dark and seemingly endless space, which was divided into a total of 13 different-sized 'Islands of Lights'. Each island zone was composed of an illuminated circular display table paired with a suspended illuminated open circle overhead and corresponding white circular base on the black carpet. Colour coding was used to clearly signal the various product areas. Lifting the dark space, these intensely illuminated colours also served as visual orientation landmarks on the stand. Floating in the darkness, the islands looked impressive from afar, enticing people onto the stand. Visitors flocked to a group of seven islands that presented new innovations for TVs, tablets and PCs. One feature island in the centre of the stand was distinguished with a different appearance to highlight the launch of the new M9/L9 series of ultra high-definition televisions. Here a cylindrical formation of illuminated red textile threads created a spectacular vertical lighting installation that shone like a beacon. This dazzling stand presented the technology company in an expressive way and wowed visitors with a multi-sensory experience. ➡

INTE
PROD

ALAPE
Heine/Lenz/Zizka Projekte

TRADE FAIR **ISH**
WHERE **Frankfurt, Germany**
WHEN **March 2015**
DESIGNER **Heine/Lenz/Zizka Projekte**
STAND CONSTRUCTOR **Holtmann**
CLIENT **Alape**
MARKET SECTOR **Sanitary/bathroom**
TOTAL FLOOR AREA **250 m²**
PHOTOGRAPHER **Achim Hatziu**

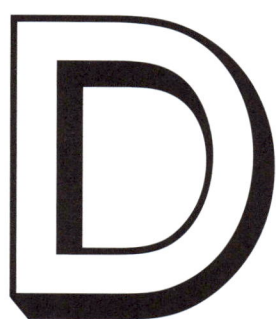

Designed by Heine/Lenz/Zizka Projekte, the Alape stand at ISH in Frankfurt, the fair for bathroom design, energy-efficient heating and air conditioning technology and renewable energies, was defined by five seemingly floating open cubes. Fashioned from fine metal framework, each island showcased a different product category or mounting option that the bathware company

was launching that year. The star of the show was a white sculptural installation positioned centrally in the space, acting almost as a main public square. Composed from stacked rectangular volumes of thin glazed steel the sculpture demonstrated the use and qualities of the material – precision, lightweight and filigree impression – that sets the company's products apart. Imprinted onto the sculpture was the motto of the exhibition: 'steel. the difference'. The black, framed metal showcases emphasised the idea of refinement and craftsmanship, each finished with a countertop/base of a different material including steel and wood, which added a feel of tactility and warmth. Here, washbasins were displayed almost like museum objects. Clever detailed, recessed bases gave the impression that

the cubes were floating to further suggest a sense of lightness. Punctuating each island was a recessed niche in the ceiling lined with copper. To maintain coherence the same thin frames were also used to encase other bath furniture and create customised bar stools. Located beside the entrance was a white wall filled with rows of mounted white maquettes. These 3D-printed scale models demonstrated the variability of the company's modular system of bathroom furniture. In contrast to the mainly pure white setting, black was used to visually differentiate the information area dedicated to architects and designers. Thoughtfully designed and detailed, the Alape stand positioned its products and strengths in a graceful, serene setting that perfectly befitted the brand. ⚊

1 The eye-catcher was a central installation made from white volumes of glazed steel mounted onto an elaborate framework.

2 The stand's minimal architecture perfectly complemented the products on display.

3

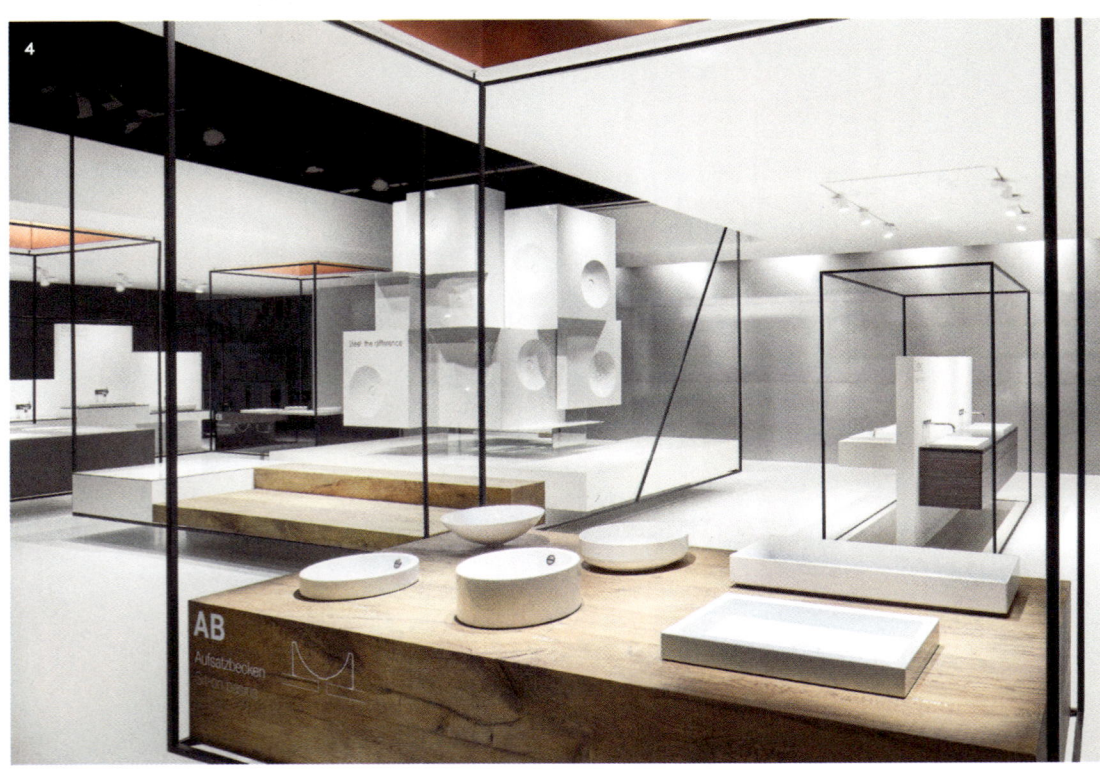

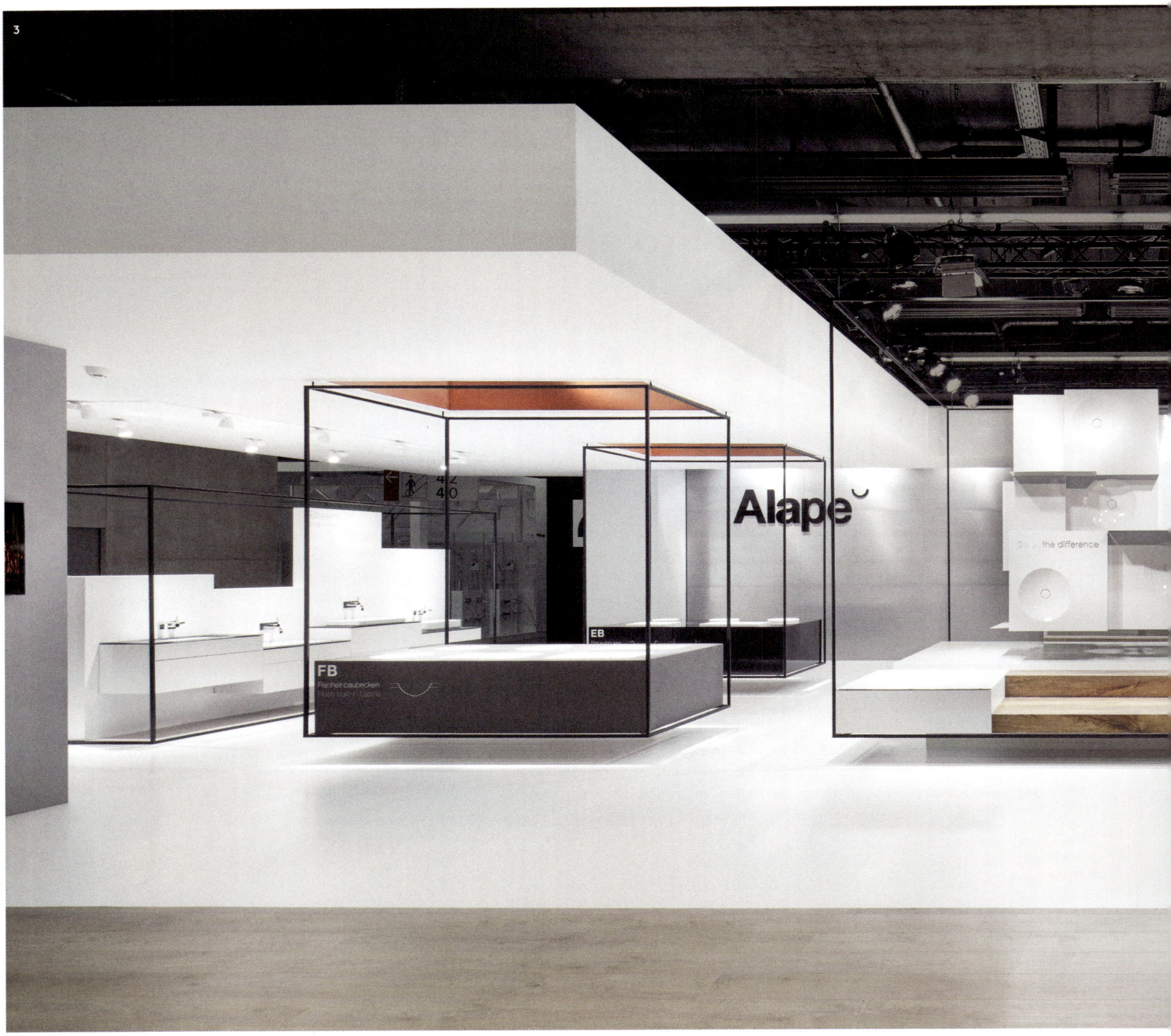
Alape
FB
Flacheinbaubecken
EB
the difference

4

AB
Aufsatzbecken

3 The stand design celebrated the brand's emphasis on the purity of aesthetics.

4 Visitors were able to meander freely between the islands, which were completely open, to view the products from all angles.

THE PRODUCTS ARE DISPLAYED LIKE MUSEUM OBJECTS IN FLOATING, OPEN-FRAMED CUBES

FLOOR PLAN

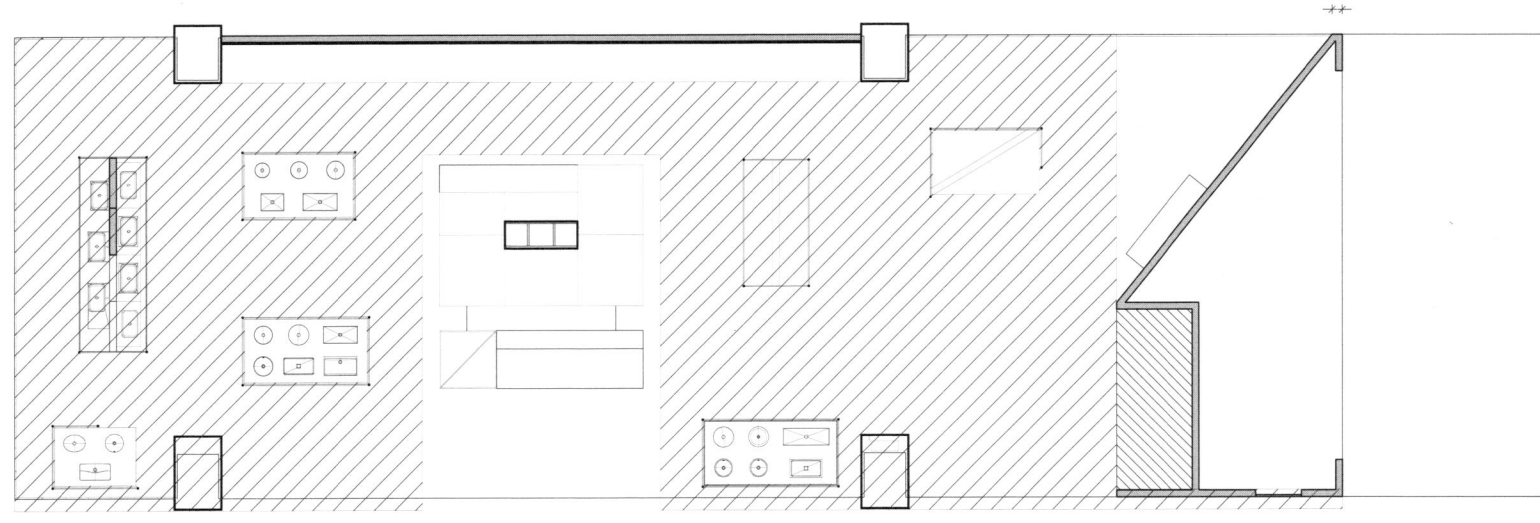

FRONT ELEVATION

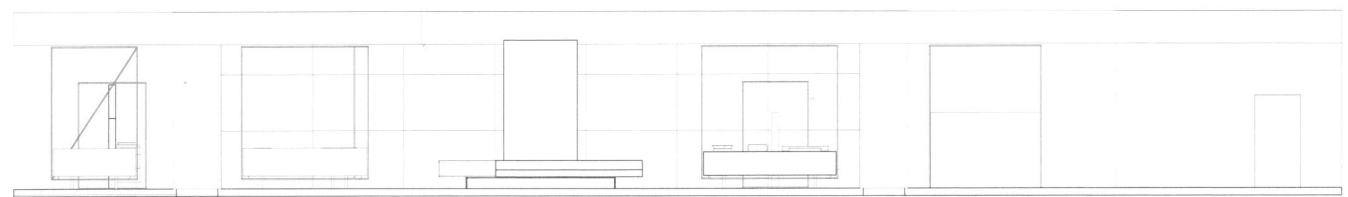

PERSPECTIVE

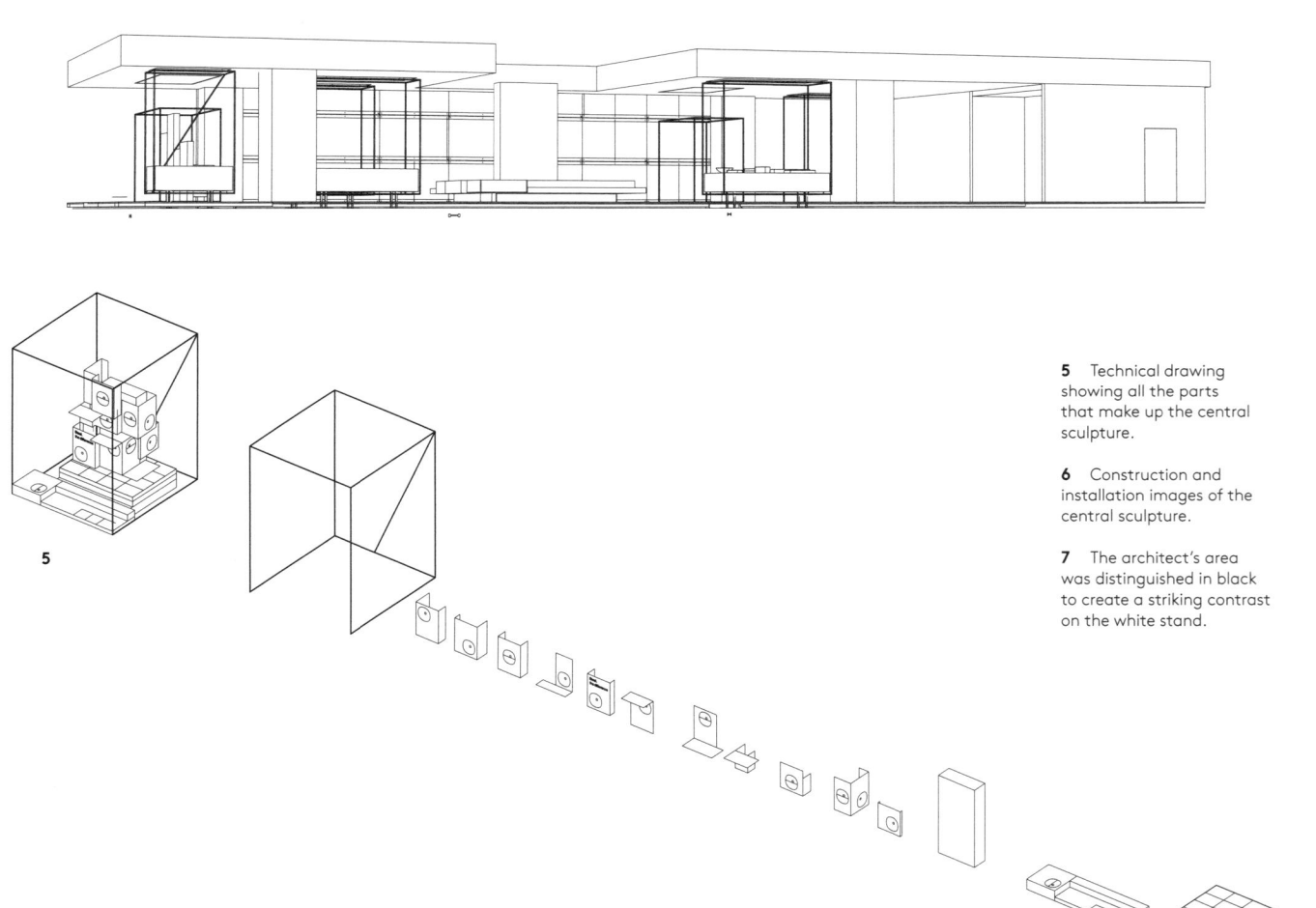

5 Technical drawing
showing all the parts
that make up the central
sculpture.

6 Construction and
installation images of the
central sculpture.

7 The architect's area
was distinguished in black
to create a striking contrast
on the white stand.

6

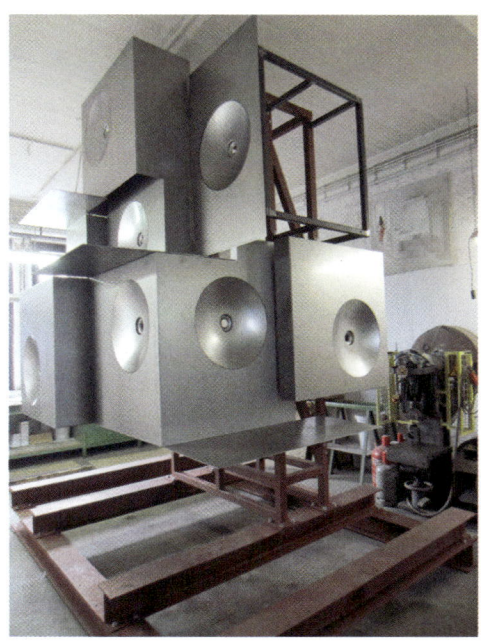

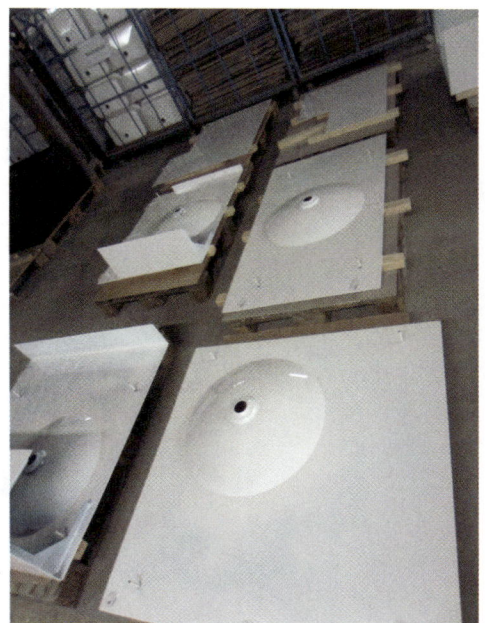

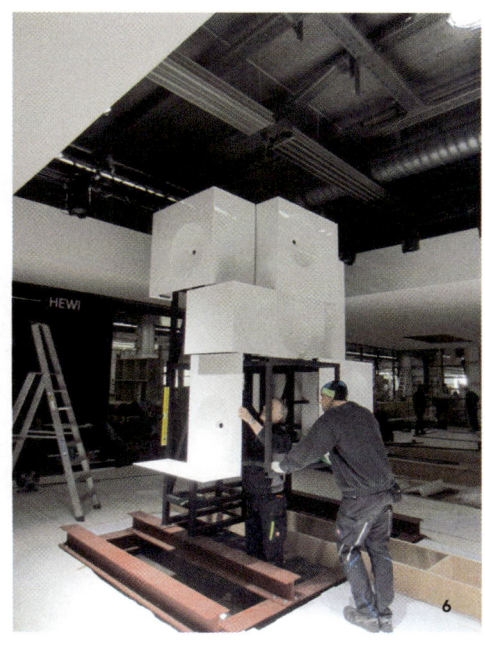

THE STAR OF THE SHOW IS A WHITE SCULPTURAL INSTALLATION

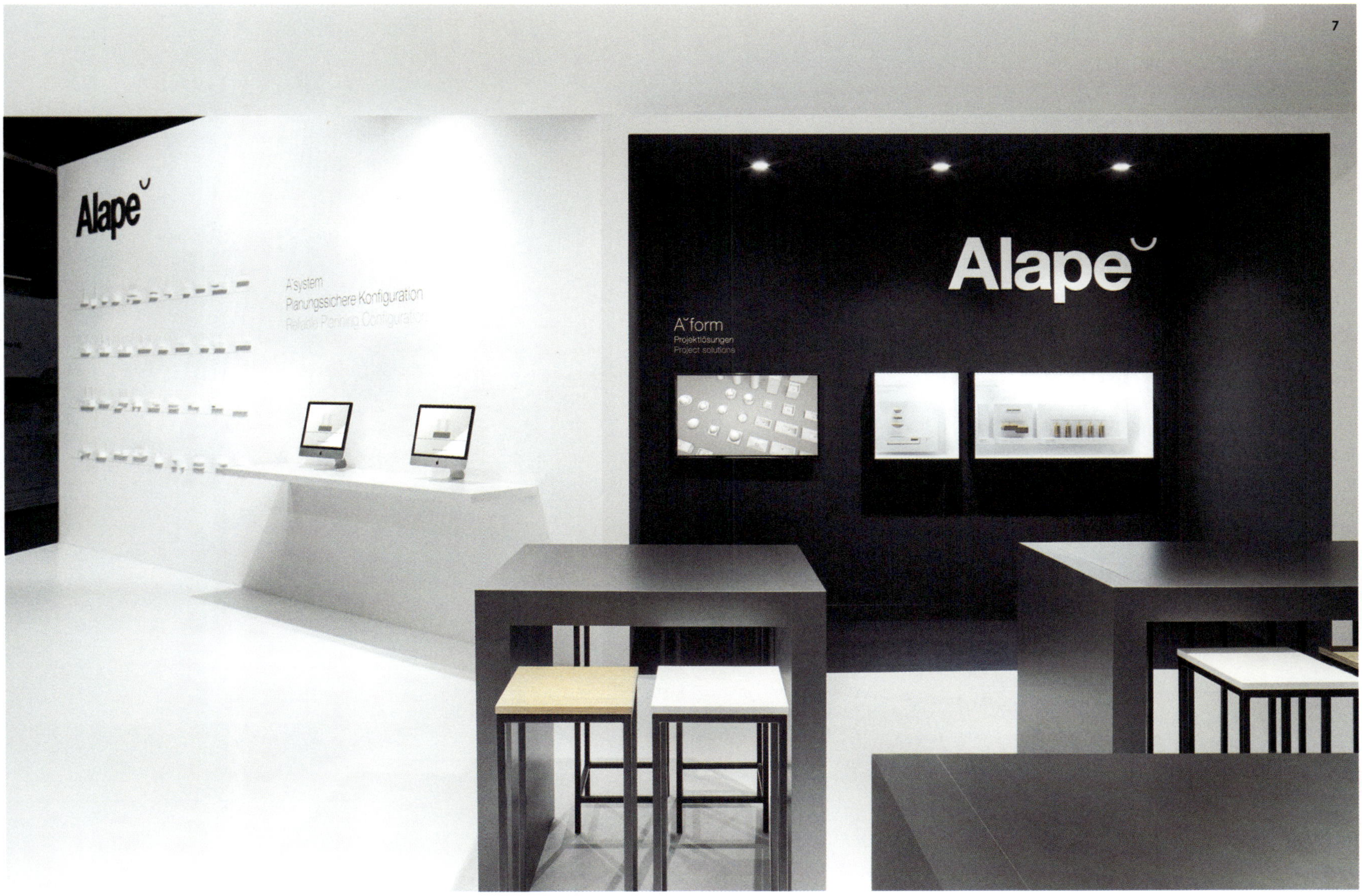

7

BRUNNER
Ippolito Fleitz Group

TRADE FAIR **Orgatec**
WHERE **Cologne, Germany**
WHEN **October 2014**
DESIGNER **Ippolito Fleitz Group**
STAND CONSTRUCTOR **Hospes Team**
CLIENT **Brunner**
MARKET SECTOR **Office furniture**
TOTAL FLOOR AREA **660 m²**
PHOTOGRAPHER **Andreas Körner**

Ippolito Fleitz's concept for Brunner's stand at Orgatec 2014 began with the question of how to introduce dramatic tension to the presentation, which showcased its new portfolio of seating and tables for office use. The graphic concept from Brunner's latest print publication provided the answer. The idea was to translate the minimal lines from those pages into an open, transparent exhibition stand as part of an integrated brand presentation. In this way, the space literally and figuratively brought the Brunner collection to life.

Lengths of black polypropylene rope were deployed as three-dimensional screens throughout the space – 18 kilometres were used in total. These ropes were formed into dense taut curtains and geometric forms that partitioned the stand into different zones, through which visitors could freely wander. A truncated cone enclosed an intimate surrounding, a chandelier-like installation suggested domesticity, delicate vertical curtains lent a lounge-like feel while diagonal sails dramatically sliced through the space.

The backdrop colours on walls, ceilings and floors were intentionally kept neutral using black, white, beige and grey to highlight the colours of the products themselves. Along the length of the stand, the dense ropes gradually became more open, creating a gradient effect. Additional dynamism was created through neon lighting strips on the ceiling and a diagonally hatched floor; its direction altered in line with different zones. The underlying theme of filigree lines not only resulted in a coherent and attractive stand, it was also synonymous with the precision and quality of Brunner's furniture. ▭

1/2 Eighteen kilometres of black polypropylene rope formed the basis of Brunner's stand.

2

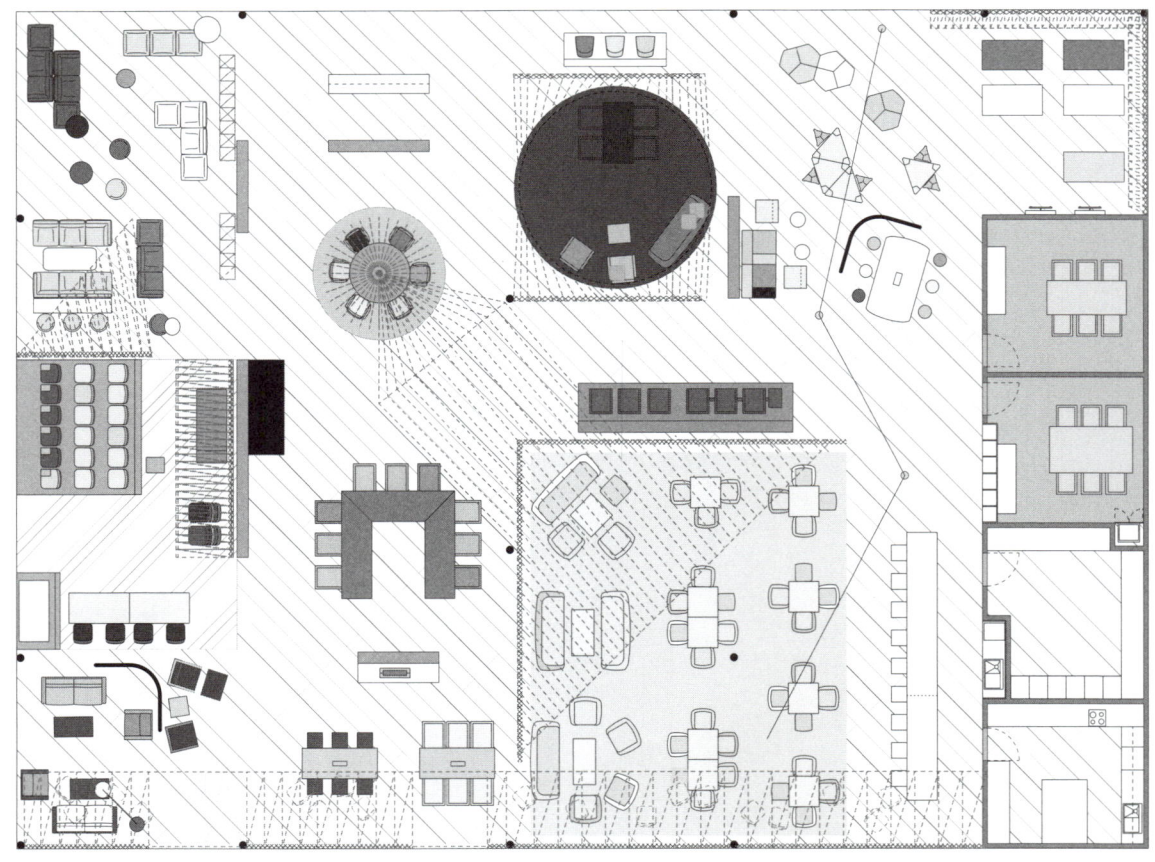

THE FILIGREE LINES ARE SYNONYMOUS WITH BRUNNER'S PRECISION AND QUALITY

FLOOR PLAN

4

3 The bright, open stand invited visitors to meander freely through the presentation.

4 Playful seating elements.

5 The workshop corner was dedicated to the craftsmanship behind the products.

6 Sweeping diagonal sails of rope screened off the lounge area.

5

6

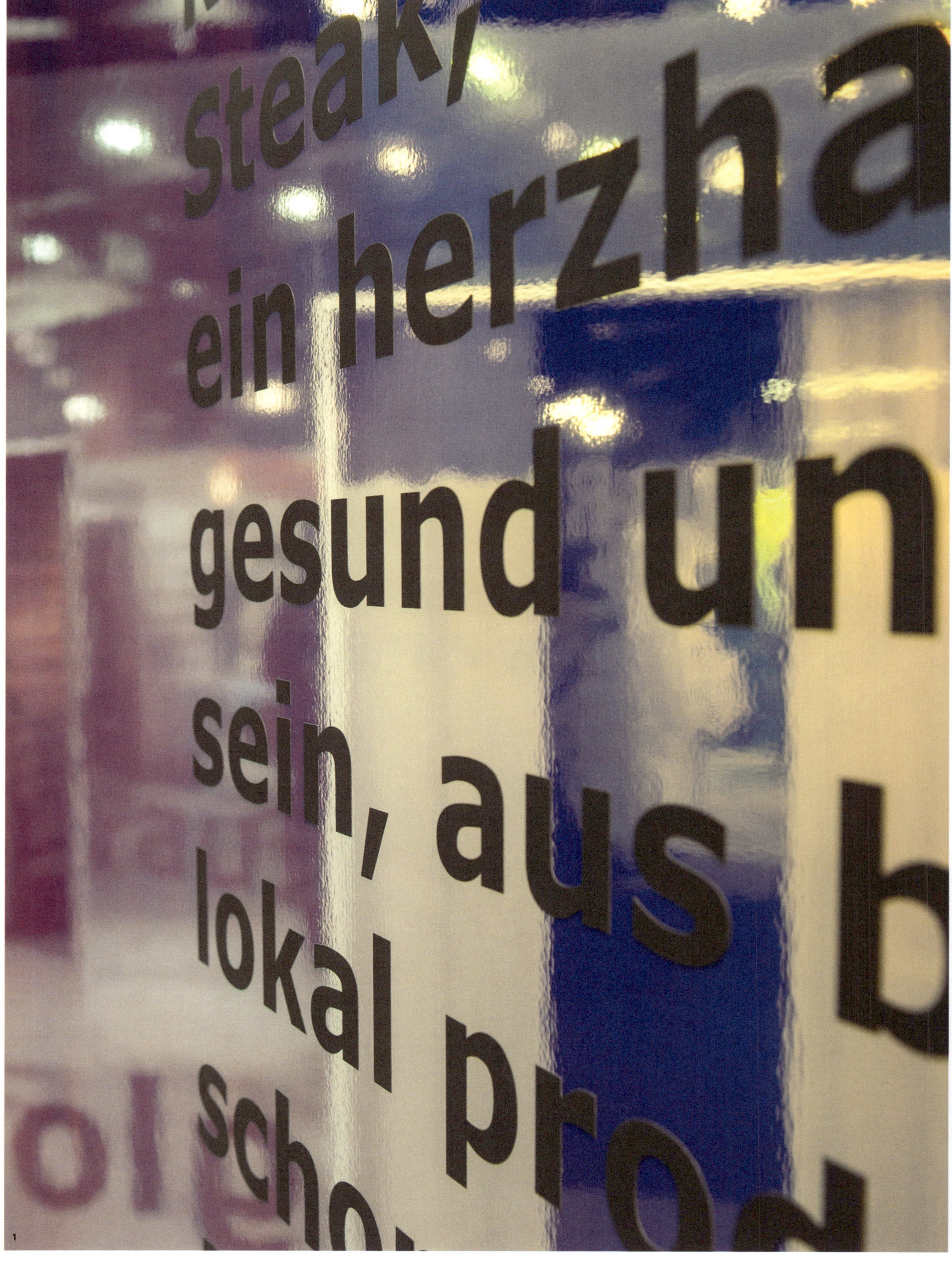

INTERIOR PRODUCTS GRAND STAND 5

COMPETENCE CENTRE SPACE

100% interior

1/2 Mirrored dichroic cubes showed different perspectives of the presentation and featured keywords and texts related to work.

2

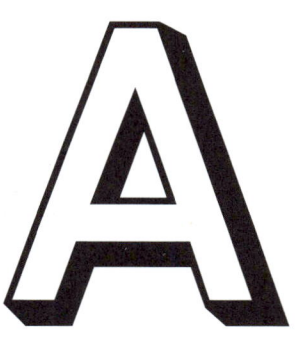

At Orgatec in 2014, Koelnmesse commissioned 100% interior to design its Competence Centre Space, a separate showcase at the fair which highlights interior components such as lighting, colours, acoustics, flooring and furniture as integral parts of modern workplaces. Communication formed the core of the concept, being a fundamental aspect of the office world. Instead of presenting typical office environments, the design aimed to do just the opposite. An art installation with imaginative interior settings took visitors through work-related themes with only a single office chair in sight. A series of minimal cubes was arranged to form a meandering route through the space. Covered in mirrored and dichroic film the cubes hinted at communication in an abstract way, reflecting the outside world. Short texts on the cubes written in different languages depicted keywords related to the themes in the cubes while longer stories gave visitors further food for thought. The reflections and colours of the cubes changed from different angles, adding a dynamic play of space. Visitors themselves became active participants in the presentation as they were mirrored on the cubes. The interiors of the cubes challenged fairgoers to think outside the office box. The concept of a think-tank was reimagined as an Arctic setting, where a pure white interior conjured up an icy landscape with plush carpet, soft velvet curtains, acoustic-damping surfaces, stark lighting and the sound of frosty winds. The concert/disco setting indicated work-life balance, the market suggested global ways of working and the organic lifestyle addressed office breaks. The presentation showed how different interior elements, from texture to sound and reflections, affected the office landscape and inspired visitors to take a different view on their working environment. ⚊

TRADE FAIR **Orgatec**
WHERE **Cologne, Germany**
WHEN **October 2014**
DESIGNER **100% interior Sylvia Leydecker**
STAND CONSTRUCTOR **Uniplan**
CLIENT **Koelnmesse**
MARKET SECTOR **Office design**
TOTAL FLOOR AREA **275 m²**
PHOTOGRAPHERS **Reinhard Rosendahl, Cor and Volker Schäffner**

INTERIOR PRODUCTS   GRAND STAND 5

4

THE PRESENTATION CHALLENGES VISITORS TO THINK OUTSIDE THE OFFICE BOX

5

3 Bamboo-fast food-plates and cutlery form a decorative ornament in the 'organic lifestyle box'.

4 Far, far away from the office, a contemplative icy landscape depicted a think-tank.

5 The market looks at globally-operating, always-on working cultures.

6 Clusters of customised lounge chairs provided intimate areas for visitors to chill out.

6

KEY VISUAL OF THE STAND LAY-OUT

ORGANIC SPACES
PEOPLE
COMMUNICATION
NATURE
EXPERIENCE BOX
LOOK.
SLOW... SPEED!
LISTEN
OPEN PLATFORM

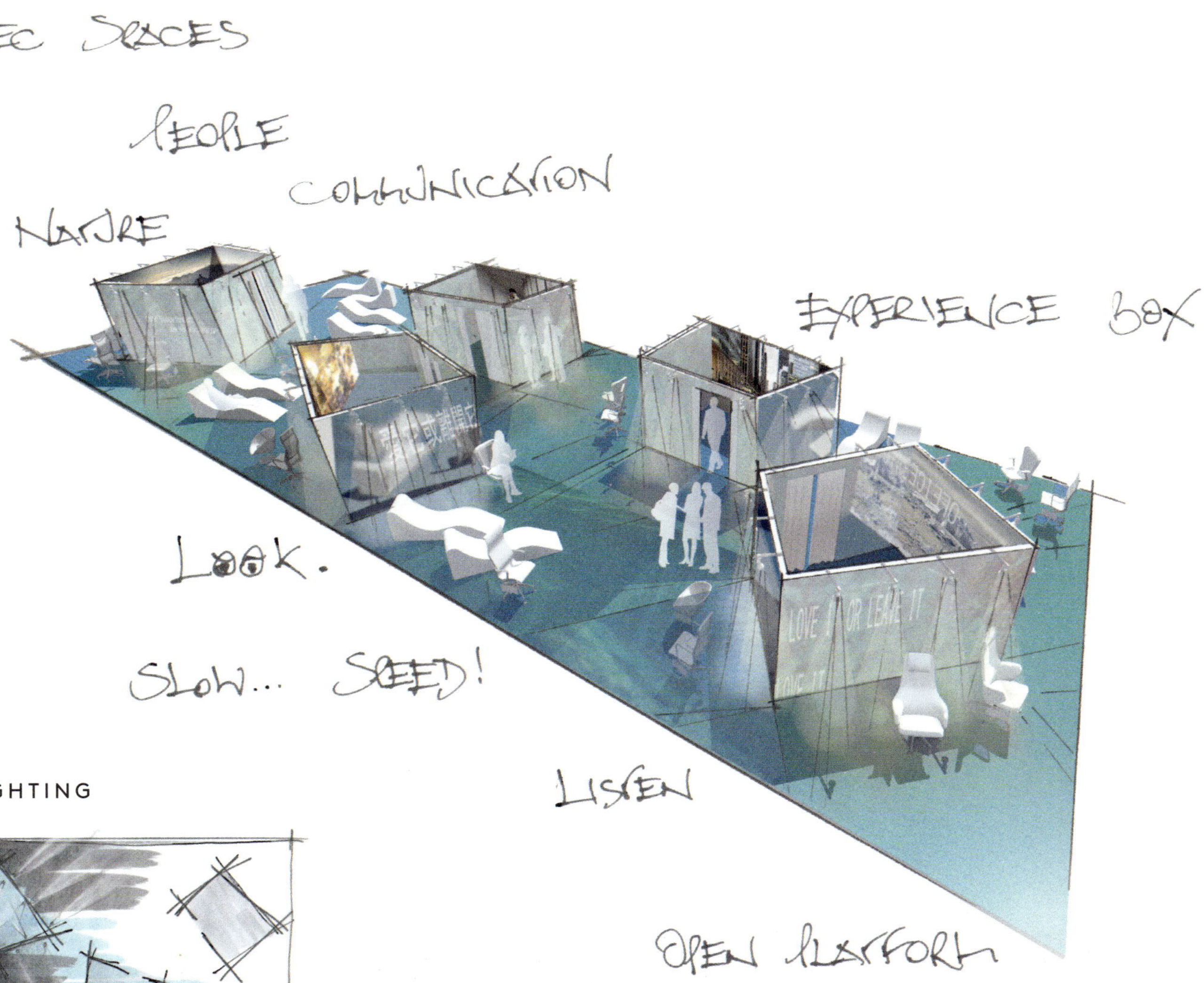

CONCEPT SKETCH LIGHTING

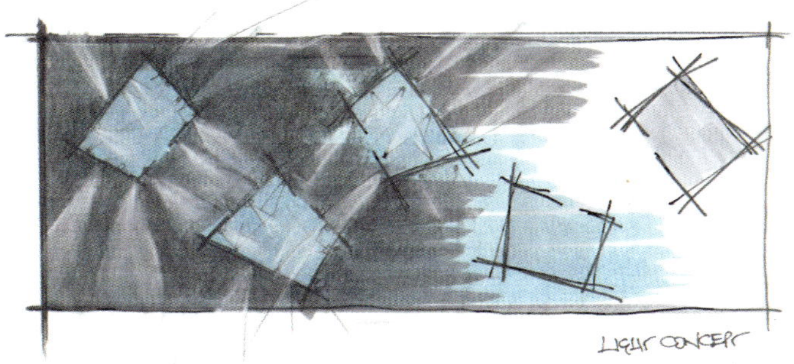

LIGHT CONCEPT

PERSPECTIVE BOX 1 ARCTIC

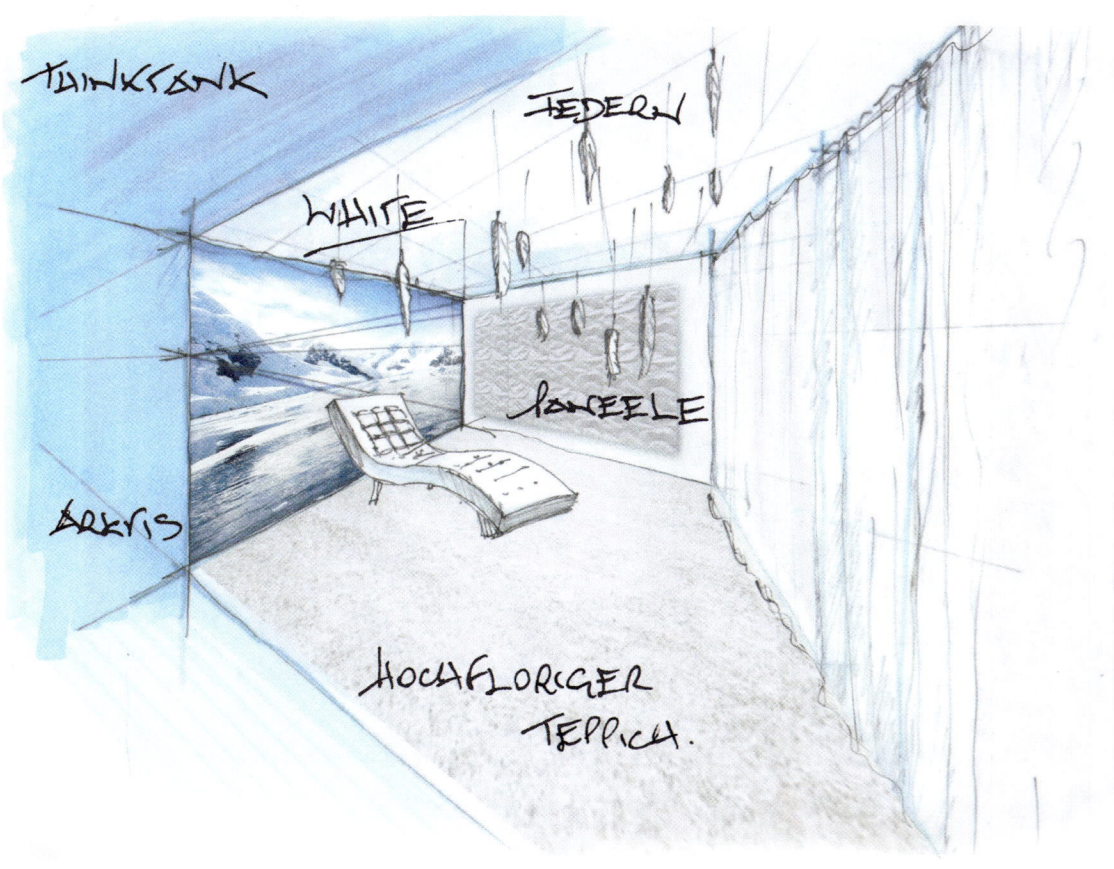

THINKTANK
FEDERN
WHITE
PANEELE
ARKTIS
HOCHFLORIGER
TEPPICH.

PERSPECTIVE BOX 2 CONCERT
DISCO, WORK-LIFE BALANCE

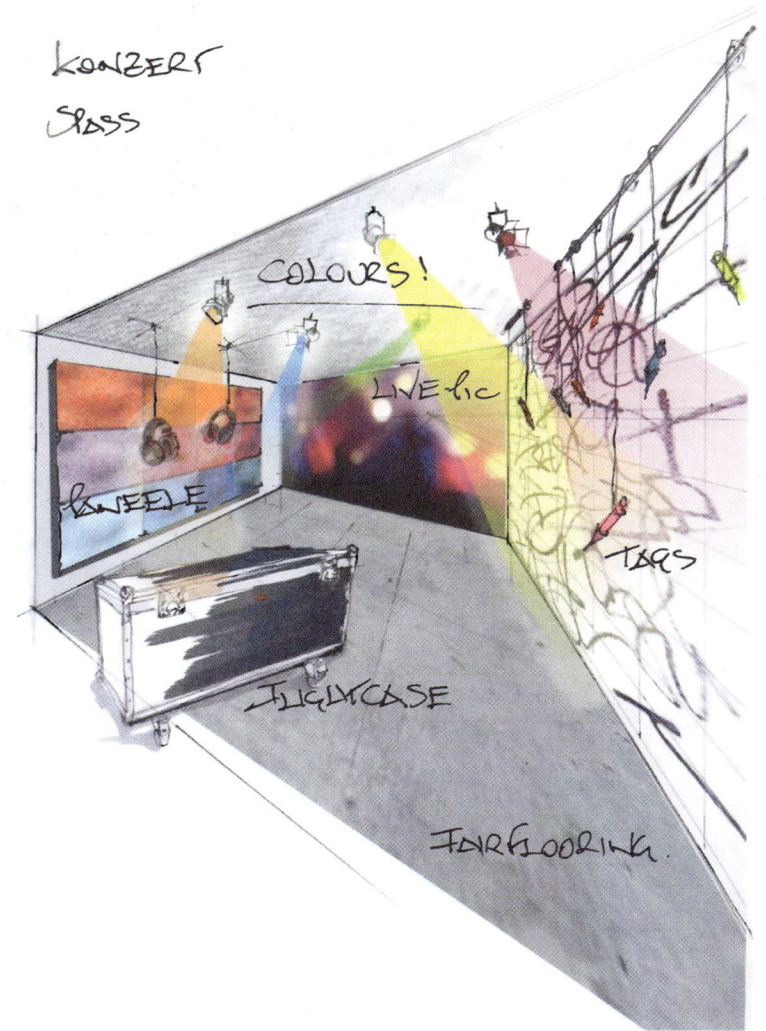

KONZERT
SPASS

COLOURS!

LIVE Pic

KOPFHÖRER

FLIGHTCASE

TARFLOORING.

TAGS

PERSPECTIVE BOX 4 BREAK

PAUSE

WOOD

ROHES HOLZ

JAP FOOD TABLEWARE HOLZ

"BREAK"

JAPANISCH!

PHILO

PEBBLES

PERSPECTIVE BOX 6
OFFICE PRODUCTIVITY

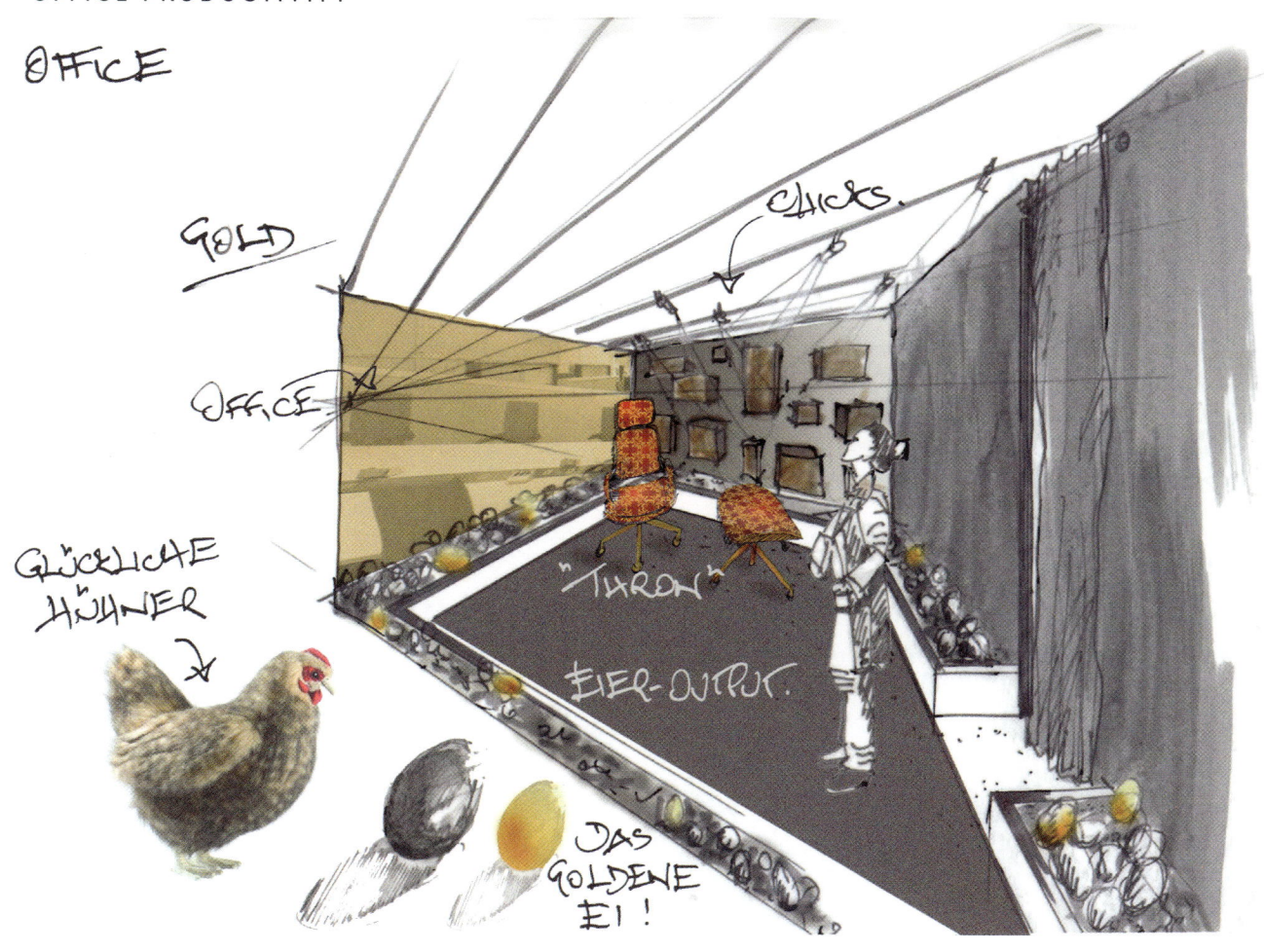

OFFICE

GOLD

OFFICE

CHICKS.

"THRON"

EIER-OUTPUT.

GLÜCKLICHE HÜHNER

DAS GOLDENE EI !

INTERIOR PRODUCTS   GRAND STAND 5

DE SEDE
Projekttriangle Design Studio and Hollin+Radoske

1 Openness and enclosure was beautifully contrasted through the open frameworks, printed and transparent glass and opaque partitions.

2 The uncluttered, minimal stand provided a calm respite from the bustle of the fairs.

2

'Memorable places' formed the focus of de Sede's new brand identity that was created in celebration of the company's 50th anniversary, and consequently informed the design of its fair stands during this period. De Sede briefed Projekttriangle Design Studio and architects Hollin+Radoske to develop a spatial system for exhibition that could be easily scaled from an intimate fair stand to a large presentation. Reflecting this theme, the concept took inspiration from special places in nature, architecture and interiors. The stands appeared as a series of rooms within rooms in a tranquil setting, where open cubes were furnished with the company's high-end leather furniture accompanied by images of dramatic Swiss mountainscapes. Recalling the structure and rhythm of Japanese tea rooms, the cubes were made from powder-coated aluminium frames of different sizes and colours. With each one showcasing different furniture this resulted in different memorable spaces on the stand. Individual surfaces in each frame functioned as background screens, either transparent or semi-transparent with printed large-format landscape photographs by Martin Grothmaak or opaque, minimally decorated with images and text. All formats, grids and compositions were guided by the Fibonacci sequence. As the frames were placed on the floor in different ways, either as a platform or integrated into the floor, this resulted in a dynamic layout that invited visitors to engage with each cube in a different way. Interplaying the open frames were more enclosed niches for meeting areas screened off by high partitions. The oak flooring added a sense of warmth that beautifully complemented the minimal space. Using this modular framework system, the stand could be easily reconfigured and expanded or reduced in size according to the specific requirements of each presentation. ⟶

TRADE FAIR **imm cologne**
WHERE **Cologne, Germany**
WHEN **January 2015**
DESIGNERS **Projekttriangle Design Studio and Hollin+Radoske**
STAND CONSTRUCTOR **Visage**
CLIENT **de Sede**
MARKET SECTOR **Furniture**
TOTAL FLOOR AREA **420 m²**
PHOTOGRAPHER **Martin Grothmaak**

5

3 The use of platforms resulted in lively variations in the floor area.

4 The configuration of the stand could be easily adapted by changing the composition and layout of the cubes.

5 Photography by Martin Grothmaak placed a central role in de Sede's new brand identity.

6 Stunning photography of the Swiss Alps also provided a dramatic setting for the private meeting areas.

4

5

6

OPEN CUBES ARE ACCOMPANIED
BY IMAGES OF DRAMATIC SWISS
MOUNTAINSCAPES

GAGGENAU
eins:33

1 Erco track-lighting and Bolich pendant lights illuminated the stand.

2 The main entrance led directly into the stand's central courtyard.

2

Gaggenau paid tribute to the roots of culinary culture at EuroCucina, the International Kitchen Furniture Exhibition, in 2014 in Milan. For this presentation the manufacturer of high-quality home appliances placed eins:33 in charge of designing its stand, which formed part of a trilogy. Beginning in 2010 with a focus on the company's production processes, the presentation concept evolved in 2012 to underline raw materials as the basis of the appliances, and ended in 2014 highlighting the 'Tradition of Manufacture'. This last chapter showcased the making of bread and wine in celebration of traditional artisanship, and communicated the sophisticated lifestyle of today's culinary culture. Attention was centred on the 400 and 200 series ovens for making bread, and the Vario cooling 400 series for storing wine. Architecturally the theme was translated by a traditional wooden Saxon farmstead comprising four open buildings clustered around a rectangular courtyard. A simple black exterior with the company's logo in white announced the stand. Warm and rustic yet contemporary and minimal, the interior beckoned invitingly to visitors – helped no doubt by the smell of freshly baked bread. A modest palette of natural materials dominated the well-crafted space, immediately making visitors feel at home. Referencing the tradition of stone ovens, the ovens were mounted in the long brick wall. A metal-and-wood working bench and shelf completed the bakery display. Showcasing wine storage and other appliances, the black kitchens added a slick modern touch. Wooden floors added continuity throughout the exhibition spaces while large black ceramic tiles defined the courtyard. Like fallen logs, two long benches fashioned from stacked natural oak planks conjured up an elemental setting. Going back to basics has never looked more appealing. ⸺

TRADE FAIR **EuroCucina**
WHERE **Milan, Italy**
WHEN **April 2014**
DESIGNER **eins:33**
STAND CONSTRUCTOR **Altmann Laden- und Innenausbau**
CLIENT **Gaggenau**
MARKET SECTOR **Kitchens**
TOTAL FLOOR AREA **300 m²**
PHOTOGRAPHER **Bodo Mertoglu**

WARM AND RUSTIC, THE INTERIOR BECKONS INVITINGLY TO VISITORS

3 Natural materials, especially brick and wood in the bakery, suggested authenticity and warmth.

4 Furnished simply with two log benches, the courtyard formed the hub of the farmstead.

5 Renowned food-and-wine experts were invited to celebrate the 'Tradition of Manufacture'.

SKETCHES

MODEL

GOING BACK TO BASICS HAS NEVER LOOKED MORE APPEALING

CONSTRUCTION

   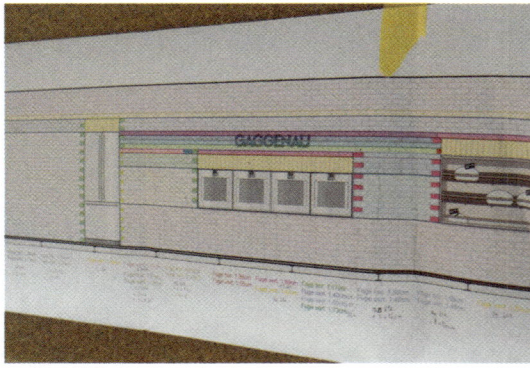

photos by Christine Neulinger.

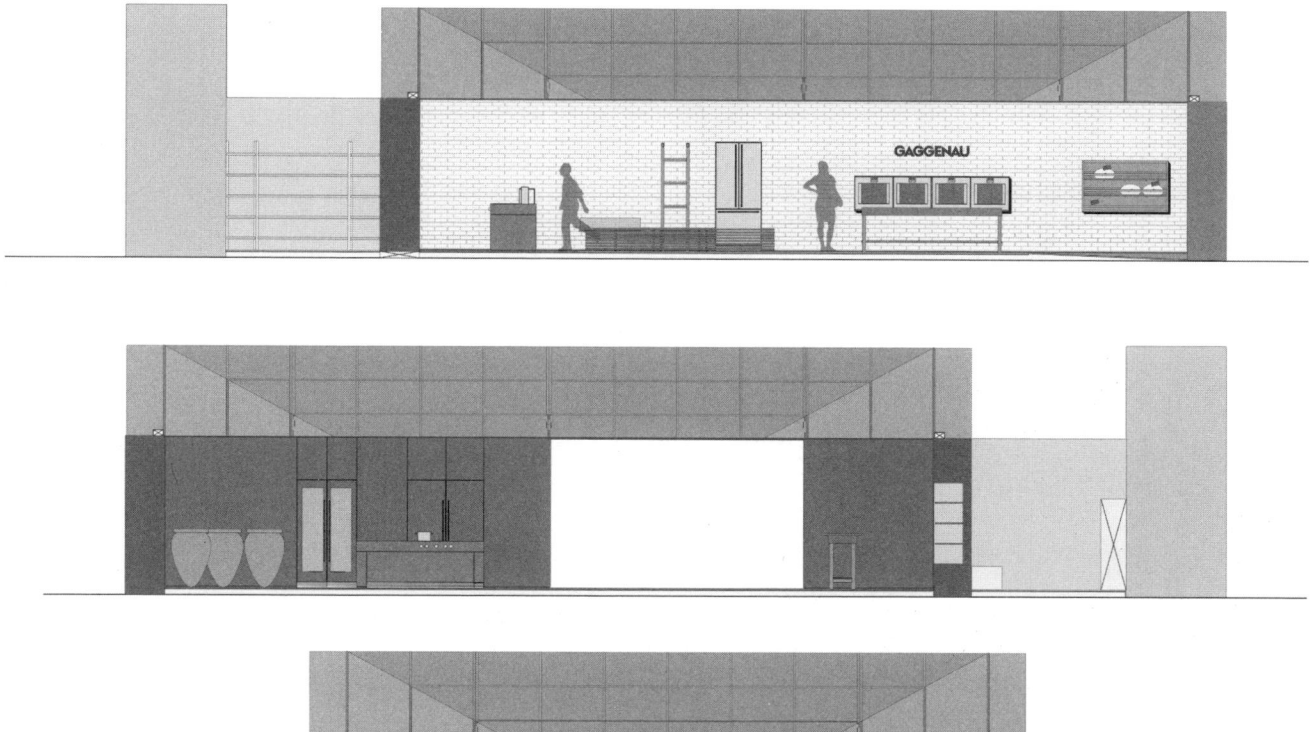

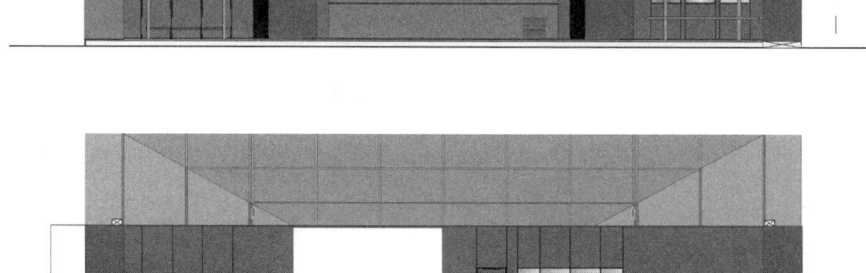

FLOOR PLAN

01 Courtyard
02 Welcome area
03 Staff and storage area
04 Live-cooking area
05 Backup kitchen
06 Bakery
07 Secondary entry (ramp)
08 Winery

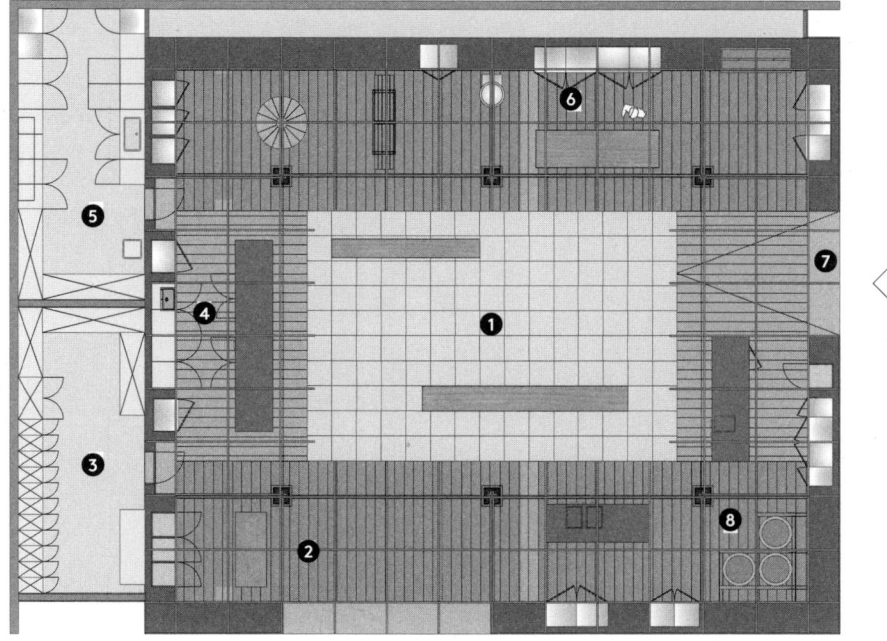

GAGGENAU SHOWCASE

eins:33

1 Nostalgic elements on display communicated the history of the brand in celebration of its 330th anniversary.

2 The stand had a strong appearance thanks to uniform dark materials and consistent forms.

2

The 2013 LivingKitchen international kitchen show provided the perfect setting for Gaggenau to showcase its new innovations under the apt title of 'Showcase'. Designed by eins:33 the stand toyed with this theme literally and figuratively, resulting in a sleek, exclusive presentation that perfectly encapsulated the brand's identity. Two parallel aisles with high black showcases formed the focal point of the stand, structuring the space into three sections. Each aisle comprised rows of moveable cabinets fitted with appliance combinations in vertical or horizontal arrangements. Niches in the cabinets were dedicated to focus themes such as aesthetics and lifestyle, materials and look and feel, function and design. Situated in the centre was the reception counter with a back wall constructed from hot-rolled steel panels. Feature presentations continued in the centre aisle. Control Concepts focused on the new touch display, and Vario 400 Ventilation featured an oversized counter with a base encased in glass to illustrate the system's ventilation components. Theatrical spotlighting focused all attention on the showcases and added a dramatic atmosphere. In contrast with the restrained design of the main stand, the rear steel stage, used for functions and events, included more nostalgic touches to underline the brand's 330th anniversary. Old photographs, appliances, enamel signs, a vintage bicycle and historic logos represented the technical side of the brand in the context of its development. Wine barrels, fine wines, past issues of the Michelin Guide and Gaggenau cookbooks hinted at the cultural aspects of the company. At the centre of the stage, a special counter hosted live cooking demonstrations. The interplay of historic and contemporary displays showcased the company in all its facets while the uniformity of materials and forms ensured a coherent brand presentation. ▬

TRADE FAIR **LivingKitchen**
WHERE **Cologne, Germany**
WHEN **January 2013**
DESIGNER **eins:33**
STAND CONSTRUCTOR **Altmann Laden- und Innenausbau**
CLIENT **Gaggenau**
MARKET SECTOR **Kitchens**
TOTAL FLOOR AREA **306 m²**
PHOTOGRAPHER **Bodo Mertoglu**

MATERIALITY

Hardened full-glass fronts in three colour variations
form a perfect unit in any combination.

Oven 200 series, BOP 250.
Oven 200 series, BOP 251.

Oven 200 series, BOP 250.
Oven 200 series, BOP 251.

IMPRESSION

3 Besides showcasing appliances, each cabinet contained displays highlighting different focus themes.

4 Theatrical lighting focused all attention on the showcases.

5/6 Feature presentations elaborated on special themes such as new touch displays and innovative ventilation systems.

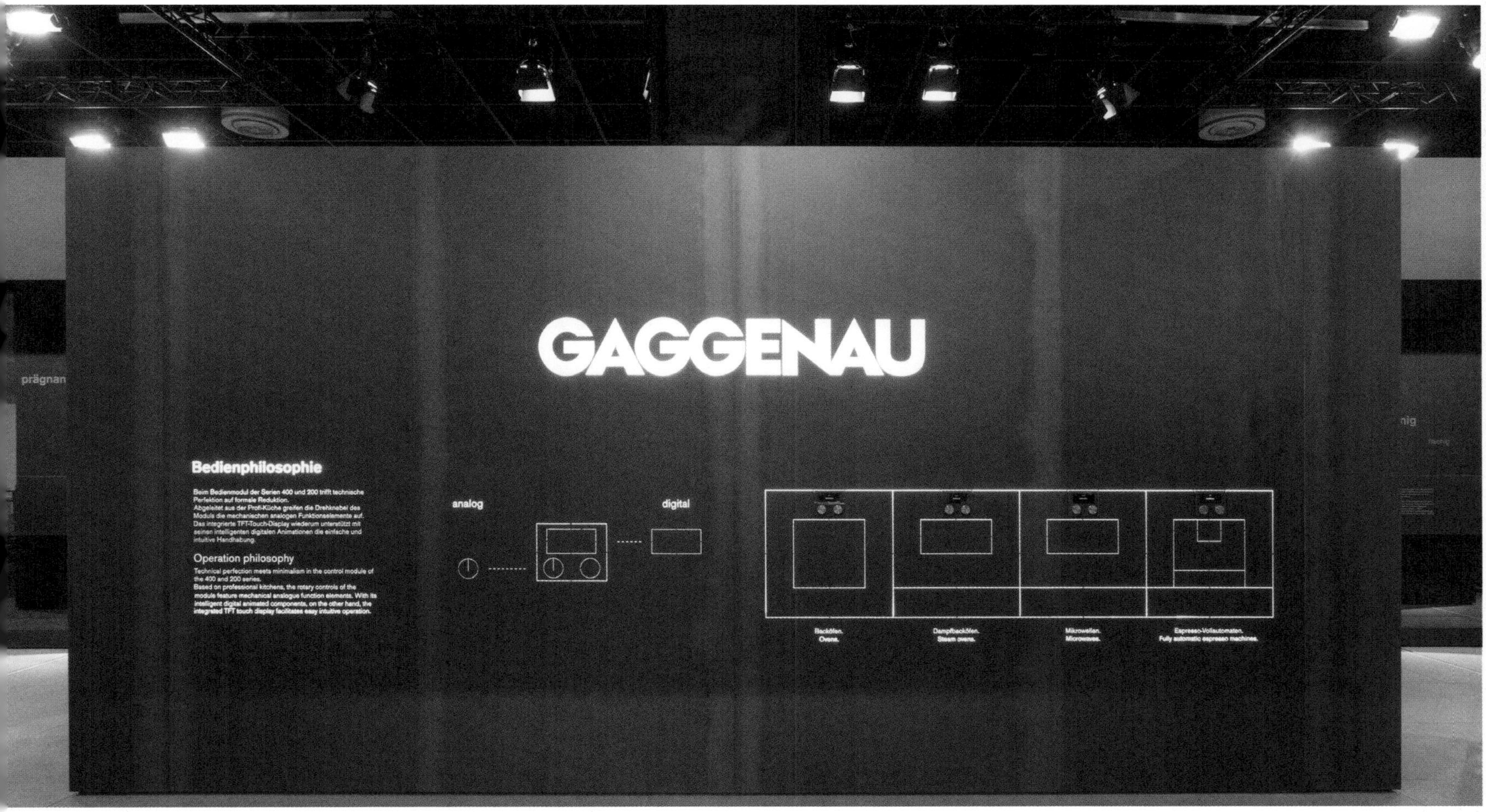

5

GAGGENAU 'SHOWCASES' ITS NEW INNOVATIONS IN EXCLUSIVE BLACK SHOWCASES

6

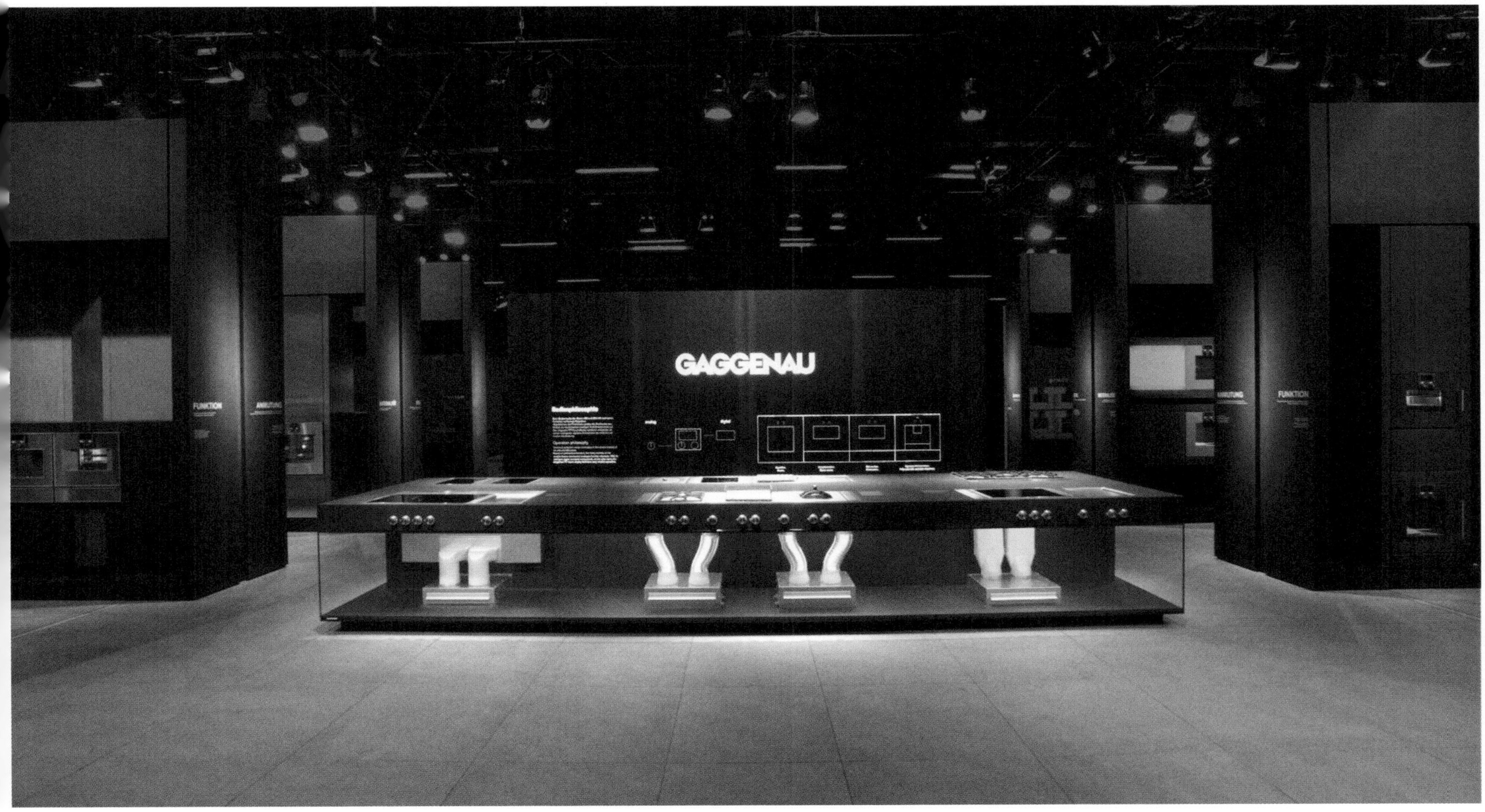

SKETCH

UNIFORMITY OF MATERIALS AND FORMS ENSURES A COHERENT BRAND PRESENTATION

Section A

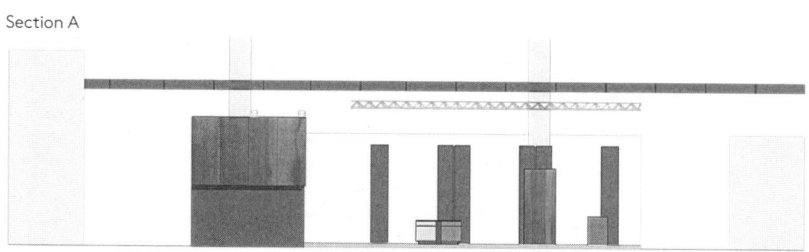

Section B

Section C

Section D

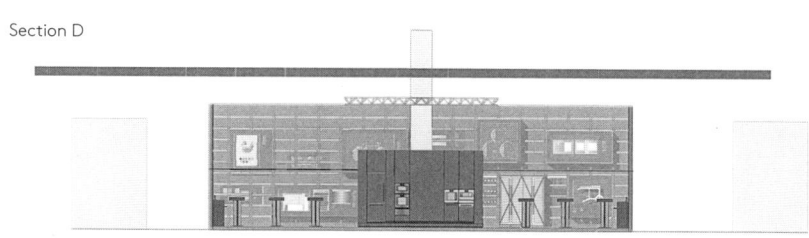

FLOOR PLAN

01 Welcome area
02 Display cases
03 Showcases Series 200
04 Showcases Series 400
05 Control concept
06 Ventilation counter
07 Secondary entry (ramp)
08 Live cooking
09 Lounge

7 Muted large-format ceramic tiles provided a light contrasting base for the dark showcases.

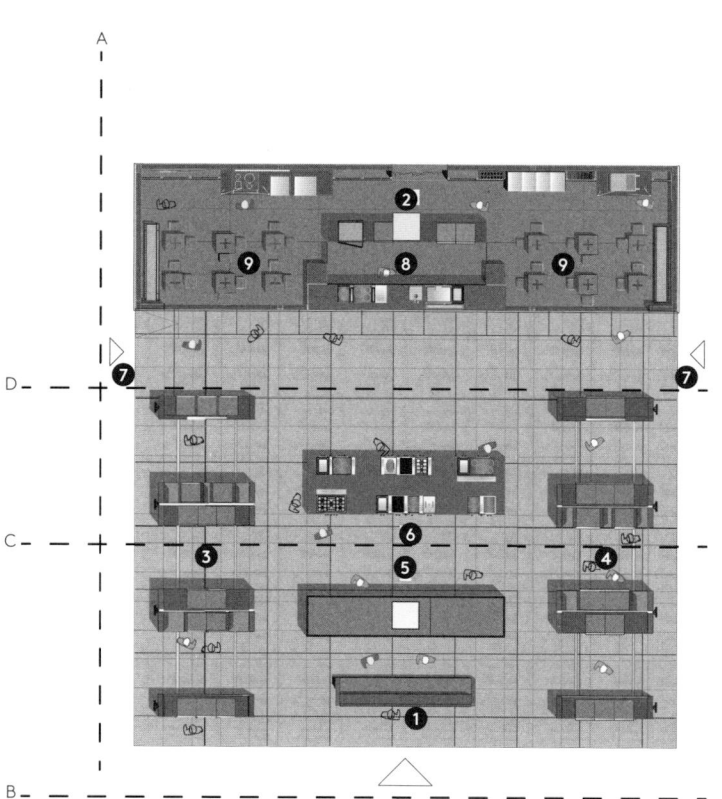

JULIUS BLUM

Arno Design

TRADE FAIR **Interzum**
WHERE **Cologne, Germany**
WHEN **May 2015**
DESIGNER **Arno Design**
STAND CONSTRUCTOR **Arno Design**
CLIENT **Julius Blum**
MARKET SECTOR **Mounting and fitting systems**
TOTAL FLOOR AREA **1028 m²**
PHOTOGRAPHER **Frank Kotzerke**

1 The faceted, crystal form of the facade was echoed on the stand in the partitions and display walls.

2 The white faceted facade was an immediate eye-catcher.

2

Julius Blum's presentation at Interzum – a fair dedicated to furniture production and interior design – focused on the launch of their Tip-On Blumotion Mechanism under the theme of 'handle-less and reliable opening'. The international manufacturer of kitchen and furniture fittings commissioned Arno Design to create an eye-catching stand that could accommodate its entire product range from the varying segments plus diverse meeting and service areas.

A three-dimensional white faceted structure formed the basis of the design, enclosing the 1028 m² space to create a private domain within the exhibition hall. With an intriguing crystal-like form, the striking facade immediately caught visitors' attentions. Two side entrances directed the flow of visitors onto the stand. Once inside, they were welcomed at the central circular reception. The main presentation formed the heart of the space, flanked by product exhibits on either side. A spacious cafeteria that spanned the entire width of the stand provided ample space to conduct meetings. The office, staff room and kitchen were located at the rear. Three main colours – white, orange and black – clearly communicated the brand

and kept the colour palette simple and strong. While white established a clean, crisp background, orange lent dynamic highlights to the furniture, displays, reception and signage. Black walls were dedicated to product presentations and the central exhibit about the Tip-On Blumotion Mechanism was bathed in white. Here, an interactive wall enabled visitors to open the drawers fitted with the special mechanism through a light touch, and in turn, activated product information projected behind a copper webbing-infused glass surface embedded in the wall. Unifying the space were two opposing paths of white and orange string curtains that lined the ceiling, which symbolized the 'Blum DNA' for quality and innovation. ➙

3

A THREE-DIMENSIONAL WHITE FACETED STRUCTURE IMMEDIATELY CATCHES THE EYE

3 Copper webbing-infused glass lent a futuristic quality to the interactive walls.

4 Lighting in the exhibition area played with contrast to highlight the products.

5 The cafeteria was decked out in vibrant orange furniture and white curtains of light.

4

KALDEWEI

Schmidhuber

TRADE FAIR **ISH**
WHERE **Frankfurt, Germany**
WHEN **March 2015**
DESIGNER **Schmidhuber**
STAND CONSTRUCTOR **Raumtechnik**
Messebau & Event Services
CLIENT **Kaldewei**
MARKET SECTOR **Sanitary**
TOTAL FLOOR AREA **750 m²**
PHOTOGRAPHER **Olaf Becker**

2

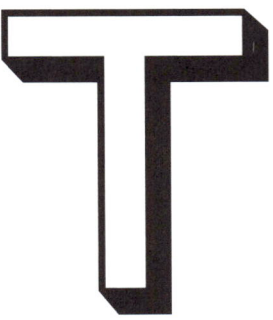

The world premiere of Kaldewei's new collection of basins took the spotlight at ISH in Frankfurt in 2015. To mark this momentous occasion, Kaldewei's stand needed to shine, both literally and figuratively. Inspired by this, Schmidhuber devised a concept of intersecting light beams to express the brand's high quality of design, setting a dramatic stage for the presentation. Invisible beams converged at three vanishing points, slicing the volume of the stand into prisms. The resulting volume appeared as a series of angular structures organised in a three-dimensional matrix – as if the whole interior was carved out by light. Walls and frames leaned towards the centre, creating a dynamic interplay of perspective and proportion. The dark architecture and atmosphere exuded an air of exclusivity and modernity and focus on the iconic presentation of the products. A central courtyard formed the focal point with the feature presentation. Here the new steel enamel basins were showcased around a large pool, which was filled with delicate white orchids. The pool's white form set against a radiant white background highlighted the presentation in the dark surrounds. Suspended above was a stunning huge globe made of white orchids, which contrasted softly with the strict geometry and dark, glossy surfaces of the space. Defined in white, the network of skewed pathways guided visitors to separate themed presentations inside the black volumes, which opened onto the courtyard. Dedicated to a different product or collection each volume was distinguished by a different atmosphere; music, scent and lighting tickled the senses. Their varying closed and open facades added a lively play of space that surprised visitors as they turned each corner. ▭

1 The design of the stand was devoid of right angles.

2 Visitors encountered mysterious black volumes that opened up into a lively mini city organised along a skewed grid of streets.

3

4

3/4 Each volume featured
a different product and
themed presentation.

DEVELOPMENT OF LIGHTBEAMS

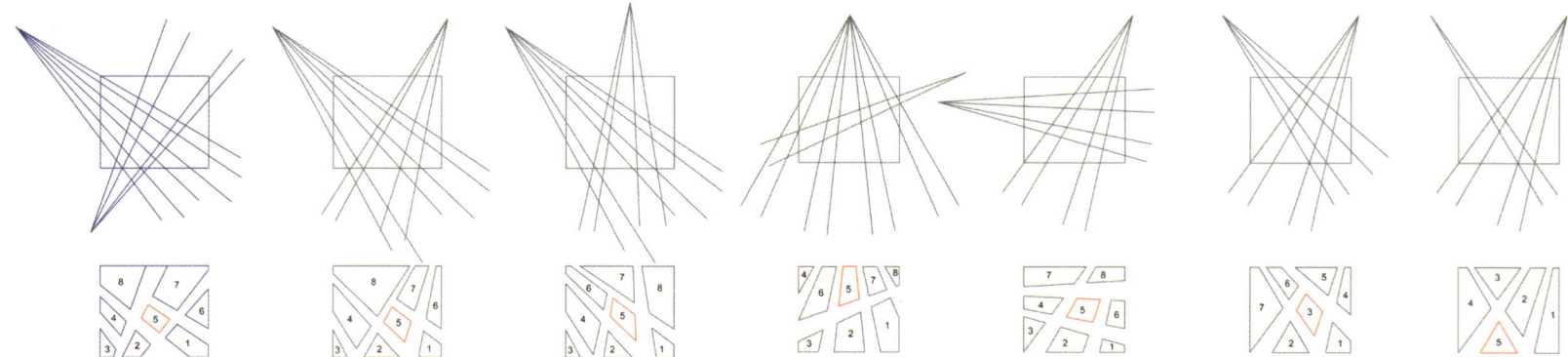

VISUALISATION OF THE CONCEPT

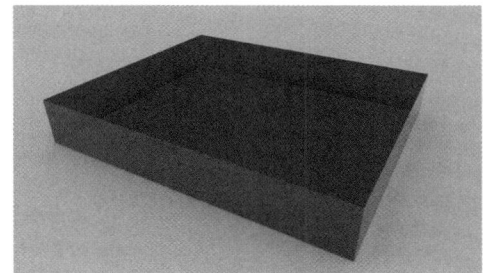

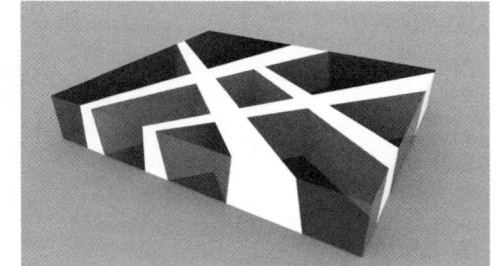

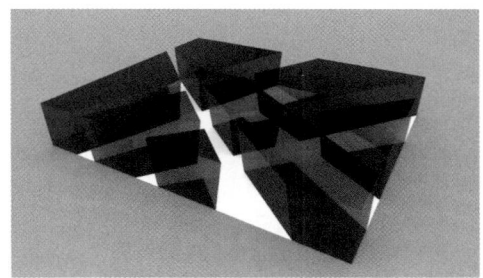

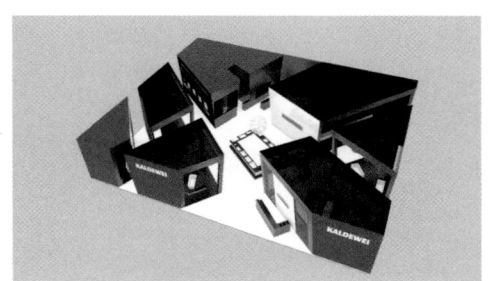

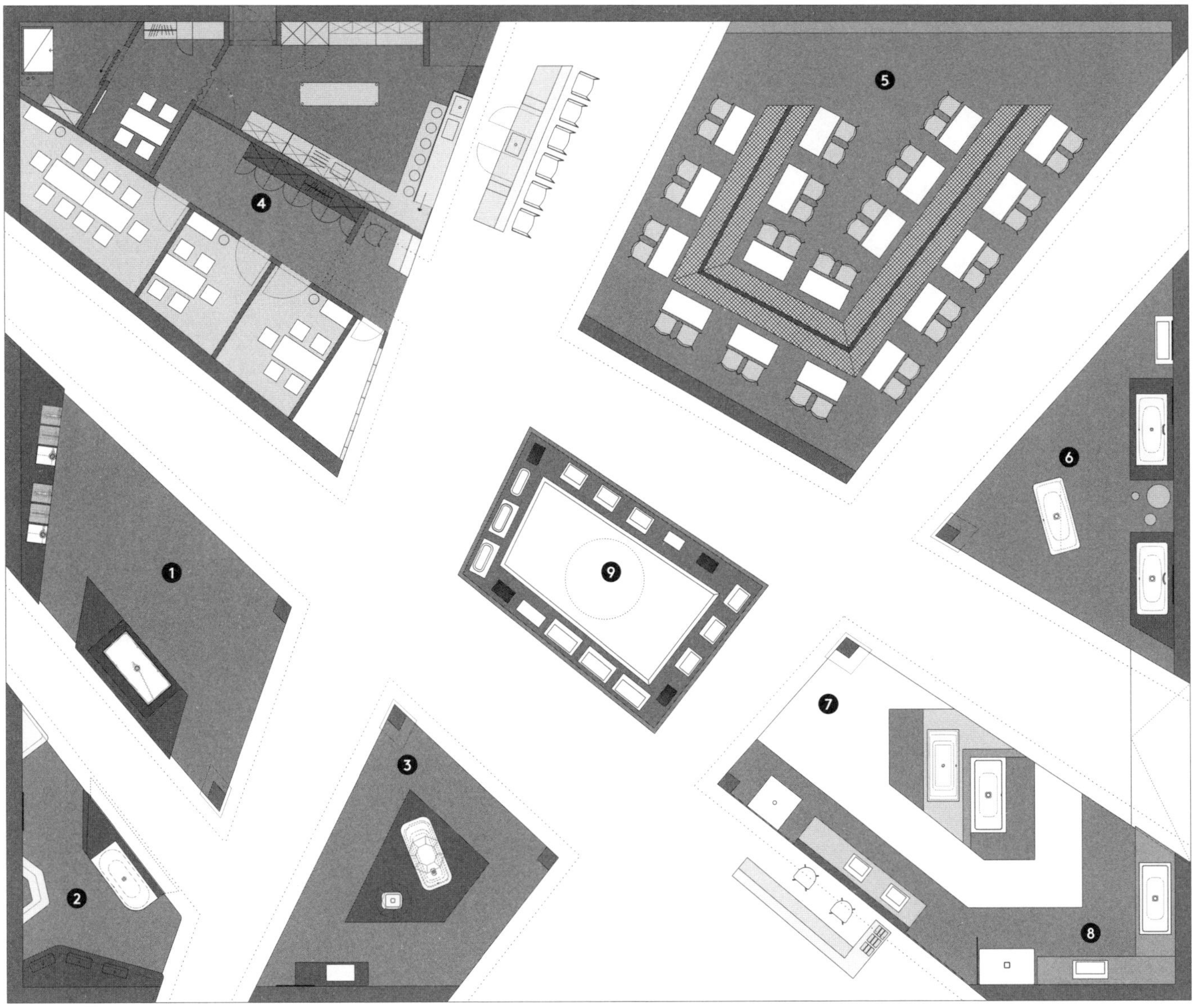

THE DARK INTERIOR IS CARVED BY INTERSECTING BEAMS OF LIGHT

FLOOR PLAN

01 Guards room
01 Shower attack
02 Skin touch
03 Arik Levy
04 Back office
05 Lounge
06 Anke Salomon
07 Puro
08 Conoduo
09 Highlight washbasins

INTERIOR PRODUCTS GRAND STAND 5

KVADRAT
Raw-Edges

TRADE FAIR **Stockholm Furniture Fair**
WHERE **Stockholm, Sweden**
WHEN **February 2013**
DESIGNER **Raw-Edges**
STAND CONSTRUCTORS **Kvadrat and Syncro Denmark**
CLIENT **Kvadrat**
MARKET SECTOR **Textiles**
TOTAL FLOOR AREA **80 m²**
PHOTOGRAPHERS **Joël Tettamanti and Raw-Edges**

1 Composed of folded vertical textile swatches, the installation took inspiration from weeping willows.

2 The designers wanted to evoke an atmosphere of nature, relaxation and warmth with a surreal touch.

3 Offering a different take on a flat display table, the angled tables faced viewers in a friendly way, much like how one holds a book.

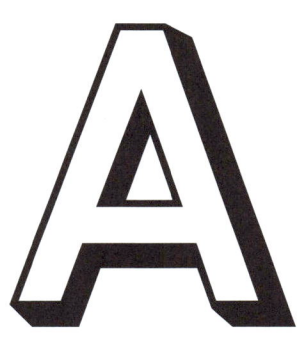

2

A t the Stockholm Furniture Fair in 2013, Kvadrat invited visitors to join a lovely picnic in an enchanted forest. Aptly entitled 'The Picnic' the eye-catching stand was designed by Raw-Edges. For its presentation Kvadrat requested a stand that would emphasise the colours, textures and variety of its textiles. In the midst of the busy fair hall, visitors encountered a calm and welcoming oasis. There were two primary elements on the stand: a solid wooden structure made from Douglas fir inside, and a stunning textile installation comprising 1500 suspended straps outside. Composed from 20 different Kvadrat textiles, the installation recalled gentle weeping willow trees. The straps were actually fashioned from textile swatches – by folding and combining them into an eye-catching installation, the designers transformed something common into a spectacular feature. Its texture resembled roof tiles or even fish scales, and the

3

colour gradient shifted from blues to whites and pinks and reds; pastel hues alternated with vibrant accents. As a screen, the beautiful curtain of drooping straps created an intimate atmosphere within the busy hall. Inside, visitors encountered a wooden cabin construction that served as the wall display for fabric swatches. Constructed from angled floor planks of Douglas fir, the structure held the samples firmly in place while visitors flipped through them. Formed like pitched roofs, long picnic tables displayed more swatches. Small trays that perched atop the tables were used for serving coffee. Playful stools made from textile cushions clamped at the ends between timber frames resembled colourful candies. The concept arose from the idea that a rolled-up sweater sleeve has a different inner and outer appearance. The varying combinations of textiles showed how different Kvadrat products could be paired in beautiful ways. ▭

ON-SITE CONSTRUCTION

ROLLS OF TEXTILE SWATCHES

POCKETS

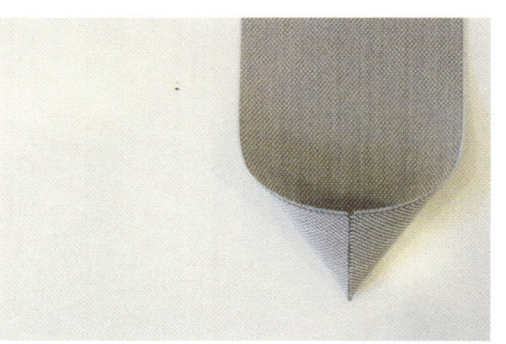

FURNITURE

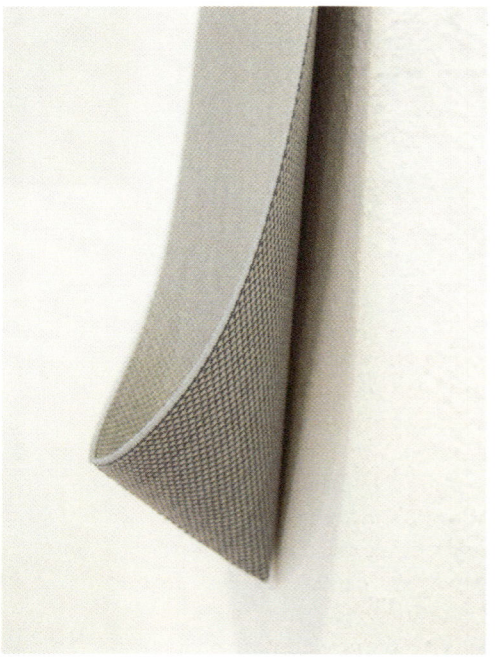

KVADRAT INVITES VISITORS TO JOIN A LOVELY PICNIC IN AN ENCHANTED FOREST

STRUCTURE/ DISPLAY FOR TEXTILE SWATCHES

INTERIOR PRODUCTS   GRAND STAND 5

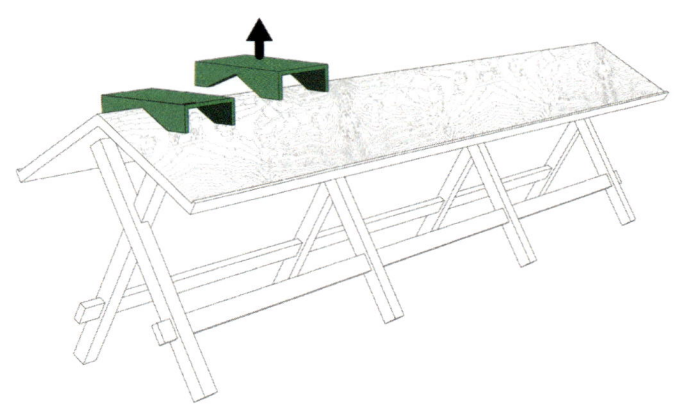

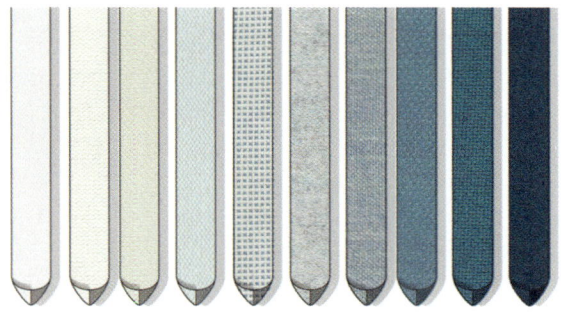

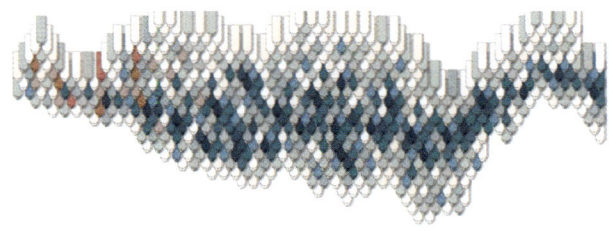

SKETCHES

ONN
VOIDplanning

1 Black mirror was placed on the floor to simulate the water's edge.

2 A simple white, paper-clad box set the scene for Onn's presentation.

2

Onn's stand at the Craft Trend Fair in Seoul transported visitors to a serene landscape that reflected the brand's pure approach. For the presentation of its premium handcrafted furniture and products, Onn wanted to recreate a scene from nature, which forms a major inspiration for the brand's designs. The ambition was also to utilise the space to showcase Korean traditions. From the outside, the stand appeared as a pure, translucent white box illuminated from within. The four-metre-high walls were constructed from traditional Korean

paper called Hanji stretched over a wooden frame. Inside, the exhibition unfolded in the long enclosed room. Walking inside the space felt like a stroll along a misty lakeside in the morning; it seemed as if the visitors had entered a majestic Korean painting. Narrow openings at each end led visitors into the space where a central gravel pathway, made of different sizes of gravel, guided them further. Also made from Hanji paper, the walls formed the main interior feature, stained to create a natural gradient that shifted upwards from dark to light. Complemented by atmospheric lighting, these beautiful walls really gave the interior an appearance of a mysterious misty landscape. A traditional ink called Muk was used to stain the paper – both originate from Jeonju, the province where Onn is based. Perfecting

the gradient across such a large surface area was the project's main challenge, which involved testing different papers with varying amounts of ink to get the right depth of colour and texture. Furniture was positioned along the edges over a dark mirrored surface reminiscent of water, further enhancing the dreamy waterside illusion. The stand's evocative, tranquil atmosphere gave visitors a poetic experience to remember Onn by. ⇒

TRADE FAIR **Craft Trend Fair**
WHERE **Seoul, Korea**
WHEN **December 2012**
DESIGNER **VOIDplanning**
STAND CONSTRUCTOR **VOIDplanning**
CLIENT **Onn**
MARKET SECTOR **Furniture**
TOTAL FLOOR AREA **90 m²**
PHOTOGRAPHER **VOIDplanning**

PALMBERG

Arting

TRADE FAIR **Orgatec**
WHERE **Cologne, Germany**
WHEN **October 2014**
DESIGNER **Arting**
STAND CONSTRUCTOR **Arting**
CLIENT **Palmberg**
MARKET SECTOR **Office furniture**
TOTAL FLOOR AREA **1230 m²**
PHOTOGRAPHER **Dirk Baumbach**

Palmberg is a producer of high-quality and contemporary office solutions for the European market. For its stand at Orgatec 2014, Palmberg specified a design should be visually eye-catching, convey an office-inspired atmosphere, include a relaxed lounge area and coherently feature the Palmberg identity throughout. Arting had the task of designing the stand after winning the design competition that

Palmberg conducted for this purpose. Arting's concept utilised contrasts – between transparency and openness, and dark and light – to create a strong architectural statement that intrigued visitors to discover more. Enveloping the stand entirely was a mysterious black screen made from PVC plates – a total of 5000 plates were suspended on a grid of steel tubes. This enclosed the space to create a more intimate atmosphere on the 1230 m² stand while allowing it to stay connected with its surroundings. In this way, the screen also remained open enough to afford glimpses into the interior to arouse visitors' curiosities, and the plates were cleverly spaced to

adhere to the level of 50% transparency that was required of all stand facades. Products were displayed in different areas that shifted between light and dark atmospheres. An open layout allowed visitors to meander freely between displays. Perforated white screens echoed the grid of the facade and functioned as playful partitions to structure the spaces. These grids were also used in the dark lowered ceilings. Other ceilings were fashioned from a light timber frame clad in delicate white fabric. An elevated section housed the cosy lounge area that was intended for hosting meetings with clients and stakeholders. ⬯

1 Warm lighting, materials and finishes created an inviting atmosphere in the lounge.

2 The striking facade provided privacy but remained open enough to reveal teasing glimpses of the interior.

2

3

3 Armchairs and bar stools offered different seating options in the lounge area.

4 A white box housed the meeting room.

5 Products were exhibited in different areas that alternated between light and dark atmospheres.

ARTING'S CONCEPT UTILISES CONTRASTS TO CREATE A STRONG ARCHITECTURAL STATEMENT

4

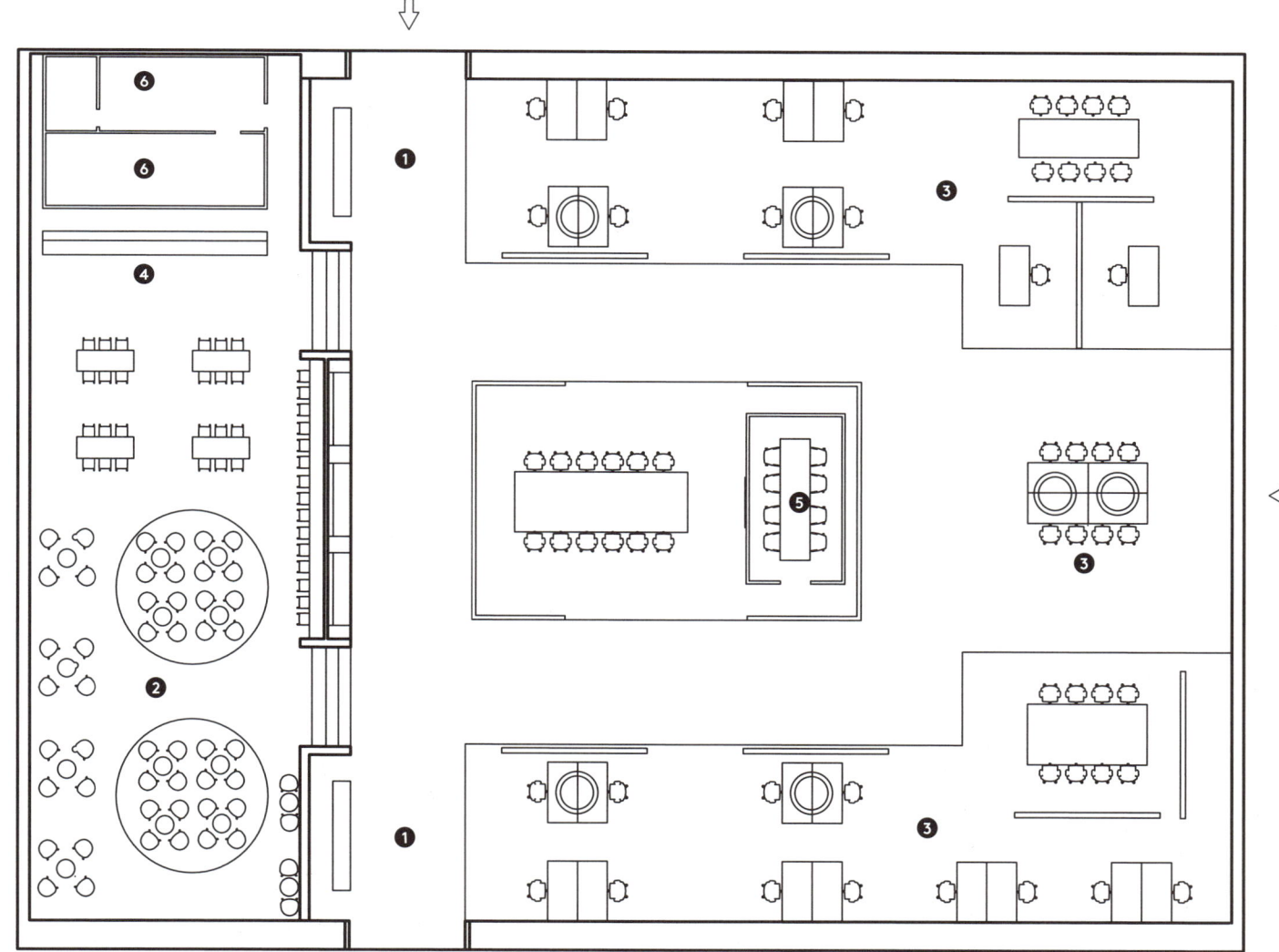

FLOOR PLAN

01 Info counter
02 Lounge area
03 Product area
04 Bar
05 Meeting room
06 Storage

SERAFINI
atelier 522

TRADE FAIR **EuroShop**
WHERE **Düsseldorf, Germany**
WHEN **February 2014**
DESIGNER **atelier 522**
STAND CONSTRUCTOR **Tischlerei Loick**
CLIENT **serafini**
MARKET SECTOR **Display systems**
TOTAL FLOOR AREA **121 m²**
PHOTOGRAPHER **Ben Decker for atelier 522**

1 The elevated corners of the booth together with its graphic exterior turned serafini's stand into a distinctive landmark at EuroShop 2014.

2 The pink bar hosted informal meetings while the meeting room offered more privacy if needed.

2

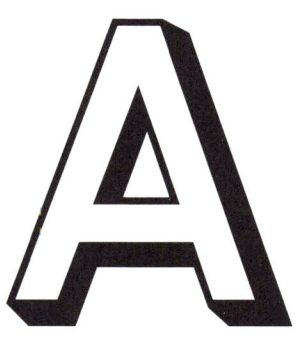

At EuroShop 2014, display systems manufacturer serafini proudly presented a diverse collection of its latest products, shop fitting systems and innovations. With so many different elements to feature, serafini sought an inviting, friendly yet innovative exhibition design that would display these varying aspects coherently. With its trademark integrated approach combining interior, graphic and product design, atelier 522 designed a bold, total environment for serafini that united the presentation and warmly welcomed visitors onto the stand.

The stand comprised a series of open and semi-enclosed display zones separated by low partitions, each with its own ambience. What united them was a clear design language and harmonious colour palette, where black and white and warm spring colours met linear and circular geometries. Serafini's dot and line system on show that year was the starting point for the design. Bar-code-like patterns were paired with regular stripes of varying thicknesses, adding a striking texture and sense of movement on the stand. Patterns of black-and-white dots also played with scale.

Complementing the grid of partitions were circular swinging windows made from copper, brass and wood that functioned like portholes into each zone. Pastel pink and unvarnished, light wood marked the meeting room volume and adjoining bar area. The candy-striped bar awning added a playful detail and an oversized rotating disc could close off the room for private meetings. Inside, the warm wood and pink accents created a warm atmosphere. The green of the material library complemented the overall palette well; brass detailing here lent a luxury touch. Unmissable in canary yellow, the central seating area invited visitors to relax and have informal meetings. Seated under the suspended yellow light sphere, they could almost feel warmed up, especially on the overcast days. A vintage yellow gumball machine added the finishing touch to this eye-catching stand. ▭

4

3 Serafini's dot and line system inspired the graphic stand designed by atelier 522.

4 Covering everything in the central meeting area from the walls, floor, furniture to the lamp and ceiling panel, the vibrant yellow brightened the entire space.

5 A peek through the porthole into the meeting room revealed an intimate, warm space made from light wood coloured with pink highlights.

5

A PALETTE OF BLACK AND WHITE WITH WARM SPRING COLOURS MEETS LINEAR AND CIRCULAR GEOMETRIES

FLOOR PLAN

01 Dot and line system presentation
02 Material laboratory
03 Seating area
04 Meeting cube

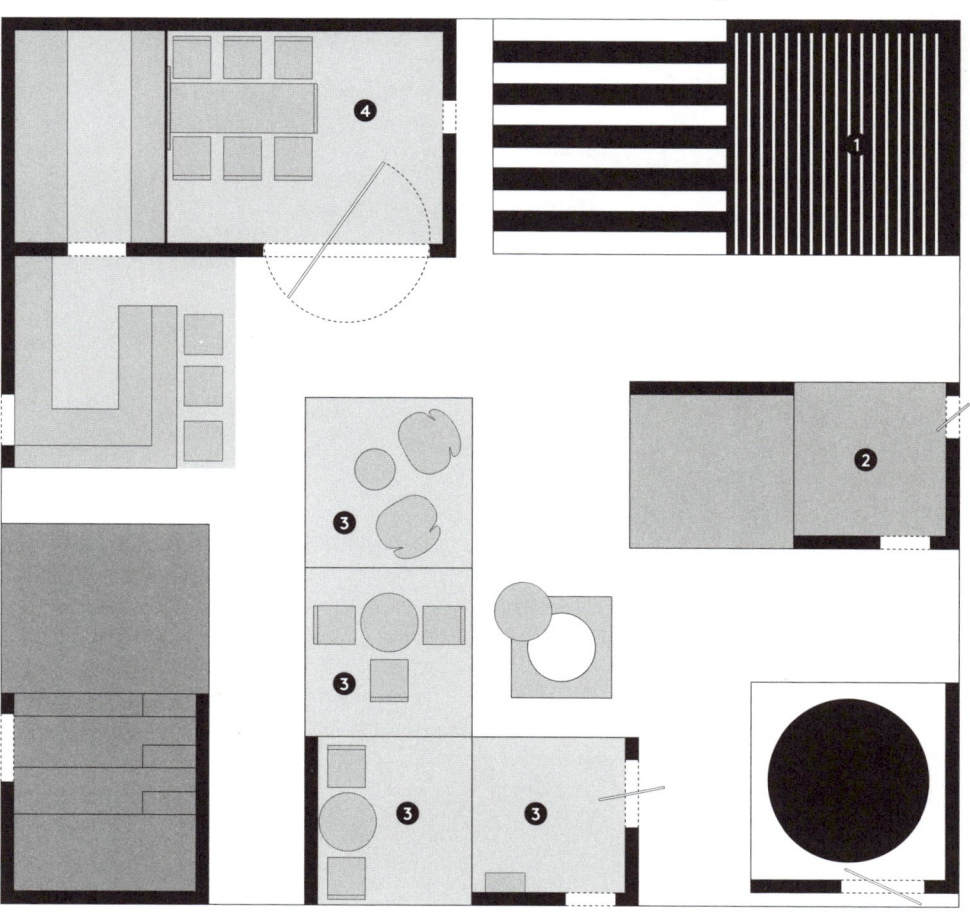

VITRA
Neo

1 A beautiful layering of space resulted as spaces flowed freely into each other.

2 The stand appeared as an ordered arrangement of interior modules inspired by the idea of photo frames.

2

VitrA's stand at Unicera, the International Ceramic Bathroom Kitchen Fair, showed the diversity of its offerings in an architectural yet intimate surrounding. Neo International Design & Communications worked in collaboration with the VitrA design team to devise a simple, elegant space to introduce the new product collections. The stand comprised two sections: 850 m² was used for exhibition and 120 m² across the corridor was dedicated to hospitality. The concept of photo frames and cells guided the design. A modular, rectilinear stand made from a white outer shell and black inner grid of aluminium profiles set up a structured framework for the presentation. Different product groups were framed in individual showcases within this grid akin to 3D photo frames. Three main areas were featured: bathroom products were displayed in rooms with stylish interior settings. The black frames captured these spaces at a specific moment, as if frozen in time. Faucets were clustered into three open cells. Tiles were showcased on smaller modular black frameworks. A grid of ceiling spotlights mounted on slim black frames perfectly complemented the theme, and ensured a warm quality of light. As the frames and rooms flowed into each other, this contributed a depth of space and sense of layering to the interior. From the exterior, alternating open rooms framed vistas into the stand. The contemporary black-and-white palette of the hospitality area suited the business atmosphere and aesthetic of the main stand. Wooden boxes with planting mounted on a black framework added a homely touch. The stand's uncomplicated, structured architecture resulted in a coherent and professional presentation. ▬

TRADE FAIR **Unicera**
WHERE **Istanbul, Turkey**
WHEN **February 2015**
DESIGNERS **VitrA and Neo International Design & Communications**
STAND CONSTRUCTOR **Neo International Design & Communications**
CLIENT **VitrA**
MARKET SECTOR **Sanitaryware/bathrooms**
TOTAL FLOOR AREA **970 m²**
PHOTOGRAPHER **Halise Özel Mahmutoğlu**

THE RECTILINEAR STAND IS MADE FROM A WHITE OUTER SHELL AND BLACK INNER GRID

3 The black frames used for mounting the tiles and spotlights complemented each other well.

4 Bathroom products were showcased in stylish interior settings.

5 The uncluttered quality of the space focused attention completely on the company's products.

5 The design of the hospitality area reflected the modular aesthetic of the stand.

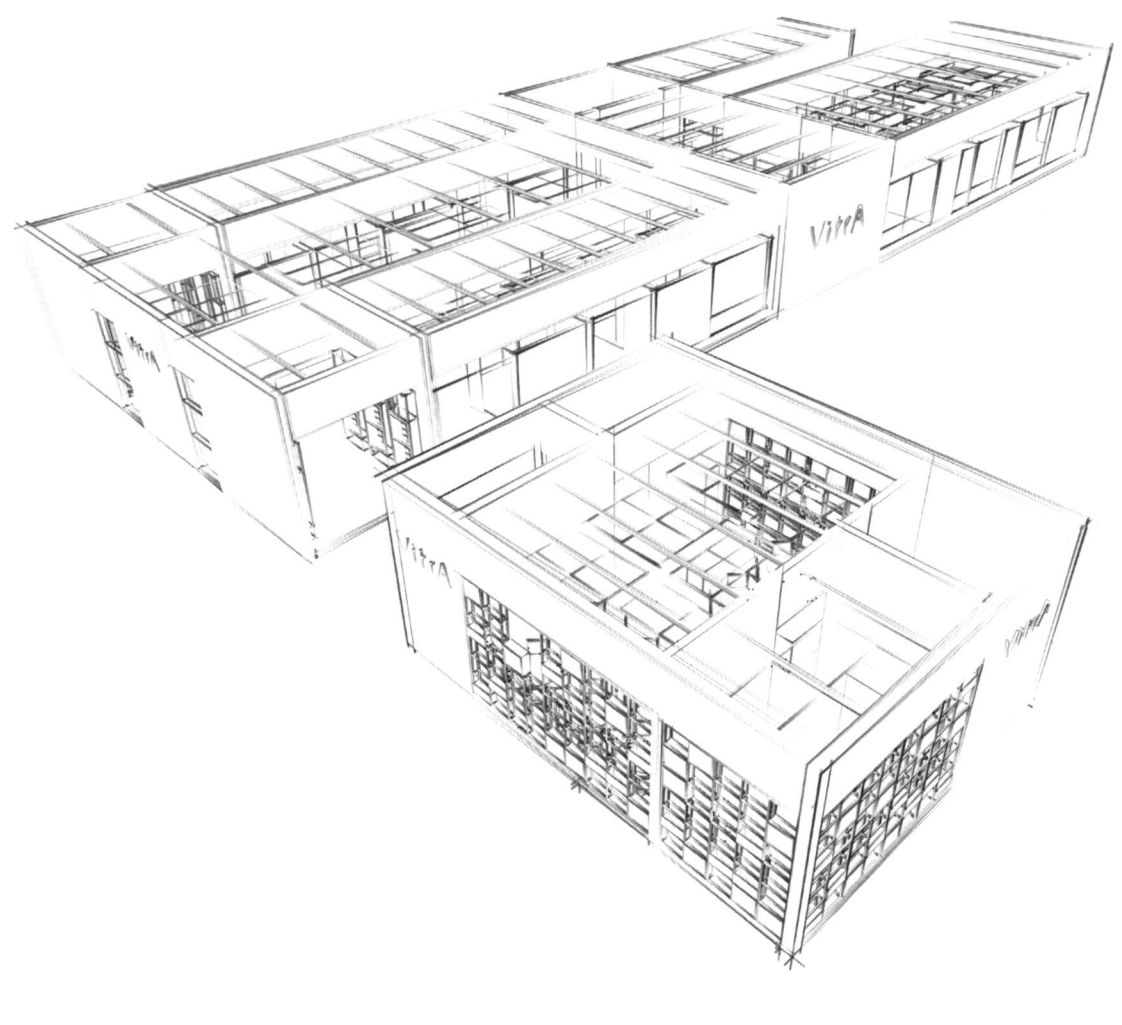

ALTERNATING OPEN ROOMS FRAME VISTAS INTO THE STAND

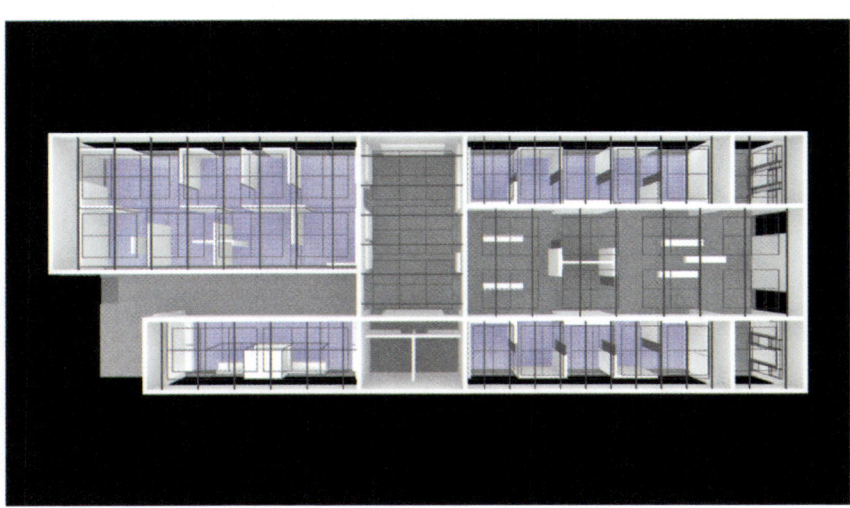

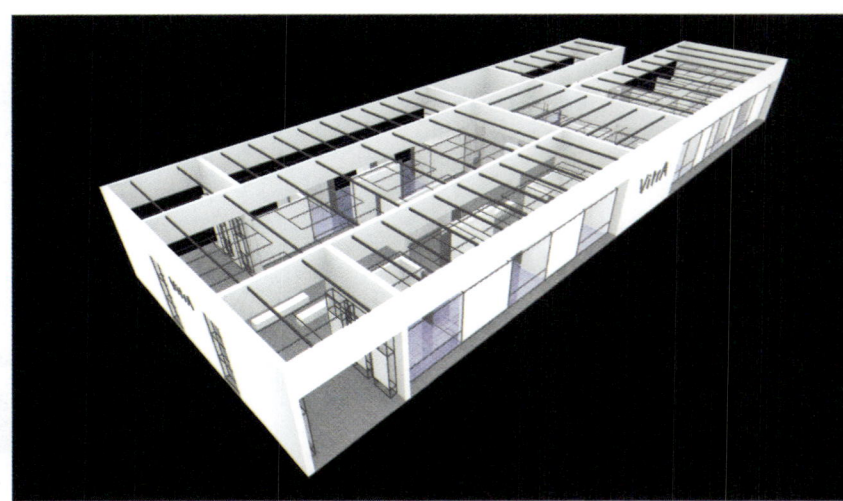

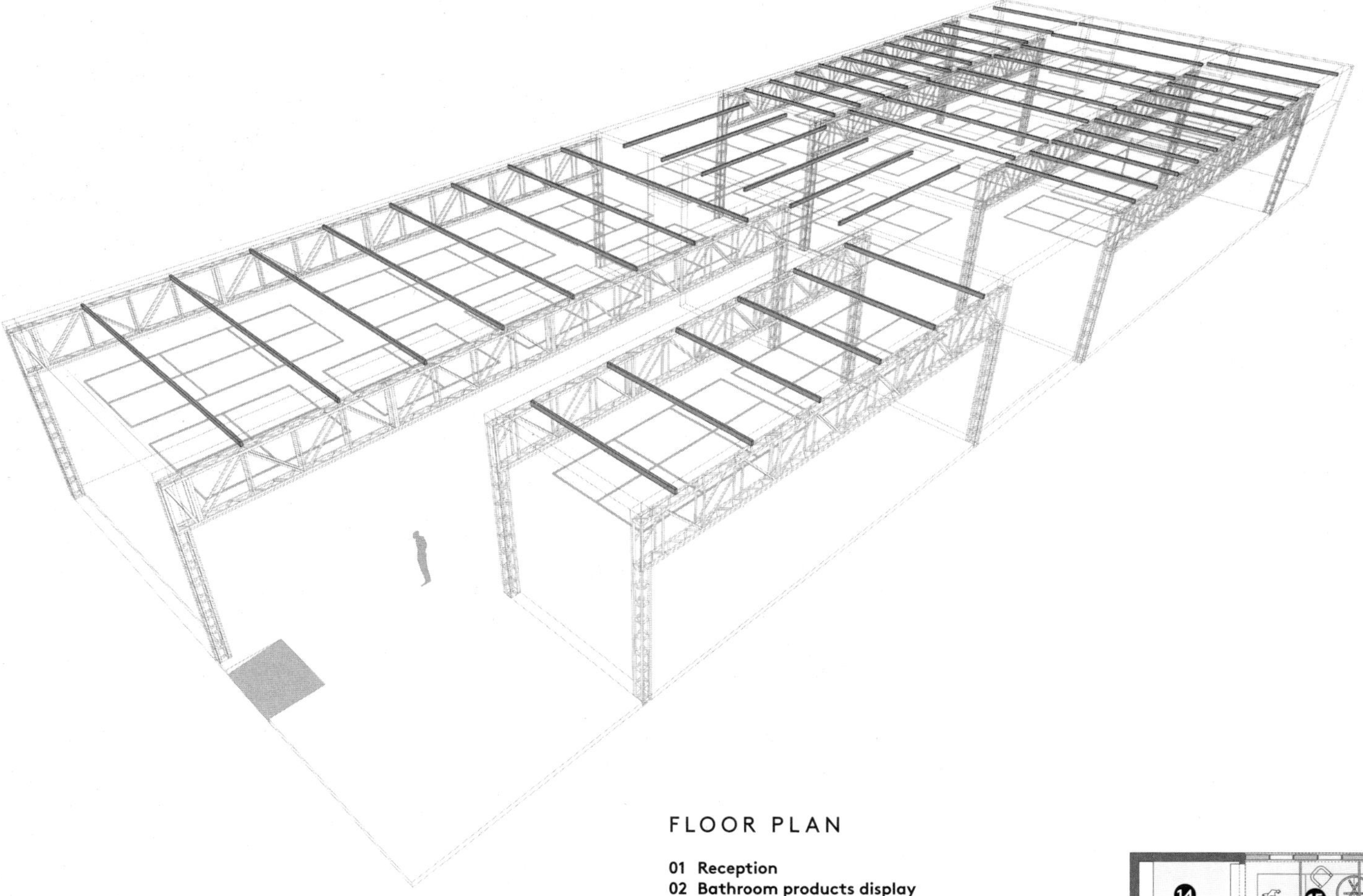

FLOOR PLAN

01 Reception
02 Bathroom products display
03 Faucet display
04 Innovation area
05 Partners reception
06 Storage
07 Tiles display area
08 Sofa
09 100x300cm tiles display
10 80x80cm tiles display
11 Simulation area
12 Hospitality area
13 Bar
14 Kitchen
15 Meeting room

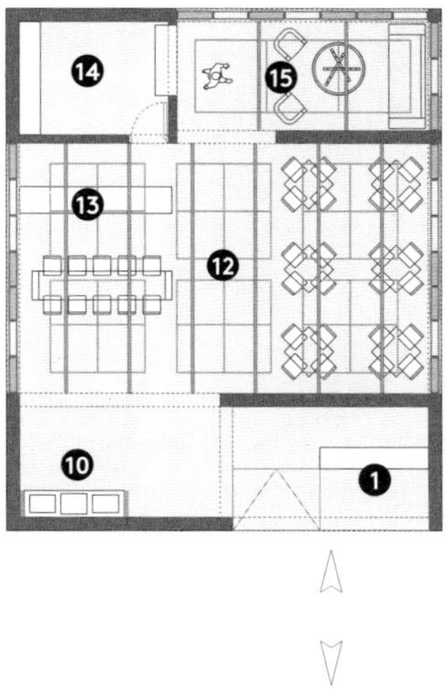

WALTER KNOLL

Ippolito Fleitz Group

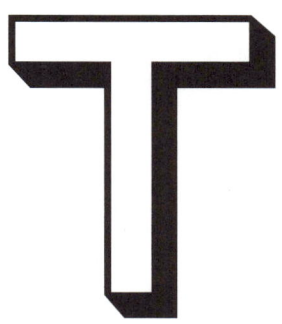

The motto for Walter Knoll's presence at Orgatec 2014 revolved around communication and identity, key themes of today's new working world. Designed by Ippolito Fleitz Group, the stand supported Walter Knoll's market presence and brand identity in the high-end office segment. At the same time, the spatial design echoed changing ways of working with less focus on classic workstations and more on social living environments.

The stand was structured into three sections: an entry zone, followed by a central axis with four scenarios and café at the rear. At the main entrance, the new organic Seating Stones collection by Ben van Berkel provided the prelude to the exhibition stand. A stunning backdrop of tropical plants wrapped in a custom-designed black carbon fibre curtain complemented the organic language of the furniture and provided glimpses into the stand beyond.

From the main entrance, a central axis accentuated by white fins on the ceiling led to the end of the stand. Grouped around this axis were four different spatial scenarios with semi-private spaces. Comprising a series of informal zones, the open middle section demonstrated the versatility of the collection through varying compositions of furniture. Spaces were cleverly zoned using suspended oversized images, also veiled behind carbon curtains, screens of black angled fins and coloured partitions that featured quotes about current and future work environments.

The rear zone highlighted communication and the increasing importance of the cafeteria within a workplace setting. Its mirrored interior adorned with lush hanging plants resembled more a chic urban bar than an office. Here, the café was the communication hub, where people had quick chats at the bar, coffee and snacks at the counter or in-depth discussions at the small tables or on comfortable lounges. With such social and dynamic workspaces, going to the office will never feel like hard work. ⧟

TRADE FAIR **Orgatec**
WHERE **Cologne, Germany**
WHEN **October 2014**
DESIGNER **Ippolito Fleitz Group**
STAND CONSTRUCTOR **werk33**
CLIENT **Walter Knoll**
MARKET SECTOR **Office furniture**
TOTAL FLOOR AREA **697 m²**
PHOTOGRAPHERS **Zooey Braun and HG Esch Photography**

1 Angled fins and mirrors coupled with atmospheric lighting resulted in a dynamic play of space.

2 The glamorous bar and café facilitated different interaction possibilities between visitors and staff.

WITH SUCH WORKSPACES, GOING TO THE OFFICE WILL NEVER FEEL LIKE HARD WORK

4 The stand design explored changing work environments.

5 The open central axis was bordered by four semi-private spatial scenarios.

6 Each spatial zone was marked by a different colour and quote on the wall.

4

COMMUNICATION AND IDENTITY ARE KEY THEMES OF TODAY'S NEW WORKING WORLD

5

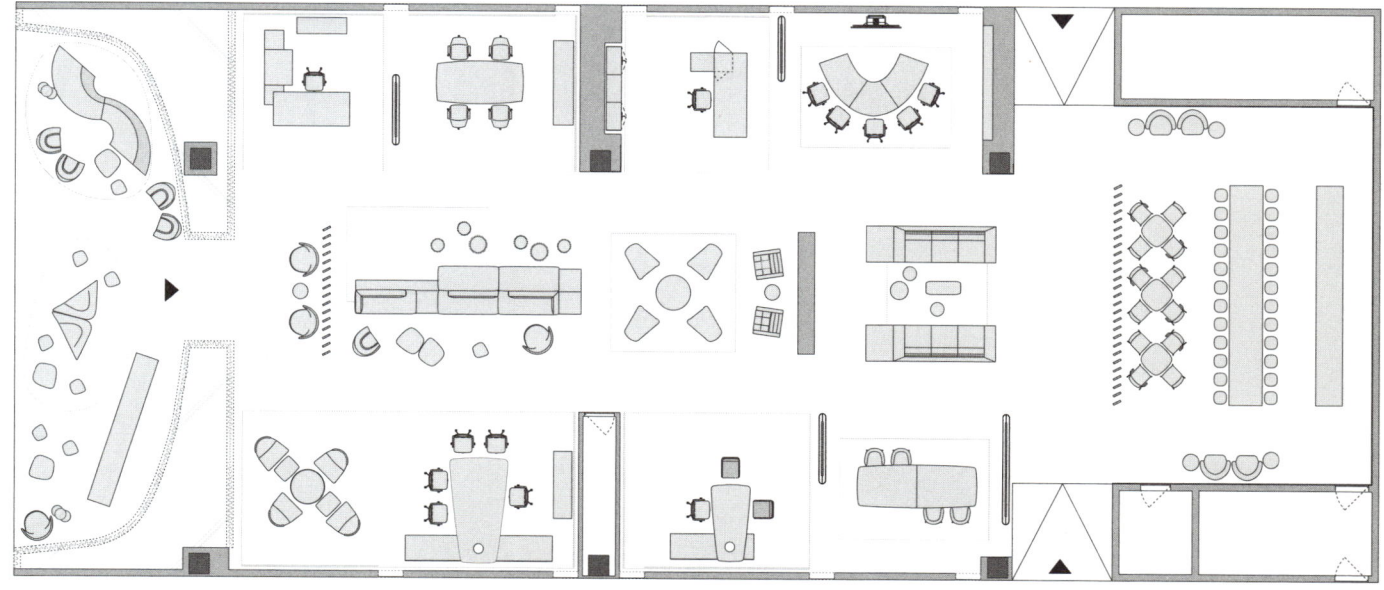

6

FLOOR PLAN

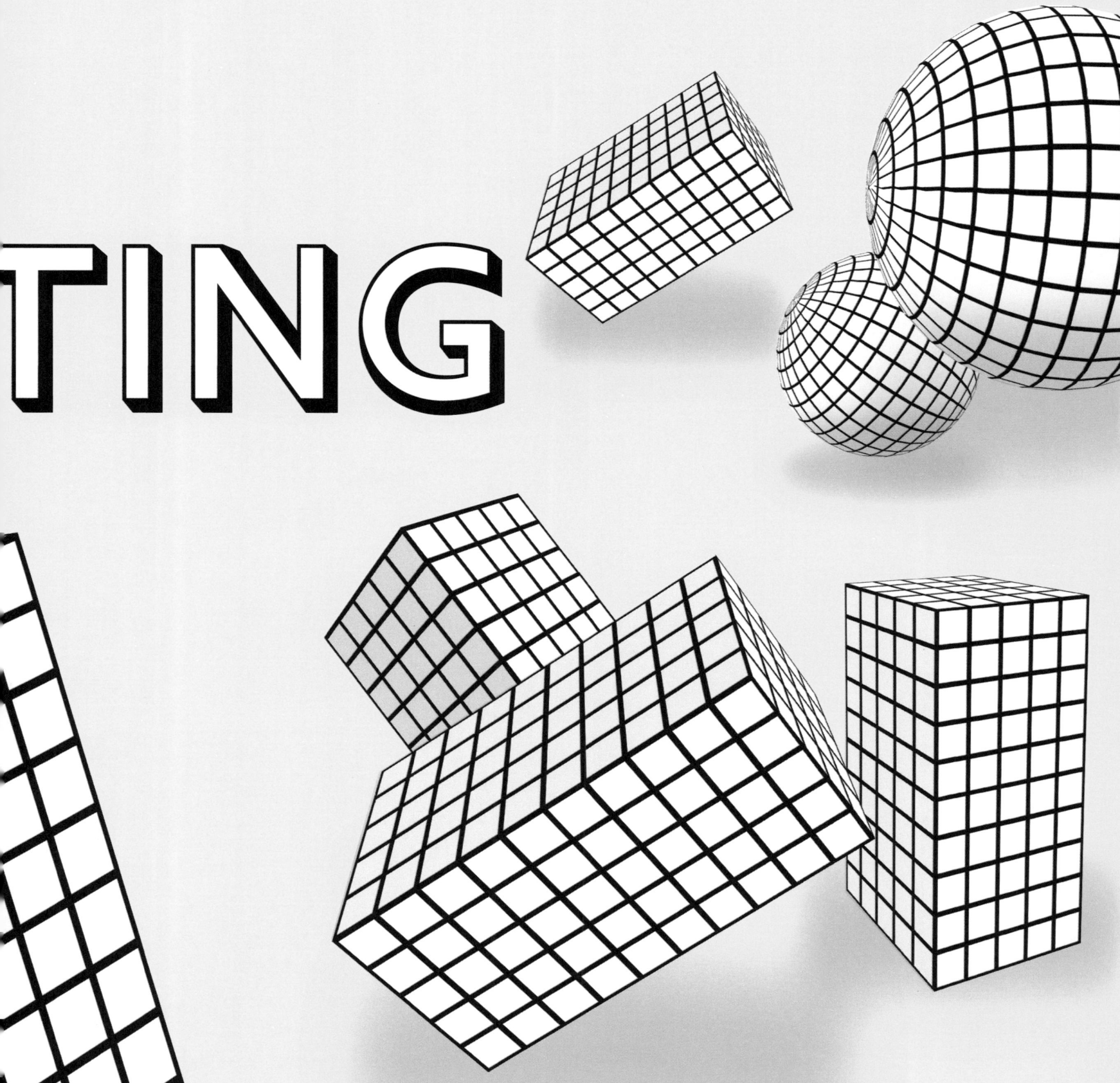

ACDC

Arting

TRADE FAIR **Light + Building**
WHERE **Frankfurt, Germany**
WHEN **March–April 2014**
DESIGNER **Arting**
STAND CONSTRUCTOR **Arting**
CLIENT **acdc**
MARKET SECTOR **Lighting**
TOTAL FLOOR AREA **240 m²**
PHOTOGRAPHER **Dirk Baumbach**

F

For its presentation at Light + Building in 2014, acdc wanted a stand that reflected its philosophy of doing things differently and challenging the norm. The client also wished for the stand to be inviting, make a strong visual impact and create a positive brand experience. It should also be easy to transport, construct and dismantle within a short time frame. Arting, the designers entrusted with this task, proposed an iconic architectural structure that interplayed transparency with privacy to intrigue visitors to experience acdc's world. The exterior

appeared as a mysterious white shell with a skin that alternated between sections of smooth panels and angled vertical slats. Dramatically illuminated the slats resembled curtains of light that seemingly slid open or lifted to form entrances onto the stand. Shifting angles of slats were used to create either more open or closed sections of facade, resulting in a dynamic eye-catching exterior. The tight rhythm of the slats combined with the gentle arch of the entrance contrasted hard and soft, and solid and diffuse elements in reference to the behaviour of and the way we experience light. Spatially the stand was organised into an outer public zone and a circular private inner domain. In continuation of the facade and to showcase the products in the best possible way, the outer section was kept pristine white. In contrast, the inner lounge had

a warm, cosy atmosphere with dimmed lighting and a dark stained plywood interior. The circular bar and library wall, along with the high and low seating areas, offered a relaxed environment for conducting informal meetings and seminars as well as for product displays. Acdc's stand made a memorable mark on visitors thanks to its sculptural, intriguing design that celebrated the brand. ⟹

1/2 Three entrances framed glimpses of the interior and directed the flow of visitors onto the stand.

2

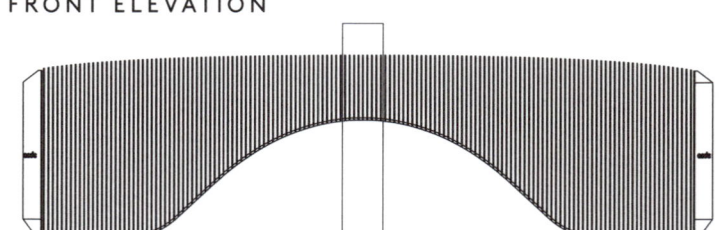

3

3 The dark inner lounge formed the circular core of the space.

4/5 The circular walls appeared to glow thanks to the dark stained plywood and warm lighting.

FRONT ELEVATION

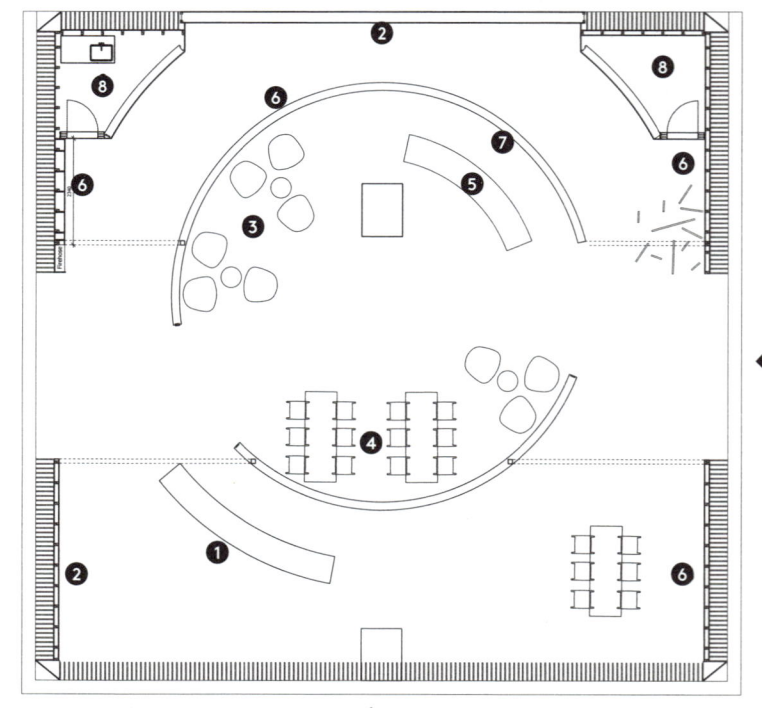

FLOOR PLAN

01 Reception
02 Info area
03 Low seating area
04 High seating area
05 Bar
06 Product display
07 Product library wall
08 Storage

AN INTRIGUING, SCULPTURAL CURTAIN OF LIGHT

4

5

OCCHIO

Drändle 70|30 and Martin et Karczinski

1 Mirrored counters also provided display surfaces.

2 Elegant white oversized graphics complemented the presentation.

3 Covered in 4000 lush plants, the green plus immediately caught the attention of visitors.

2

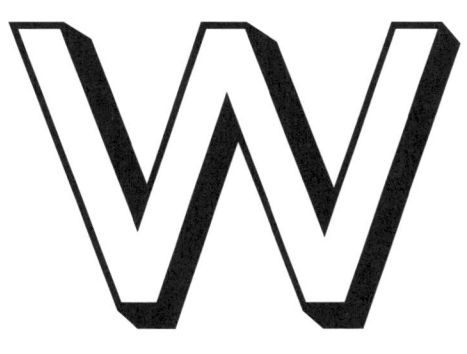

With its statement 'evolution plus' Occhio demonstrates its ability to innovate with its stand at Light + Building 2014, the international trade fair for lighting and building technology. The stand was conceived, designed and implemented by Jürgen Drändle of Drändle 70|30 in close collaboration with designer Axel Meise and the brand agency Martin et Karczinski.

The central symbol of the fair presentation was the plus sign, which symbolises how the company approaches technological change. Occhio uses it to generate added value for its users and demonstrate the successful symbiosis of design, function and lighting technology. On one half of the 364 m² stand, oversized plus signs served as presentation areas for forthcoming new Occhio products. One highlight was the presentation of the extended Occhio 3d family. These three luminaire series are based on basic geometric shapes, which use the patent-pending Occhio 3d kinematics for 3-dimensional movability, all in LED: io, lui and lei.

On the other half of the stand was the communications platform. Here a green plus sign covered in 4000 plants was suspended above an illuminated pool of water. This bold element set the scene for the brand motto 'light is evolution'. An Italian bar with two eight-metre-long wooden tables made from Agate oak with Permadur finish and custom-made chairs invited visitors to linger a while and enjoy the serene atmosphere of the stand. ⇒

TRADE FAIR **Light + Building**
WHERE **Frankfurt, Germany**
WHEN **March-April 2014**
DESIGNERS **Drändle 70|30 and Martin et Karczinski**
STAND CONSTRUCTOR **Steffen Jastrob**
CLIENT **Occhio**
MARKET SECTOR **Interior lighting**
TOTAL FLOOR AREA **364 m²**
PHOTOGRAPHER **Robert Sprang**

THE PLUS SIGN SYMBOLISES HOW OCCHIO APPROACHES TECHNOLOGICAL CHANGE

5

4

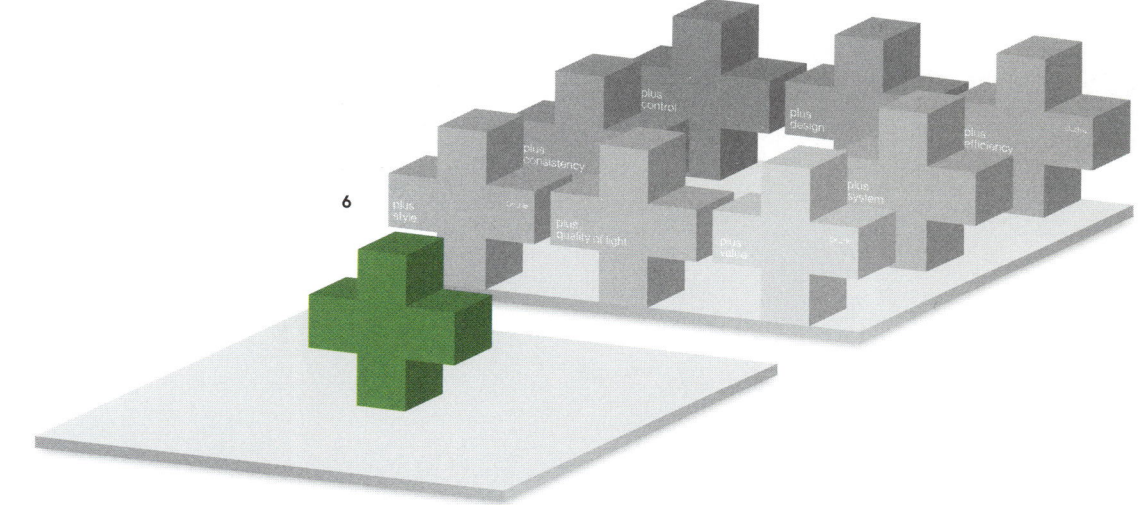

4 Mirrored bases created an illusory play of space.

5 The warm oak bar invited visitors to pause and take a break from the bustle of the fair.

6 Rendering showing the placement of the main symbol of the fair presentation: the plus sign.

COMMUNICATION ZONE

01 Reception and Information desk
02 Infotainment area
03 Bar

PRODUCT PRESENTATION

04 Exhibition area 'future' of upcoming products, future lab

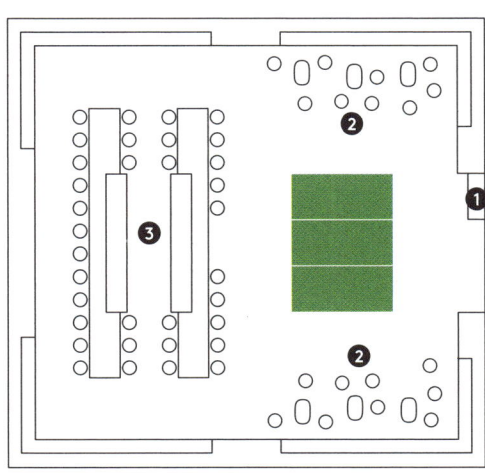

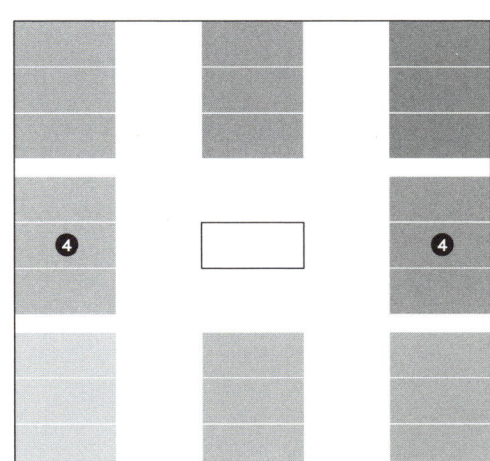

OLIGO
BachmannKern & Partner

1 All the different product families were showcased in their own individual setting.

2 The mysterious dark outer shell revealed little of the presentation inside.

2

Oligo was keen to showcase its diverse new product range and passion for lighting at its appearance at Light + Building 2014 in Frankfurt. BachmannKern & Partner was commissioned to orchestrate the presentation in line with the corporate philosophy, 'Feel the Light'. From the exterior, the stand appeared as deconstructed rectangular black volume, illuminated dramatically from within. Gaps in the mysterious volume framed interior views and invited visitors to discover the presentation further. Inside, a radiant all-white landscape was revealed, filled with a collage of different displays. In order to accommodate the large number and variety of products to be displayed, the stand was divided into a series of different settings that each hosted an individual product presentation. These settings were contained in high white cubes, all slightly angled in a different way. In combination with graphics and objects that were used to create different atmospheres in each cube, this resulted in a lively presentation landscape. The cubes were open to each other to facilitate a flow of space and overlapped in certain sections to show the connection between products. Floors, walls and ceilings were utilised to maximise the exhibition area and demonstrate the diversity of the products. Centrally placed was a work table that featured integrated product showcases and formed the communication hub, where seating around the table invited visitors and staff to meet and interact. ⚊

TRADE FAIR **Light + Building**
WHERE **Frankfurt, Germany**
WHEN **March-April 2014**
DESIGNER **BachmannKern & Partner**
STAND CONSTRUCTOR **Visage Messe- und Ausstellungsbau**
CLIENT **Oligo Lichttechnik**
MARKET SECTOR **Luminaires**
TOTAL FLOOR AREA **247 m²**
PHOTOGRAPHER **Alexander Ring**

3 Oligo's railing system was mounted as a sculptural installation, showcasing the product in an innovative way.

4 The inner face of the black volume revealed a vibrant presentation.

5 A central work table formed the communication hub of the stand.

A COLLAGE OF DIFFERENT PRODUCT DISPLAYS FILLS THE RADIANT, ALL-WHITE PRESENTATION

4

5

LIGHT IS
OPENING UP NEW DIMENSIONS

LIGHT IS
CONNECTING

LIGHT IS
PIONEERING

OSRAM

BachmannKern & Partner

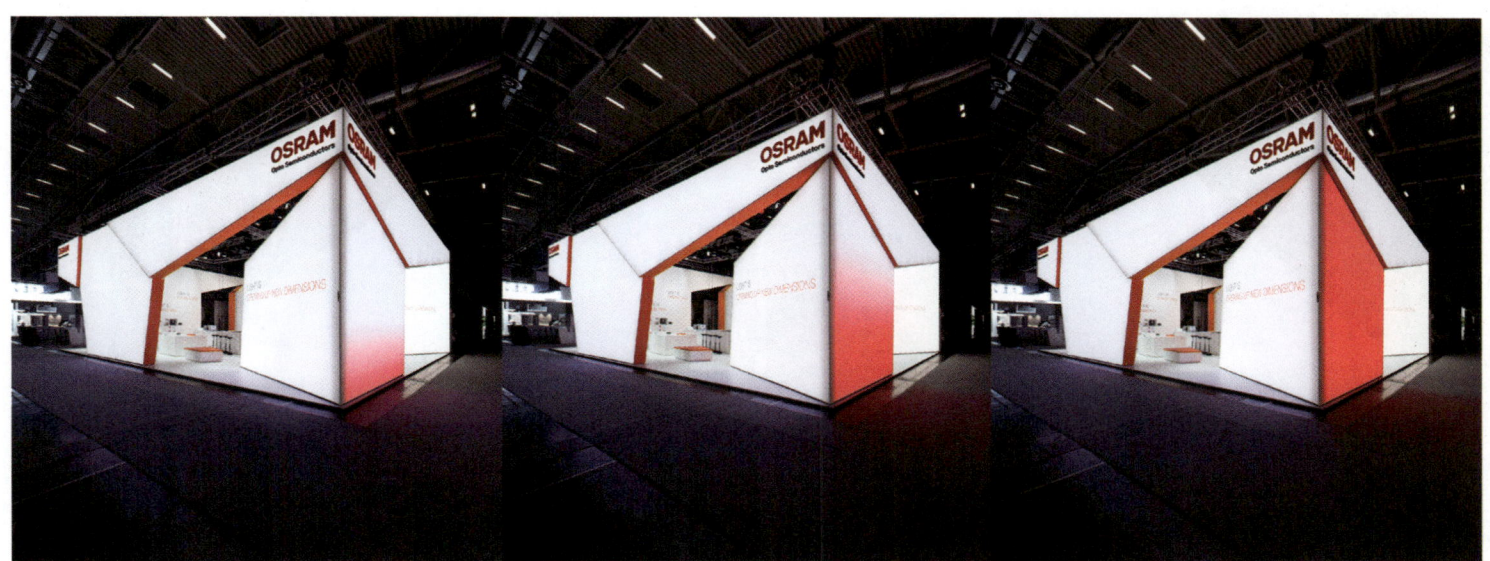

2

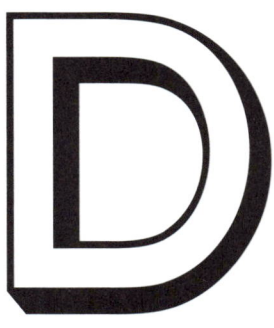

During the Electronica fair in 2014, Osram Opto Semiconductors wanted its presentation to convey the message that 'there is more beyond lighting' with regards to the company's operations and its portfolio. The task of designing the stand was entrusted to BachmannKern & Partner who used the element of surprise as a starting point. The striking, luminous stand was unmissable at the 26th edition of this International Trade Fair for Electronic Components, Systems and Applications, and set the stage for a stunning multimedia presentation. With its strong architecture composed from staggered angular planes, the structure expressed the dynamics of the company and showed that there is more than meets the eye. Its illuminated facades made of backlit fabrics glowed intensely, immediately attracting visitors' attentions. The edges of the wall planes were defined in orange resulting in a dynamic structural outline which pointed to a prominent element of the company's corporate identity. As the planes shifted, views opened into the interior inviting visitors to explore the presentation further. Inside, the stand was divided into five domains, each displaying different scopes of application with a unique claim beginning with, 'Light is....' Each of the five claims – Connecting, Pioneering, Enriching, Stunning and Inspiring – was communicated by a distinguishing light colour and wall space and had its own counter. A large LED wall in the centre of the booth showed accompanying films relating to each of the domains. During each of the relevant film sequences, both the internal and external walls of that particular domain were illuminated in its distinguishing colour, dramatically transforming the appearance of the stand. A sixth film sequence united the presentation and bathed the whole booth at the end in the iconic Osram orange hue. ⬤

TRADE FAIR **Electronica**
WHERE **Munich, Germany**
WHEN **November 2014**
DESIGNER **BachmannKern & Partner**
STAND CONSTRUCTOR **Manuel de la Rosa**
CLIENT **Osram Opto Semiconductors**
MARKET SECTOR **LED lighting**
TOTAL FLOOR AREA **224 m²**
PHOTOGRAPHER **Frank Dora**

3 A dramatic cantilevered corner formed the main entrance onto the stand.

4/5 Made from backlit textile, the structure itself formed the canvas for an hour-long multimedia presentation.

THE STRIKING LUMINOUS STAND SHOWS THAT THERE IS MORE THAN MEETS THE EYE

4

5

PERFORMANCE IN LIGHTING

Bongiana Architetture

1 One meeting area had an open structure while the other was clad in perforated panels.

2 The combination of minimal forms with embellished wooden screens resulted in a vibrant space.

2

Performance in Lighting debuted its new identity with a radiant stand at Light + Building in 2014 designed by Bongiana Architetture. The main aim was to communicate the integrated form of the new brand that fused five established technical lighting companies. In celebration of this launch that took place in Germany, the design took inspiration from the Low Saxon house with its characteristic timber frame and hip roof. Varying structures were clustered on the stand to create a village-like setting, each intended for a different function or family of lighting.

Most prominent were five white pointed houses that contained the displays for indoor lighting. Immediately drawing attention to the stand, the eye-catching houses interplayed open and closed facades that invited visitors to meander between. Dotted along the perimeter of the space were high grey showcases that framed the outdoor lighting products. Informal meeting areas were housed in two elongated pointed wooden houses that recalled the vernacular timber-framed architecture. Other shared spaces such as the VIP lounge, bar and reception as well as the storage and kitchen were accommodated in the largest structure. The striking wooden structure was clad in perforated wooden screens with a fine pattern of different sized circles. When illuminated from within the magical effect of the facade made the structure appear like an oversized lantern. As some

panels were closed – their surface milled with the same circular pattern to create a relief – the screens together contrasted openness with enclosure to create a dynamic sense of space. Juxtaposing the abstract, minimal structures with the twinkling wooden facades, the stand acknowledged the individuality of the brands while uniting them as one coherent family. ⸺

TRADE FAIR **Light + Building**
WHERE **Frankfurt, Germany**
WHEN **April 2014**
DESIGNER **Bongiana Architetture**
STAND CONSTRUCTOR **Eurostands**
CLIENT **Performance in Lighting**
MARKET SECTOR **Lighting**
TOTAL FLOOR AREA **600 m²**
PHOTOGRAPHER **Boutique Creativa**

3 Open and closed facades added liveliness to the village.

4 Located prominently the white houses immediately attracted visitors onto the stand.

AN ABSTRACT VILLAGE-LIKE ATMOSPHERE PERVADES THE STAND

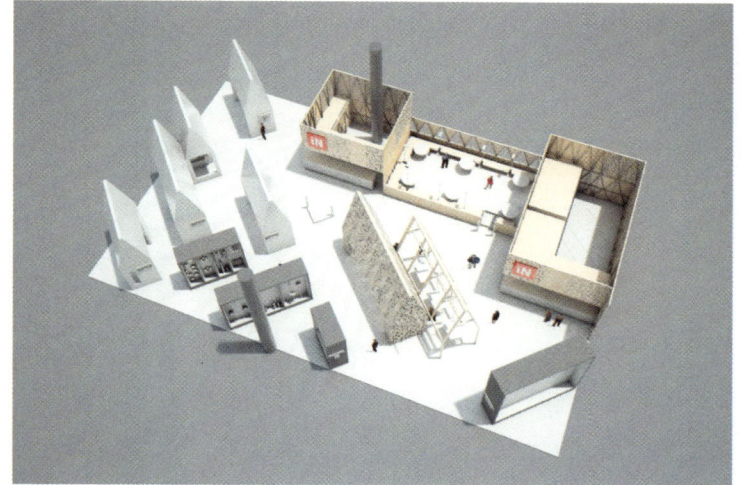

FLOOR PLAN

01 Reception
02 Lumis
03 SBP Urban Lighting
04 Prisma Architectural
05 Spittler
06 Bar / Alehouse
07 VIP Lounge
08 Kitchen
09 Counter
10 Lockers

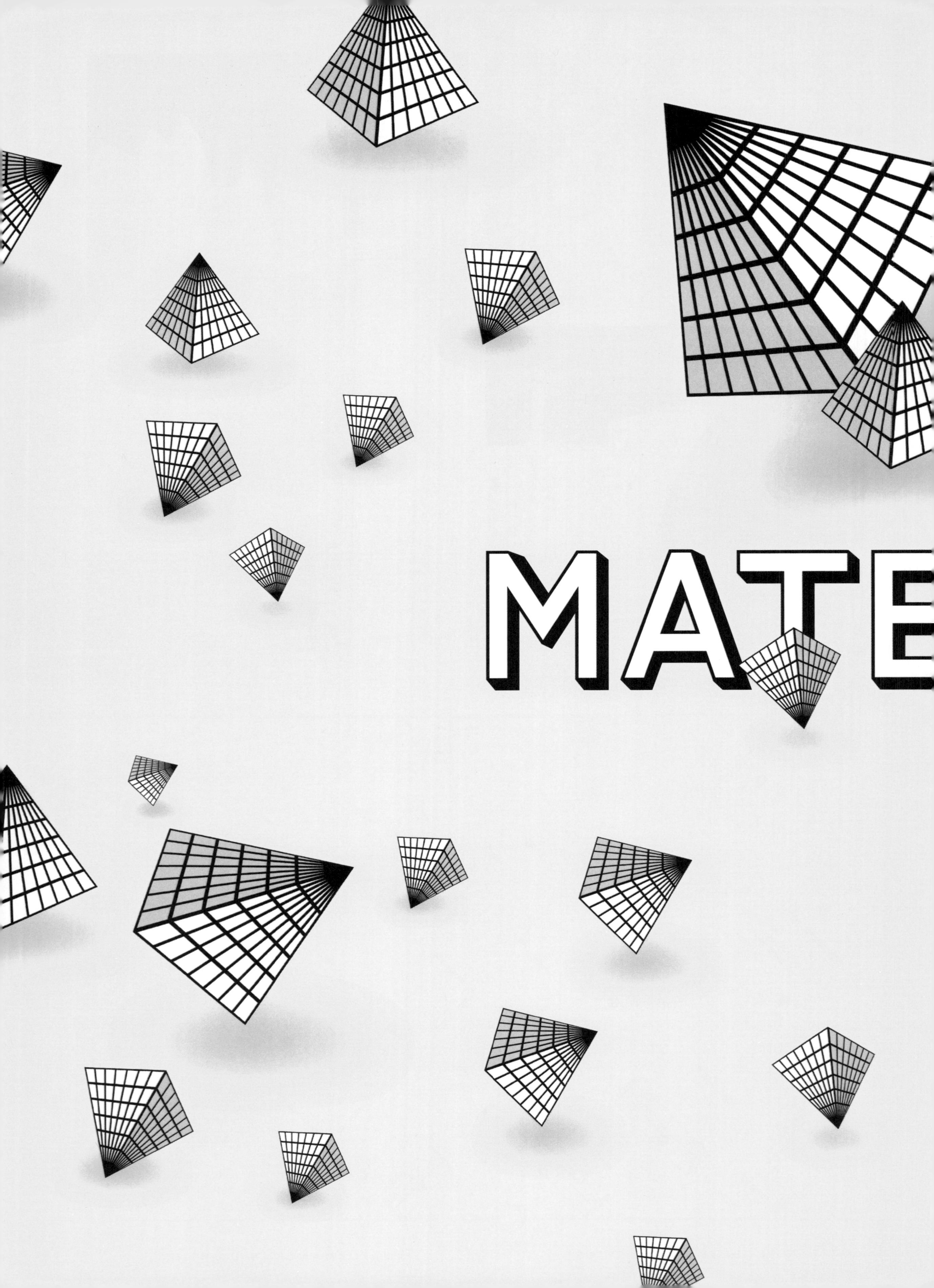

MATE

RIALS

MATERIALS

ARPA INDUSTRIALE

ArpaLab

1 A central corridor formed the spine with a double reception.

2 Backlit textures on the stand's exterior created an intriguing, eye-catching effect that further showcased the material's properties.

2

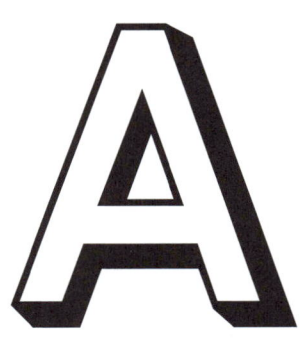

Arpa Industriale's stand at Interzum 2015 presented two distinct faces that communicated the duality of the presentation while respecting the unity of the brand. Sandro Marini, Filippo Manetti and Fausto Donato of ArpaLab were responsible for the design. The client wished for the stand to not only exhibit the materials but also show real-life applications and engage visitors to experience the innovations first hand. The winning combination of black and white visually distinguished the two 'souls' of the company through the use of its two materials, which have different brands and personalities. Two separate shells (or 'spaceships') made entirely from these respective materials cohabited one stand and were connected by a central corridor. The white back half was dedicated to Arpa Industriale's High Pressure Laminate (HPL) while the black front half presented Fenix NTM® (Nanotech Matt material for interior design). Visitors could enter from three sides. The black volume was open at the front where a huge X from the Fenix NTM® logo marked the entrance. Two side entrances at the ends of the spine guided visitors into the heart of the presentation where a double reception – in black and white – awaited. In the Fenix NTM® volume the big X showcased the collection of colours and thicknesses of the material. Left of the X was an interactive desk where people could experience the features of the material with live demonstrations. To the right were examples of vertical applications including engraved walls, partitions, a wall system and door. Across the corridor the white half showcased new and existing HPL collections combined with wall displays featuring examples of applications including a sink, kitchen counter and vanity. As the white realm represented the corporate face of the company, the two meeting rooms were placed here, each one featuring bespoke furniture made from the two materials – in black and white. ⚊

TRADE FAIR **Interzum**
WHERE **Cologne, Germany**
WHEN **May 2015**
DESIGNER **ArpaLab**
STAND CONSTRUCTOR **Chiaradia Exhibitions**
CLIENT **Arpa Industriale**
MARKET SECTOR **Interior design materials**
TOTAL FLOOR AREA **224 m²**
PHOTOGRAPHER **Buchwald & Jankowski Fotografie**

3

FENIX
Follow us
Ar

4

OPEN YOUR MIND
AND CREATE SURFACES
FOR NEW THOUGHTS
FENIX NTM.
Nanotech Matt Material.
Made in Italy.
Arpa
FENIX NTM®
2015 | 2018
Awards and Honours
FENIX NTM®

5

FENIX NTM®

NANOTECH MATT MATERIAL
FOR INTERIOR DESIGN

6

3 X marks the stand: the bold Fenix NTM® logo triggered visitors' curiosities.

4 The stand not only exhibited the company's materials, but the spatial elements were also constructed from them.

5 The design of the demonstration counter incorporated real-life applications of the material.

6 Bespoke furniture made from black FENIX NTM® furnished one of the meeting rooms.

7 Arpa Industriale's High Pressure Laminates (HPL) took the spotlight in the white volume where new decors and finishes were showcased.

7

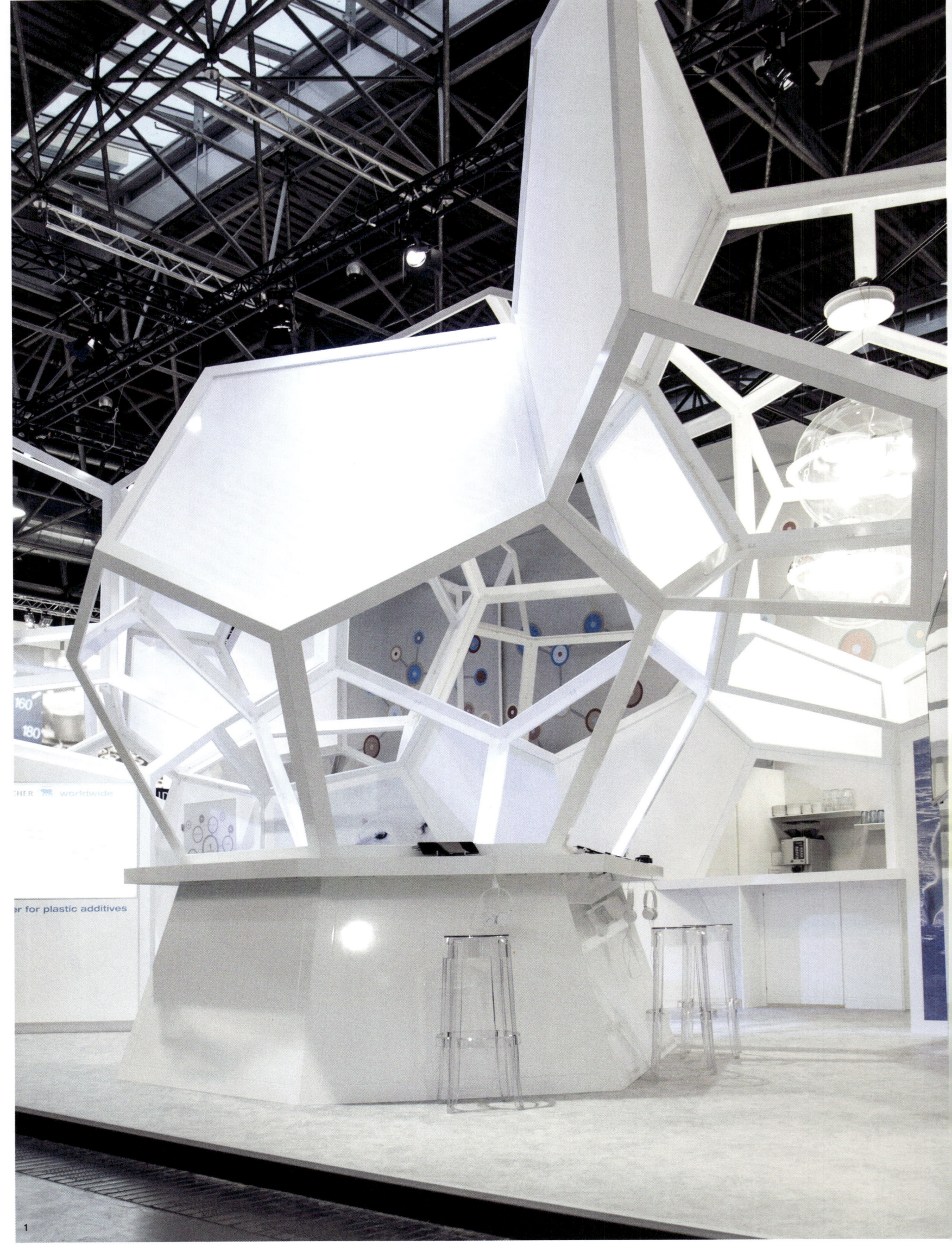

BAERLOCHER

wroom

1 The structure was designed to become more open towards the ceiling.

2 Like real plastic molecules, the structure was self-supporting, modular and expandable.

2

Wroom was commissioned by Baerlocher, a leading supplier of plastic additives, to design its stand at K 2013, the international trade fair for plastics and rubber. The main challenge was to find a unique way to present a company that doesn't produce any tangible goods which can be easily displayed. Instead, Baerlocher's expertise was visualised in the form of the stand itself that became the exhibited product. Wroom's concept played with Baerlocher's motto – 'We add character to plastics' – in a fresh and innovative way. The chemical symbol of a plastic molecule was playfully interpreted to form the main element of a complex, modular structure. Polyhedrons units were linked and grouped – like real molecular chains of plastics – to create small self-supporting structures. Digitally designed, the frames were made from PVC that was CNC-milled and then folded into shape. Each group housed a specific function and was also strategically positioned to structure the flow of visitors onto the stand. Simultaneously each polyhedron had a more open or closed structure that corresponded to its function. Doors could also open or close the molecules, also changing the atmosphere of the space throughout the day. Bordering the corridors the stand had a more open front to attract the public, with an information counter, media screens and entry points. The inner section contained the private areas such as meeting rooms, the kitchenette and service areas. Here side sections of the polyhedrons were enclosed by opaque PVC panels to create privacy but upper sections remained open for light and air. A bar at the rear hosted informal meetings. Translucent panels overhead were illuminated by LEDs to increase the stand's visibility from a distance. Placed throughout the stand were media screens and tablets that displayed additional information about the company's expertise. ▬

TRADE FAIR **K 2013**
WHERE **Düsseldorf, Germany**
WHEN **October 2013**
DESIGNER **wroom**
STAND CONSTRUCTOR **Winkels Messe- und Ausstellungsbau**
CLIENT **Baerlocher**
MARKET SECTOR **Plastics additives**
TOTAL FLOOR AREA **144 m²**
PHOTOGRAPHERS **wroom and Thomas Lünen**

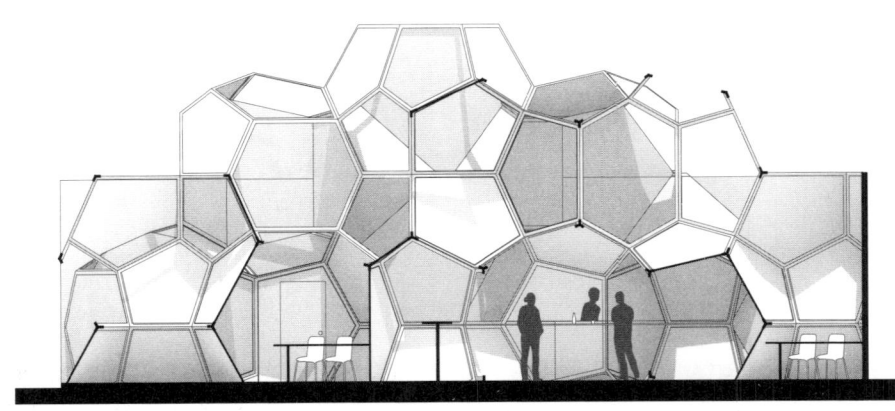

THE DESIGN PLAYFULLY INTERPRETS THE CHEMICAL SYMBOL OF A PLASTIC MOLECULE

MODEL

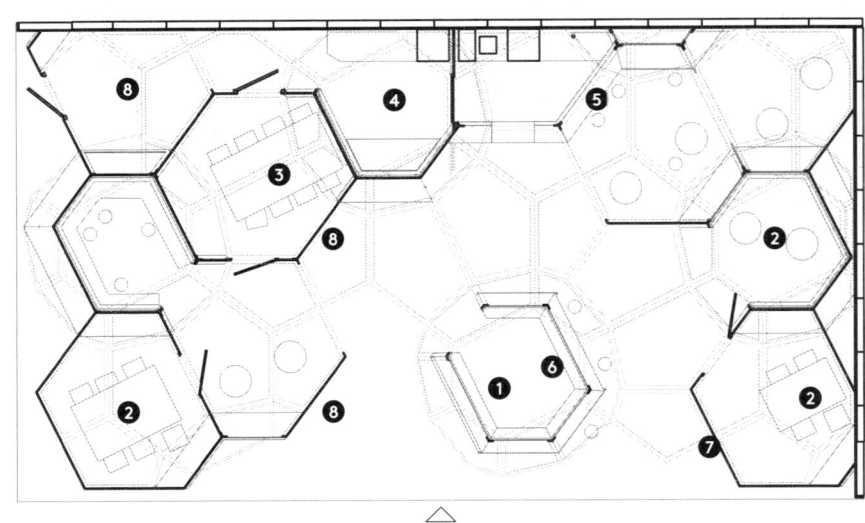

FLOOR PLAN

01 Reception
02 Meeting room
03 Conference room
04 Kitchenette
05 Bar
06 iPad info stations
07 Flat screen
08 Key messages
09 Staff room

FOLDED FRAME CONSTRUCTION

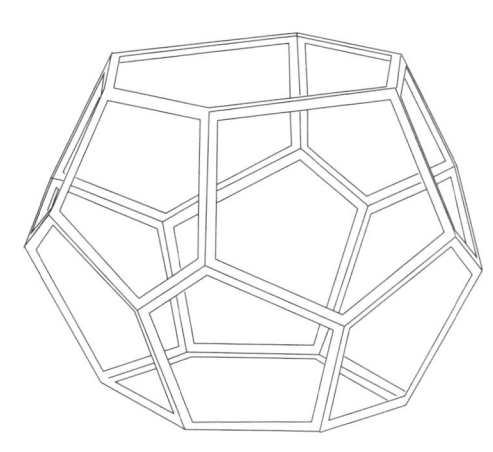

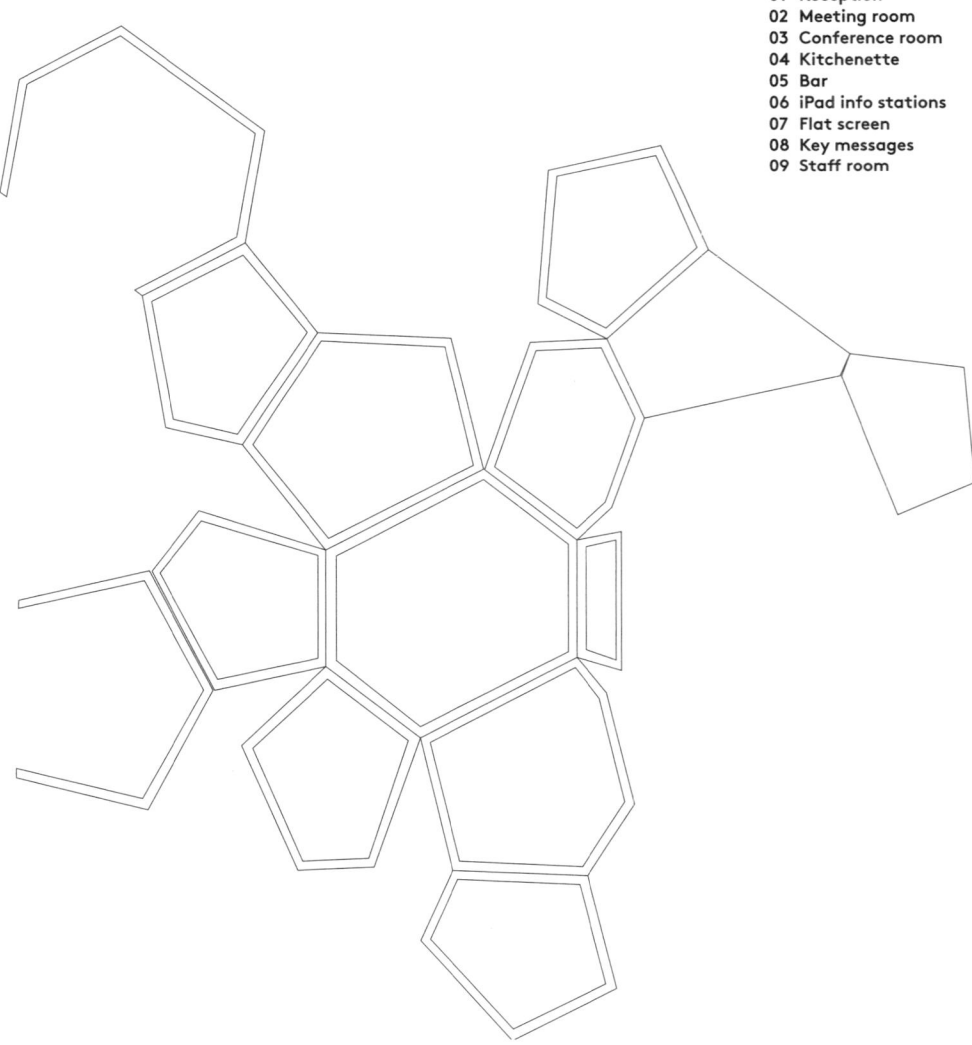

TECHNICAL DRAWINGS

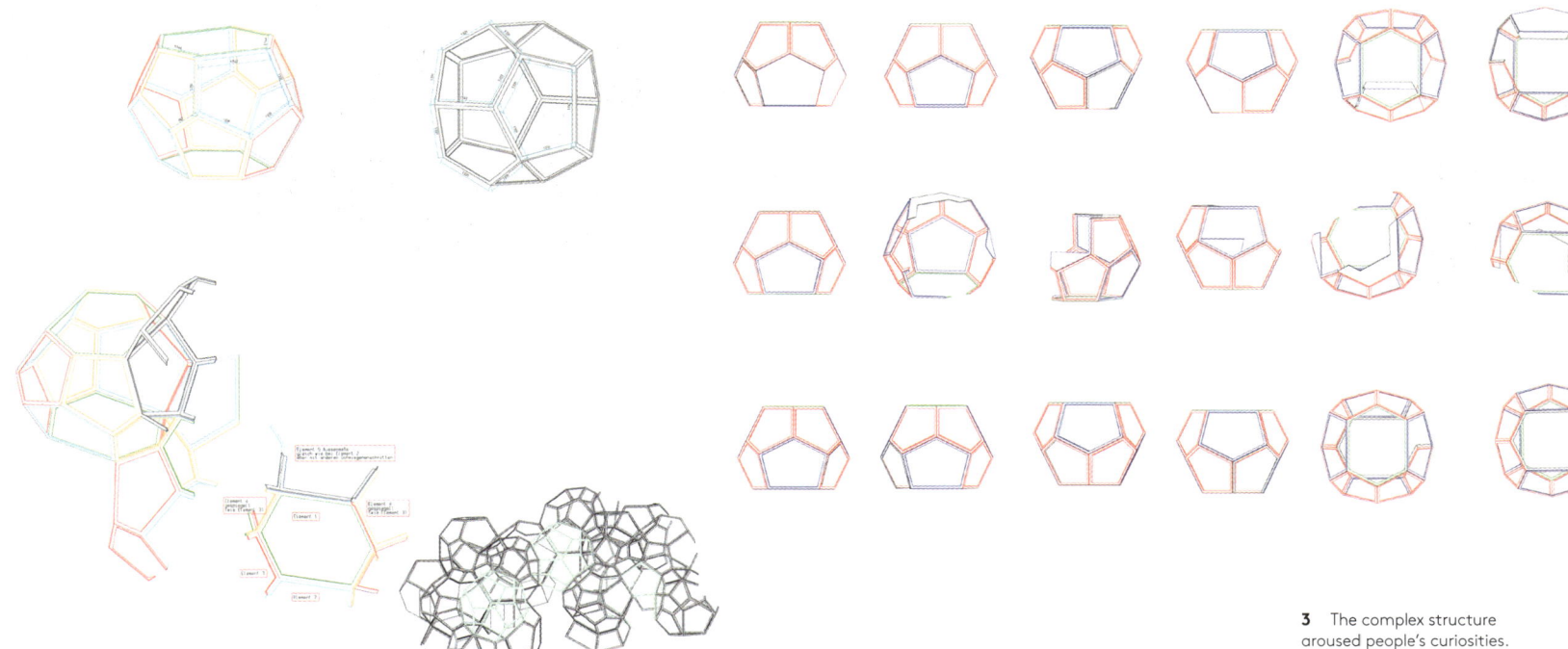

3 The complex structure aroused people's curiosities.

3

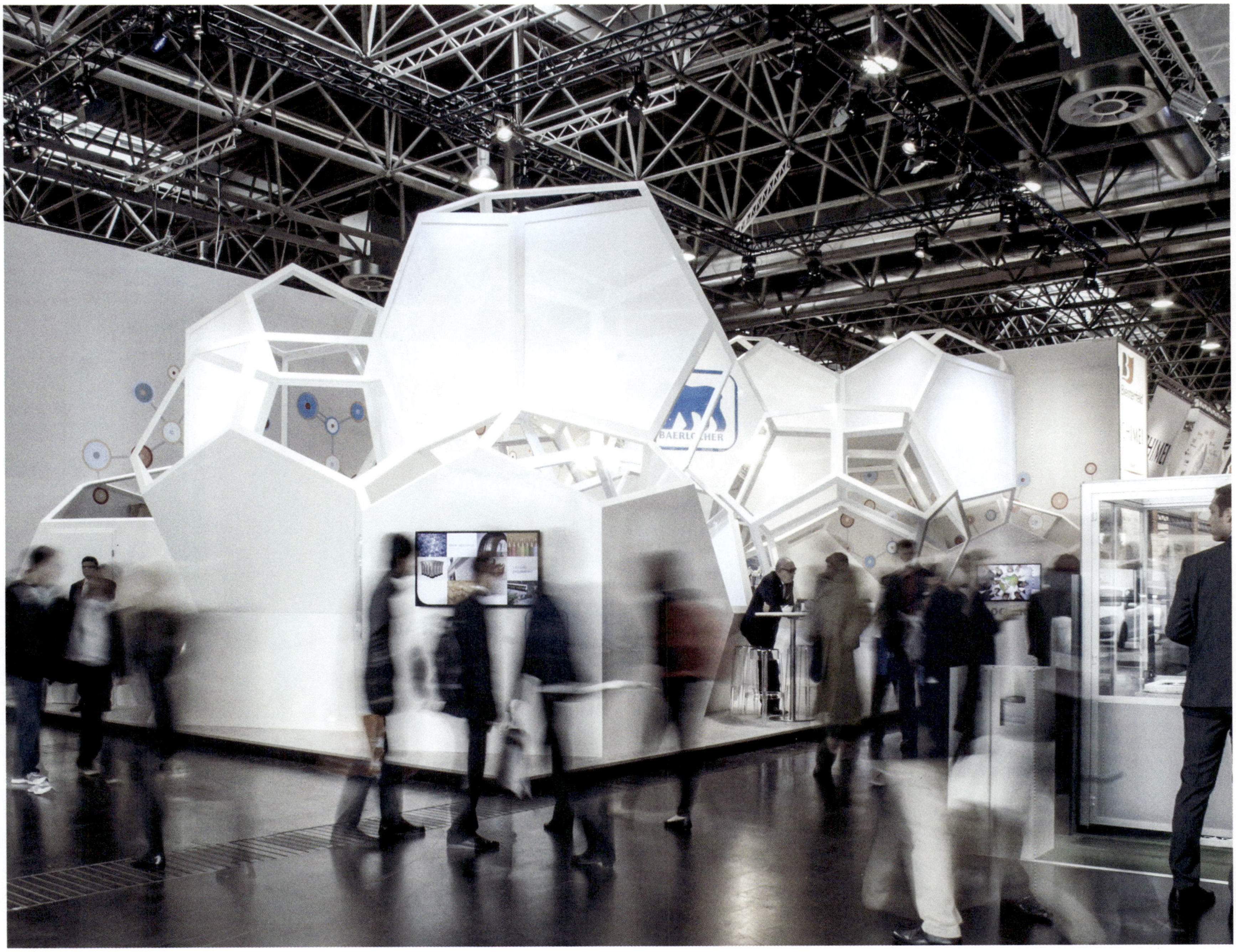

W.L. GORE & ASSOCIATES

Atelier Seitz

1 The sculpted surface of the stand incorporated displays of products made from ePTFE.

2 Red, the corporate colour dominated the space, giving the brand a prominent visual presence.

2

Atelier Seitz was set an interesting challenge for the design of W.L. Gore & Associates' stand at Achema 2015, the world forum for chemical engineering and the process industry. The stand needed to present the qualities and advantages of the non-descriptive bare polymer PTFE, a soft white material that the company uses to manufacture numerous sealing products. Simultaneously the space should also stage a positive brand experience on a compact footprint of 64 m². Conceived by Atelier Seitz, the design of the rather unusual stand echoed the structure of expanded PTFE (ePTFE) from magnified images; the entire booth appeared as a large, closed, white surface made of polygons. Bar tables, counters, pedestals for exhibits and even monitors emerged seamlessly from the surface resulting in an almost monolithic structure. Examples of products made using ePTFE were displayed throughout. On this compact area, the use of one material and colour made the space appear coherent and calm. Visually, the fluidity of the surface communicated the plasticity and adaptability of the PTFE material while the angular shapes of the booth hinted at Gore's distinctive logo. Red accents in the shelving and image frames drew attention to the focus themes and, together with the red bar seating, further underlined Gore's corporate identity. ▬

TRADE FAIR **Achema**
WHERE **Frankfurt, Germany**
WHEN **June 2015**
DESIGNER **Atelier Seitz**
STAND CONSTRUCTOR **Atelier Seitz**
CLIENT **W.L. Gore & Associates**
MARKET SECTOR **Polymer sealing**
TOTAL FLOOR AREA **64 m²**
PHOTOGRAPHER **Olaf Schiemann**

3 Product samples were displayed throughout.

4 Stand entry.

5/6 Construction of the booth. Emerging from the sculptural wall, several display surfaces communicate the qualities of the promoted material.

3

4

5

6

DISPLAY FURNITURE AND EXHIBITS EMERGE SEAMLESSLY FROM THE FLUID SURFACE

FLOOR PLAN

01 Information desk
02 Standing table
03 Workbench
04 Screen
05 Kitchen / storage
06 Hall column

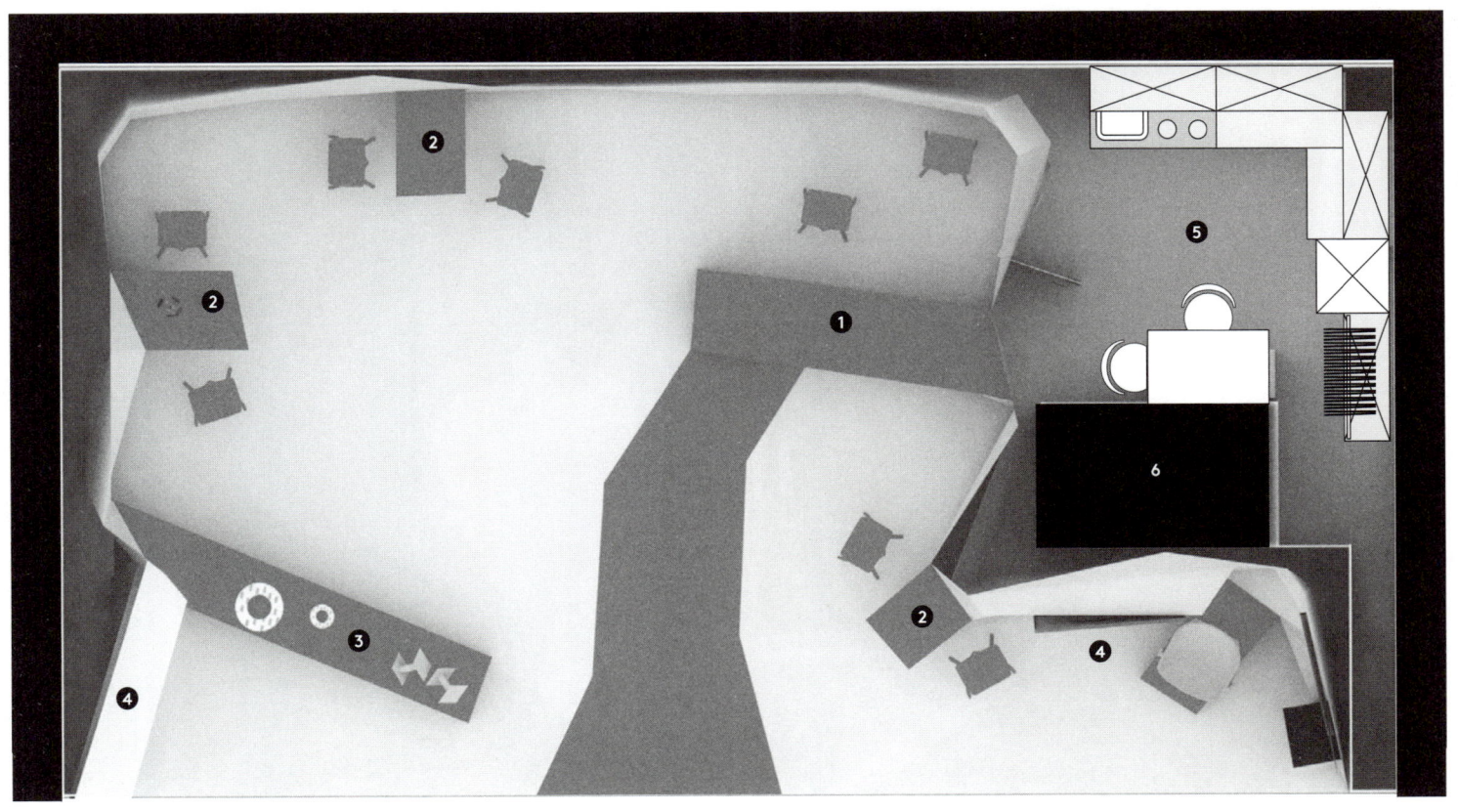

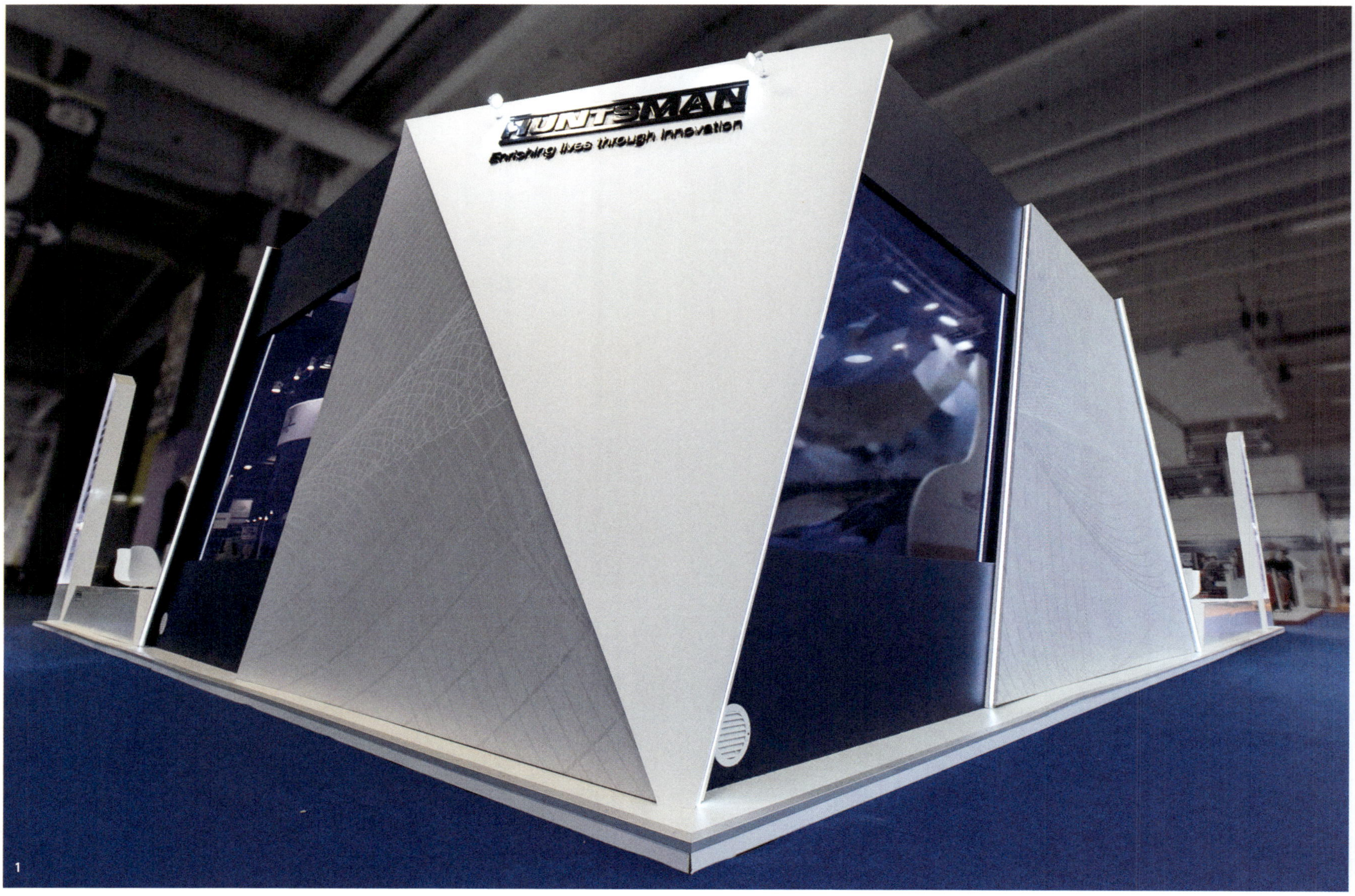
HUNTSMAN
Enriching lives through innovation
1

HUNTSMAN
Enriching lives through innovation
Araldite
build
bond
protect
Araldite
build
bond
protect
2

HUNTSMAN
DSA

TRADE FAIR **JEC Europe**
WHERE **Paris, France**
WHEN **March 2014**
DESIGNER **DSA**
CLIENT **Huntsman**
MARKET SECTOR **Composite materials**
TOTAL FLOOR AREA **137.5 m²**
PHOTOGRAPHER **Dupif Photo**

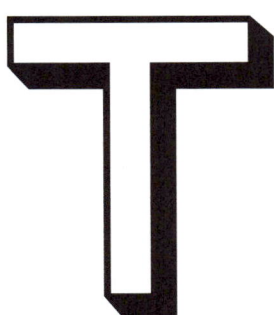

3

1 The closed corner anchored the presentation and incorporated private meeting rooms.

2 Suspended centrally, the eye-catching starburst chandelier acted as a beacon.

3 Surfaces of the angular display elements rose to form wall surfaces and graphic content.

The moment of creation formed the starting point for DSA's concept for Huntsman's presence at JEC Europe, the largest international annual gathering of composites professionals. The designers wanted to capture a sense of dynamism and excitement, for example, at the instant that precedes an innovative discovery. A series of angular structures occupied the stand, their geometric forms with facets and strong angles referencing the molecular level at which Huntsman products perform. A deliberately disarranged backdrop allowed for a structured presentation of the Huntsman product portfolio, as if to bridge the journey from inception to realisation, from chaos to perfect order. Anchoring the presentation was a high structure in the corner composed of tilted and angled triangular planes. This was the only enclosed part of the space. The rest of the presentation radiated from here into an open landscape of floating angular plinths. Situated off a main aisle, the plinths displayed specific products supported by interactive touchscreens and acrylic panels that communicated technical specifications. Approaching from the main open corner, the contrasting two-tone floor in white and dark blue immediately caught the eye and functioned as a visual trigger to direct visitors onto the stand. The generous sense of space enabled people to meander around freely, allowing for maximum visitor engagement. At the rear a large format video wall was orientated in portrait format for maximum visual impact and two meeting rooms were set within the main structure. Positioned centrally the reception counter formed the greeting and hospitality hub. Punctuating the structure was a suspended lighting feature positioned above the central display. Its starburst form represented the point of creation, addressing the moment an idea becomes real and tangible. ⬱

Infinite inspiration
Decor Paper by Munksjö

MUNKSJÖ DECOR

hw.design

1/2 The well-structured layout comprised three distinct zones that transitioned smoothly from public to private.

2

For the ninth consecutive year, hw.design was in charge of designing the stand for Munksjö Decor, a producer of premium decor papers, at Interzum. For the designers, the ambition is always to produce creative synergies between architecture and paper, presenting new opportunities for presentation. In 2015, 'Infinite Inspiration' formed the motto, referring to the expanded new product and colour range of Munksjö's papers.

In this way, colour was to be introduced to the presentation while maintaining the recognisability of traditional white. This theme was poetically interpreted through a striking floating paper cloud that hovered over the entire stand, illuminated in different colours by a changing LED installation. Paper of varying sizes was suspended in a seeming random arrangement, resulting in a beautiful texture and layering as light bounced off it in different ways. The minimal all-white stand radiated an air of contemplation that provided a calm respite from the busy fair. It was also the ideal blank canvas for a multimedia experience; thanks to the changing light installation the atmosphere of the space dramatically transformed as cool blues and warm reds took over. A simple restrained architecture, orientated diagonally, maintained focus on the cloud and structured the stand into three distinct sections. An open public

lounge with benches occupied the front corner, indicating the main entry point. The mid section hosted a more enclosed area for informal meetings with clusters of seating enveloped by a low curved partition. Behind was the bar with a series of private spaces including a meeting room and service spaces. The stand's original design completely wowed visitors and showcased the beauty of Munksjö's paper in an ethereal new light. ⚊

TRADE FAIR **Interzum**
WHERE **Cologne, Germany**
WHEN **May 2015**
DESIGNER **hw.design**
STAND CONSTRUCTOR **i.xpo**
CLIENT **Munksjö Decor**
MARKET SECTOR **Surface paper for panels**
TOTAL FLOOR AREA **200 m²**
PHOTOGRAPHER **Erik Chmil**

Infinite inspiration
Decor Paper by Munksjö

4

THE PAPER CLOUD SHOWCASES THE BEAUTY OF MUNKSJÖ'S PAPER IN AN ETHEREAL LIGHT

5

3 Mirroring the cloud, the use of curved, all-white forms for the furniture and partitions resulted in a coherent aesthetic.

4/5 With a cycle that lasted 20 minutes, the LED installation transformed the space dramatically through changing colours.

WEVO-CHEMIE
Projekttriangle Design Studio and Von M

1 The combination of the minimal white design, cool lighting and elemental volumes painted a coherent image of the company.

2 Displays were integrated into the multipurpose white furniture elements.

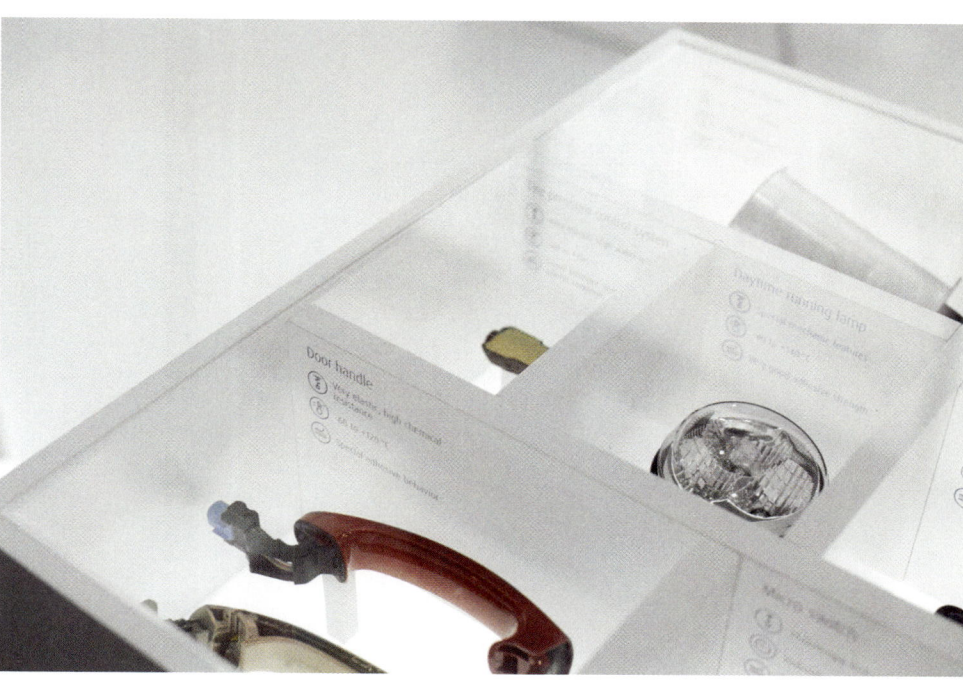

2

Wevo-Chemie develops and produces solutions for casting, bonding and sealing. Bondexpo, the international trade exhibition for bonding technology, provided the ideal platform for the company to unveil its new brand identity along with its latest product offerings. It commissioned Projekttriangle Design Studio and Von M to design and construct its exhibition stand in accordance with the new identity developed by Projekttriangle. The company's products such as grouting systems and industrial adhesives posed a challenge to present on a visual level. So the designers opted for a stand that would primarily illustrate the products' areas of application, their characteristics

and the company's high-tech image. The futuristic white aesthetic conveyed the innovative nature of the company, combining the atmosphere of a laboratory with the appearance of a museum. Due to the limited floor area of 24 m² the stand's layout was kept as open and uncluttered as possible. White floors, walls and furniture established a coherent basis. A series of white rectangular volumes dominated the space. These multipurpose elements incorporated vitrines, were used as high tables and displayed brochures. Two feature walls anchored the presentation. One wall featured oversized illuminated symbols of the product applications – Filters, Electronic/ Electric and Automotive. Upon closer inspection, the images were composed of thousands of dots, a concept used in the new identity. The other wall incorporated six screens that showed nine short films about the characteristics of Wevo's grouting compounds. A rather unusual

location was devised for storing the product catalogues: a baking oven. As the brochure had been treated with a thermo-sensitive varnish, it changes colour when it cools down. This display cleverly drew attention to heat conductivity, the main theme of the exhibition. Through its surprising details, the stand successfully showcased the company's products in a new light. ▬

TRADE FAIR **Bondexpo**
WHERE **Stuttgart, Germany**
WHEN **October 2013**
DESIGNERS **Projekttriangle Design Studio and Von M**
STAND CONSTRUCTOR **Bluepool**
CLIENT **Wevo-Chemie**
MARKET SECTOR **Resins and adhesives**
TOTAL FLOOR AREA **24 m²**
PHOTOGRAPHERS **Dennis Mueller and Martin Grothmaak**

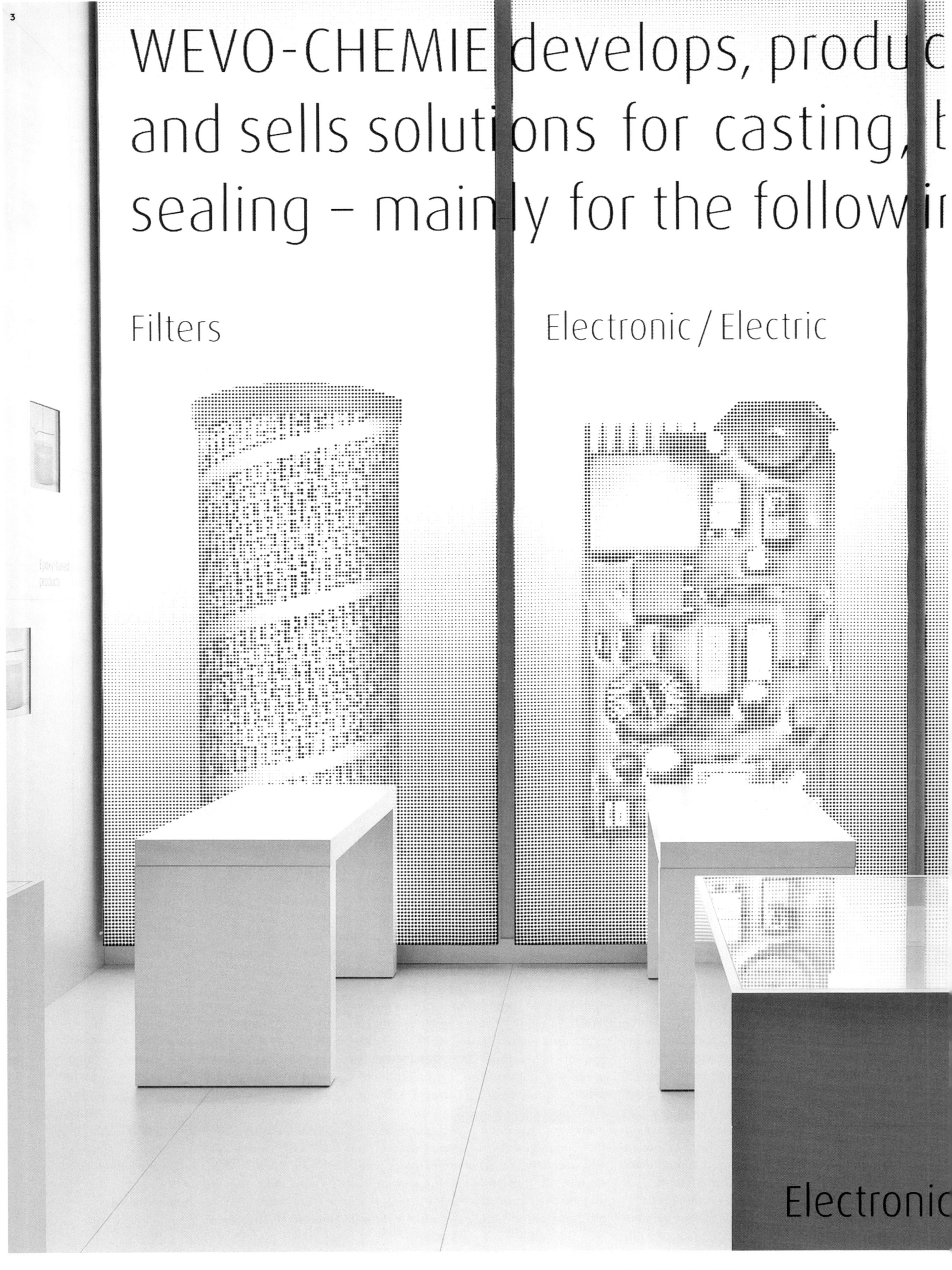

WEVO-CHEMIE develops, produc
and sells solutions for casting, b
sealing – mainly for the follow i

Filters

Electronic / Electric

Electronic

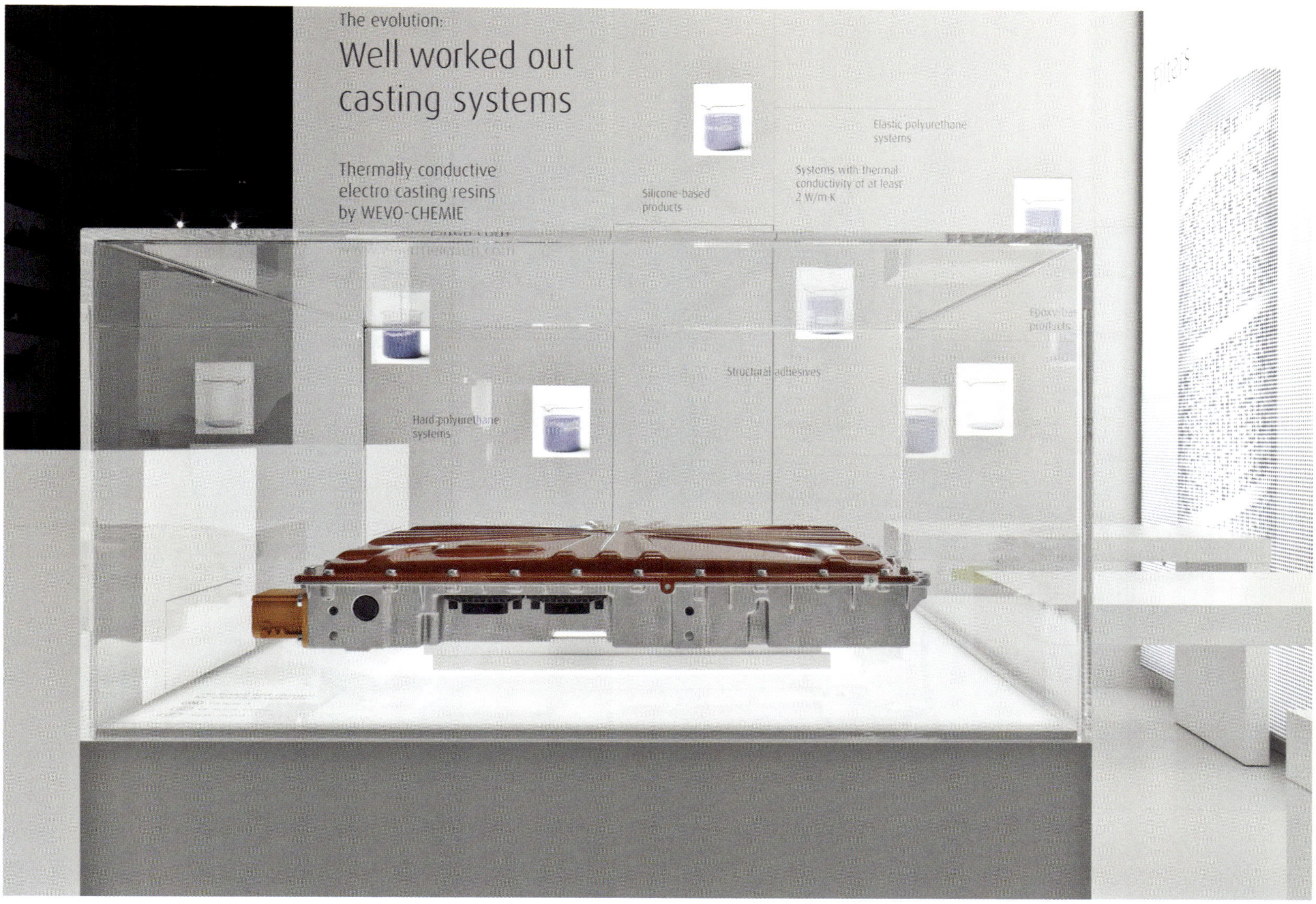

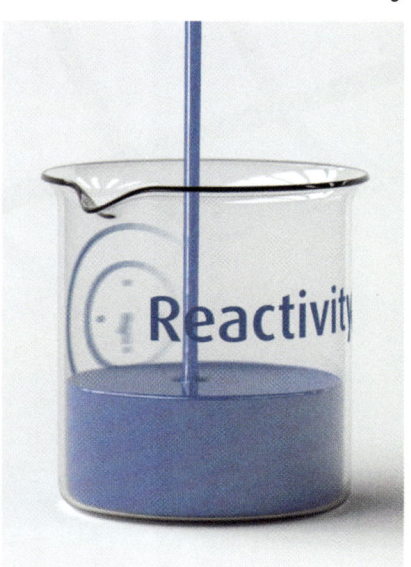

[Figure 4 — display showing:]

The evolution:
Well worked out casting systems

Thermally conductive
electro casting resins
by WEVO-CHEMIE

Elastic polyurethane
systems

Silicone-based
products

Systems with thermal
conductivity of at least
2 W/m·K

Epoxy-based
products

Structural adhesives

Hard polyurethane
systems

4

3 The three main
application areas were
presented by means of
symbolic images on the
back wall.

4 The main vitrine
displayed a casing for a
rechargeable battery of an
electric car.

5 Stills from short
films that illustrated the
characteristics of Wevo's
grouting compounds.

THE FUTURISTIC WHITE STAND COMBINES THE ATMOSPHERE OF A LABORATORY WITH THE APPEARANCE OF A MUSEUM

5

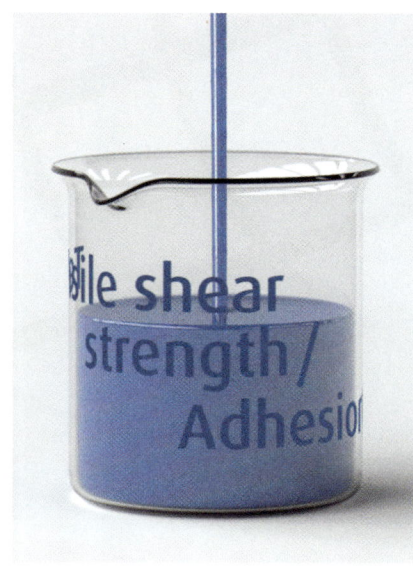
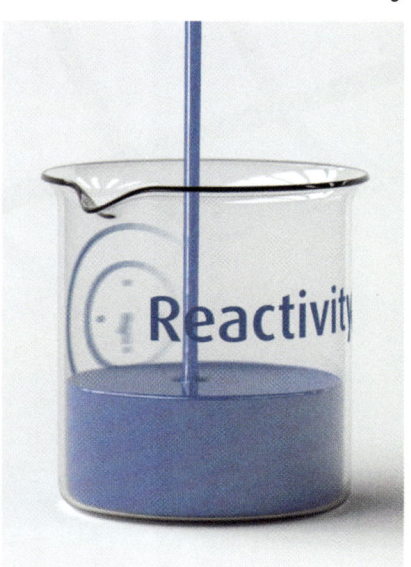

products can be processed
using 3 simple...

tensile shear
strength/
Adhesion

Reactivity

MOB

LITY

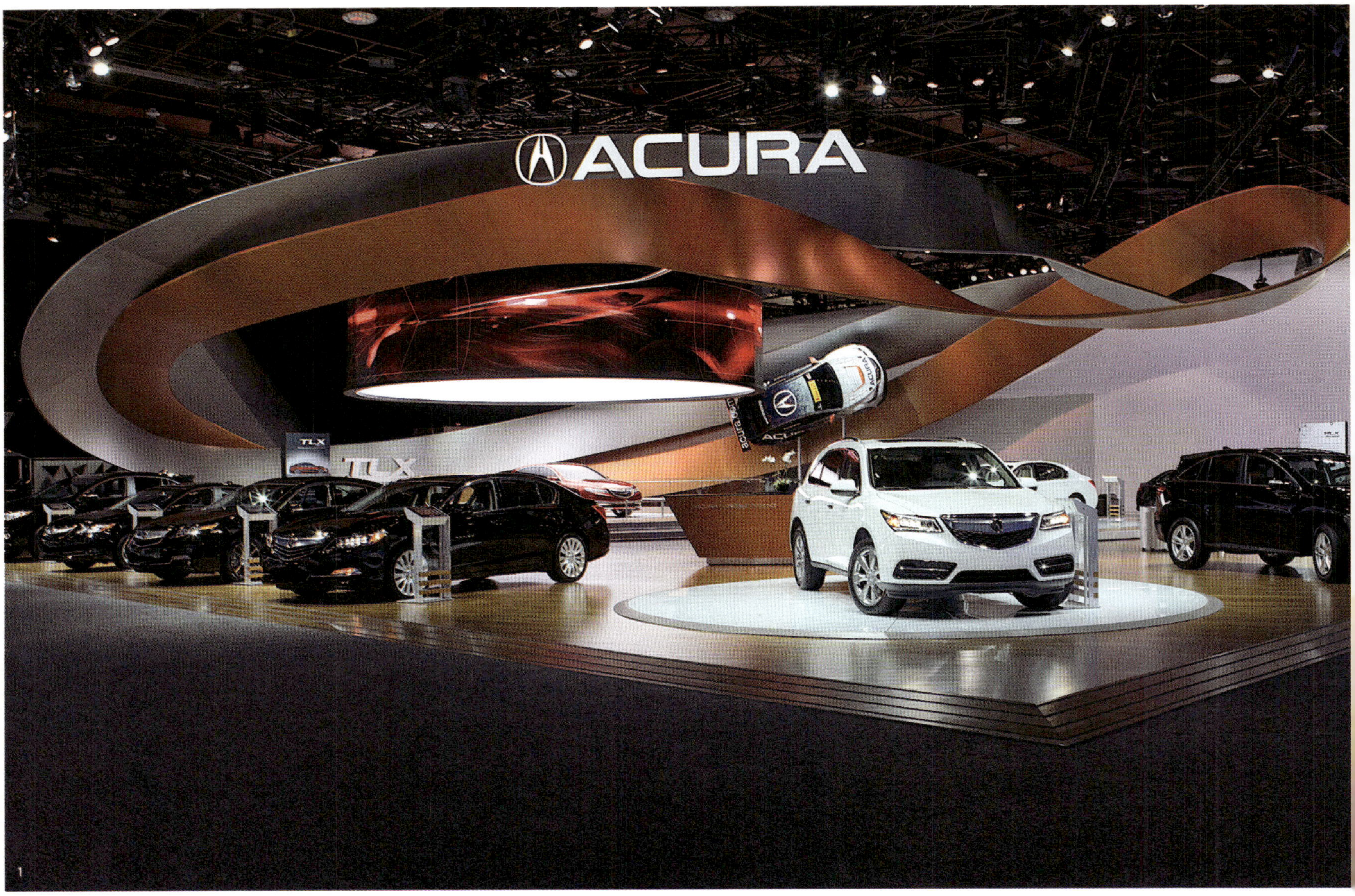

1

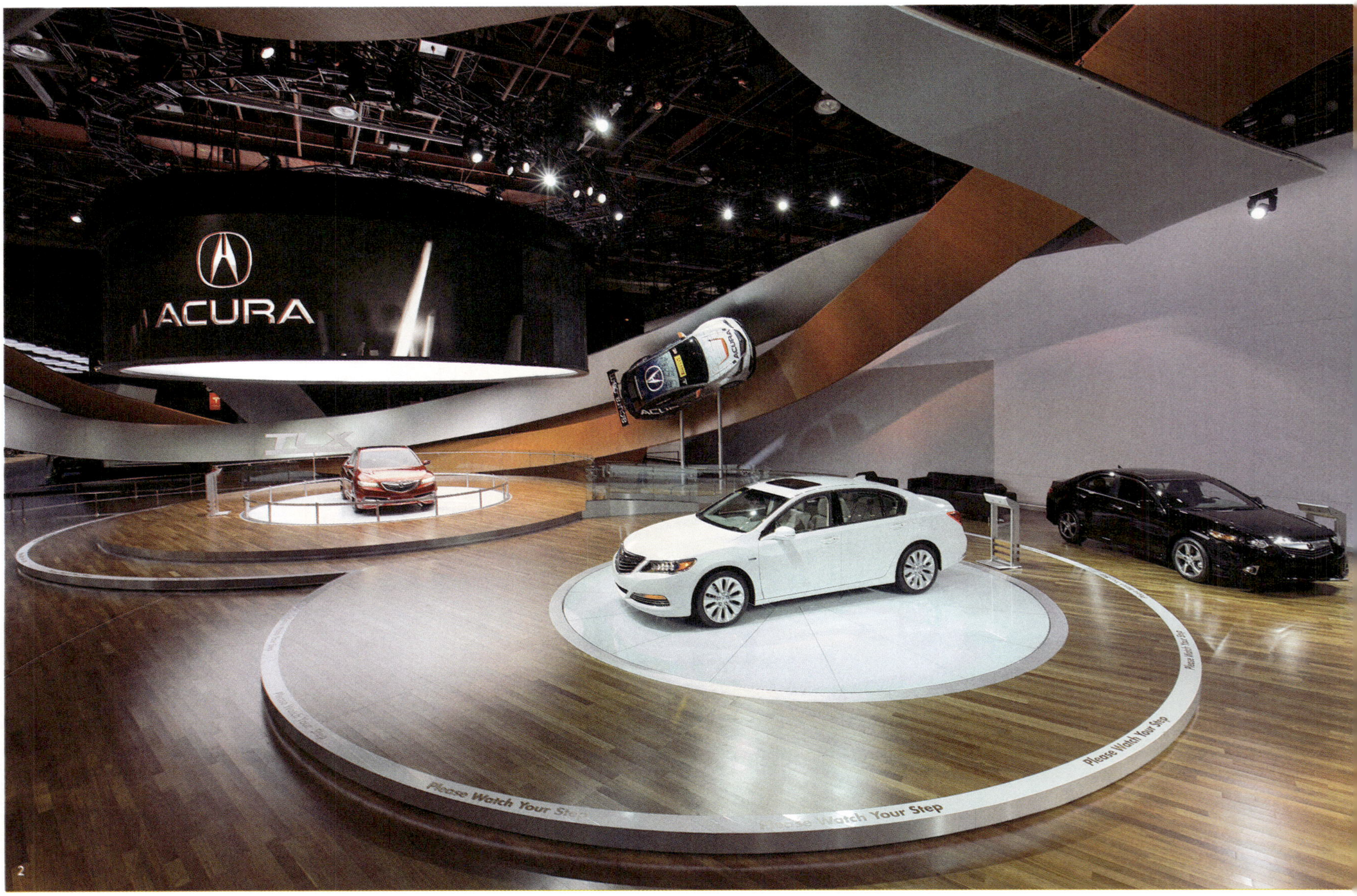

2

ACURA
George P Johnson
Experience Marketing

1 The looping ribbons encapsulated the company's ethos that positions man and machine in sync.

2 Complementing the ribbons were turntables and a suspended round LED screen that together formed the main presentation area.

3/4 The car launch was marked by a dynamic interactive show that featured holographic water vapour and augmented reality.

George P Johnson Experience Marketing (GPJ) realised a bold presentation for Acura at the North American International Auto Show in 2014 that was rooted in the automotive company's core values. Its 'Man-Machine Synergy' principle proposes that man and machine work in synergy for ultimate performance. GPJ brought this theme to life with a striking stand that truly celebrated the company's DNA. Two suspended intertwined looping ribbons formed the main feature of the stand. One ribbon signified the organic 'man' – with the natural colour of wood – and the other in metal – a technical material – symbolised

'machine'. Functioning not only as an eye-catching immersive backdrop, the ribbons also doubled as a gravity-defying racetrack for an Acura TLX race car. Constructing the ribbons from real wood and metal would have been too heavy. So an ingenuous structure was engineered to emulate the ribbons, made from custom polymer textile stretched over lightweight aluminium frames. Fabric was chosen to suggest the tints and textures of wood and metal. Directly under the ribbons was a central presentation area that featured two turntables and a 40-inch-diameter high resolution LED screen. With the form of a rotunda the suspended screen acted as a beacon, which displayed visuals as part of a spectacular show focused on the Acura TLX prototype. The visuals were complemented with interactive segments featuring a holograph water vapour display and an augmented reality-enabled tabletop. A palette of wood and metal dominated the stand and lent the space an atmosphere of both luxury

and warmth. The acacia wood floor contrasted beautifully with the glass and metal-trimmed turntables, and the furniture and walls were made from teak and glass. The experience brought visitors closer to Acura's inner workings and reinforced its image as a prestigious, innovative brand. ⚊

TRADE FAIR **North American International Auto Show**
WHERE **Detroit, United States**
WHEN **January 2014**
DESIGNER **George P Johnson Experience Marketing**
STAND CONSTRUCTOR **George P Johnson Experience Marketing**
CLIENT **Acura**
MARKET SECTOR **Automotive**
TOTAL FLOOR AREA **1000 m²**
PHOTOGRAPHER **Kathryn Rapier**

3

4

1

2

AUDI

KMS Blackspace

3

An unfamiliar darkened room in Frankfurt set the scene for the market launch of the new Audi TT. Clients and the general public were invited to experience the innovations of the new model first hand at a special presentation designed by KMS Blackspace. Located across the Skyline-Plaza, a black freestanding building called the 'Heartbeat' was specifically made to house the presentation. The dark exterior gave away nothing of what was to come. Inside visitors were first welcomed in a futuristic, stark white space where they could register their details. Afterwards they proceeded into a dark room with a curved and tilted panoramic wall that was unveiled as a custom-built indoor racetrack. With a radius of 35 metres, it had Germany's steepest curve with a bank angle of 58°. The motordrome was teamed with a live show comprising a 180° cinema experience, light show, 8.1 surround sound and four real vehicles that drove on the track at top speeds. The spectacular multi-sensory event, which told the story of the TT with a journey through galaxies, seemed to reverse the laws of gravity, allowing visitors to experience a world of weightlessness. Films and imagery were projected onto the track by high-performance projectors. Choreographed sound and lighting further enhanced the thrilling atmosphere of the show, which was executed with pure precision. Such a daring design also had its fair share of challenges to consider relating to the substructure of the track, track surface and finish, venting of car emissions, accident and fire prevention and, of course, audience safety. After the show, every visitor enjoyed the chance to test drive the high-performance car and experience the sensations of the sharp curve first hand. For the audience and the client, this turned out to be a breathtaking launch like no other. ▬

TRADE FAIR **Audi TT 360°**
WHERE **Frankfurt, Germany**
WHEN **October 2014**
DESIGNER **KMS Blackspace**
STAND CONSTRUCTOR **Adunic**
CLIENT **Audi**
MARKET SECTOR **Automobile**
TOTAL FLOOR AREA **2840 m²**
PHOTOGRAPHER **Stefan Bösl**

4

4/5 Visitors were wowed
with a live choreographed
show that unfolded on the
racetrack.

6 A tracking system
sensed the presence of
the cars to activate the
projection of the right film
clip at the right moment.

THE DARK INTERIOR REVEALS
A STEEP INDOOR RACETRACK
AS PART OF A SPECTACULAR
MULTI-SENSORY SHOW

KMS BLACKSPACE   AUDI   251

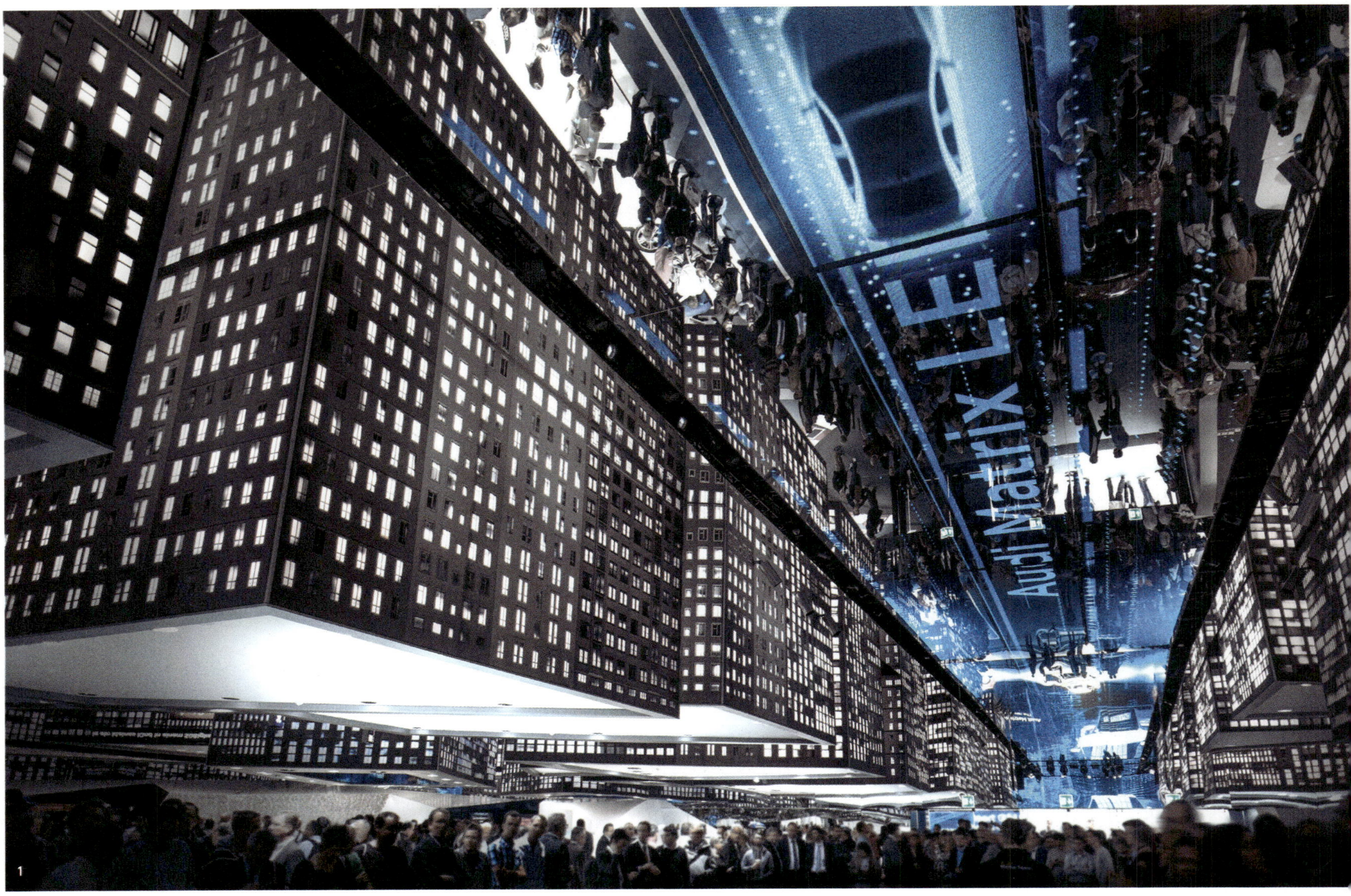

1

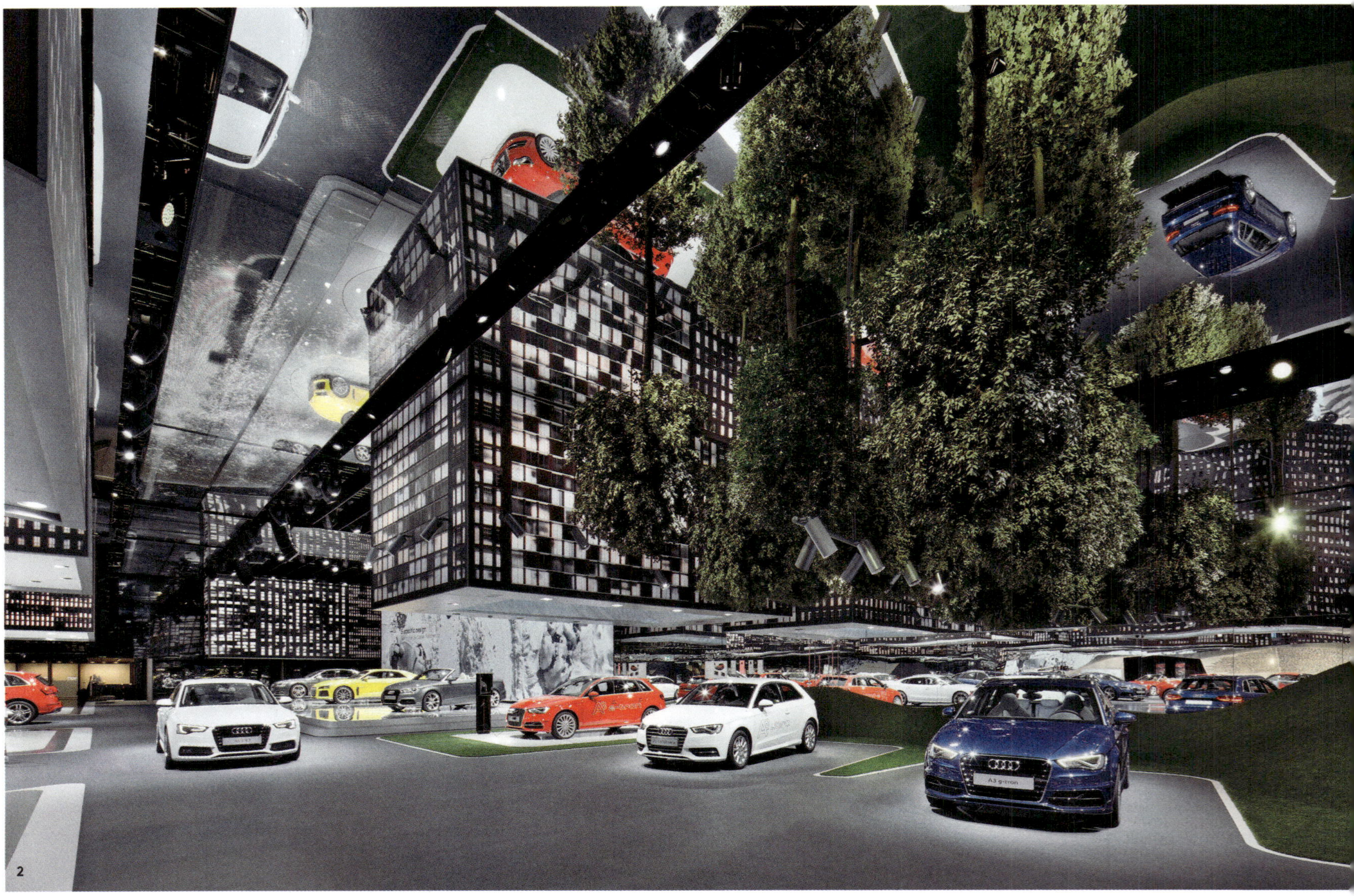
2

AUDI
KMS Blackspace

TRADE FAIR **IAA**
WHERE **Frankfurt, Germany**
WHEN **September 2013**
DESIGNER **KMS Blackspace**
STAND CONSTRUCTOR **Nüssli**
CLIENT **Audi**
MARKET SECTOR **Automobile**
TOTAL FLOOR AREA **3400 m²**
PHOTOGRAPHER **Andreas Keller Fotografie**

Entitled 'A New Point of View' Audi's spectacular presentation at the 2013 International Motor Show showed new perspectives of future mobility. For its booth, Audi envisioned a space where visitors could literally and figuratively experience the brand from a new angle. Here, the spotlight was on the city as the symbol of urban and mobile living. Designed by KMS Blackspace 'A New Point of View' turned the city on its head, exploring the need for a change in perspective to address urban challenges related to mobility, for instance concerning urbanisation, sustainability or networking. While the exterior of the freestanding exhibition structure appeared as a minimal, white geometric cube, the interior revealed a luminous futuristic city. Visitors felt like they had stepped into Blade Runner or Metropolis – only upside down. Entire neighbourhoods multiplied from the ceiling. Mirrored ceilings and walls reflected endless cityscapes that cleverly showcased the Audi models on display. The presentation was structured into four main themed neighbourhoods: Exclusivity, Quattro, Efficiency and Design/Technology. As the entire installation was elevated, visitors could meander underneath, between the buildings and cars. The flooring resembled a real streetscape with roads, footpaths zebra crossings, parking spaces and grassy knolls. Construction-wise the city was ingenuously fabricated from printed textile spanned across an extensive framework and reflective foil on the ceilings. Projected images totalling 11,2 million LED pixels brought urban scenes to life. Projectors were also placed inside windows to animate the building 'interiors'. Actual cityscapes from four international cities provided the inspiration for the neighbourhoods, lending the installation a sense of familiarity and realism. Visitors hopped between Copenhagen, New York, Tokyo and Munich while leaving their passports behind. This impressive installation showed fairgoers that urban mobility has very a bright future. ⟶

1 Upside-down LEDs were installed behind the reflective foil on the ceilings.

2 Seeing double: through the clever use of reflective foil, the city appeared to float from the ceiling.

3 Unexpected vistas and glimpses of the cars appeared with the turn of every corner.

4 The installation transported visitors into a buzzing fictional metropolis.

VISITORS FEEL LIKE THEY HAVE STEPPED INTO BLADE RUNNER OR METROPOLIS

BPW
Walbert-Schmitz

1 The 14-metre-long transparent truck visually communicated the inner workings of a trailer. A moveable monitor and interactive displays supported the exhibit.

2 Two interactive circular islands formed the other dominant features on the stand.

2

The BPW Group is a reliable international mobility and system partner for the transport industry. The portfolio ranges from axles, suspension systems, brake technologies, closure systems, body technology, lighting systems and plastic technologies through to user-friendly telematics applications for trucks and trailers. This holistic way of working was reflected in the theme 'we think transport' which guided the company's presentation at the IAA (International Motor Show)

Commercial Vehicles in 2014. BPW briefed the designers Walbert-Schmitz to design a stand that would encapsulate the company's innovative character and future-orientated thinking, echo its main showroom and comprehensively present the company's entire product assortment, including the subsidiary products. The booth should also appear bright, technological and inviting. An eye-catching glass truck forms the showpiece on the stand, accompanied by several larger display elements. The rest of the space is kept uncluttered and open to maintain the focus on the main presentation. White, silver and glossy materials complemented the company's corporate colour blue, forming a consistent palette and adding a modern look. The life-sized transparent truck ingenuously showcased the company's entire product range by placing them in their actual position in the truck, as well as represented the company's future visions. It successfully engaged visitors'

attentions by demonstrating the intricate inner workings of the vehicle in a creative, playful way. Its diagonal positioning at the front of the stand ensured extra prominence. Additionally, two circular islands explained the company's range of services and displayed detailed models. Anchoring the presentation was a curved rear wall with a 19-metre-long LED light box that visualised the exhibition themes. Concealed behind the wall were closed conference rooms and an open catering area for entertaining guests. ⊐

TRADE FAIR **IAA**
WHERE **Hannover, Germany**
WHEN **September 2014**
DESIGNER **Walbert-Schmitz**
STAND CONSTRUCTOR **Walbert-Schmitz**
CLIENT **BPW Bergische Achsen**
MARKET SECTOR **Automotive**
TOTAL FLOOR AREA **934 m²**
PHOTOGRAPHER **BPW**

nouvelle Classe S Coupé
Das neue S-Klasse C
La nouvelle Classe S C
Das neue S-Kla

1

2

MERCEDES-BENZ

jangled nerves

3

Mercedes-Benz had much to celebrate at the 2014 Geneva International Motor Show. The event marked the world premiere of the new S-Class Coupé and V- Class as well as the European premiere of the new C-Class. With this in mind jangled nerves set about to design a stand that would place the full spotlight on these new vehicles and ensure high visual impact. The 'brand ribbon' forms a consistent element of Mercedes-Benz's brand architecture at every trade fair appearance. For the first time, the ribbon appeared here as a completely digital medium in the form of a huge LED wall. Composed from seven million pixels, this surface spanned the entire width of the stand, opening up like a triptych. Dynamic changing visuals, accompanied by a matching soundtrack and light installation, animated the ribbon setting an immersive multimedia stage for the presentation. As an eye-catcher the impressive ribbon also ensured the stand had substantial visual presence and was well visible from afar. On the exhibition floor, 33 vehicles were showcased in an open, uncluttered space that was kept deliberately minimal to focus full attention on the cars and the ribbon. The layout was structured into a series of angular zones that arranged the cars according to priority, relevance and vehicle class. Varying floor materials defined these zones to create a dynamic floorscape.

Behind the first zone, a low zigzagging black partition emerged from the floor as a display wall to present exhibits around focus themes, and also functioned as an extra information counter. The rear of the stand accommodated a back office and two-storey structure that contained the function rooms.

TRADE FAIR **Geneva International Motor Show**
WHERE **Geneva, Switzerland**
WHEN **March 2014**
DESIGNER **jangled nerves**
STAND CONSTRUCTOR **Raumtechnik, Messebau & Events services**
CLIENT **Daimler**
MARKET SECTOR **Automobile**
TOTAL FLOOR AREA **3100 m²**
PHOTOGRAPHER **Andreas Keller**

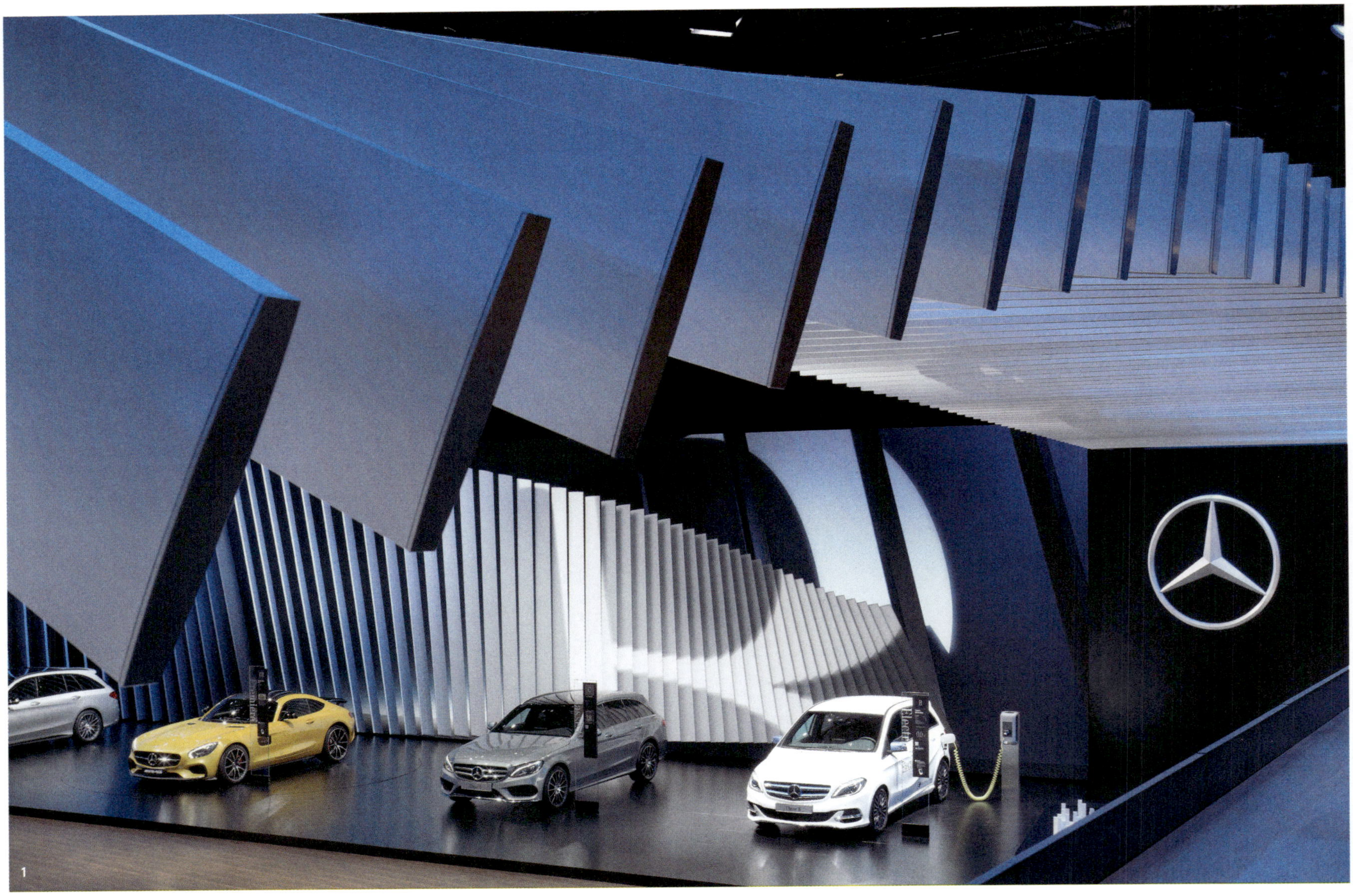
1

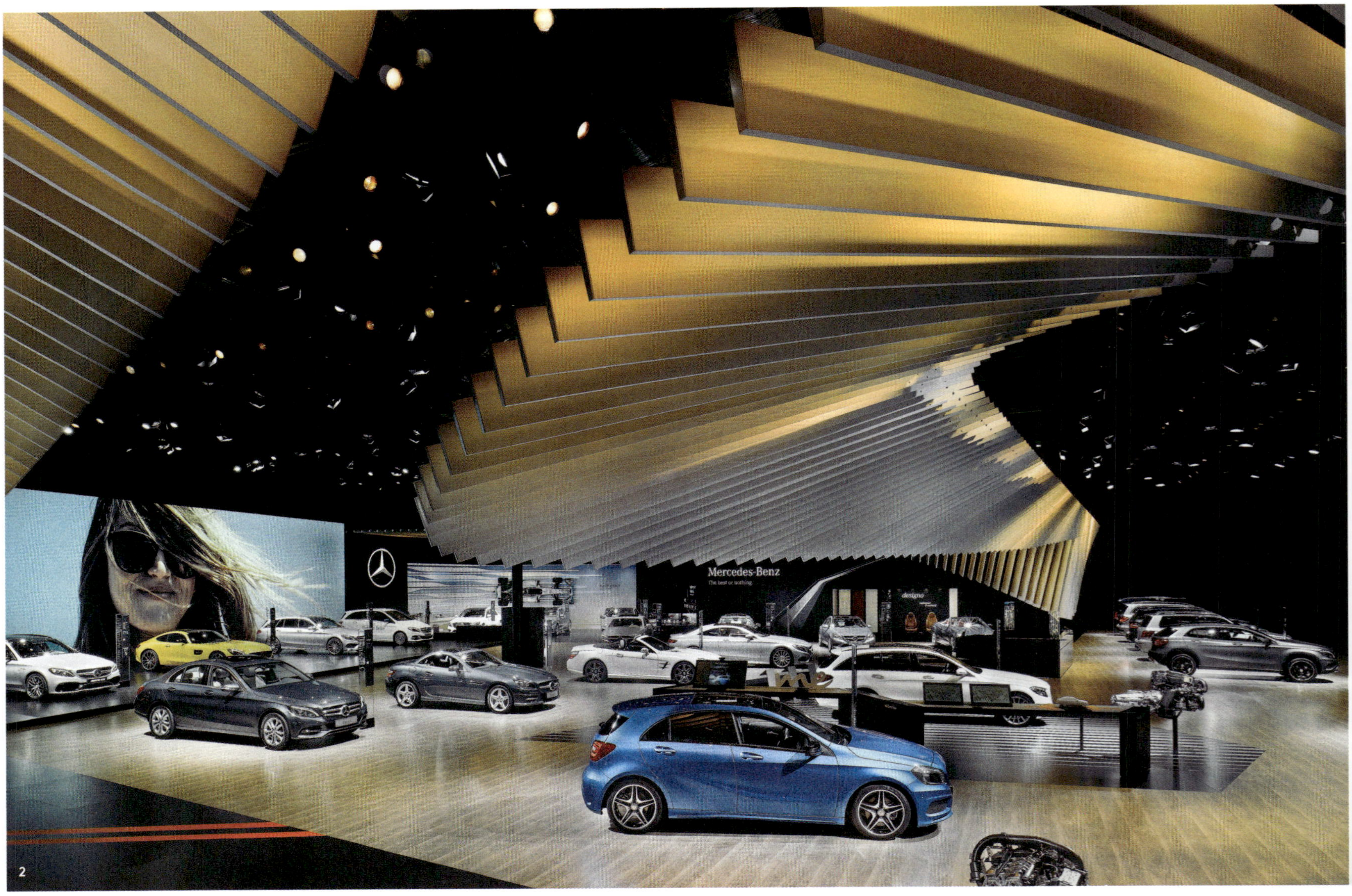

2

MERCEDES-BENZ SILVER FLOW

Atelier Markgraph and jangled nerves

1 Changing colours of lights animated the sculpture, further playing with the idea of motion.

2 Conjuring an atmosphere of lightness and elegance, the structure weighed 21 tonnes.

3 The architectonic installation was well visible from afar, immediately attracting visitors' attentions.

3

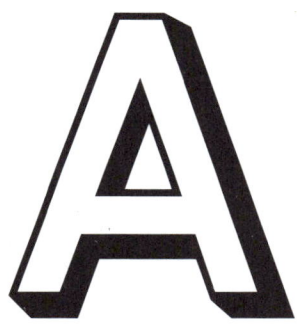

At the 2014 Mondial de l 'Automobile fair in Paris, Mercedes-Benz not only proudly launched a range of new vehicles, it also premiered a dynamic new exhibition concept. In its briefing to the designers Atelier Markgraph and jangled nerves, the client requested a new trade fair concept that should have high brand recognition but be adaptable for different events. The design should also match the company's design philosophy of 'Sensual Purity'. The result was the 'Silver Flow', a stunning suspended sculpture composed of twisting silver-coloured louvres which set a dramatic background for the presentation. Generating immediate visual impact, the flexible sculpture wound along the ceiling in an elegant, continuous gesture, suggesting the fluidity of vehicular motion. The skeletal structure was composed from 300 aluminium louvres, some spanning 7.5 metres in length. Despite weighing more than 21 tonnes, the installation appeared to move with lightness and ease through the space. Besides the architectonic element, the installation also functioned as a seamless media surface, where changing light projections accentuated and animated the sculptural form, intensifying the idea of flow. Animated this way, the constructed Silver Flow extended the central media display, and the media display continued the architecture with an animated Silver Flow. Flexibility not only applied to the visual character of the installation but also to its construction. Thanks to specially-designed adjustable connections, the installation can be easily dismantled and reconfigured into varying complex geometric shapes for each changing presentation. The design cleverly enabled the consistent brand presence and high recognition that Mercedes-Benz sought with a unique stand for every event. ⇒

TRADE FAIR **Mondial de l 'Automobile**
WHERE **Paris, France**
WHEN **November 2014**
DESIGNERS **jangled nerves (architecture);**
Atelier Markgraph (communication,
exhibition and media design)
STAND CONSTRUCTOR **Metron Vilshofen**
CLIENT **Daimler**
MARKET SECTOR **Automobile**
TOTAL FLOOR AREA **2500 m²**
PHOTOGRAPHER **Andreas Keller**

FASCINATION MERCEDES

Kauffmann Theilig & Partner and Atelier Markgraph

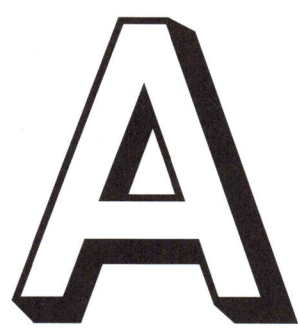

At the 2013 International Motor Show Mercedes-Benz set itself the challenge of creating a unique experience for visitors that would far exceed all expectations. And they succeeded with a bang: Entitled 'Fascination Mercedes' the presentation combined an impressing architecture with a spectacular choreographed multimedia production and an innovative interactive exhibition

For the tenth time in a row, Mercedes-Benz put architecture office Kauffmann Theilig & Partner and spatial communication ageny Atelier Markgraph in charge of its presentation, with Frankfurt's historic Festival Hall returning as the venue. The design conjured up a vibrant urban setting, where three levels with over 8,000 m² of exhibition space created a luminous architectonic panorama. The centrepiece was an extensive stage lined with a 55-metre-long LED screen and LED floor. But the real stars were 15 premiere vehicles that drove onto the stage from a five-metre-high LED carwalk for the 25-minute-long show. Thanks to a clever tracking system, the motion and position of the cars were meticulously synchronised with changing light effects, music and images.

Not only the setting and show were choreographed but also the routing through the presentation. After entering the hall, visitors immediately saw the impressive stage front on. From here, they travelled up two escalators to level 2 to join the guided tour. A terraced structure led people down to level one and ground floor along a 600-metre-long route. Visitors could follow the stage show throughout their tour as the surrounding exhibition circuit doubled as the spectator grandstand. The adjacent exhibitions provided in-depth and supplementary information about themes from the stage production. Visitors were also invited to participate by uploading images of the show live via social media. The vibrant presentation brought the experience of the brand to life, exuding intensity and dynamism in an absolute showstopper that will keep visitors talking about Mercedes-Benz for years to come. ▭

TRADE FAIR **IAA**
WHERE **Frankfurt, Germany**
WHEN **September 2013**
DESIGNERS **Atelier Markgraph and Kauffmann Theilig & Partner**
STAND CONSTRUCTOR **Display International**
CLIENT **Daimler**
MARKET **Automobile**
TOTAL FLOOR AREA **12,400 m²**
PHOTOGRAPHERS **Kristof Lemp and Andreas Keller**

1 Cleverly choreographed interaction between the vehicles and light, images and music continually focused the attention onto centre stage.

2 The stage show presented premiere vehicles and brand themes in a series of chapters, each with its own atmosphere.

3 The spacious architecture of the exhibition provided ample space to gaze and stroll.

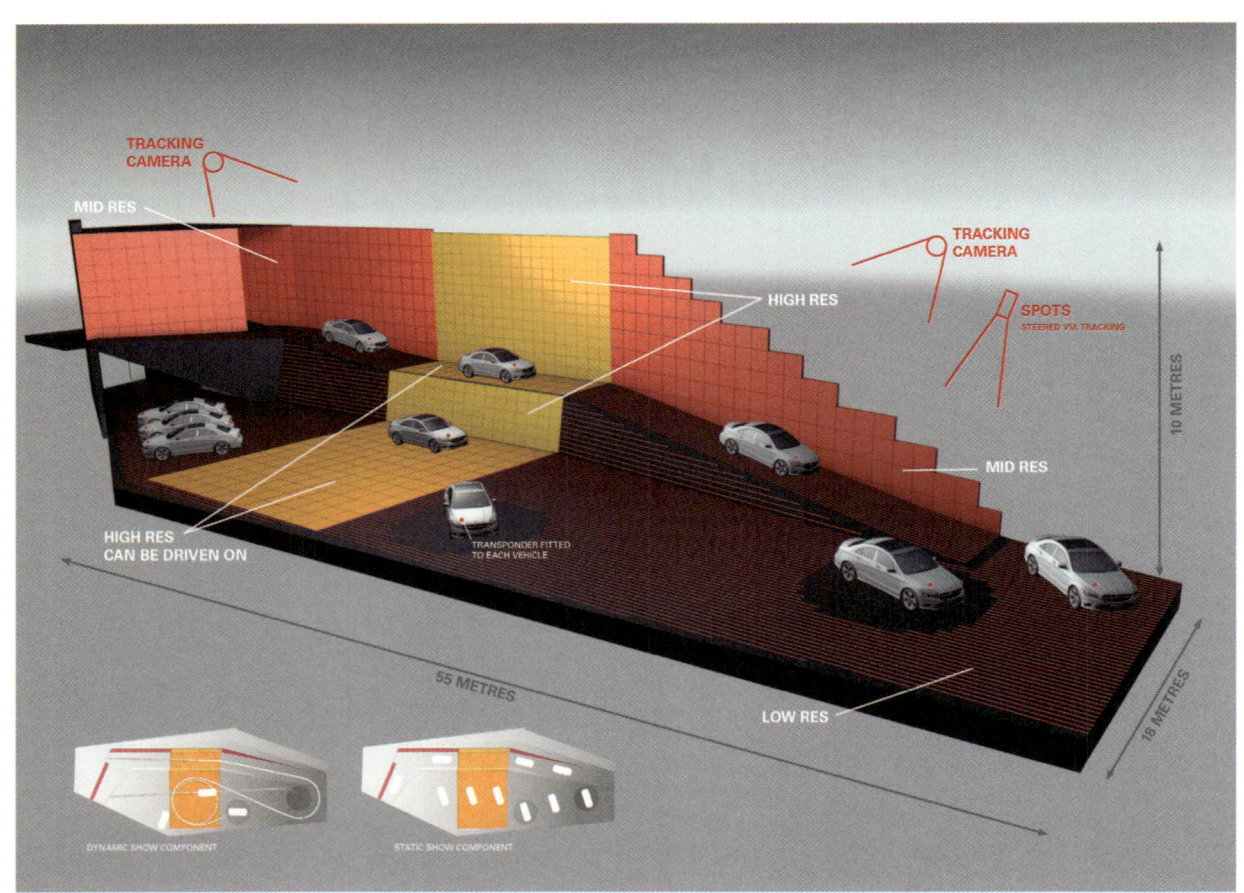

4 The cars became conductors that directed their digital surroundings.

5 Diagram of the tracking system.

6 Around 70 vehicles, themed presentations and interactive exhibits were featured in the adjacent exhibition. Engineers, designers, product experts and sales personnel were on hand to assist visitors.

SECOND FLOOR

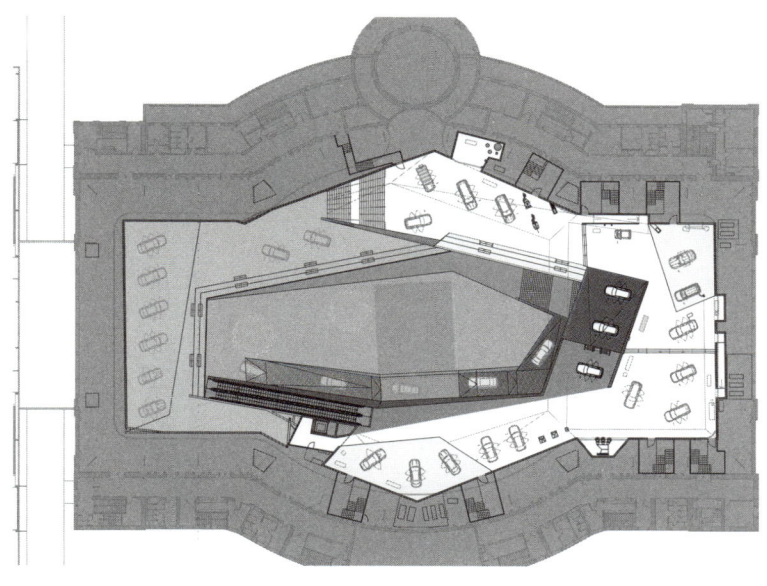

6

A SHOWSTOPPER THAT KEEPS VISITORS TALKING ABOUT MERCEDES-BENZ FOR YEARS TO COME

FIRST FLOOR

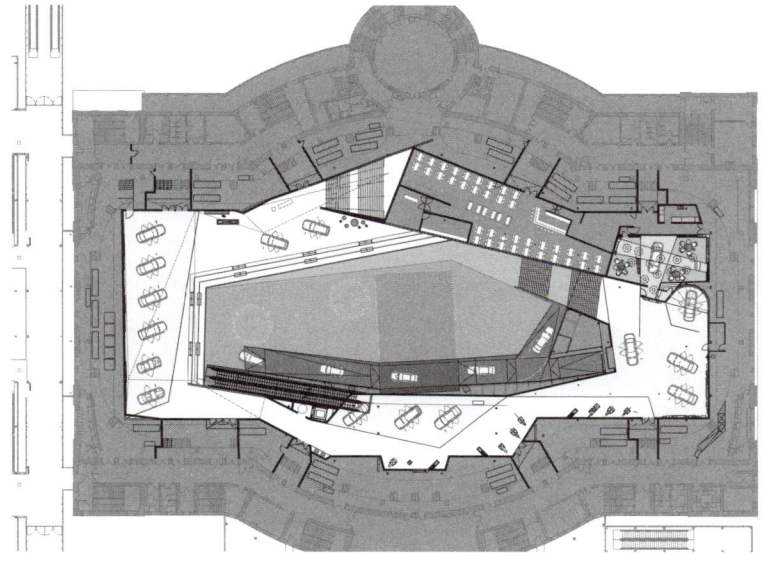

LONG SECTION

GROUND FLOOR

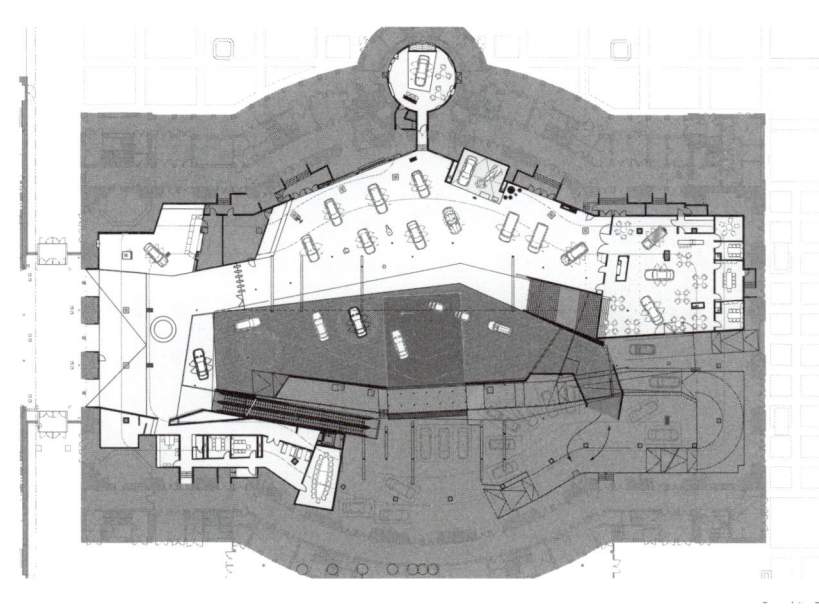

CROSS SECTION

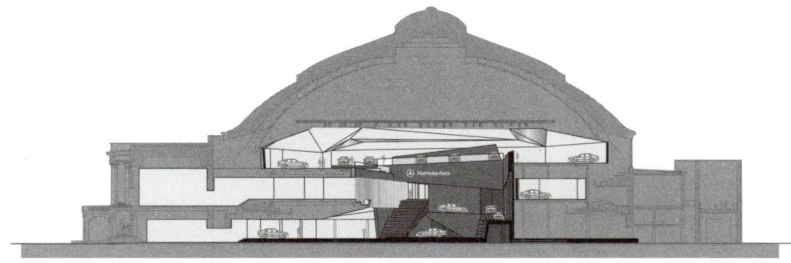

HITACHI CONSTRUCTION MACHINERY

Gielissen

1 An unconventional approach showcased the machines in a semi-closed domain without external distractions.

2 Hitachi's corporate identity was prominently featured on the stand, resulting in a bold and coherent presentation.

2

'Meet the Stars' was Hitachi Construction Machinery's promise to visitors at Intermat in 2015. At this International Exhibition for Equipment and Techniques for the Construction and Materials Industries, the company's trademark orange machines stole the show. Designed by Gielissen Interiors & Exhibitions the vast 2590 m² stand immediately caught visitors' attentions with its bold orange-and-black setting that perfectly encapsulated the identity of the brand. The main aim was to put the spotlight entirely on the machines. To achieve this, the designers developed a concept that focused the stand inwards to separate the presentation from the bustle of the hall. In this way the machines could be showcased in their own branded world against a calm background without external distractions. A four-metre-high black banner wrapped the top half of the front of the stand, leaving the base open to give visitors a glimpse of the interior. Two openings at each end invited visitors onto the stand where they were guided along the 'Walk of Fame'. Lined by the impressive machines this diagonal black carpet path meandered through the space, marked with orange stars. Spotlights shone theatrically on each machine to showcase it in the best light. Behind the back wall was an enclosed zone that incorporated meeting and service spaces. Besides the machines, the other highlight was the orange information desk at the centre of the stand with a 3D cinema behind that transported fairgoers into Hitachi's construction world. Topping off the showbiz theme were popcorn dispensers placed at the entrances that got visitors into the swing of the theme. ▬

TRADE FAIR **Intermat**
WHERE **Paris, France**
WHEN **April 2015**
DESIGNER **Gielissen Interiors & Exhibitions**
STAND CONSTRUCTOR **Gielissen Interiors & Exhibitions**
CLIENT **Hitachi Construction Machinery**
MARKET SECTOR **Construction equipment**
TOTAL FLOOR AREA **2590 m²**
PHOTOGRAPHER **Adriaan van Dam**

3 A succession of black ceiling banners complemented the rhythmic procession along the 'Walk of Fame'.

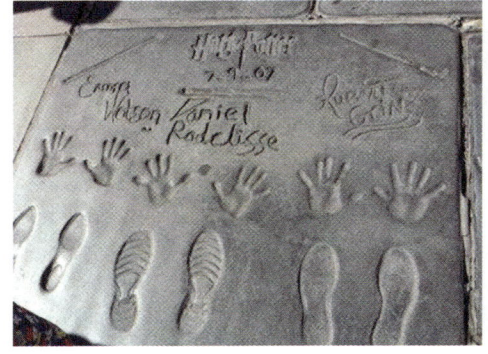

VISITORS WERE GUIDED ALONG THE 'WALK OF FAME' LINED WITH HITACHI'S IMPRESSIVE MACHINES

RENDERINGS

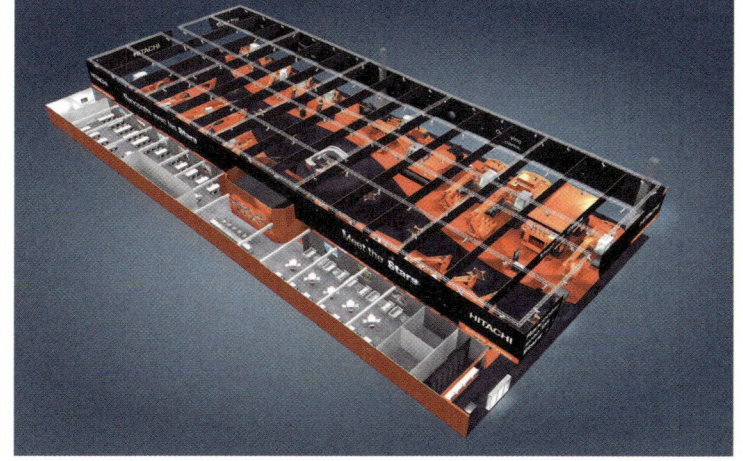

STAND CONSTRUCTION

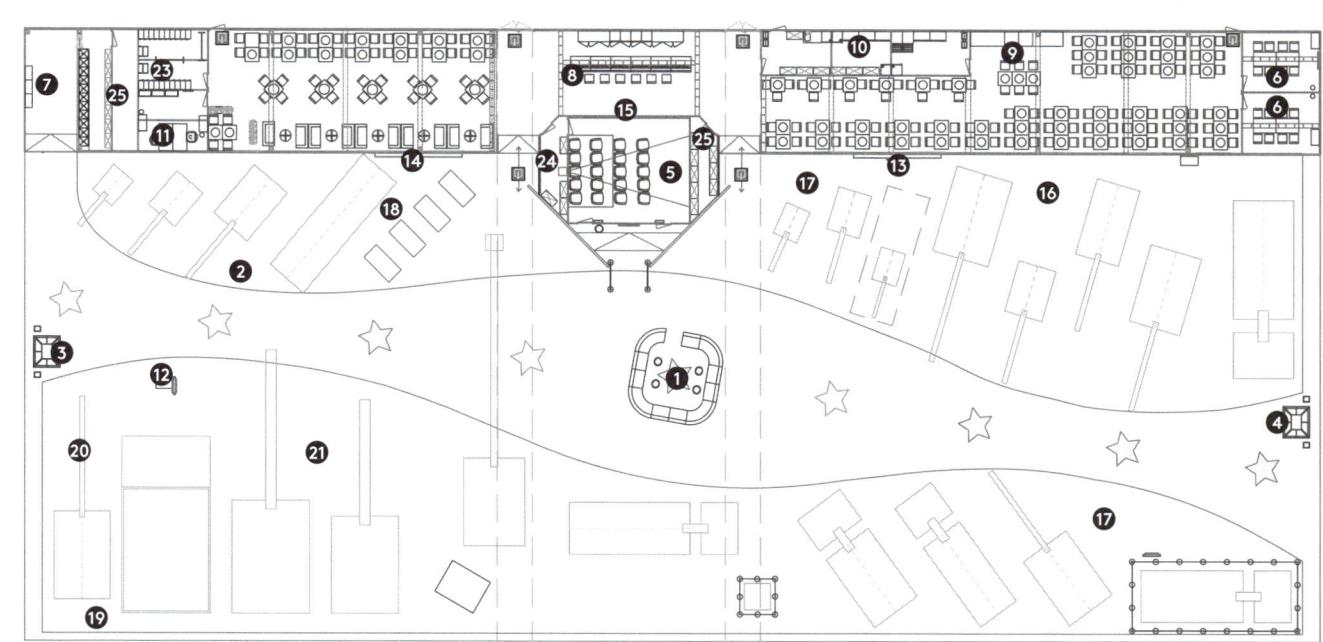

FLOOR PLAN

01 Information desk
02 Road
03 Slt popcorn
04 Sweet popcorn
05 Cinema
06 Meeting room
07 Shop
08 Bar
09 Buffet
10 Kitchen
11 Back office
12 LCD screen
13 Sumitomo wall
14 Europe map wall
15 Wall of fame
16 Construction/
    earthmoving
17 Sumitomo
18 Camino corner
19 Africa corner
20 Africa
21 Quarry
22 Recycling
23 Lockers
24 Tech
25 Storage

Mercedes-Benz
Test the new
A-Class now.
Take a picture
with the A-Class
and win it.
A-Klasse
1

Wow*
2

MERCEDES-BENZ

Liganova

1 Each structure was customised on location with changing vehicles, visuals and interior accessories according to a different campaign.

2 Presentations were hosted in public spaces in major European urban centres. Here at the Central Station Zurich.

3 The streamline structure echoed the dynamic architecture of the brand.

Mercedes-Benz sought an innovative spatial concept to launch its new A-Class compact car in the European market. The specifics of the brief were: Develop a mobile pavilion that is easy to transport, has a modular structure, can be assembled and dismantled at little cost and can be deployed all year in different contexts. As a starting point for the design Liganova was triggered by the concept of 'Captured Energy', which the client used to describe the development of its new generation compact cars. The result was an aerodynamic structure whose architecture was informed by dynamic natural elements such as wind and waves, and automotive and aircraft design. The elegant streamlined profile derived from a single movement that morphed the floor into the wall, then the ceiling and back to the floor. Designed for maximum flexibility and adaptability the structure suited both indoor and outdoor contexts, travelling roadshows or site-specific events during both summer and winter. Using the basic pavillion as a foundation, each presentation could be modified with changing visuals according to the relevant campaigns along with different vehicles and interior accessories. The modular pavillion was composed of a steel substructure with a segmented facade made from aluminium elements. A clever system of magnets easily attached and detached the facade from the structure. Internally the open layout featured a flexible wall and a fixed wall with a video screen. Bolon, a durable material suitable for indoor and outdoor applications, was used to clad the floors, walls and ceilings. A total of 16 pavillions were made, with the launch encompassing 82 stops in 22 European countries covering 70,000 km. The design successfully showed how temporary architecture could make a long-lasting impression. ⌐

TRADE FAIR **A-Class Roadshow**
WHERE **22 countries across Europe**
WHEN **May-December 2012**
DESIGNER **Liganova. The BrandRetail Company**
STAND CONSTRUCTOR **Nüssli**
CLIENT **Daimler**
MARKET SECTOR **Automobile**
TOTAL FLOOR AREA **128 m²**
PHOTOGRAPHER **Liganova. The BrandRetail Company**

3

MERCEDES-BENZ TRUCKS

Uniplan

TRADE FAIR **bauma**
WHERE **Munich, Germany**
WHEN **April 2013**
DESIGNER **Uniplan**
STAND CONSTRUCTOR **Uniplan**
CLIENT **Daimler**
MARKET SECTOR **Trucks**
TOTAL FLOOR AREA **1569 m²**
PHOTOGRAPHER **Stefan Schilling**

1 Suspended LED panels distinguished the information counter as a visual landmark.

2 High brand recognition was integral to the design.

Uniplan was once again responsible for designing the stand for Mercedes-Benz trucks at bauma. At this trade fair for construction machinery, building material machines, mining machines, construction vehicles and construction equipment, the focus was on the Arocs heavy-duty truck. Its motto 'The new power in construction' was also adopted as the guiding force of the design. The trucks appeared completely at home on the spacious stand that took visual cues from the construction site. Black walls and floors dominated the stand, marked by white graphics that lent the space a contemporary feel. Bright spotlights focused all attention on the trucks against the dark background, conveying an atmosphere of quality and prestige. Silhouettes of cranes, buildings and other construction elements decorated the walls, made from printed mesh. Thick white arrows were used to help structure the space and became the visual symbol of the stand. Starting on the walls and continuing onto the floors, the bold arrow markings contributed a dynamic sense of space. Signage pillars were fashioned from real construction materials such as concrete, gravel, cables, folding rulers and screws – the materials used cleverly corresponded with the vehicle's function. Stencilled text, which is used mainly on building sites, further suggested a genuine construction atmosphere. Oversized fonts throughout enabled signage to be well visible from afar. Above the information counter, a double-sided LED panel displayed changing texts about vehicle features on both sides. The stand's clear and structured set up, bold aesthetic and strong atmosphere clearly communicated the position of Mercedes-Benz trucks as a first-class manufacturer of construction vehicles. ⇒

2

Vito 116 CDI
Kombi 4x4

Der Kombi, der sich in jeder
Gebiet zuhause fühlt.

The crewbus that feels at ...

Trucks you can trust.

THE TRUCKS APPEAR COMPLETELY AT HOME ON THE CONSTRUCTION SITE

3 Signage pillar made of folding rulers.

4 Walk this way: bold white arrows became the visual symbol of the stand.

5 Different materials used on the pillars indicated the functions of the trucks.

5

OPEL
Bellprat Associates

TRADE FAIR **Paris Motor Show**
WHERE **Paris, France**
WHEN **October 2014**
DESIGNER **Bellprat Associates**
STAND CONSTRUCTOR **Ambrosius Deutschland**
CLIENT **Opel**
MARKET SECTOR **Automotive**
TOTAL FLOOR AREA **2014 m²**
PHOTOGRAPHERS **Oliver Oettli and Dietmar Gapp**

To celebrate the world premiere of the Opel Corsa at the 2014 Paris Motor Show, Bellprat Associates took inspiration from the glitz and glamour of the fashion world for the design of the Opel stand. The designers transformed the whole space into a giant catwalk using the cars as models. This worked perfectly in tune with Corsa's youthful target audience. A sea of high-gloss black glass flooring was combined with reflective ceilings to set the stage for the slick stand. This spectacular mirrored effect showed off the cars from every angle – with help from spotlights – and also served to extend the space visually. At one end of the stand, the long white stage displayed the cars in a selection of vibrant colours. During the press conference the Corsas were paraded on this catwalk, accompanied by Claudia Schiffer who acts as a brand ambassador for Opel. Behind the stage was an extensive video wall that broadcasted dynamic images, textures and videos during the event, further immersing visitors in the brand. Here, dramatically hung on its side, was a bright red Corsa, suspended in motion.

On other parts of the stand, an array of futuristic looking, interactive pods invited visitors to take selfies that were incorporated into the video animation in real time, and thus allowed visitors to become part of the show. Fairgoers could share their thoughts with Opel designers in a live design studio, and discover material and colour samples. In addition to the Corsa presentation, the stand also offered various other exhibits like engine displays and merchandising products that were, of course, all modelled on a fashion display. ⌐

1/2 Reflective ceilings created an illusory sense of space that showcased the cars from every angle.

2

THE STAND IS MODELLED ON THE GLITZ AND GLAMOUR OF THE FASHION WORLD

3 Paparazzi crowd around the catwalk to get their first glimpses of the new cars.

4 Visitors could see behind-the-scenes of the Corsa in the design studio.

5/6 Selfies were incorporated into the video animation in real time.

FUSION OF VISUALS AND ARCHITECTURE

HAUTE VOITURE

CONCEPTUAL SKETCH

6

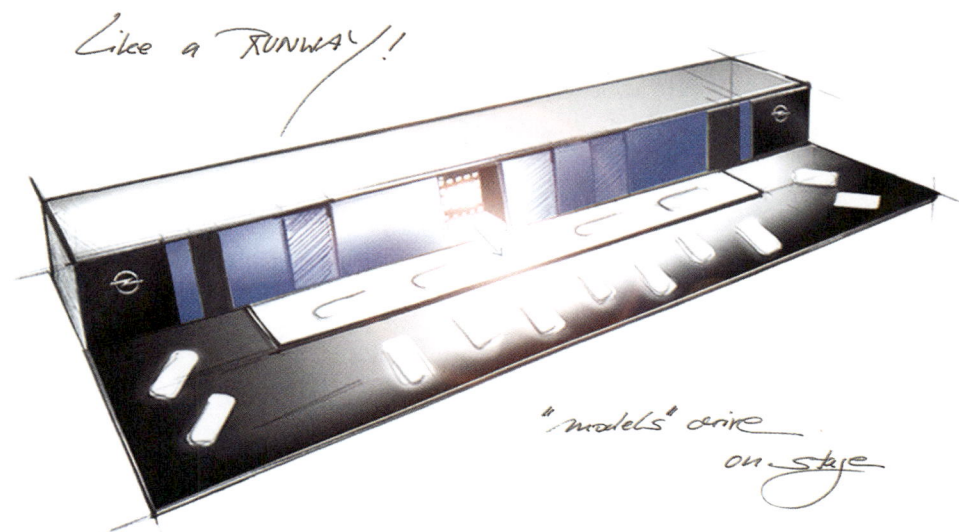

Like a RUNWAY!

"models" drive on stage

CONCEPT RENDERING

SMART
Braunwagner

TRADE FAIR **IAA**
WHERE **Frankfurt, Germany**
WHEN **September 2013**
DESIGNER **Braunwagner**
STAND CONSTRUCTOR **Klartext**
CLIENT **Daimler**
MARKET SECTOR **Automobile**
TOTAL FLOOR AREA **3350 m²**
PHOTOGRAPHER **Andreas Keller**

1 smart's stand was a celebration of mobility.

2 Bold, colourful graphics were integral to the design, strategically applied throughout the stand.

2

Braunwagner developed the concept 'smart move' for the IAA in 2013 to visualize smart's dynamic brand strategy and prepare for the launch of a new product family. This presentation also set the tone for the following year's shows. The Forum once again hosted the 3350 m² stand, with mobility and individuality as key themes.

The stand was planned as a series of themed open experience areas. Spatially these areas were defined by dynamic elements that freely transformed into floors, ceilings and walls throughout the space. On the ceiling fluid illuminated green lines, also echoed in the floor, teamed with bold horizontal white fins that shifted through the space. High gloss floors lent a slick feel, beautifully reflecting the cars and lights. The energetic architectural language used throughout the whole design from the counters to showcases, platforms, typography elements and niches for media screens ensured a coherent overall brand experience.

Complementing the strong architecture was a clear graphic concept that consisted of oversized typography and vivid colour accents. Colour codes were used to identify different themes and the main graphics combined neon hues with transparent overlays of colour. Accent colours corresponded with the cars on display. The way colour contrasted with the dynamic white architecture resulted in a spatial experience full of surprise. Various collaborations that highlighted individualization and lifestyle were showcased in separate spaces on the edge of the stand. Towards the rear of the space, the DesignLab gave an insight into the conception of a new car from sketch to final product using enlarged renderings. The clever play of lines, bold colours and shifting surfaces clearly exuded a sense of vibrancy, fun and mobility synonymous with smart. ⌐

THE CONCEPT 'SMART MOVE' VISUALISES SMART'S DYNAMIC BRAND STRATEGY

3

4

5

3   Green is the feature colour of smart electric drive. It was reflected in the dynamic lines, the typography and furniture.

4   The eccentric smart forjeremy lounge upstairs was inspired by the showcar created by fashion designer Jeremy Scott.

5   The executive lounge showcasing the smart BRABUS tailor made had a more pared-back look.

6   A neon light installation expressed the theme Neon Accent.

6

SUBARU
TECHINTACTO®
technically invincible
1

SBARRO
TECHART
HALLE
2
ALLÉE
210C
2

TECHINTACTO

Arno Design

Classic, exclusive and luxurious: Techintacto's stand brought a bit of old-school glamour to the 85th edition of the International Geneva Motor Show in 2015. Techintacto equips vans and mini-vans with luxurious bespoke interiors. As the company operates in a high-end segment, it wanted its stand to reflect its motto of 'Don't travel less than first class'. In response to this request, Arno Design opted for a luxurious, classic design that encapsulated the essence of the company, and differentiated the stand from the mostly high-tech approach of other exhibitors. The classic smoking bar as seen in glamorous 1940s Hollywood movies formed the inspiration for the design. Interior elements such as dark-panelled wood, gilded walls and classic Chesterfield sofas set the scene. Dark materials like the smoked oak parquet floor and dark leather together with the dark-coloured cars contributed a sense of luxury. With an open fireplace and small clusters of armchairs and sofas, the lounge area offered a cosy backdrop for informal client meetings, perhaps over a glass of whisky. Finished in gold and furnished with vintage bar stools, the gentlemen's bar added a touch of class. While spotlights focused on the cars, the rest of the stand was more subtly illuminated with warm freestanding lamps to keep the mood more intimate and personal while maintaining the atmosphere of exclusivity that befits the brand. ▬

TRADE FAIR **International Geneva Motor Show**
WHERE **Geneva, Switzerland**
WHEN **March 2015**
DESIGNER **Arno Design**
STAND CONSTRUCTOR **Arno Design**
CLIENT **Techintacto**
MARKET SECTOR **Automotive**
TOTAL FLOOR AREA **125 m²**
PHOTOGRAPHER **Ben Grna**

1 Techintacto wanted their space to evoke the exclusivity of the company's operations.

2 The gold gentlemen's bar added the finishing touch to the space.

3 Dark colours and finishes conveyed a sense of luxury and sophistication.

3

TOYOTA
Let's Go Places
#ToyotaCES
TOYOTA
TOYOTA FV2

1

TOYOTA
Let's Go Places
#ToyotaCES
On the roads of Southern California

2

TOYOTA

George P Johnson Experience Marketing

1/2 Toyota's corporate branding was prominently visible on the stand.

3 Occupying a prominent position, the three-wheeled i-Road zipped around the stand on a compact track.

3

With technology increasingly finding a home within the family vehicle, the Consumer Electronics Show (CES) in 2014 represented an opportunity for Toyota to debut three new advanced concept cars. The space needed to highlight Toyota's position as a leader in automotive innovation while embracing the culture of the CES through immersive and educational environments. On board to design the stand was George P Johnson Experience Marketing who took a future-focused approach to show visitors a glimpse of Toyota's visions. A prominent Toyota-branded header suspended above the stand and an

aerodynamic structure with integrated large format LED panoramic back wall set the scene. The minimal white background perfectly complemented the red accents of Toyota's iconic corporate colour. Three zones structured the space to highlight the story behind each concept. The Toyota i-Road, a three-wheeled vehicle, zipped around a track within the space, suggesting a new future for city driving with fewer traffic headaches. The display for the Toyota FCV, a hydrogen fuel cell vehicle, took an educational approach. Interactive tables and LED displays led visitors through the history of Toyota FCV development and testing, assuring attendees that this technology was not only real, but also reliable and safe. Topping off the presentation was the Fun-V2, a vehicle that took Toyota's 'Fun to Drive' concept even further into the future. The vehicle responds to body movements and uses voice and image

recognition to determine driver mood. Its LED surface and interactive features were showcased through a camera that projected images onto the surface of the vehicle, demonstrating the real-time visualization of the relationship between driver and vehicle. This engaging experience showed that technology and automotives have a bright, fun future together. ▭

TRADE FAIR **Consumer Electronics Show**
WHERE **Las Vegas, United States**
WHEN **January 2014**
DESIGNER **George P Johnson Experience Marketing**
STAND CONSTRUCTOR **George P Johnson Experience Marketing**
CLIENT **Toyota**
MARKET SECTOR **Automotive**
TOTAL FLOOR AREA **1676 m²**
PHOTOGRAPHER **Kathryn Rapier**

VIRGIN ATLANTIC

Dijon Designs

TRADE FAIR **Business Travel Show**
WHERE **London, United Kingdom**
WHEN **February 2014**
DESIGNER **Dijon Designs**
STAND CONSTRUCTOR **Dijon Designs**
CLIENT **Virgin Atlantic**
MARKET SECTOR **Aviation**
TOTAL FLOOR AREA **50 m²**
PHOTOGRAPHER **Courtesy of Dijon Designs**

1 The high attention to detail throughout gave visitors a taste of Virgin Atlantic's exceptional hospitality.

2 With its bold architecture, the stand easily stood out at both fairs.

2

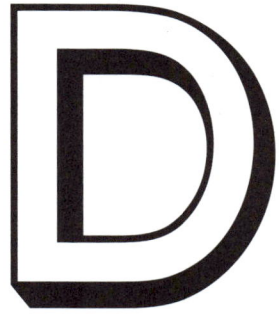

Dijon Designs was tasked with delivering an eye-catching, travelling exhibition stand for Virgin Atlantic at the Business Travel Show 2014 in London and Global Business Travel Association (GBTA) 2014 in Los Angeles. The focus of the brief was to exemplify the Virgin Atlantic brand and the instinct of the company to do things differently, and give visitors an experience of Virgin's exceptional hospitality. Cool, contemporary, glamorous and fun were keywords that guided the design,

which also took inspiration from Virgin's Upper Class Lounge. The angular white structure presented an intriguing front, its unexpected form with unusual cutouts and LED lighting teasing visitors to step 'on board'. A luxurious, immersive experience awaited them inside, where they were treated to a feast for the senses. Guests were welcomed by a member of the crew (dressed in Vivienne Westwood-designed uniforms) and guided through the stand with Google Glass. This gave a taste of the technology used on real flights to inform passengers about their travel plans. Sounds, aromas, textures together with travel books and catering hinted at the destinations serviced by the airline. Three bespoke bench-seating areas structured the space, upholstered

with fabric that matched the seating in the Upper Class Lounge to ensure authenticity. Quality materials, designer furniture and fittings and atmospheric lighting were key to achieving an exclusive feel. A feature wall was constructed using 3D sculptured materials and bronze and gold laminates with recessed 32 inch plasma screens displaying inflight content and destination information. The stand's modular construction enabled ease of assembly/ disassembly and transportation as the exhibition travelled from London to Los Angeles. The stand was reinstalled in a slightly modified configuration due to a different context, thereby also giving visitors across the Atlantic the exclusive Virgin Atlantic experience first hand. ⇒

4

virgin atlantic

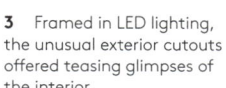

3 Framed in LED lighting, the unusual exterior cutouts offered teasing glimpses of the interior.

4 Eddison pendant lights were used in the stand.

5 Crew in Vivienne Westwood designed uniforms on board the stand.

5

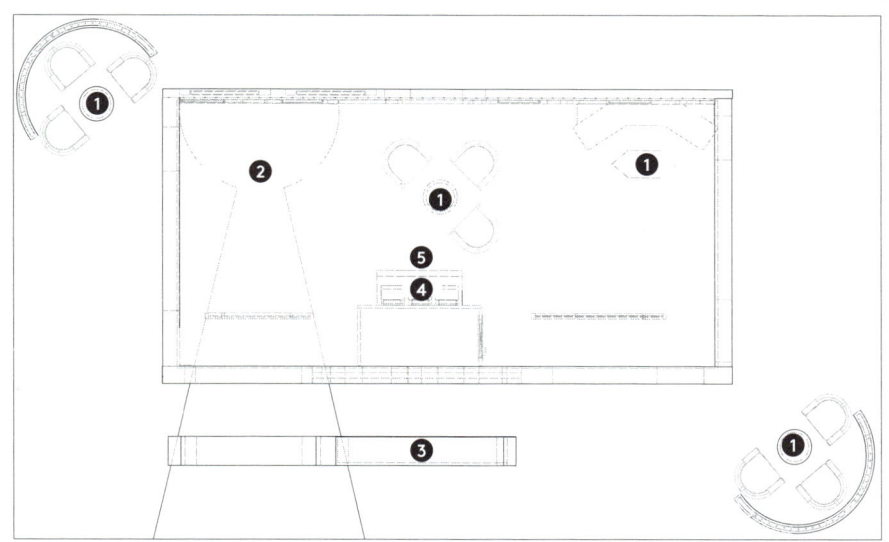

FLOOR PLAN

01 Seating area
02 Interactive area
03 Bar
04 Store
05 Wanderwall

SECTIONS

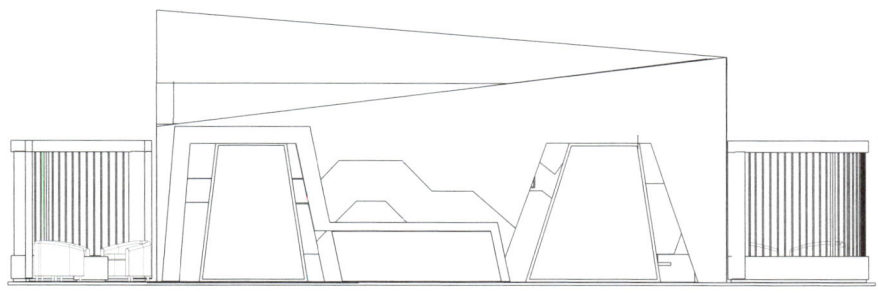

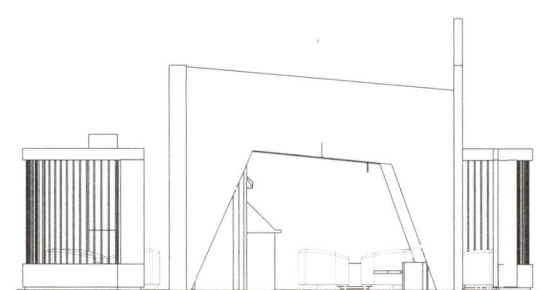

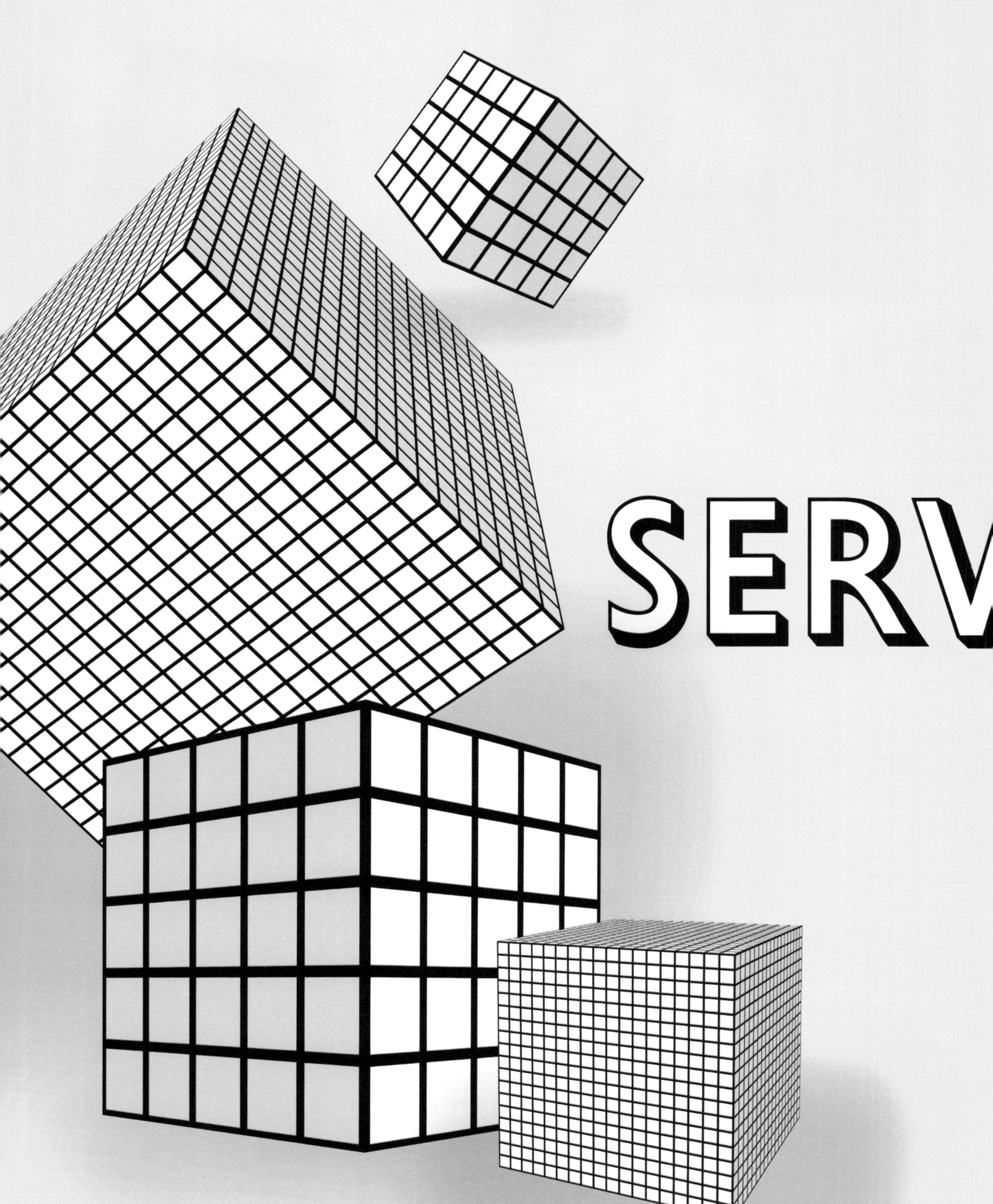

SERV

ICES

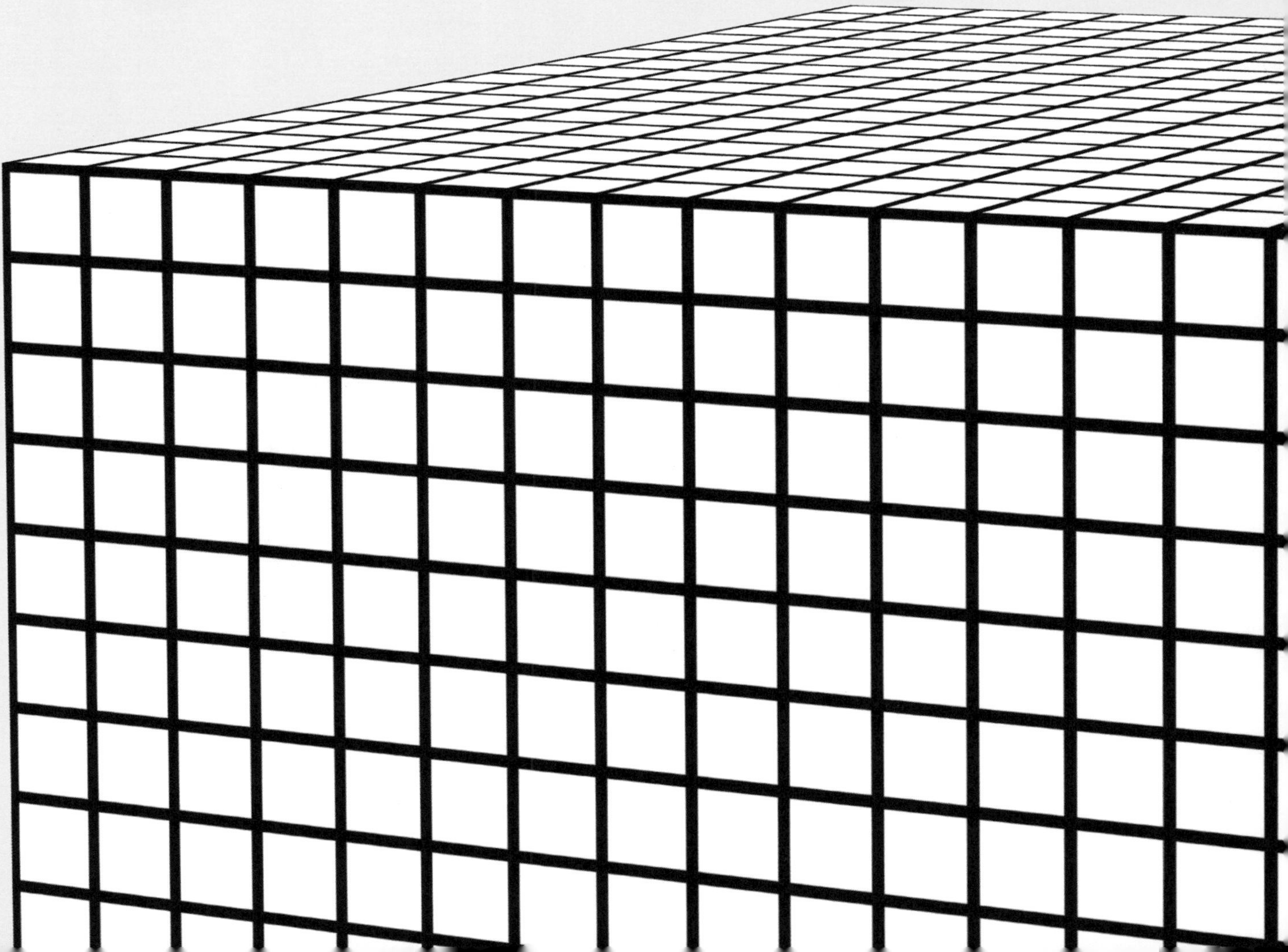

ARTING

Arting

TRADE FAIR **EuroShop**
WHERE **Düsseldorf, Germany**
WHEN **February 2014**
DESIGNER **Arting**
STAND CONSTRUCTOR **Arting**
CLIENT **Arting**
MARKET SECTOR **Design**
TOTAL FLOOR AREA **170 m² (over 2 floors)**
PHOTOGRAPHER **Dirk Baumbach**

1 The chic material and colour palette and detailing perfectly conveyed the atmosphere of a modern home.

2 Welcome to the House of Arting.

2

The 'House of Arting' aptly described Arting's own presentation at EuroShop in 2014. As a design office that offers retail & exhibition solutions, Arting wanted its stand to proudly represent its many positive qualities and core values, which include dialogue, passion, hard work, process, concept and craftsmanship. The challenge was to highlight the company's identity and showcase its design capabilities particularly with attention to complexity and details. With the set-up of a modern house, the House of Arting felt more like a warm inviting home than a conventional exhibition booth. A white cube with high narrow windows and high main entrance formed the basis of the stand. From the outside, curious visitors could peer into the windows to get a glimpse of the interior. Made of white vertical wooden slats that varied in thickness, the textured facade resulted in an eye-catching exterior, like an elegant curtain enveloping the structure. Inside, the house had a contemporary, high-end look with a strong Scandinavian accent, particularly through the use of light wood, light colour palette and iconic Danish furniture and lighting. Visitors were welcomed into the double-height hall area where they could chat with staff in the meeting area and bar. An adjacent lounge area hosted informal chats, and the walls throughout were adorned with digital screens – almost like artworks – that displayed Arting's portfolio. Wall panelling reflected the residential theme. During the fair, some of the design team relocated to the first floor design studio where they presented their work to potential clients face-to-face. The upper balcony offered a great overview of the interior. Arting successfully welcomed visitors into their personal world by making them feel completely at home, thus creating the positive brand experience they set out to achieve. ⟶

3 A balcony on the first floor provided the perfect vantage point to survey the interior.

4 The cosy lounge invited visitors to sit back and relax.

5 Seating areas were positioned throughout the house to host casual meetings.

3

4

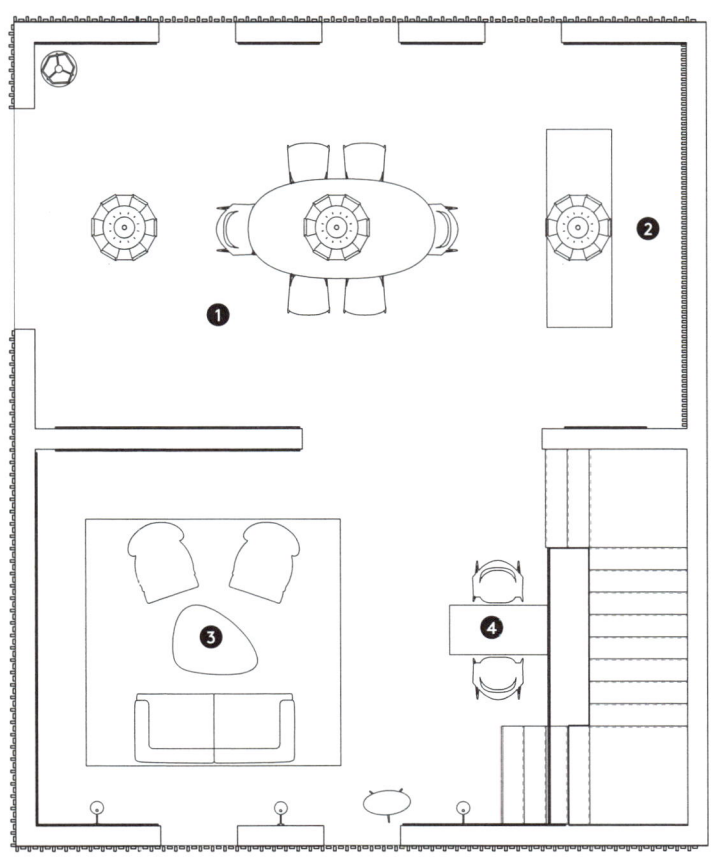

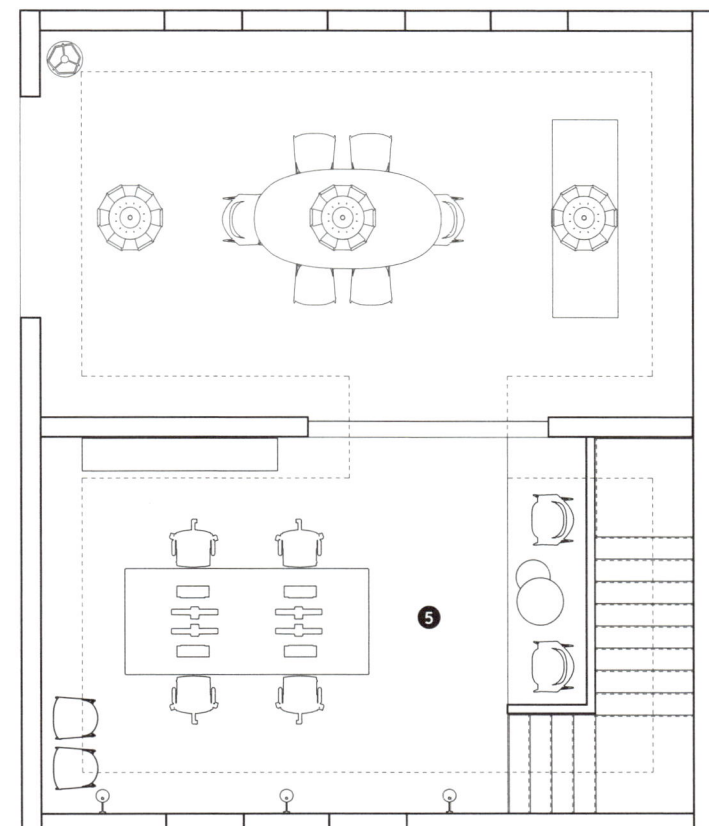

FLOOR PLAN

01   Hall
02   Bar
03   Lounge area
04   Sales area
05   Design office

5

VISITORS FEEL COMPLETELY AT HOME INSIDE THE 'HOUSE OF ARTING'

1

Drei Farben
für ein
besseres
Leben
Brot
für die Welt

2

Brot
für die Welt
2.700
Liter
Wasser werden für
die Herstellung von
1 Baumwollhemd
benötigt.
800
Millionen
Menschen weltweit
können weder lesen
noch schreiben.

3

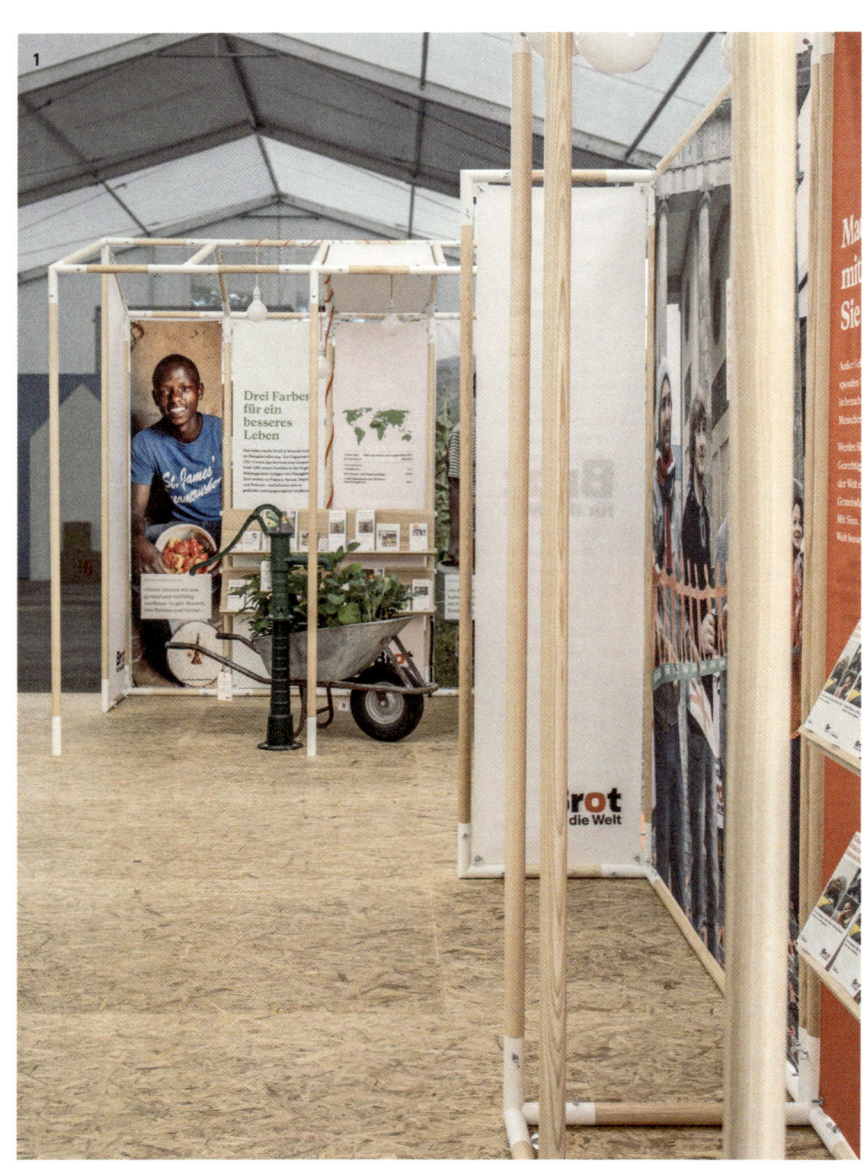

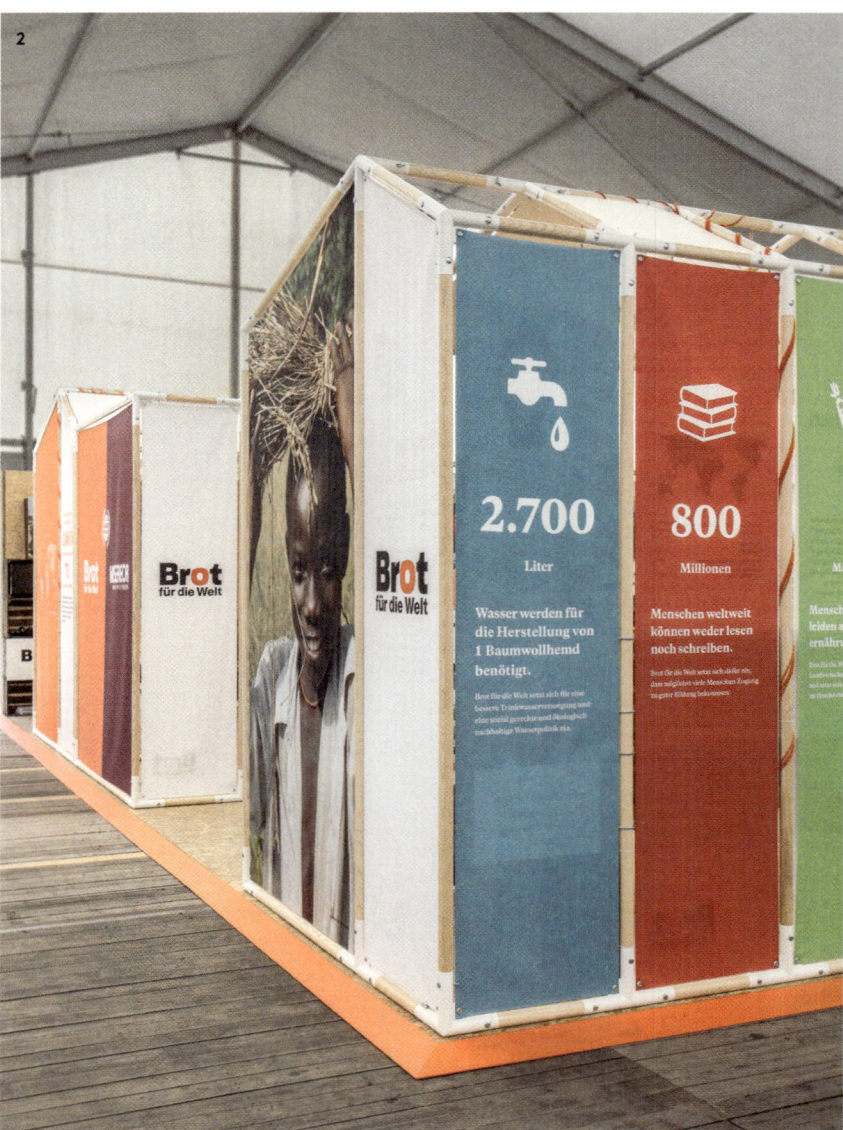

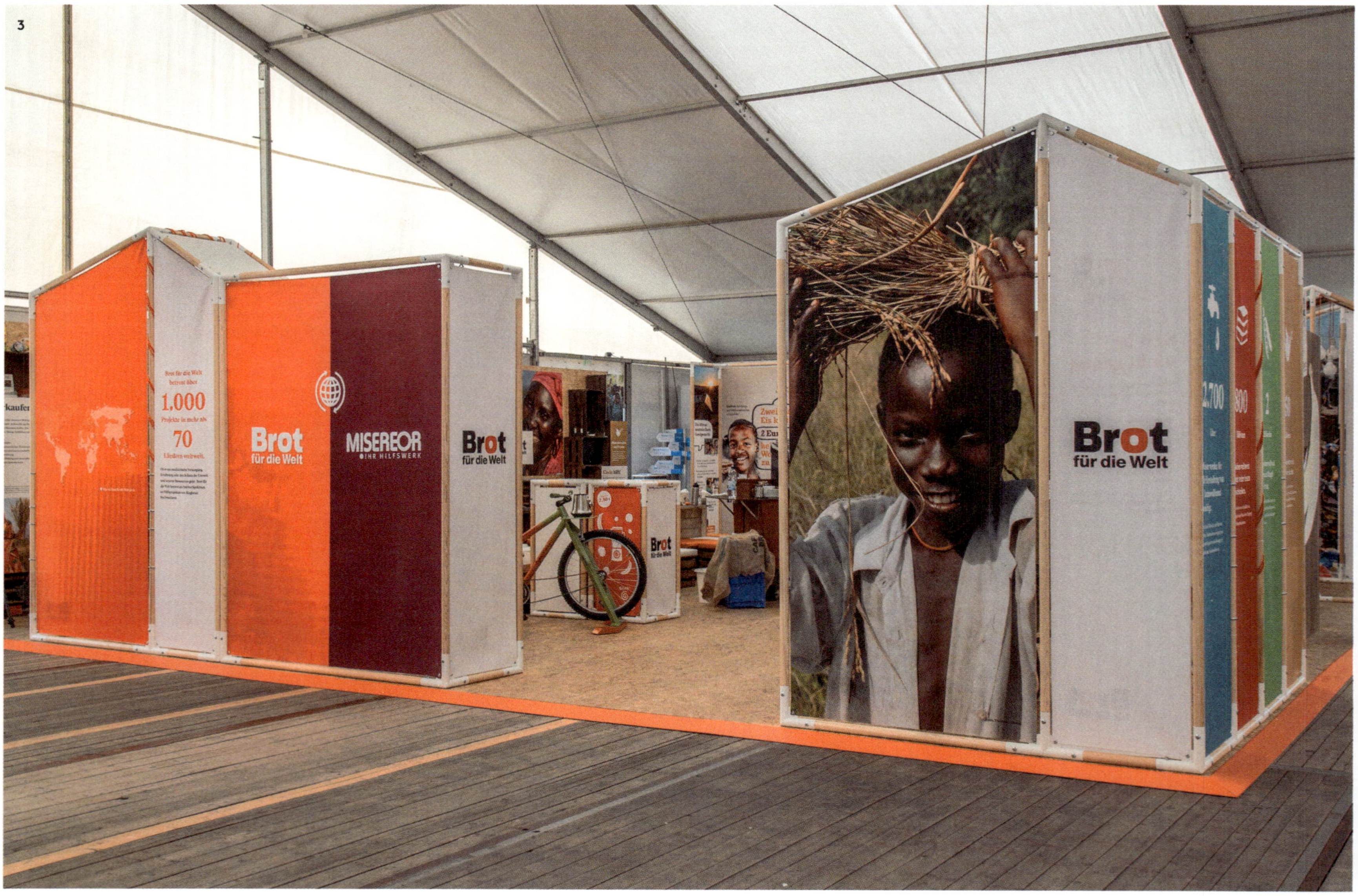
1.000
70
Brot
für die Welt
MISEREOR
IHR HILFSWERK
Brot
für die Welt
Brot
für die Welt

BROT FÜR DIE WELT

VON M and Gold & Wirtschaftswunder

4

1 The houses can be used on their own or combined to create a community.

2 Made from printed textile, engaging panels of content clad the houses and could be easily changed when needed.

3 Complementary displays can be easily added to the base presentation.

4 The stand was design with an easy, tool-free assembly in mind.

Brot für die Welt is the development and relief agency of the Protestant Churches in Germany. Active globally the organisation works in the fields of food security, promotion of health and education, access to water, strengthening of democracy, respecting human rights, keeping peace and integrity of creation. It's also a regular participant at different presentations ranging from small solo shows to large stands. For this reason the organisation needed a flexible exhibition system that could be adapted to the changing contexts of each event. VON M and Gold & Wirtschaftswunder were asked to develop a solution, which also should be assembled easily without any tools, is transportable and constructed from modest and sustainable materials. The system was to be launched at the German Protestant Kirchentag, a five-day biennial festival, where the organisation had a large stand. The designers looked to the tradition of basic mountain huts that provide shelter from the elements. Their design comprised a modular system based on the primary unit of a house, which functioned as a metaphor for shelter and safety, important themes of the organisation. Combining these units resulted in a village with, for example, a communal courtyard, which addresses the theme of community, another core focus. Custom designed, the base structure was constructed from ash wood rods joined with white metal connectors. Content could be easily added (and altered) as cladding on the walls and ceilings using printed textile panels fastened onto the connectors. Freestanding products, props and displays could furnish the houses and stand as and when needed. No tools were required for assembly or disassembly and the whole structure could be easily transported flatpack. This simple, modest presentation not only fulfilled the brief functionally, it wonderfully captured the social spirit of the organisation. ⌐

TRADE FAIR German Protestant Kirchentag
WHERE Stuttgart, Germany
WHEN June 2015
DESIGNERS VON M and Gold & Wirtschaftswunder
STAND CONSTRUCTOR Id3d
CLIENT Brot für die Welt
MARKET SECTOR Development assistance
TOTAL FLOOR AREA 120 m²
PHOTOGRAPHER Dennis Müller

CENTRICA ENERGY
Garp Design

1 The white and lime green palette of the structure, graphics and furnishings contributed a coherent aesthetic.

2 The stand maximised its compact footprint with a minimal, fresh design.

2

'Seismology and geology are not about one answer or one result, as different people see different things.' This quote from a geologist at Centrica Energy inspired the theme of the energy company's exhibition stand at ONS, the offshore oil and energy exhibition in Stavanger. As the event is important for meeting and establishing contacts for the future the company wanted to utilise the opportunity for building its brand and conveying its story. Centrica also wished for its stand to appear visually interesting and attractive to attract potential employees and collaborators.

The task for designing the stand was entrusted to Garp Design who used the quote as a starting point. Led by the theme 'Different Perspective' the design played with different perspective lines on the walls and floors. Open on two sides the compact stand was kept minimal with a fresh colour palette of lime green and white. Extending to the maximum allowable height, the high white folding walls drew attention to the stand. The distinctive green patterns and lines were derived from seismic/geological patterns from one of Centrica's big discoveries. On the wall a visual timeline depicted Centrica Energy's three main disciplines: Exploration & Discovery (light blue line); Development (dark blue line); and Production (green line). Suspended above was a prominent typography installation. Viewed from different directions the letters appeared as a cloud of white

spheres but when viewed frontally, the message of the theme appeared. The stand further accommodated an information desk, a back room and a small meeting area. A screen divider fashioned from blue and green textile ropes was used create more privacy for the seating area. Continuing the spherical theme and colour palette, coloured stress balls were distributed to visitors as branded giveaways. ⇒

TRADE FAIR **ONS**
WHERE **Stavanger, Norway**
WHEN **August 2014**
DESIGNER **Garp Design**
STAND CONSTRUCTOR **Garp Design**
CLIENT **Energy**
MARKET SECTOR **Energy**
TOTAL FLOOR AREA **42 m²**
PHOTOGRAPHER **Joakim Bjerk**

COSTA GROUP

Costa Group

Pizza, mozarella, gelato, polenta, desserts, cheese and coffee. The Costa Group's mouthwatering stand at Host delighted visitors with its delectable design, bustling vibe and focus on Italian delicacies. As a supplier of fittings and furnishings for the hospitality industry, the company wanted to showcase its wide spectrum of services at this international hospitality exhibition. The overarching concept presented a marketplace/food court composed of different hospitality concepts. In this way, the designers hoped to show how varying styles and atmospheres could coexist and complement each other. The interior

design took visitors on a sensorial journey through colours, textures, flavours and sounds to communicate the emotional appeal of the concepts and ingredients. Technology also played an important role in the experience. At Nando il Lattaio – the dairy – freshly creamed yogurts, fresh cheeses, ice cream and mozzarella were produced onsite in a lively open plan laboratory. The pizzeria was characterised by a rustic atmosphere and the classic cocktail bar featured dark timber finishes, dim lighting and a wall collage of old picture frames. In contrast, the bakery was designed like an elegant parlour. With its ornately carved timber counter and wood-panelled wall – and not to mention the scrumptious pastries exhibited in the chic glass display – the bakery exuded both warmth and sophistication. The organic brewery featured recyclable beer barrels and an industrial feel pervaded

the coffee section. Central to the presentation was a contrasting modern meeting area where clients could meet the managers of the different areas. Digital imagery on the wall behind the bar changed to convey different atmospheres and the dining table told stories about food through projections of three-dimensional textures. Visitors could also discover the production chain through a special mobile app. ⬌

TRADE FAIR **Host**
WHERE **Milan, Italy**
WHEN **October 2013**
DESIGNER **Costa Group**
STAND CONSTRUCTOR **Costa Group**
CLIENT **Costa Group**
MARKET SECTOR **Design**
TOTAL FLOOR AREA **636 m²**
PHOTOGRAPHER **Stefano Aiti**

2

3

4

A BUSTLING MARKETPLACE
WITH A DELECTABLE DESIGN
AND FOCUS ON ITALIAN
DELICACIES

3 With its contrasting contemporary feel the central meeting area utilised digital projectors to change the atmosphere of the space.

4 Dark metal coffee silos contributed to the industrial feel of the coffee section.

5 The light, elegant bakery complemented the dark, classic cocktail bar.

6 The bakery's high level of detailing was accompanied by an irresistible display of pastries.

5

D'ART DESIGN GRUPPE

D'art Design Gruppe

1 Wooden toy blocks playfully echoed the architecture of the stand.

2 Planes of spruce were artfully slotted together to create the stand.

2

For its own presentation at EuroShop 2014 D'art Design Gruppe chose the theme of 'Undo' to visualise the design process. Wanting to provide an insight into how creatives think and work, the spatial communication studio developed a thoughtful multimedia concept for visitors to experience its brand.

Considering this was D'art Design's eighth consecutive appearance at EuroShop, the challenge was to create a unique experience that would once again surprise visitors and improve upon previous years' efforts; this year's stand did not disappoint. A huge wooden structure composed of stacked spruce walls housed the presentation. The strong architecture of the 5.6-metre-high installation recalled a playful tower of children's wooden blocks, immediately triggering people's curiosity. Access points were created in the structure through strategically staggering the planes. Playing with the theme, the semi-finished look of the architecture suggested that the building had the potential be reworked or redone with ease at any moment.

Inside a light, warm atmosphere pervaded the space thanks to the singular use of spruce across the entire interior, from the floors, walls and ceilings to the furniture. Instead of seeing an 'analogue' portfolio of D'art Design's work, visitors surprisingly encountered a digital presentation. Equipped with tablets, they were directed along a path of QR codes on the surrounding exhibition walls. These codes gave access to D'art Design's digital realm that explored creative processes and showcased its work. Afterwards visitors were invited for drinks and bites at the communal table, and to play the game of 'Undo' by stacking the wooden blocks – or take one home for inspiration. With its innovative stand that was both a digital and tangible playground D'art Design yet again set itself big shoes to fill for the coming years. ▬

TRADE FAIR **EuroShop**
WHERE **Düsseldorf, Germany**
WHEN **February 2014**
DESIGNER **D'art Design Gruppe**
STAND CONSTRUCTOR **Projektpilot**
CLIENT **D'art Design Gruppe**
MARKET SECTOR **Design**
TOTAL FLOOR AREA **247 m²**
PHOTOGRAPHER **Lukas Palik**

4

5

3 Key words associated with the design process were printed onto the blocks.

4 Using tablets, visitors entered D'art Design's digital presentation following a trail of QR codes.

5 The design skilfully contrasted technology with the tangible, human quality of the space and material.

6 A communal table with desktops and central lighting installation was the focal point of the interior.

THE STAND IS BOTH A DIGITAL AND TANGIBLE PLAYGROUND

6

1

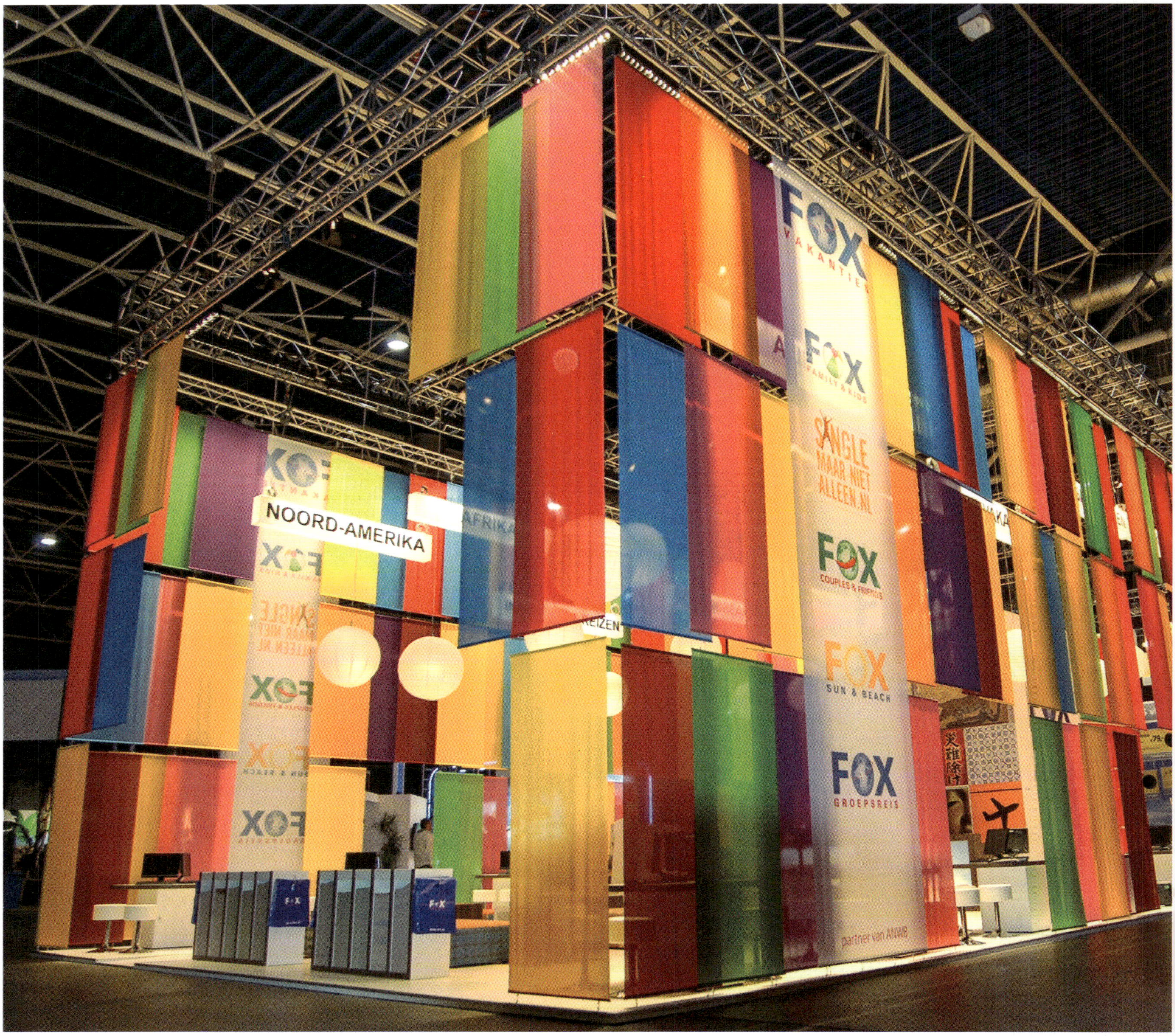
NOORD-AMERIKA
AFRIKA
REIZEN
FOX
VAKANTIES
FAMILY & KIDS
SINGLE
MAAR NIET
ALLEEN.NL
COUPLES & FRIENDS
SUN & BEACH
GROEPSREIS
partner van ANWB

2

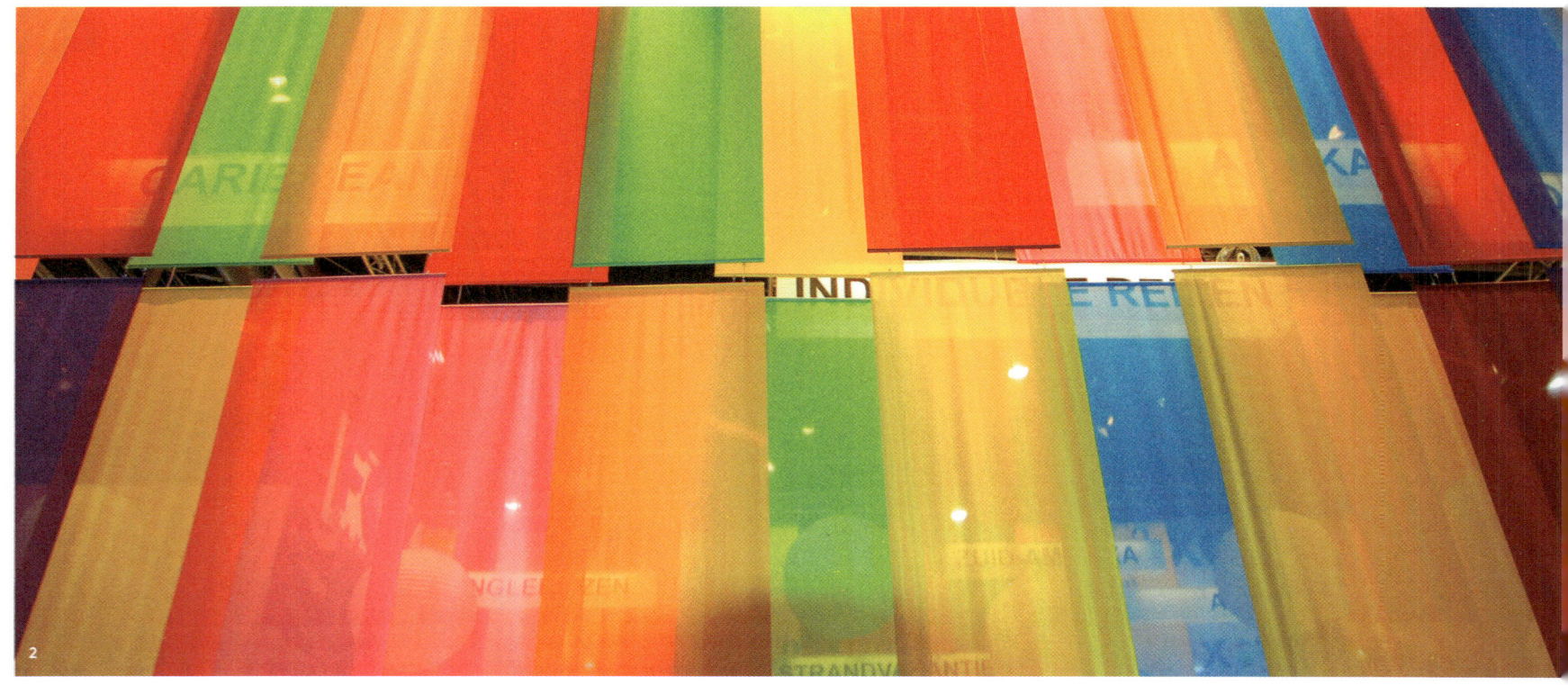

FOX
Qupix

TRADE FAIR **Vakantiebeurs**
WHERE **Utrecht, the Netherlands**
WHEN **January 2014**
DESIGNER **Qupix**
STAND CONSTRUCTOR **Yaro Interieurbouw**
CLIENT **Fox**
MARKET SECTOR **Travel agency**
TOTAL FLOOR AREA **220 m²**
PHOTOGRAPHER **Qupix**

Fox is a European tour operator specialising in high quality, long-distance package holidays. Qupix were onboard in 2014 to design Fox's stand at the Vakantiebeurs, a Dutch consumer travel fair. As the company operates an online booking platform, its presence at Vakantiebeurs is important for engaging both suppliers and clients directly. In this way, it was important that the design of the stand be engaging, inviting and interactive, and especially cater to the consumer audience. Pragmatically, the brief required sufficient computer terminals to serve the high number of visitors. Design-wise, the client wanted the spatial concept of the stand to reflect its corporate office. In this way Qupix incorporated architectural elements from the building into the design, combining it with a lively travel experience. A striking layered skin of colourful textiles immediately made a big impression – this referred to the glazed facade of the company's office building. At either end of the stand two openings guided visitors into the space while smaller openings on the lower tier of textiles framed the interior. Inside a burst of colour and imagery awaited, creating a holiday-like mood. Travel snapshots adorned a high partition, the furniture and flooring underneath it, evoking the spirit of travel. Circular paper lanterns added an exotic touch. Two long rows of computers lining the perimeters of the stand ensured there were enough terminals for visitors to research destinations or make bookings. Behind the wall at the back of the stand was the Theatre, which resembled an oversized lantern. Covered in textiles, this voluminous curved red structure hosted the Wheel of Fortune which tempted clients to win a trip or discounts on their bookings. With its cheerful, fun interior Fox's stand gave visitors a festive start to their dream holiday. ⇒

1/2 The stand's multicoloured facade was unmissable at the Vakantiebeurs.

3 Casual seating in the central zone offered space for informal chats and chilling out.

3

A BURST OF COLOUR AND IMAGERY CREATED A HOLIDAY-LIKE MOOD

4 Fox's new head office by William McDonough & Partners was a source of inspiration for the stand design.

CONCEPT SKETCHES

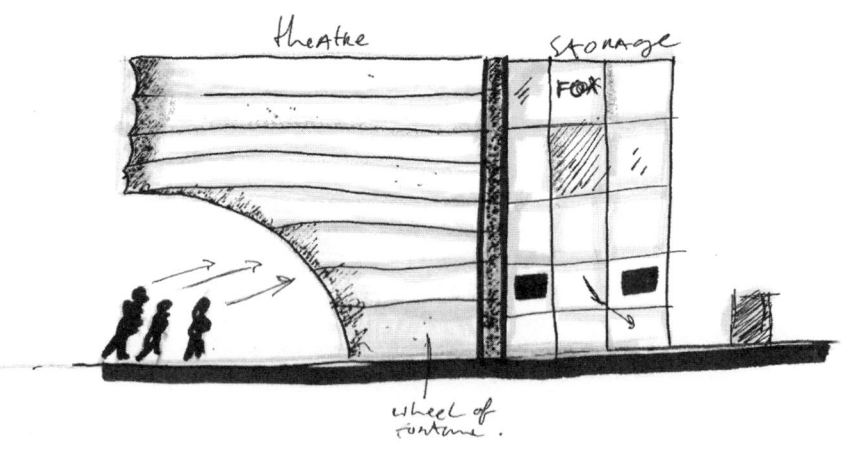

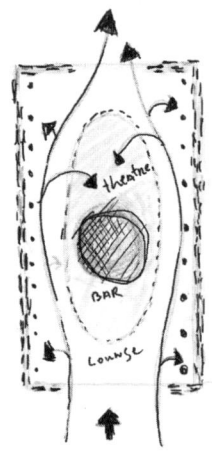

FLOOR PLAN

01 Workstations
02 Lounge area
03 Bar
04 Storage
05 Wheel of fortune
06 Destinations

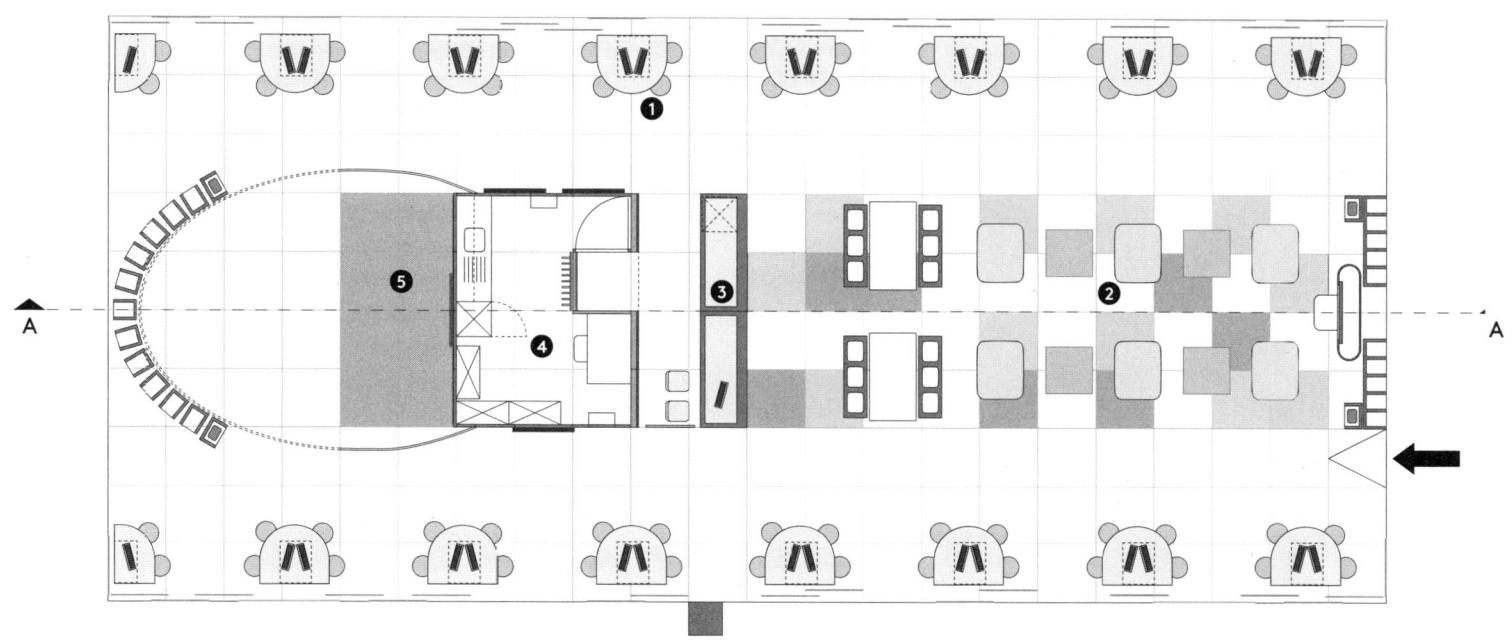

SECTION A

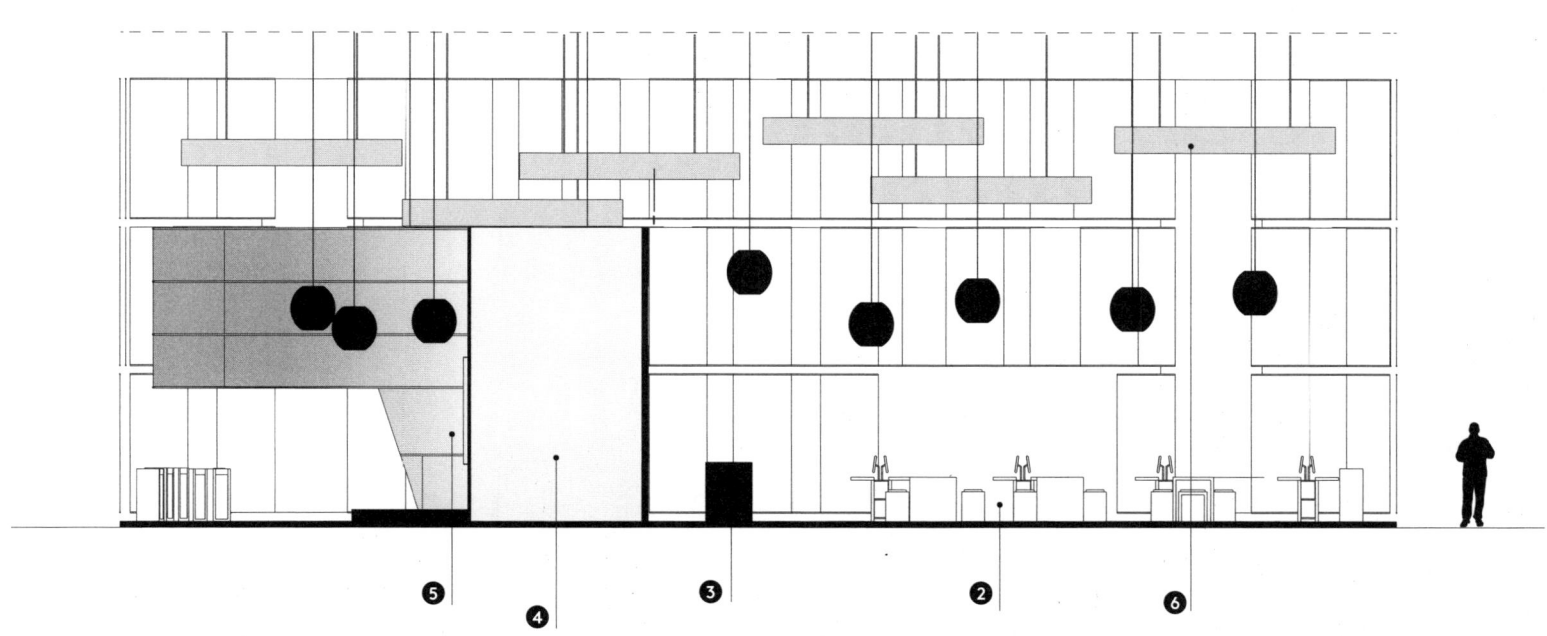

GASSCO
Garp Design

TRADE FAIR **ONS**
WHERE **Stavanger, Norway**
WHEN **August 2014**
DESIGNER **Garp Design**
STAND CONSTRUCTOR **Garp Design**
CLIENT **Gassco**
MARKET SECTOR **Gas transportation**
TOTAL FLOOR AREA **155 m²**
PHOTOGRAPHER **Joakim Bjerk**

1 The stand was characterised by an open uncluttered design and focus on natural materials.

2 'About a Stool' barstools from Hay furnish the reception desk

2

Gassco and Garp Design have a longstanding relationship regarding the gas transporting company's stand at the international offshore oil and energy exhibition Offshore Northern Seas (ONS) in Stavanger. In 2014 it was Gassco's wish to have an open and inviting stand, a highly functional meeting point for both visitors and staff. The stand's main purpose was to communicate a positive brand experience and uphold the company's reputation as a reliable gas transporter in Europe. Timeless natural materials, used against an elegant curved black backdrop, expressed its identity and core values. Elements like wood and stone represented the reliability, credibility, genuineness and nature of Norway. The curved information desk formed a spectacular eye-catcher, composed from 196 slats of natural and painted birch. Emerging from the wall, the sculptural desk had a floating form that echoed the organic shape of the stand. The natural wall cladding and upstairs screen made from slim timber battens complemented the desk well. On the wall a striking installation fashioned from Norwegian slate and oak formed a graphic map of Gassco's gas transportation system. Visitors were immediately drawn to its tactile quality. The map plays an important role in depicting Norway's gas export and the company's activities, and each year it takes on a different form. The slate was cut into strips that were mounted in milled grooves in the wall while rounded oak dots indicated the destinations. A trivia game on a large touch screen encouraged activity and interaction on site. The upstairs lounge area – a first for the stand – furnished with brightly coloured furniture that reflected the corporate colours worked perfectly for more private meetings. The warm, inviting atmosphere of the stand successfully captured Norway's down-to-earth nature. ➥

TIMELESS NATURAL MATERIALS EXPRESS THE COMPANY'S IDENTITY AND CORE VALUES

3 Thanks to its organic design, the space changed appearance depending on the angle of the viewer.

4 A generous use of wood created a warm, down-to-earth atmosphere.

5 Upstairs, the meeting area invited clients and guests for more private meetings.

6 The map of Gassco's transportation network was beautifully crafted from slate and oak from Norway.

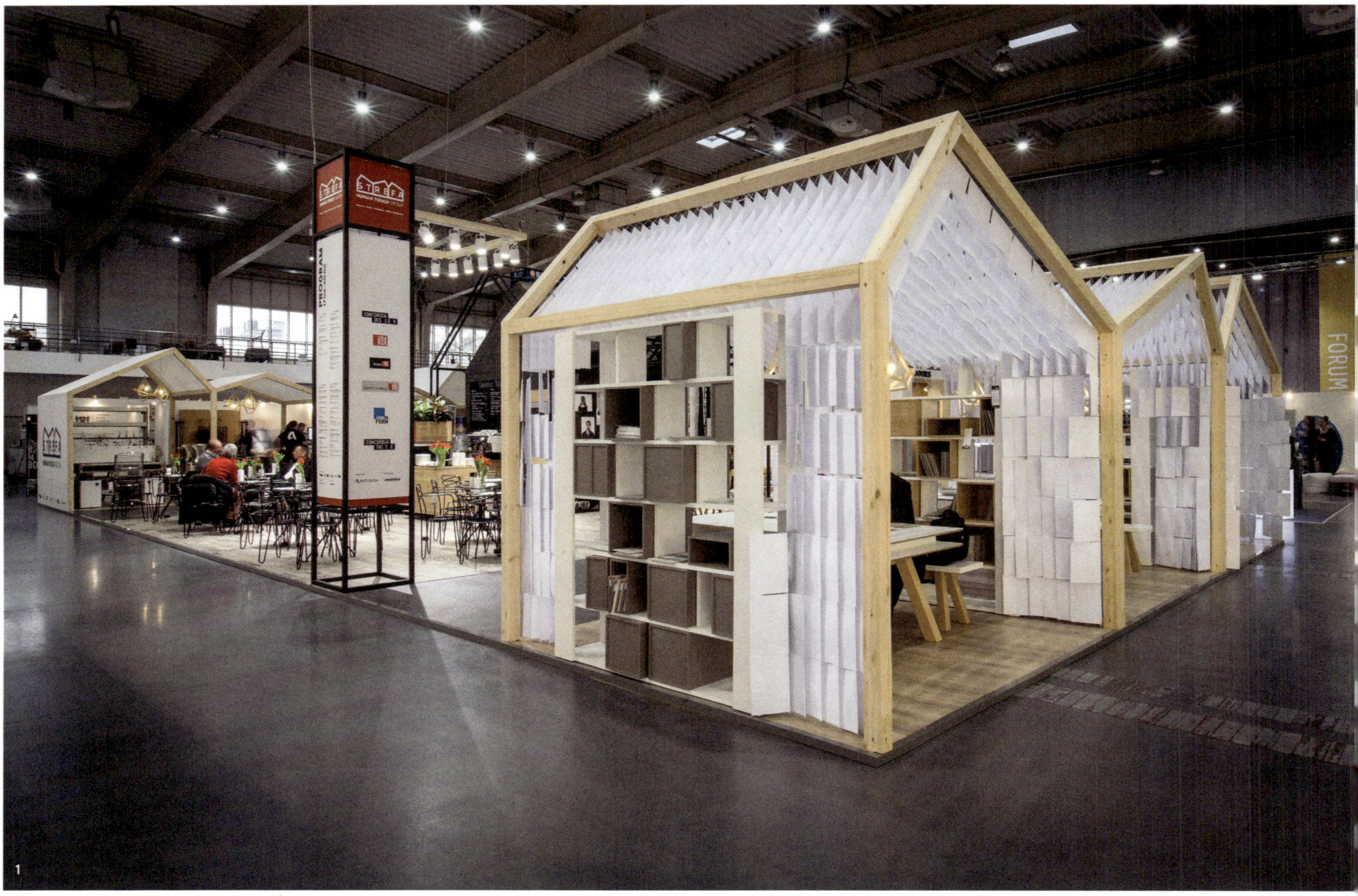

1

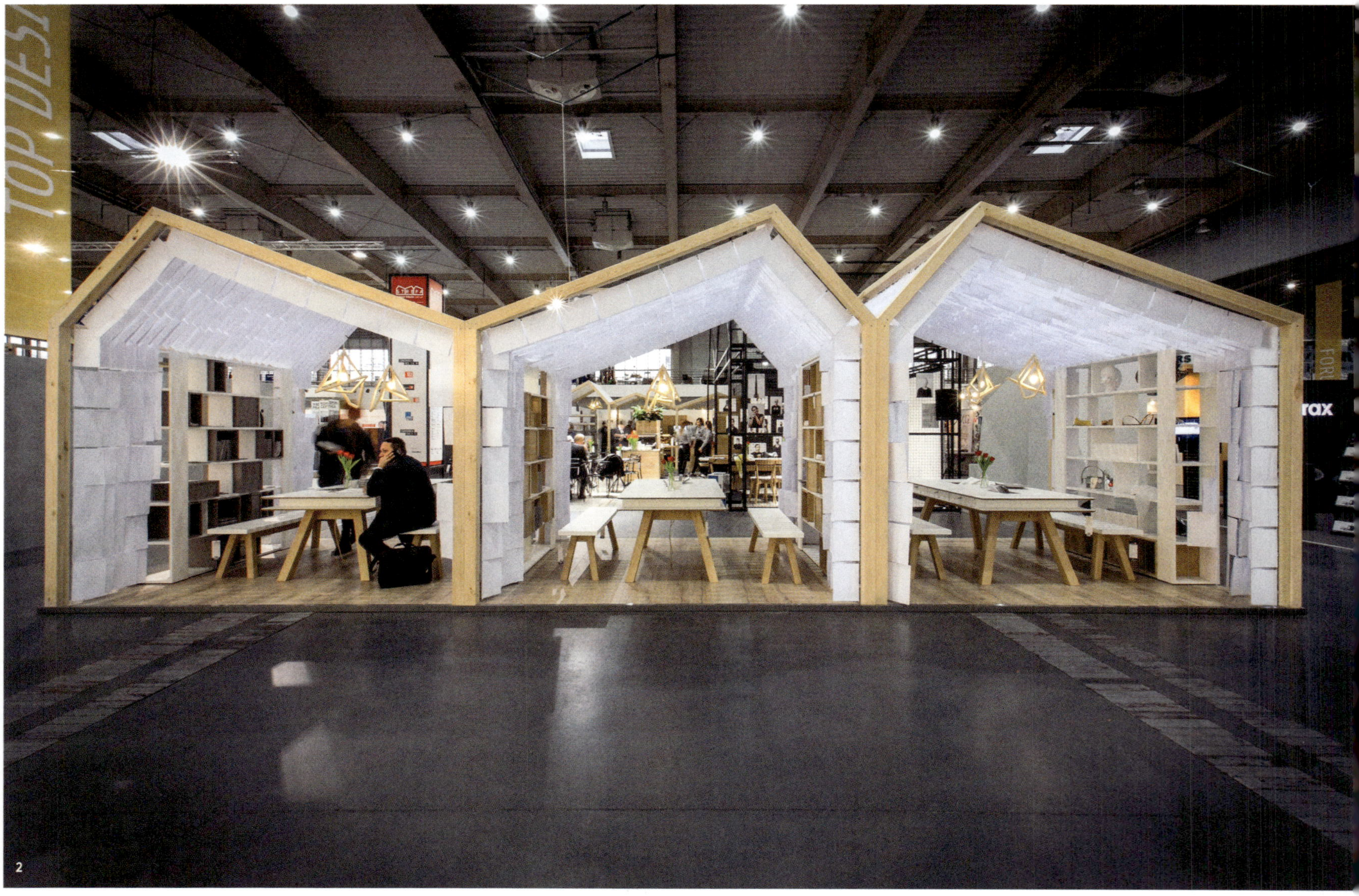

2

HUMAN TOUCH GROUP
mode:lina architekci

1/2 Open structures maintained a flow of space through the stand and resulted in a lively layered dynamic.

3 The biggest houses were constructed from black steel while the perimeter houses were made from wood, textile and paper.

3

Human Touch Group (HTG) is a business-focused connection between companies, schools and organisations that cooperate with the Vox Capital Group, which operates in the construction materials and interior design sector. At Arena Design in Poznań, a business forum for producers and designers, HTG wanted to demonstrate the multifaceted quality of the organisation to an audience of architects, designers and design graduates and students. For the design of the stand, mode:lina architekci took a cue from its location at the event. HTG was allocated a very central space in the fair hall beside important activity areas and pedestrian routes – this prompted the designers to start with an open format to maintain an uninterrupted flow of space. Furthermore, as the client requested a restaurant area, this supported the idea of a public square to capture a communal atmosphere. The result was a lively micro-city that was anchored by a piazza surrounded by a cafe and a series of small-scale houses. Each of the houses accommodated different functions ranging from meeting rooms to exhibition stalls. Natural, tactile materials and warm lighting created an inviting and intimate atmosphere. A visual highlight was the wooden houses clad with rows of 'tiles' made from stapled paper – 4500 sheets in total. In order to maintain the openness of the stand and flow of space, the houses were also designed with open structures, especially for elevations facing the corridors. Throughout the day the stand buzzed with activity as visitors arrived to take part in workshops and meetings, browse the presentations or simply enjoy a coffee – visitors probably felt so at home in this mini-city that they didn't want to leave. ⬭

TRADE FAIR **arena Design**
WHERE **Poznań, Poland**
WHEN **February 2015**
DESIGNER **mode:lina architekci**
STAND CONSTRUCTOR **Smart Design Expo**
CLIENT **Meble Vox**
MARKET SECTOR **Education**
TOTAL FLOOR AREA **200 m²**
PHOTOGRAPHER **Marcin Ratajczak**

4

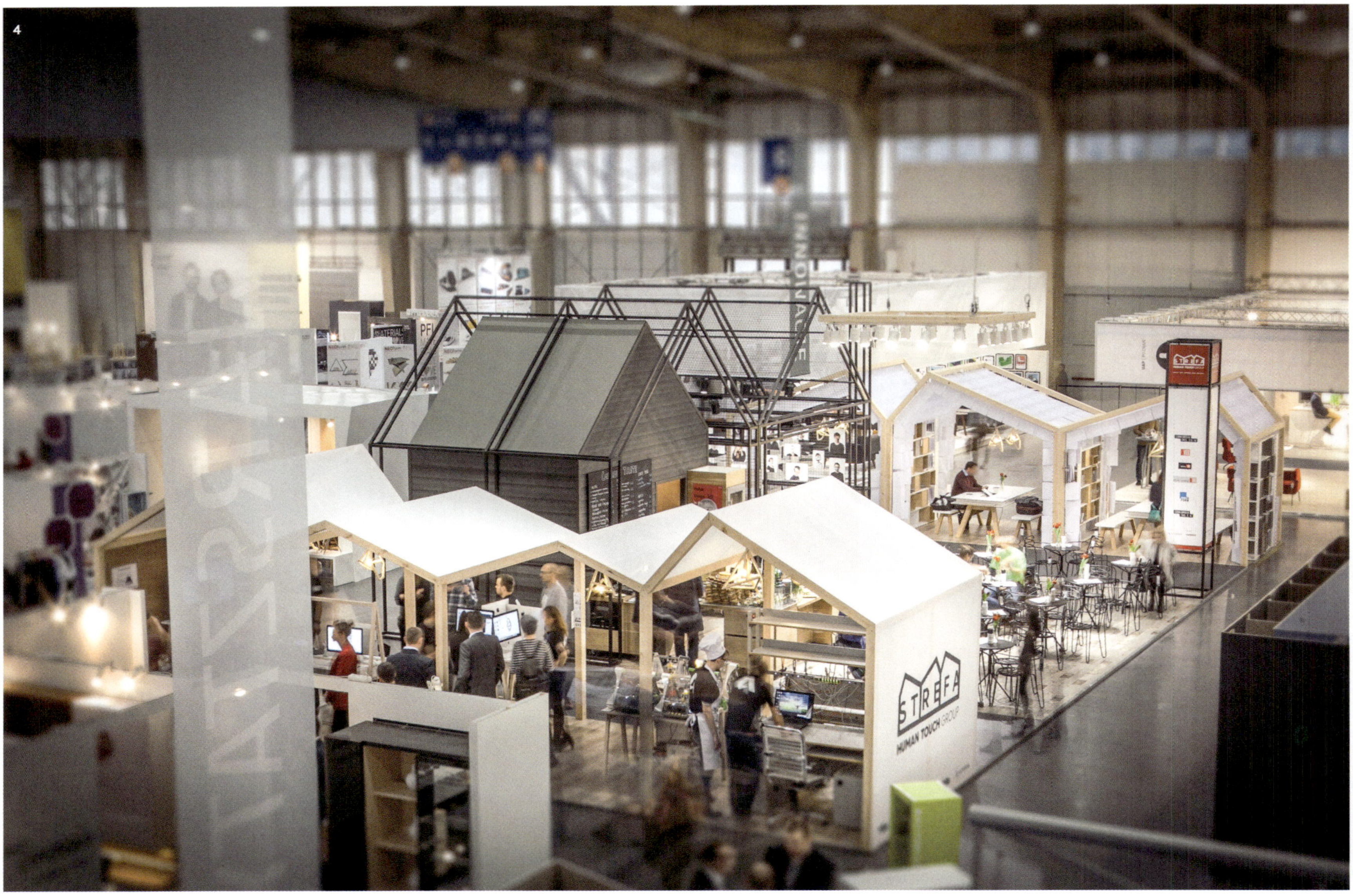

5

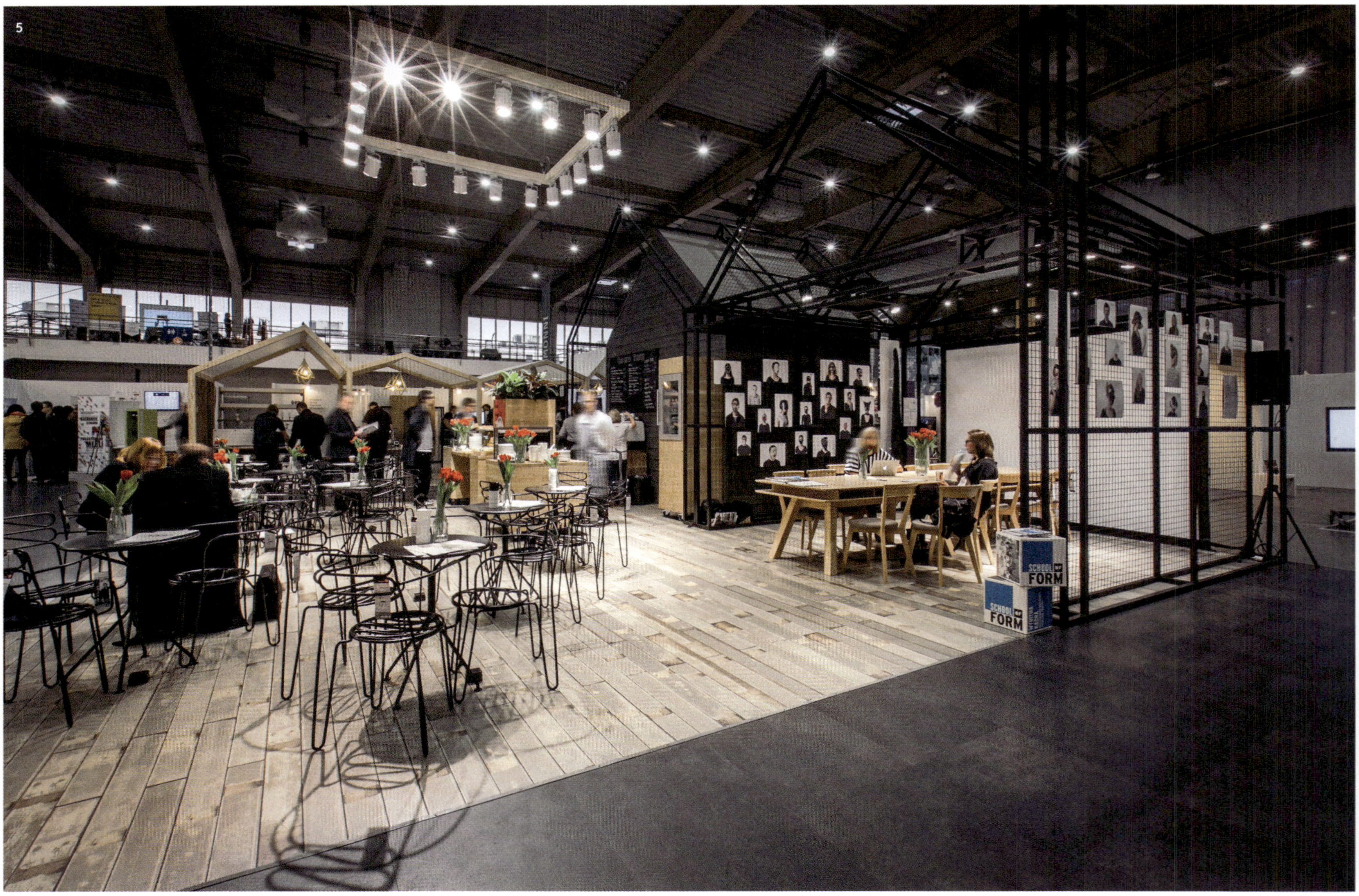

4 The stand was a buzzing micro-city that showcased the multifaceted quality of the organisation.

5 Visitors were invited to engage in various activities on the stand ranging from meetings and workshops to simply enjoying lunch.

6/7 Details of the wood-and-paper houses.

8 With a wonderfully textured surface, the paper cladding was fashioned from 4500 stapled sheets of paper.

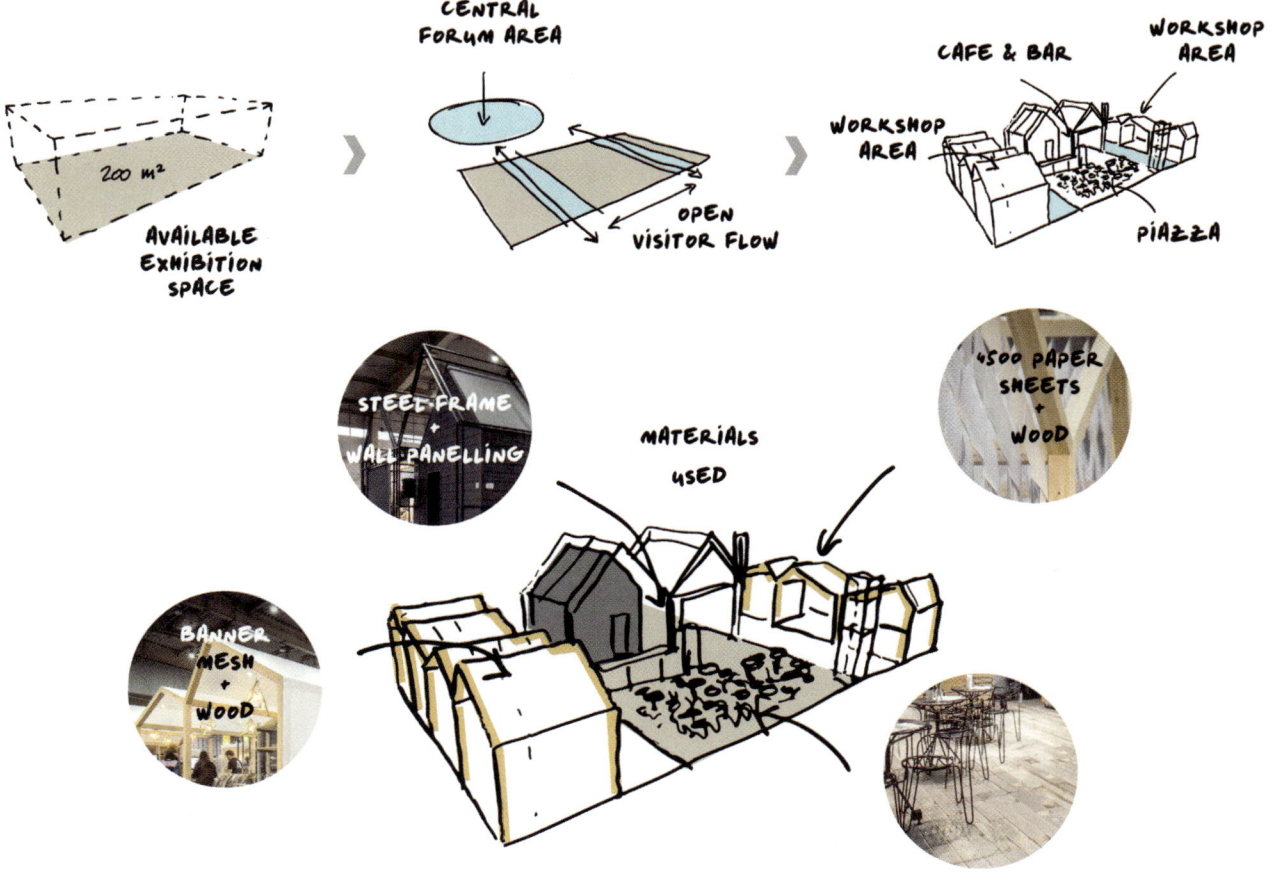

THE LIVELY MICRO-CITY
BUZZES WITH ACTIVITY

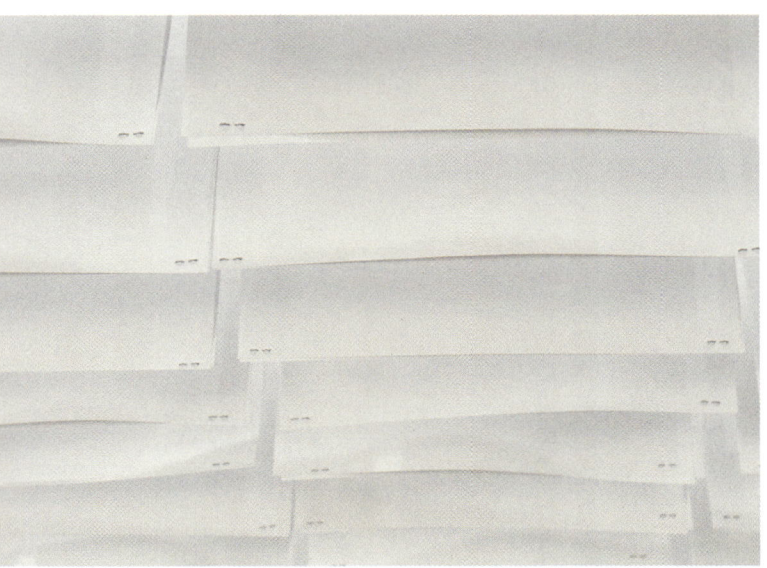

6

7

8

KPLUS KONZEPT

kplus konzept

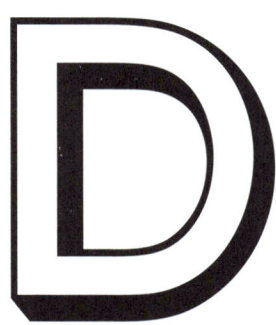

D

'Discover New Spaces' was the motto of kplus konzept's first presentation at EuroShop. This creative guiding principle reflected the company's expertise in staging brand environments; here visitors were invited to discover the experience for themselves. The objective was to communicate the kplus konzept approach to the target group, and give it maximum presence on a compact stand of 18 m². The main aim was to arouse curiosity and appeal to the senses. In this way the stand was designed as a multi-sensory experience that opened up new perspectives for the audience.

The booth was structured into three themed worlds that corresponded with three mysterious elevated white boxes positioned centrally in the space. Visitors accessed these worlds by climbing up the ladders and poking their heads inside. Each box revealed a different landscape of scents and sounds, with the colours used representing the company's visual identity. The 1970s pink pop world was filled with plush disco balls, spotlights, lava lamps and the smell of candy. The green world was a humid jungle inhabited by 32 different cultivars, sound and scent landscapes of humming flies, chirping birds, musty nature and RGB LED lamps that simulated the changing daylight. A third contrasting black-and-white techno world had a matching soundscape and semi-transparent mirrors that reflected kaleidoscope-like optical effects. Pink, the main corporate colour, was reiterated

on the stand's bright backdrop that was composed of a bold grid filled with colours and textures. This graphic and sensory format worked across all cultures without any language barriers, ideal for the international clientele of the show. By allowing visitors to interact with the presentation, kplus konzept successfully achieved its aim to initiate dialogue with its target audience. ▬

TRADE FAIR **EuroShop**
WHERE **Düsseldorf, Germany**
WHEN **February 2014**
DESIGNER **kplus konzept**
STAND CONSTRUCTOR **Carpentry Tischlerei Grünert**
CLIENT **kplus konzept**
MARKET SECTOR **Design**
TOTAL FLOOR AREA **18 m²**
PHOTOGRAPHER **Kratz Photographie**

1 The graphic and sensory design appealed to the target audience and enticed people onto the stand.

2 The company's logo in black was cleverly integrated onto exterior of the white boxes.

2

VISITORS POKE THEIR HEADS INTO MYSTERIOUS WHITE BOXES TO DISCOVER THEMED WORLDS

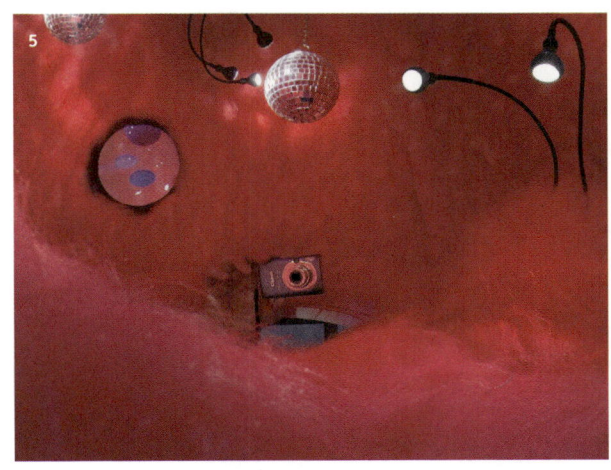

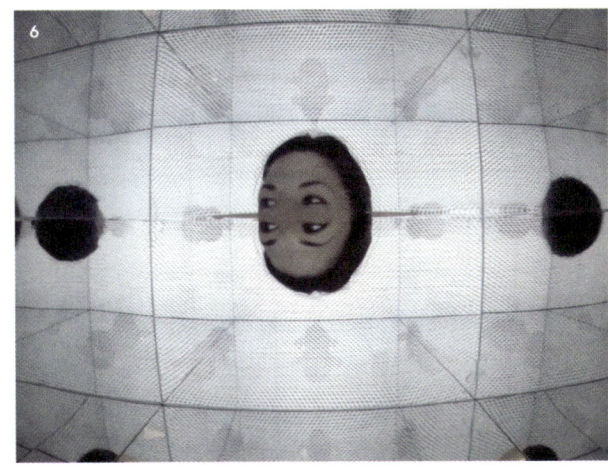

3 The interactive stand was popular with fairgoers.

4 The green jungle box.

5 The pink pop box.

6 The black techno box.

GROUPE
Caisse desDépôts
TRANSITION ENERGETIQUE ET ECOLOGIE
Immobilier public
Actualité
1

GROUPE
Caisse desDépôts
INFRASTRUCTURES
Projets de long terme
Retraite des collectivités locales
GROUPE
Caisse desDépôts
GESTIONNAIRE DE CONFIANCE
Consignations
ECO CONÇU
2

LE GROUPE CAISSE DES DÉPÔTS

3Design and eko Design

1 A palette of bright colours was used to structure the presentation into clear themed areas.

2 The curved ceiling shifted form in response to the different zones below.

3 The lanterns also concealed unsightly services and underceilings.

3

The Caisse des Dépôts group is a public group serving the general interest and economic development of France. Its brief to 3Design and eko Design for its presence at the Salon des Maires et des Collectivités Locales – a fair for the public sector in France – was to design a booth that represented the complexity and sizeable nature of the organisation in a simple and playful way. It was integral that the presentation be easily understandable for visitors – a challenge given the diverse identity of the organisation, which is composed of over 20 brands and services. The exhibition hall's low ceilings also restricted the ceiling height to a maximum of four metres. As a starting point, five themes were identified that covered every activity of the organisation: housing, information, infrastructure, mandate manager and energy transition. Subsequently these themes were used to structure the space in combination with different colours assigned to identify each theme. Applied to the signage pillars and carpets, the colours ensured the clear distinction of each zone. Unifying the stand was an undulating ceiling of illuminated white paper lanterns. Echoing the form of the signage pillars, the lanterns served multiple functions at different levels. Viewed from a distance, the glowing ceiling marked the stand and caught the attention of visitors. Internally, the ceiling ensured good lighting and sound insulation, curved according to the zones below to further define the spaces and created an intimate atmosphere. Sustainability was an integral part of the design hence every element was designed to avoid waste and produce low carbon emissions. Environmentally friendly paint was used, rented carpet tiles were installed on a recycled platform, lighting was designed to minimise energy consumption and the use of paper and cardboard reduced transportation weight. ▬

TRADE FAIR **Salon des Maires et des Collectivités Locales**
WHERE **Paris, France**
WHEN **November 2014**
DESIGNERS **3Design and eko Design**
STAND CONSTRUCTOR **Mythiqs**
CLIENT **Le Groupe Caisse des Dépôts**
MARKET SECTOR **Public sector**
TOTAL FLOOR AREA **180 m²**
PHOTOGRAPHERS **Jean-Yves Giscard and David Durand**

CONTENT THAT USERS EXPECT
Firefox

1

Firefox OS
UNLEASH THE FUTURE
EXTINTOR

2

MOZILLA

2LK Design

1 Immediately recognisable by visitors, Mozilla's playful fox successfully attracted attention to the stand.

2 Participants gathered in the Fox Den for forums, discussions, product launches and other events.

3 The lounge provided a private and completely soundproof room to conduct meetings.

3

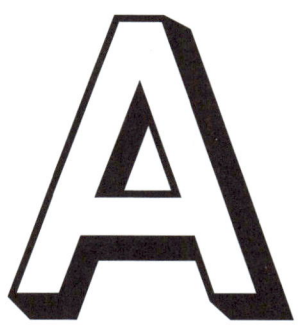

At the 2015 Mobile World Congress, Mozilla aimed to leverage the event as an opportunity to inspire brand advocates and drive business growth. The purpose was to articulate the power of 'open mobility' – enabled by Firefox OS, launch new devices, welcome partners and showcase future applications that go 'beyond mobile'. The brief to designers 2LK Design was to translate the company's core values and qualities – fun, confident, spirited and playfully disruptive – into an engaging and connected visitor experience, with a special focus on the B2B audience. 'Unleashing the Fox' was

the main design strategy – literally and figuratively. Suspended playfully above the stand, Firefox's signature brand icon formed the unmissable focal point of the space. With its giant illuminated tail wrapping around the 400 m² stand, the fiery orange beast definitely put a big smile on visitors' faces. The rest of the space was intentionally kept simple, with wide use of bold blue to reflect the brand personality and maintain focus on the fox. Square white pedestals were positioned centrally to clearly present devices showcasing the new OS. Integral to the stand was the 'Fox Den' – a mini event space that hosted presentations, product trials and technology forums. The trademark blue and orange colour scheme was applied here to the low seating and walls with vibrant, eye-catching graphics. Adjacent was the lounges and meeting rooms that were

designed to meet the client's rigorous requirements for soundproofing. External walls were transformed into a gallery where huge canvas prints by international artists depicted visions of inspiration, innovation and freedom – values integral to Mozilla's mission. ⚊

TRADE FAIR **Mobile World Congress**
WHERE **Barcelona, Spain**
WHEN **March 2015**
DESIGNER **2LK Design**
STAND CONSTRUCTOR **Central Display**
CLIENT **Mozilla**
MARKET SECTOR **Online**
TOTAL FLOOR AREA **400 m²**
PHOTOGRAPHER **Steve Eastell**

NÜRNBERGMESSE

Ueberholz

1 Floating bottles were given away as souvenirs to visitors.

2 The 3000 empty PET water bottles were reused after the exhibition.

Ueberholz was commissioned to create a special exhibition at CO-Reach 2014 for the event organizer NürnbergMesse, who wanted to highlight the rebranding of the dialogue marketing fair. The presentation should also focus on the topic of cross-media. Research for the design of the stand was led by the question: 'How do we communicate in 2030?' The response 'There is a message in a bottle for you on the web' referred to the use of cross-media, whereby an old-fashioned message in a bottle and digital communication are both communicative devices. At the exhibition, visitors encountered a luminous cloud suspended over a dark pool of water. Floating in the pool were small bottles containing printed answers to the question. At the same time, visitors were invited to use the iPad to formulate their own answers, which were then projected onto the water surface. Above the water, a large cloud of 3000 suspended PET water bottles visualised both the idea of a digital cloud but also the bottles used for placing messages. Spotlights above shone through the upside down bottles to simulate the effect of a luminous cloud. Stepped plywood seating allowed visitors to rest by the water and take a break from the busy fair. By pairing the digital theme and projection technology with natural experiences such as the play of light, lapping water and tangible materials, this created an accessible way for visitors to relate to the complex theme of cross-media. ⚊

2

TRADE FAIR **CoReach**
WHERE **Nuremberg, Germany**
WHEN **June 2014**
DESIGNER **Ueberholz**
STAND CONSTRUCTOR **Ueberholz**
CLIENT **NürnbergMesse**
MARKET SECTOR **Dialogue marketing**
TOTAL FLOOR AREA **47 m²**
PHOTOGRAPHER **Frank Dora**

SRG DEUTSCHSCHWEIZ

Space4

1 The maze was filled with life-size images of Swiss public figures.

2 The roadshow travelled to five trade fairs in Switzerland.

2

SRG Deutschschweiz (the German-speaking division of the Swiss Radio and Broadcasting Corporation) used its roadshow entitled A Mirror of Switzerland to present itself to the general public as a trustee for the country's public service radio and television stations at various large consumer exhibitions in Switzerland. The roadshow travelled to five fairs starting in St Gallen at OLMA, the Swiss Trade Fair for Agriculture and Food, and ending in Bern at BEA, Switzerland's largest spring fair. Designed by Space4 the exhibition illustrated the significance of radio and television through a multisensorial experience. The concept evoked the hall of mirrors and played with people's memories of Swiss media. The mirrors are infamous attractions from funfairs and carnivals, which share roots with the origins of consumer trade fairs, and also functioned to visualise the depictive qualities of radio and television. The main part of the stand was set up as an intriguing maze of mirrors. Navigating through the maze visitors saw not only their own reflections but encountered life-size models of public figures from Swiss media history from politics, film and entertainment, sports and business. At the same time, visitors themselves became part of the exhibition while reflected in the installation. In this way, everyday people and celebrities merged to form one overall picture of the Swiss German media landscape. The heart of the maze concealed a special surprise. In this black room, hidden projectors showed iconic footage from Swiss television history taken from the SRG archives. Using a white A3 piece of cardboard visitors moved through the space until they could 'catch' and view the film clips, which brought fond memories for many Swiss television viewers. ⬢

TRADE FAIR **BEA**
WHERE **Bern, Switzerland**
WHEN **April 2015**
DESIGNERS **Space4 with teamstratenwerth**
STAND CONSTRUCTOR **Hospes Team**
CLIENT **teamstratenwerth on behalf of the Regional Board of SRG Deutschschweiz**
MARKET SECTOR **Media**
TOTAL FLOOR AREA **80 m²**
PHOTOGRAPHER **Damian Poffet**

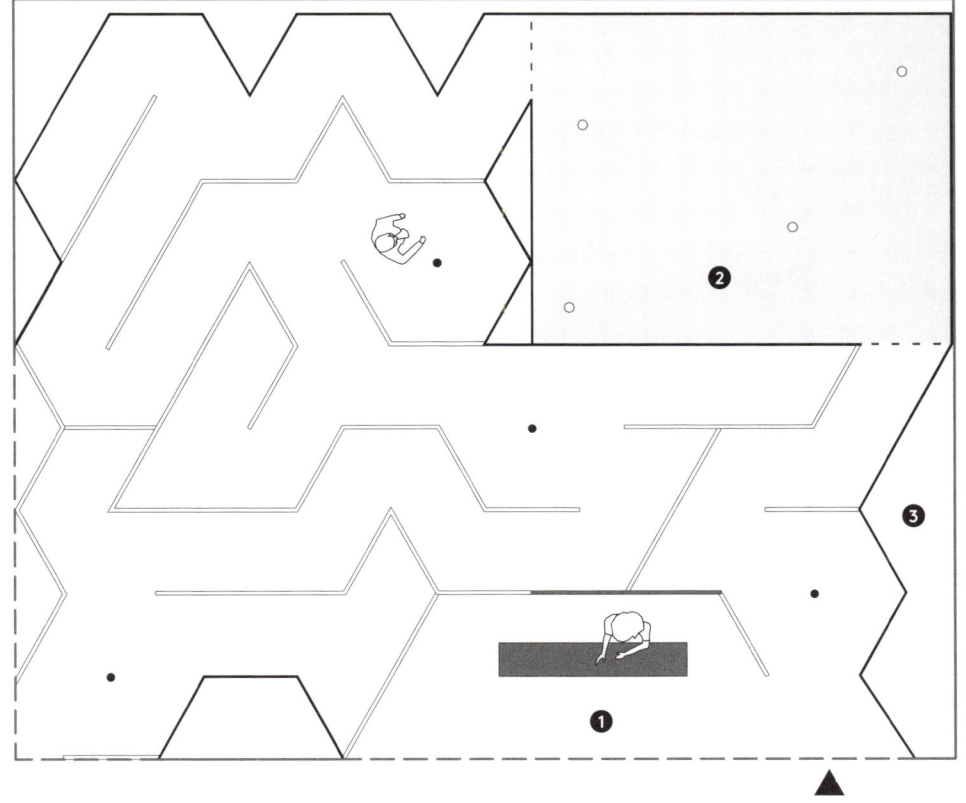

SPIEGEL DER SCHWEIZ

SRG Bern Freiburg Wallis

SRG Deutschschweiz

4

THE INSTALLATION EVOKES
A HALL OF MIRRORS

FLOOR PLAN

01 Reception
02 Room of exclusive images
03 Technical room

5

3 Visitors themselves became part of the installation as their reflections merged with those of the public figures.

4 SRG's corporate colour red was immediately recognisable on the stand.

5 Inside the room of exclusive images.

YOURWAY2GO

Con'fetti

1 Peru, Indonesia or Cuba? YourWay2GO's stand celebrated the personal experiences of travel.

2 The colour scheme of the continents was informed by the objects hanging above.

3 Typical souvenirs and signboards represented the cultures and destinations on the continents.

2

TRADE FAIR **Vakantiebeurs**
WHERE **Utrecht, the Netherlands**
WHEN **January 2013**
DESIGNER **Con'fetti**
STAND CONSTRUCTOR **Con'fetti**
CLIENT **YourWay2GO**
MARKET SECTOR **Travel**
TOTAL FLOOR AREA **50 m²**
PHOTOGRAPHER **Hans Zijffers**

3

As a travel specialist for individual organised tours, YourWay2GO places great emphasis on the personal experience of the traveller. For this reason, experience was the focus of its stand at the Vakantiebeurs in Utrecht, a consumer fair for holidays and travel. A warm, personal approach was immediately felt on the stand which was designed by Con'fetti. A 3D world map anchored the compact space. On the floor, the map appeared as wooden furniture elements in the form of continents, each distinguished with a different colour, height, decoration, and thus a different experience. The continents were set on the ocean floor, made from vinyl adorned with a graphic water print. The lower elements provided seating for informal chats while the higher elements functioned as standing tables and information/booking points. Suspended above each continent were groups of objects typically found in countries on that continent. For instance sombreros from South America, ice skates from North America and boomerangs from Australia. The colours of these objects determined the colours of their respective continents below. Hung under the souvenirs were the company's trademark signboards that pointed in different directions to countries on that continent. The cloud of signboards created a lowered ceiling that added an intimate atmosphere to the space. The back wall featured a printed collage of travel highlights from different countries, heightening the theme of the stand. The stand was designed to be flexible to adapt to changing exhibition requirements at upcoming fairs. For example the modular MDF floor was composed of square panels that could be connected in different ways and the back wall could be easily extended or shortened without affecting the graphic. The fun, friendly design of the stand definitely got visitors in the right holiday mood to book their dream getaway. ▭

SHO
ACCES

SHOES & ACCESSORIES GRAND STAND 5

BLACKFIN
Anidride Design

TRADE FAIR **Mido**
WHERE **Milan, Italy**
WHEN **February 2015**
DESIGNER **Anidride Design**
STAND CONSTRUCTOR **Deimos**
CLIENT **Blackfin**
MARKET SECTOR **Eyewear**
TOTAL FLOOR AREA **96 m²**
PHOTOGRAPHER **Giovanni De Sandre**

1   Rhythmic, suspended strips of black fabric punctuated the central presentation area.

2   The raw architecture of the stand drew inspiration from the latest campaign images shot at a disused military base.

3   The enclosed quality of the structure heightened the experience of the space and two side openings provided controlled entry points.

2

Blackfin Titanium Eyewear's stand appeared as an impressive black armoured structure at the Mido international eyewear show in Milan. Designed by Anidride Design the stand took centre stage as a powerful 'machine' that represented the rapid journey of the young company's development, in this sense, a machine that never stops. The industrial aesthetic underlined the brand's strong design and performance values and simultaneously echoed its latest marketing campaign. The campaign visuals were shot in an abandoned military base, a somewhat dangerous and futuristic place but with its own charm and strong visual impact. The stand recalled abandoned metal structures at the base and presented something never seen before at the fair. Large perforated metal panels fitted together to form an enclosed angular volume of metal shards – hence the name of the stand 'Black Shard'. The use of metal strongly linked to the raw material of the eyewear and expressed the idea of the strength of titanium. A huge moving turbine on the front of the stand formed the centrepiece, immediately attracting visitors' attentions. With a diameter of three metres, the turbine heightened the industrial atmosphere. Two side entrances controlled the flow of traffic into the space. Once inside visitors encountered a beautiful play of light thanks to the perforated panels; this delicate skin contrasted strikingly with the dark machine aesthetic. Clever detailed, the perforations are actually cutouts of eyewear frames. Behind the turbine, an oversized graphic panel featured an image from the latest campaign. A series of black freestanding angular pedestals of varying heights structured the front of the stand while a bar and storage room block surrounded by two rows of meeting tables occupied the back. The expressive stand definitely made sure that visitors kept a keen eye on this dynamic young brand. ◁

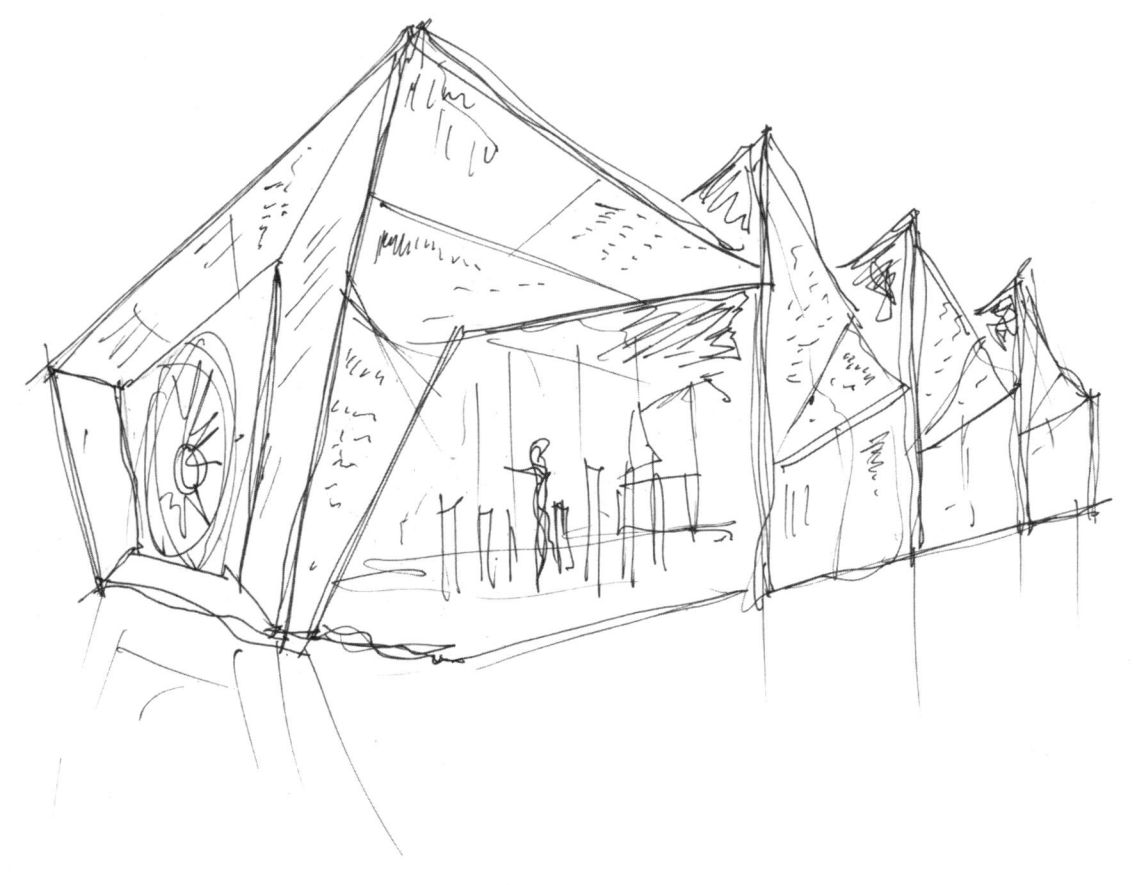

THE IMPRESSIVE BLACK ARMOURED STAND RECALLS ABANDONED MILITARY STRUCTURES

FLOOR PLAN

01 Freestanding display
02 Graphic panel
03 Freestanding display
04 Cipriani's bar
05 Closet
06 Monitor with new campaign photos
07 Tables
08 Turbin
09 Box truss

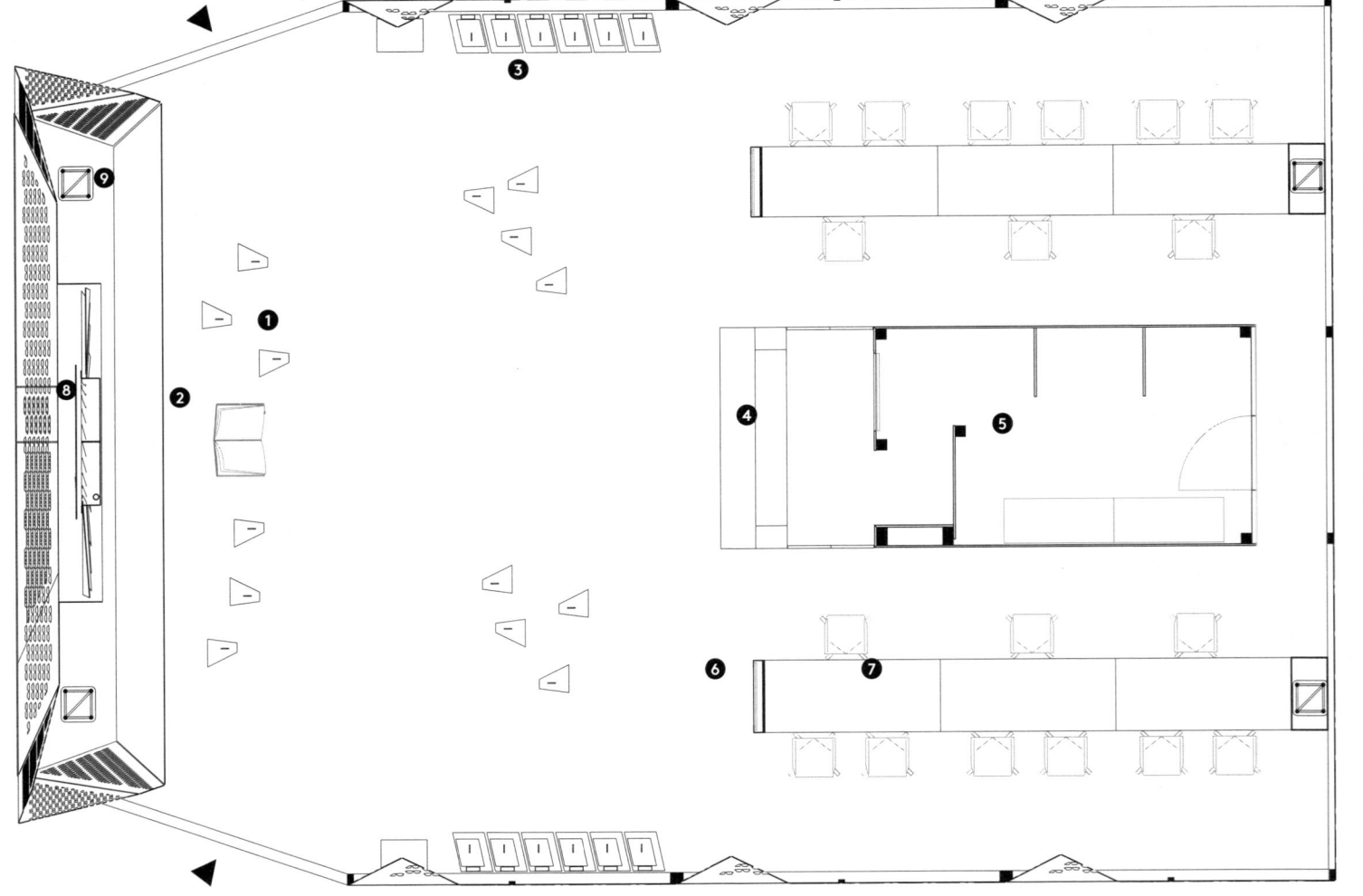

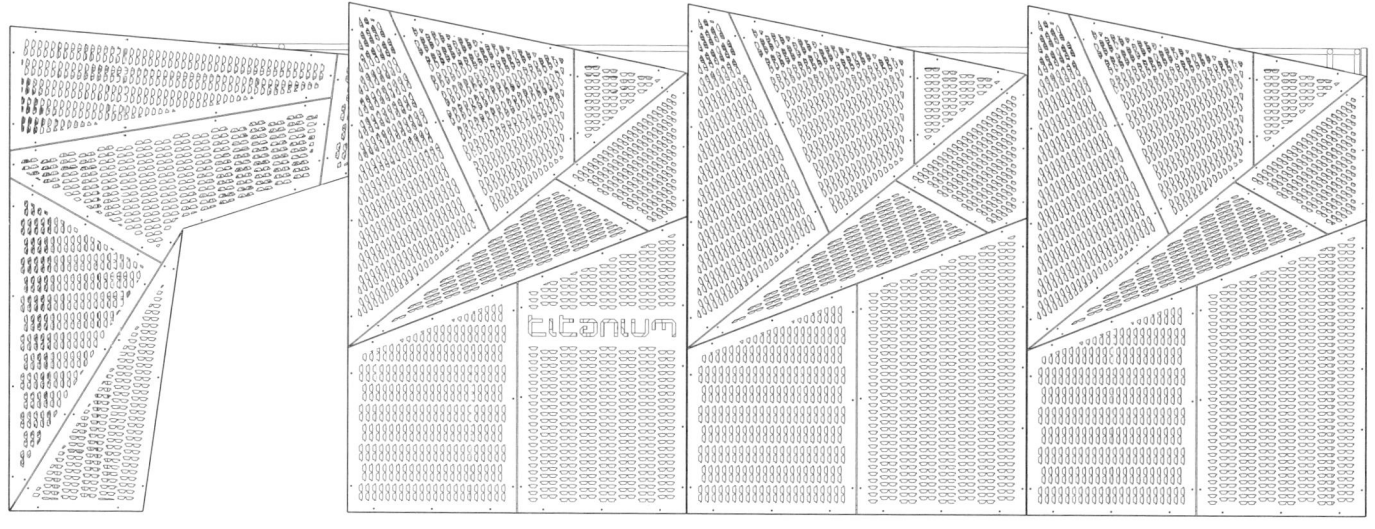

AXONOMETRIC VIEW

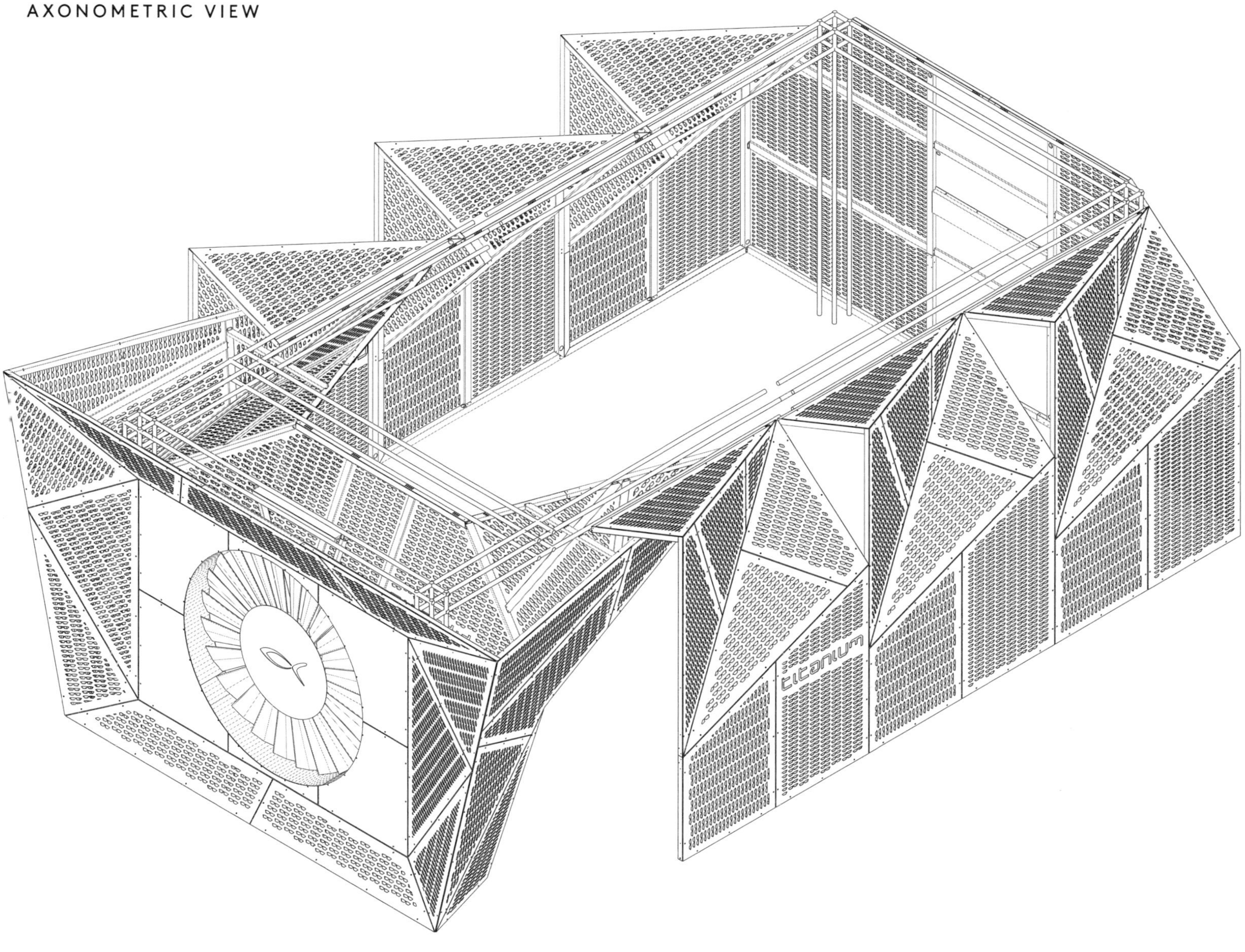

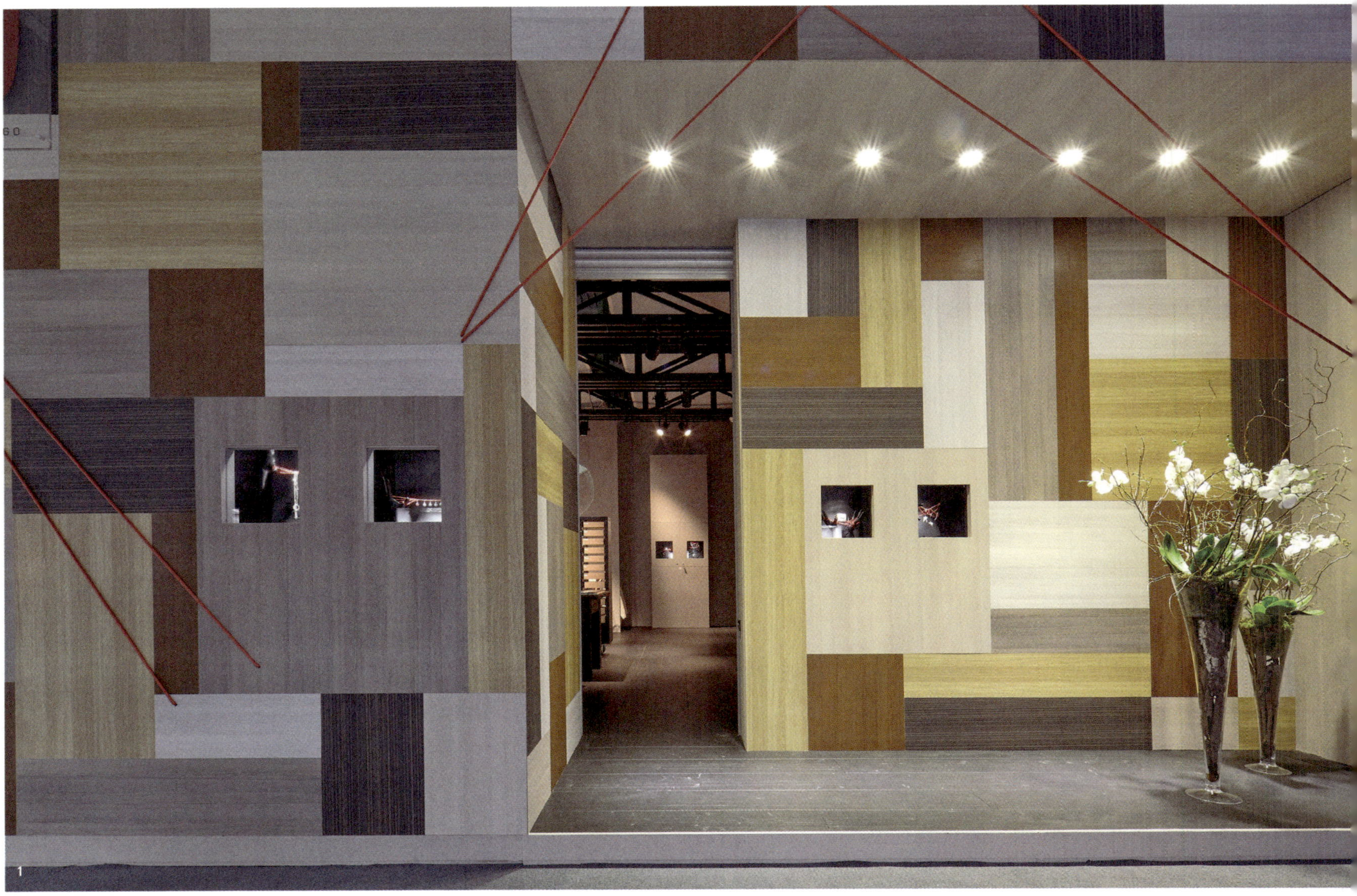
1

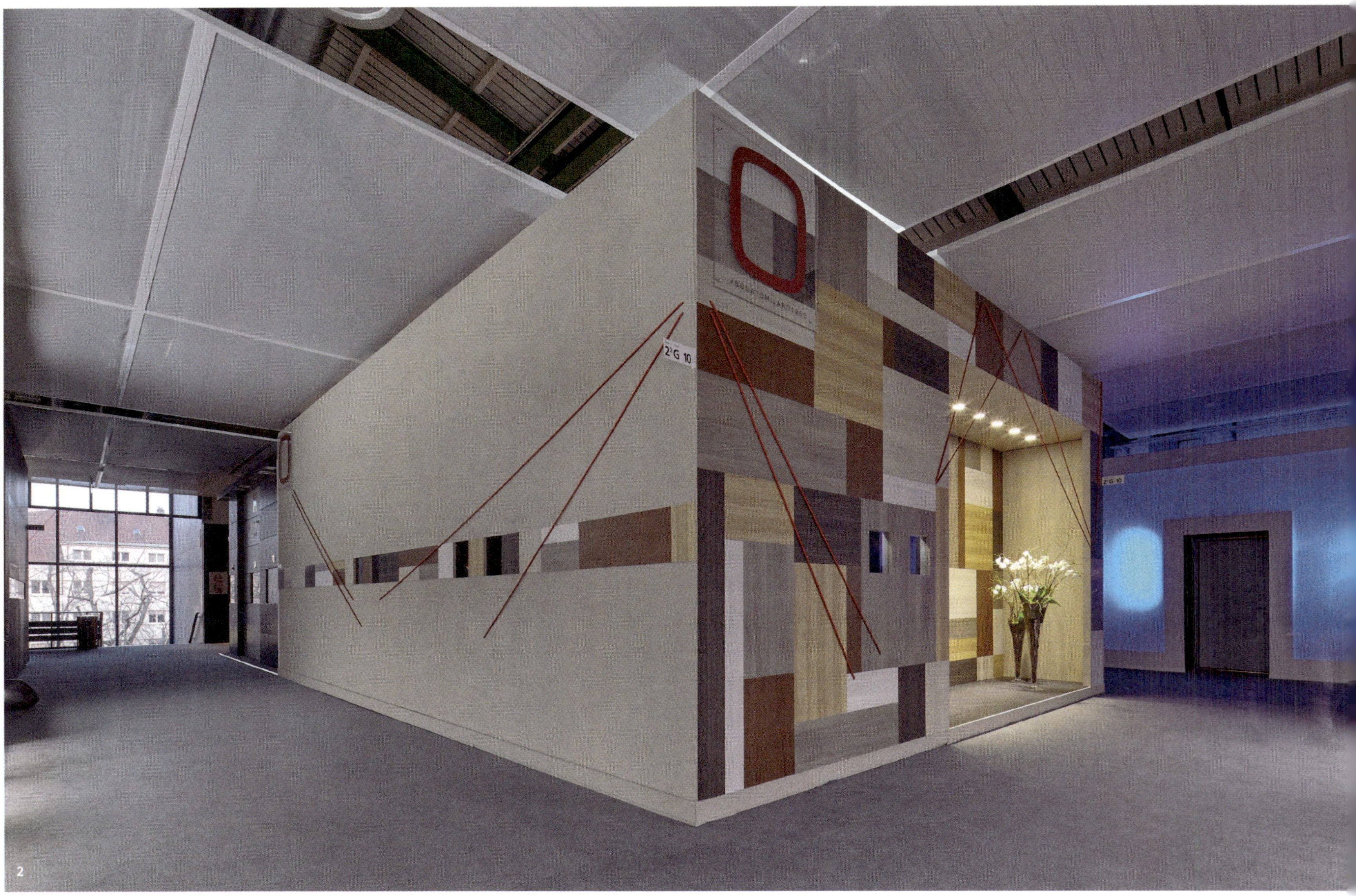
2

BONATO MILANO 1960

Arquitect Studio

1 The patchwork of wooden textures signified the union of different elements of the company.

2 Red thread was used as the visual connecting element of the stand.

3 The interior was characterised by an elegant, dark ambience.

4/5 In the showcases black 3D-printed hands threaded with red thread cradled the precious jewellery.

3

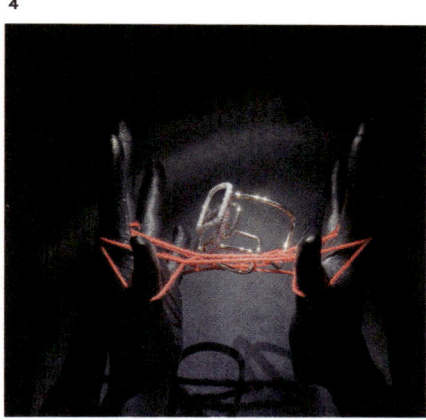

4

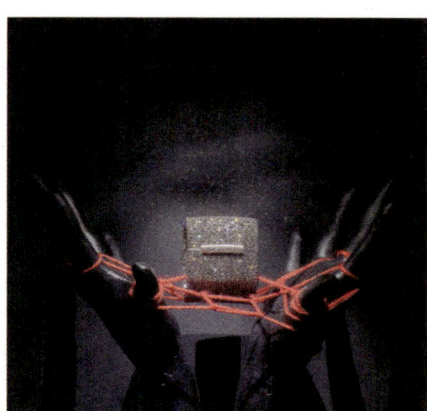

5

A

At Baselworld, a leading international event for the watch and jewellery industry, Bonato Milano 1960 wanted its stand to not only display its elegant high-end jewellery but also communicate the new energy of the company. This design task was entrusted to Arquitect Studio. The most recognisable element of the stand was its striking facade. Carefully composed from varying textures of wood the facade represented the union of different elements of the company by the new owner. This patchwork was accompanied by lines of red thread that signified the continuity of the company's work which is projected towards a new future. This literal and figurative red thread held together the stand and created a visual path between the windows, entry and company logos on the facade. The stand was open to the corridor on three sides. The facades incorporated a series of small showcases that each displayed a single piece of precious jewellery. Inside each showcase was a black box from which a pair of black hands emerged, holding a bed of braided red thread for the jewellery to delicately rest on. An LED spotlight focused directly on the jewellery to accentuate its brilliance, the reflecting light on the black walls lending each showcase a warm, theatrical glow. Inside, the grey plastered walls and fabric ceiling and black-painted wooden floors created a neutral backdrop for the bespoke feature furniture that included black tables with luxurious dark marble tabletops and customised Ghost chairs. The facades and showcases were designed in collaboration with Antonina Lopresti. ⚊

TRADE FAIR **Baselworld**
WHERE **Basel, Switzerland**
WHEN **March 2015**
DESIGNER **Arquitect Studio**
STAND CONSTRUCTOR **Arquitect Studio**
CLIENT **Bonato Milano 1960**
MARKET SECTOR **Jewellery**
TOTAL FLOOR AREA **65 m²**
PHOTOGRAPHER **Maria Gambino**

1 The installation aimed to show that technology is meaningless without beauty.

2 Literally and figuratively, visitors got lost in time.

LIGHT IS TIME

Dorell.Ghotmeh.Tane/Architects

TRADE FAIR **Milan Furniture Fair**
WHERE **Milan, Italy**
WHEN **April 2014**
DESIGNER **Dorell.Ghotmeh.Tane/Architects**
STAND CONSTRUCTOR **Xilografia**
CLIENT **Citizen Watch**
MARKET SECTOR **Watches**
TOTAL FLOOR AREA **423 m²**
PHOTOGRAPHER **Takuji Shimmura**

2

'Light Is Time' is an interpretation of time's origin and connection to light. Without light, time would not exist. Designed by Dorell.Ghotmeh.Tane/Architects for the watch brand Citizen at the Milan Furniture Fair, the stunning installation encapsulates Citizen's philosophy of 'watches for all citizens' with a universal theme that captured the essence of time and light. Hosted at the Triennale di Milano Exhibition Hall, the exhibition revealed a shimmering microcosm that appeared suspended in time. Visitors entered a mysterious dark space occupied by a huge elongated cloud of sparkling particles. These particles were composed from 80,000 circular brass base-plates (the basic mechanical component of a watch) suspended from fine metal wires. These wires were organised geometrically into 36 different sequences, which appeared like lines of music notes, that together ensure sufficient variation in the installation's composition. More than 4000 individual wires were installed by hand on site. Teamed with a choreographed soundscape and extensive lighting design by Luftzug, the installation took on a dream-like emotive atmosphere. Strung at different angles, the base-plates bounced light in all directions to create the glittering effect. Sounds conveyed the timeless movement of light in space. Walking around the sides, visitors encountered openings that led them into a maze-like interior. Seemingly carved from light, cavernous internal hollows further in housed the exhibition spaces. Here was Citizen's heritage on show, starting from its origins with its very first pocket watch through to the latest satellite-synchronised timepiece. Evoking curiosity and wonder, the exhibition was an unforgettable experience that gave visitors a spectacular glimpse into Citizen's world of watch-making. ⇁

SHOES & ACCESSORIES GRAND STAND 5

3 Cavernous hollows in the maze revealed the exhibition spaces.

4 Detail of a base plate.

4

A SHIMMERING MICROCOSM THAT APPEARS SUSPENDED IN TIME

FLOOR PLAN

01 Origin
02 Parts
03 Watches
04 Office

A1 A2 A3 A4 A5 A6 A7 A8 A9 A10 A11 A12   B13 B14 B15 B16 B17 B18 B19 B20 B21 B22 B23 B24   C25 C26 C27 C28 C29 C30 C31 C32 C33 C34 C35 C36

FRAAS
Blocher Blocher Shops

TRADE FAIR **Panorama**
WHERE **Berlin, Germany**
WHEN **July 2014**
DESIGNER **Blocher Blocher Shops**
STAND CONSTRUCTOR **Starker**
CLIENT **Fraas**
MARKET SECTOR **Scarves**
TOTAL FLOOR AREA **72 m²**
PHOTOGRAPHER **Joachim Grothus for Blocher Blocher Shops**

1 Threads suspended from two oversized warp beams created an elegant canopy and screen.

2 The focus on craftsmanship was clearly felt in the design of the stand.

3 Thistles, the company's emblem, featured prominently in the presentation.

2

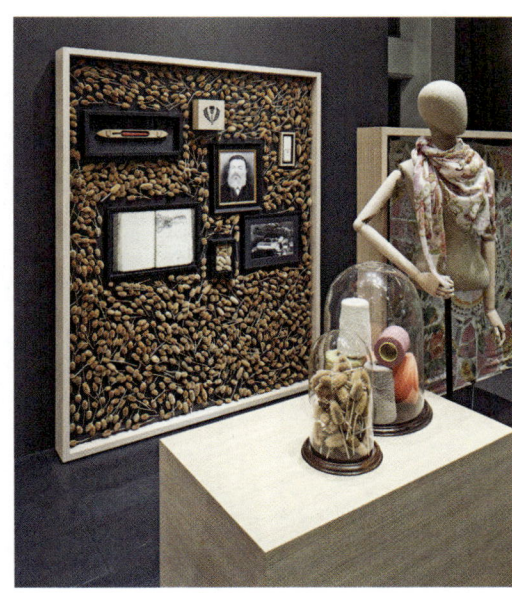

3

T

The scarf company Fraas stands for tradition and innovation. These core values were translated into the firm's exhibition stand at the fashion trade fair Panorama Berlin in 2014. Designed by Blocher Blocher Shops, the stand depicted the delicate art and craftsmanship of scarf manufacturing. Two main elements dominated the space. Defining the interior were two suspended sections of longitudinal warp threads held by oversized warp beams – parts of the loom on which transverse weft threads are interwoven. Placed centrally these elements clearly communicated the textile context of the presentation.

Forming a delicate canopy over the stand the suspended threads also cast beautiful shadows on the back wall. The grey walls and black steel floor provided a dark background to accentuate the colourful scarves. The other main design element comprised a series of wooden displays placed around the perimeter of the space. Here, some scarves were clamped between wooden frames to show the prints at their best and others were tied on metal rods. Other frames featured campaign images and collages of documents and thistles, recognisable as Fraas' logo. Special recessed black frames showcased precious company mementos. The bar was also fashioned from wood. The various wooden structures were complemented by a visual merchandising concept developed by Blocher Blocher View. On the wooden display stand custom-made glass bell jars held yarn bobbins and thistles that symbolise the heritage of the company. Custom-made papier-mâché mannequins perfectly fitted the focus on craftsmanship and showed different ways to wear Fraas' beautiful scarves. ▬

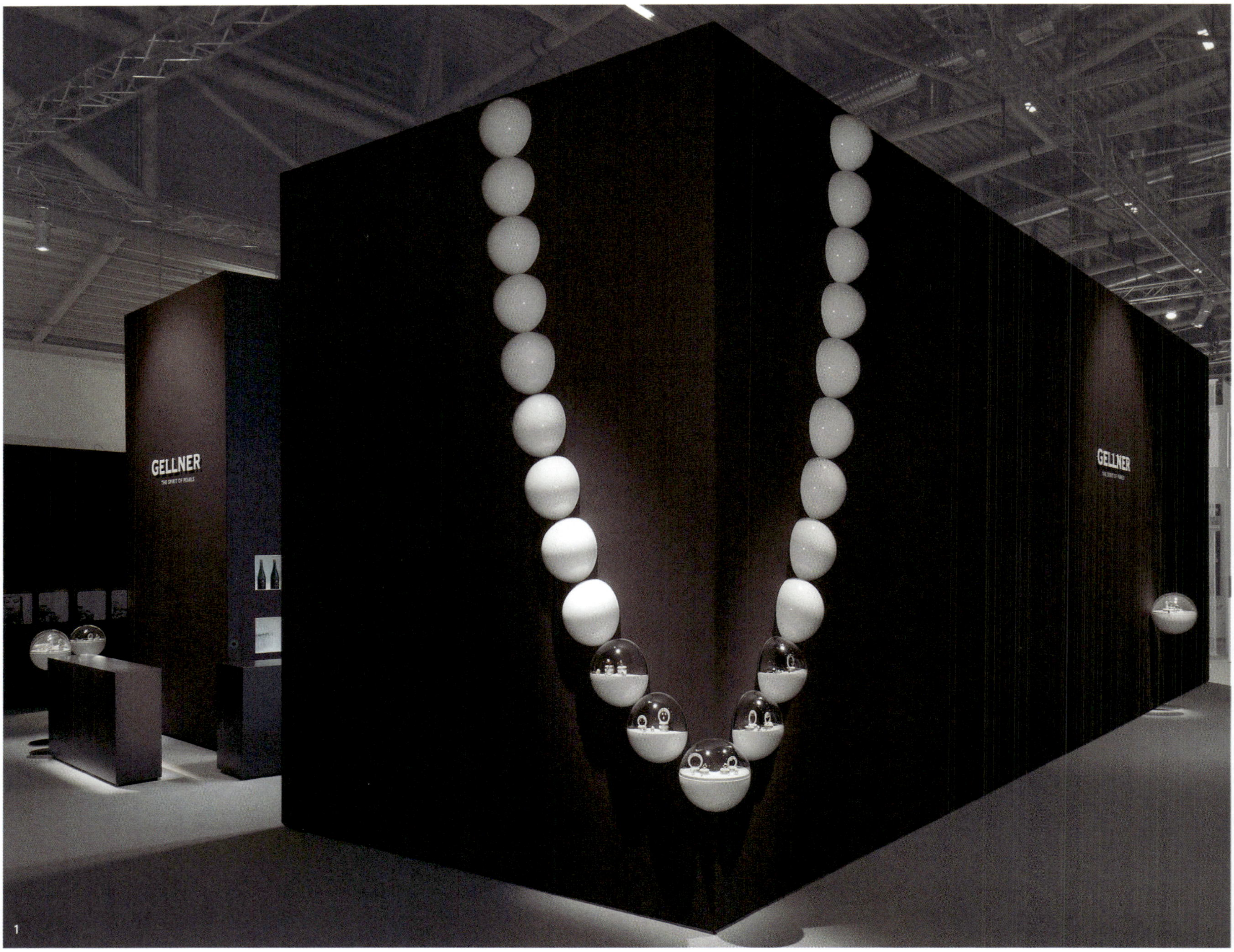

1

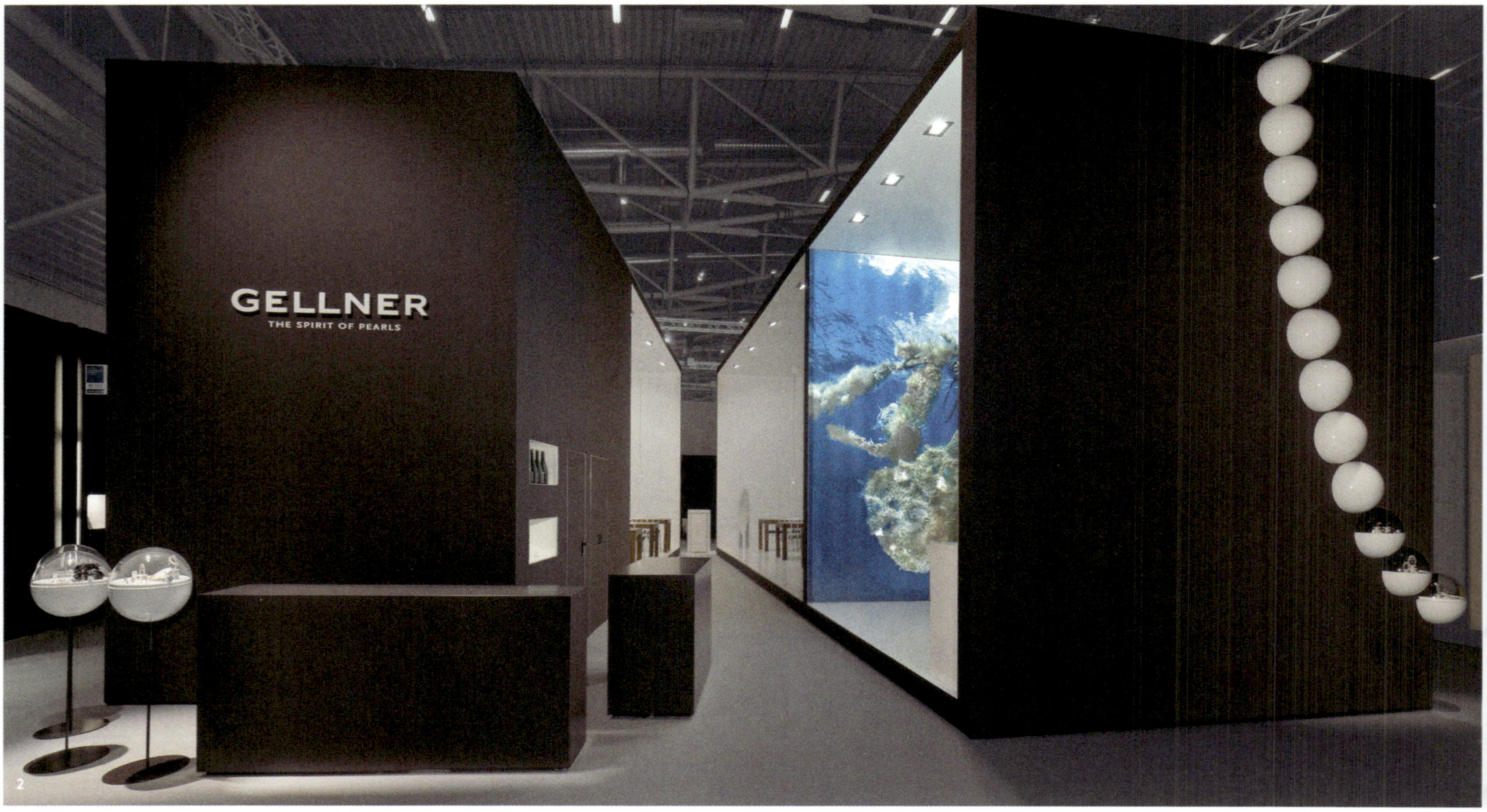

2

GELLNER

Atelier Seitz

TRADE FAIR **Inhorgenta**
WHERE **Munich, Germany**
WHEN **March 2013**
DESIGNER **Atelier Seitz**
STAND CONSTRUCTOR **Atelier Seitz**
CLIENT **Gellner**
MARKET SECTOR **Jewellery**
TOTAL FLOOR AREA **150 m²**
PHOTOGRAPHER **Olaf Schiemann**

Visitors were invited to step inside Gellner's oversized jewellery box at the Inhorgenta fair for jewellery and timepieces in Munich. Designed by Atelier Seitz, the elegant stand encapsulated the company's slogan, 'The Spirit of Pearls' to display the products in a unique way. Two parallel inward facing rectangular volumes were positioned in a slightly tapered arrangement to create the box. This opened up a corridor through the interior, where an intimate inner realm unfolded. Here a series of compartments contained semi-enclosed and enclosed rooms. Inside the lounge, the backlit underwater panel, which showed the context of pearl diving, created a luminous, mysterious atmosphere. Views into the stand shifted depending on the angle of the viewer, revealing different parts of the interior. The set up of the stand also recalled the architecture of the life form from which pearls originate: the pearl oyster. While this inner domain hosted mostly private spaces, the presentation of jewellery dominated the exterior. Four types of jewellery – necklaces, earrings, rings, and bracelets – were showcased in a sculptural way inside oversized white pearls. A huge strand of pearls hung over one corner of the stand while other pearls were elevated on thin black stands. Dark grey fabric enveloped the stand completely to present a coherent, dark exterior and provide privacy for the inner exhibition and meeting areas. Spotlights focused strategically on the jewellery and company logo. The outer fabric can be easily replaced for changing presentations as the structure is designed to be used for the coming five years. The minimal design, focus on the product and high attention to detail resulted in an elegant stand that exuded luxury, preciousness and timelessness in the true spirit of the brand.

1/2 An oversized strand of pearls was the eye-catcher on the stand.

3 A mysterious jewellery box awaited visitors.

GORE-TEX
mbco

TRADE FAIR **OutDoor**
WHERE **Friedrichshafen, Germany**
WHEN **July 2014**
DESIGNER **mbco**
STAND CONSTRUCTOR **mbco**
CLIENT **W.L. Gore & Associates**
MARKET SECTOR **Footwear**
TOTAL FLOOR AREA **230 m²**
PHOTOGRAPHER **Peter Schaffrath**

1   The radiant white setting perfectly showcased the products and campaign imagery.

2   Circular forms ensured a cohesive design concept.

3   Each furniture element was dedicated to a collaborating outdoor footwear manufacturer.

2

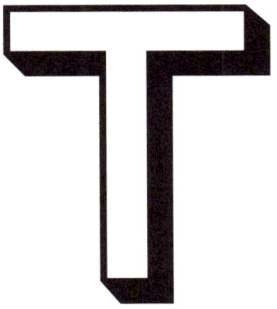

3

The European outdoor trade show OutDoor marked the occasion of the world premiere of Gore-Tex's new all-round breathable, waterproof hiking shoes. To set the stage for this event, mbco developed a concept for the fair stand that encapsulated both the high tech nature of the products and the emotion of the great outdoors where they're used. The aim was also for the stand to be as informative as possible to introduce the new innovations to visitors and trigger their curiosities. A clean, crisp white setting and a series of product circles formed the basis of the stand. The back wall was kept simple, featuring the two main campaign images and highlight text. In this way, the minimal, uncluttered space functioned to maintain sole focus on the product. Clusters of custom-made round illuminated display furniture structured the presentation and flow of traffic onto the stand. A total of 40 circular furniture elements were used to represent 40 partners. Each element exhibited shoes from a leading outdoor footwear brand that partnered with Gore-Tex to develop hiking shoes using its new technology. The circular forms alluded to the 360° surround feel and freedom of being in the outdoors, their radiance contributing a striking cool glow that caught visitors' attentions. An informative multi-touch table was positioned centrally, inviting visitors to discover more about the products' technical information and applications. Above, a suspended circular LED screen captivated visitors with an emotional outdoor film featuring stunning landscapes in different weather conditions, accompanied by a natural soundscape including thunderstorms and bird songs. Lighting was designed to showcase the product circles, the cool tone carefully fine-tuned to accentuate the colours of the products. —

K2 SNOWBOARDING
mbco

1 Windows allowed visitors a glimpse into the workshop.

2 mbco's concept metaphorically and figuratively brought K2's product catalogue to life.

3 The products were completely integrated into the snowboarder's workshop which was furnished with old tools and furniture.

For the 2013 edition of ISPO, the international trade exhibition for the sports industry, K2 Snowboarding tasked mbco with designing a trade fair booth that would translate the narrative of its product catalogue into reality. True to its slogan 'seek & enjoy' K2 has been seeking out the next frontiers in snowboarding and ways to grow the sport, and wanted to communicate that spirit in its presentation. The catalogue tells the story of an older experienced snowboarder who owns an old snowboard workshop, a well-loved space where he builds and prepares his own snowboards. He's someone who is dedicated to the sport and still loves to go out to 'seek and enjoy'. The concept for the stand was to recreate the setting of the snowboarder's workshop just moments after he had left the house to go for the next ride, while simultaneously incorporating the pragmatic requirements for a trade fair stand. Inspired by archetypal American sheds, the workshop was constructed from artificially weather timber planks. The planks were spaced quite widely to open up the facade and enable sneak peeks into the interior. While it was important that the interior should be visually engaging, it should also clearly structure the product presentation. In this way the layout was planned according to the various product chapters of the catalogue to give coherence and clarity. The products were integrated into the setting complete with old workshop tools and furniture to give authenticity to the space. The lighting installation was mounted onto the roof trusses, thereby rendering additional scaffolding unnecessary. K2's presentation shared an intimate insight into a company that is clearly passionate about snowboarding. ⏤

TRADE FAIR **ISPO**
WHERE **Munich, Germany**
WHEN **February 2013**
DESIGNER **mbco**
STAND CONSTRUCTOR **mbco**
CLIENT **K2 Snowboarding**
MARKET SECTOR **Sports equipment**
TOTAL FLOOR AREA **100 m²**
PHOTOGRAPHER **Peter Schaffrath**

PETER KAISER

mbco

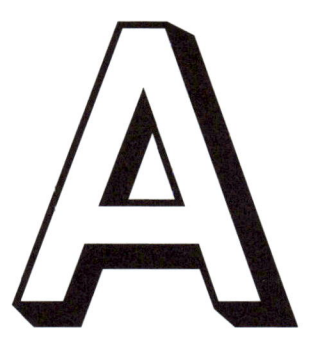

TRADE FAIR **GDS**
WHERE **Düsseldorf Germany**
WHEN **July 2014**
DESIGNER **mbco (shop design by marcbetz)**
STAND CONSTRUCTOR **mbco**
CLIENT **Peter Kaiser**
MARKET SECTOR **Footwear and handbags**
TOTAL FLOOR AREA **210 m²**
PHOTOGRAPHER **Peter Schaffrath**

2

3

At 2014 edition of GDS (Global Destination for Shoes & Accessories) Peter Kaiser was proud to launch its new collections to clients in a completely new retail setting. The rebranding was designed by marcbetz architektur and presented an elegant, living room-like atmosphere for all the shoe brand's shops. For its presentation at GDS, Peter Kaiser didn't want a completely new design for its booth but instead wished to translate the retail identity of the shop into the design of the exhibition stand, which was entrusted to mbco. The brief also stated that the booth should reuse an existing stand design and its spatial elements and be flexible for future use. For the layout the aim was to maintain an open flow through the space, and keep the zones for display and ordering separate. In this way, the stand focused on the highlight shoe presentation area. A soft palette of greys and beiges immediately established a chic yet warm setting. A series of new partitions clad in coloured sheer textile structured the space. By placing the shoe displays on the perimeter, this kept the centre of the space free for circulation and seating. Plush carpet and upholstered furniture added a feel of luxuriousness. Positioned at the end of this zone was the bar. Located in the background, adjacent to the presentation area, was the client/ordering area with meeting tables and samples on display. All the elements were modular, thereby enabling the entire stand to be easily reconfigured according to different spatial requirements for upcoming exhibitions. The unity of the retail identity with the stand design ensured the company succeeded in having a coherent brand presentation at GDS. ⚊

1 The bar and bar seating formed the social hub of the stand.

2 Varying tones of elegant greys and beiges characterised the new retail identity.

3 Guests were welcomed at the information counter.

SEIKO
EYEWEAR THAT PERFORMS
SEIKO Digital Solutions
Frage
SEIKO
Premium Partner
Programm
SEIKO
SUPERIOR Xcel
STARVISION
the collection

1

SEIKO
Walbert-Schmitz

TRADE FAIR **opti**
WHERE **Munich, Germany**
WHEN **January 2015**
DESIGNER **Walbert-Schmitz**
STAND CONSTRUCTOR **Walbert-Schmitz**
CLIENT **Seiko Optical Europe**
MARKET SECTOR **Optics**
TOTAL FLOOR AREA **117 m²**
PHOTOGRAPHER **Schiemann Fotodesign**

1   An open layout with a bright, modern interior created an inviting atmosphere.

2   The circular geometries framed the space in different ways.

2

Seiko Optical Europe specialises in modern lenses that can be customised to meet the wearer's individual and specific needs. For its presentation at opti, the international trade show for optics and design, in 2015, the company wanted to present its latest products in a creative, informative and accessible way. The stand should also have an inviting architecture that referred to optics and glasses. In its concept for the stand design, Walbert-Schmitz took inspiration from the curved geometry of lenses to truly celebrate the product. Three large circular frames structured the space, each frame hosting a different presentation. Depending on the viewing angle, the frames showed different perspectives of the space – again alluding to the qualities of lenses. The open organic structures also invited visitors to meander around the stand freely. The crisp white surrounds lent the space a modern look. Marking the stand was a suspended circular frame lined internally with Seiko's corporate colour blue, which added a vibrant accent and ensured good long-range visibility of the booth. In order to communicate the properties of the lenses, an interactive game was developed which was integrated into one of the frames. Visitors were invited to pick a question card from the wall that outlined one of the product's advantages and hold it in front of a camera. A screen listed the multiple choice answers, and the answer could be selected from a different set of cards on another wall. An augmented reality animation rewarded a correct answer. This game enabled visitors to experience the product in an engaging, playful way and also formed an effective tool for the company to increase its brand awareness at fair presentations. ▬

SWAROVSKI

Tokujin Yoshioka

Swarovski's stand at Baselworld 2013 wowed visitors with its luminous architecture. Designed by Tokujin Yoshioka, the impressive stand extended more than 2000 m² over two levels in the fair's new hall. Entitled 'Wings of Sparkle' the design made a poetic reference to two primary elements at the core of Swarovski's brand. Tokujin Yoshioka: 'The inspiration comes from natural light and sparkle that randomly shines, such as sunlight dancing on the water and the twinkle of the stars. I wanted to create the space from the luminance itself. My intention was to express the space by the dazzle of light, and not by forms.' The curvature also evokes images of a swan on a lake gracefully extending its wing, like the symbol of Swarovski.

The stand is enveloped by a seven-meter-high curved sparkle wall with a circumference of 155 meters. To create the dazzling surface 253,231 mirrored reflectors, which symbolised Swarovski's characteristic crystal facets, were embedded in the facade. Positioned on these 60 mm reflectors were 22,856 computer-controlled LEDs that emulated the twinkling effect. Visitors were immediately bathed in the most beautiful light, as if entering a huge crystal. Inside, an inner wall completely made of crystals unfolded around the space. This created a sparkling double height screen between the open stand and VIP area and bar upstairs, which were accessed by two sweeping staircases. Here 34,000 cut crystals adorned the wall, their forms mirroring the same hexagonal form as the facade reflector. Further in the stand, 40 display cases for watches and jewellery reiterated the crystal theme. These elegant freestanding hexagonal steel-and-glass cases were custom designed, also by Tokujin Yoshioka, in differing heights. Truly celebrating the essence of the brand, the spectacular stand was no doubt a major highlight of this year's show. ⇔

1 Displays were also integrated into the outer wall.

2 The dazzling stand shone like a beacon at Baselworld.

3 Curved gallery spaces led visitors through the world of Swarovski.

4 The challenges of executing the sparkling wall were expertly resolved by Swarovski's technical team.

TRADE FAIR **Baselworld**
WHERE **Basel, Switzerland**
WHEN **April-May 2013**
DESIGNER **Tokujin Yoshioka**
CLIENT **Swarovski**
MARKET SECTOR **Watches and jewellery**
TOTAL FLOOR AREA **1088 m²**
PHOTOGRAPHER **Courtesy of Tokujin Yoshioka**

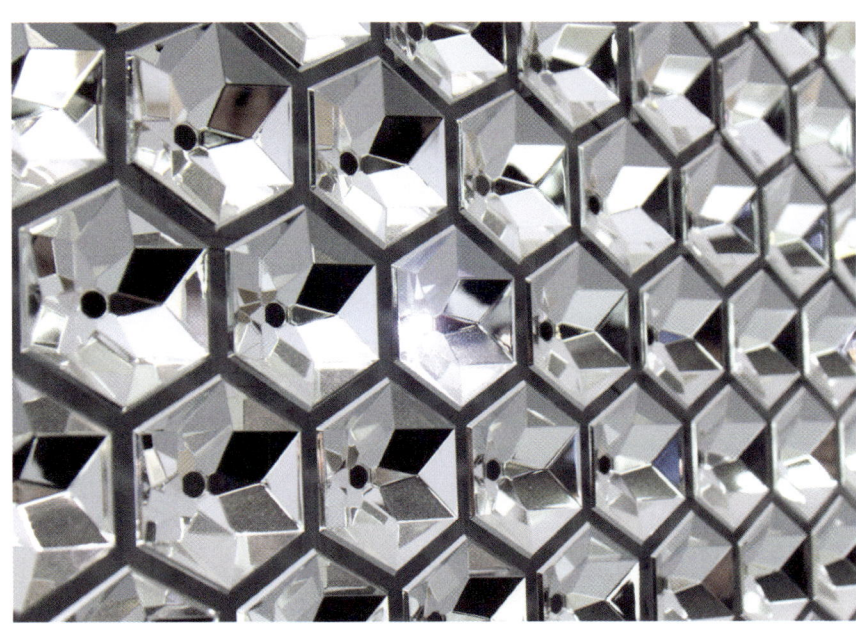

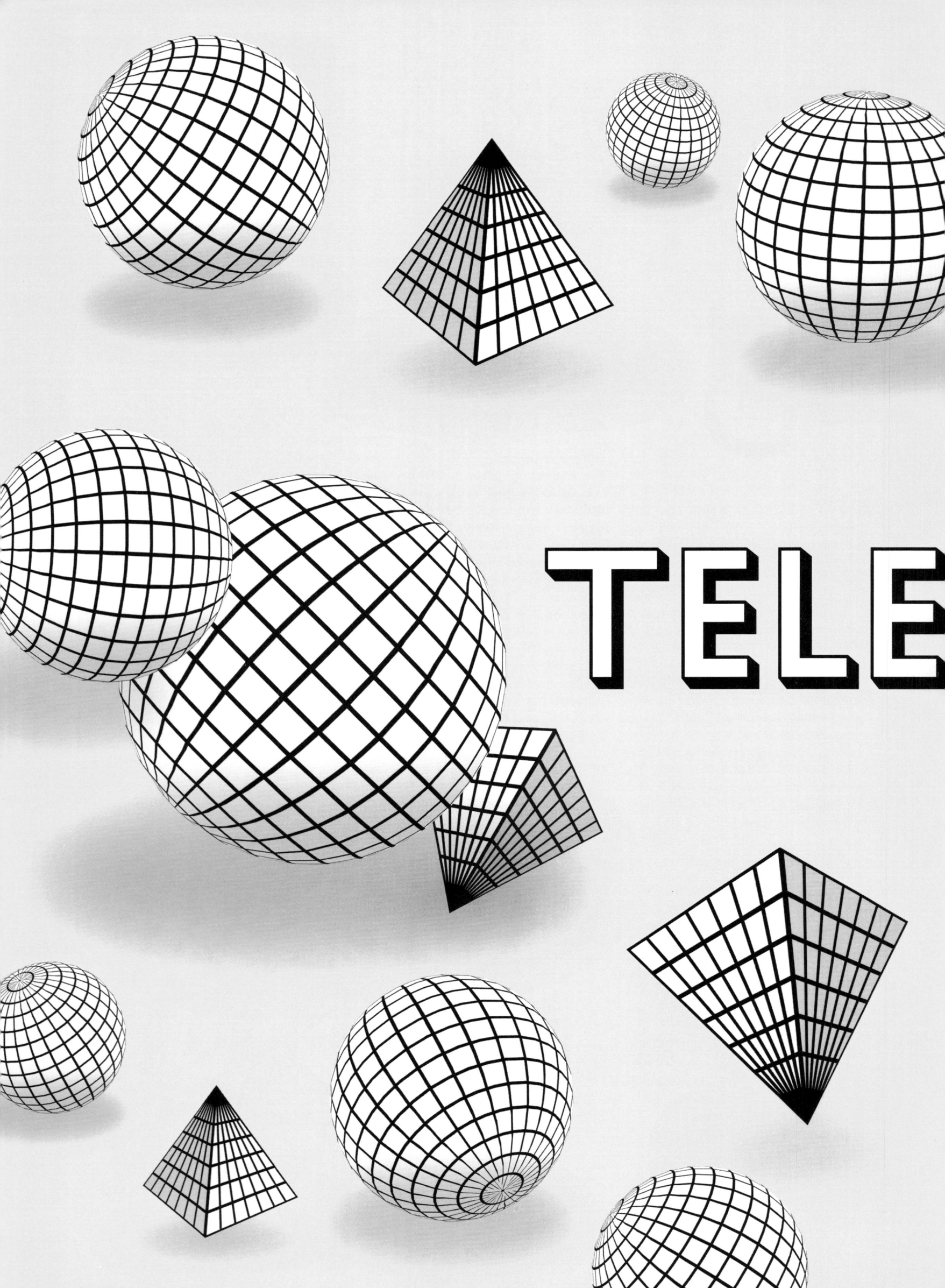

WIRTSCHAFTS-WUNDER 4.0

q-bus Mediatektur

1/2 The Industry 4.0 metatheme was the central idea of the fair presence – in addition to the 'industrial charm meets digitisation' design key, six industrial robots and a moving umbrella canopy formed the key visual.

2

How do a huge canopy of magenta umbrellas and interactive robots relate to telecommunications? These two elements formed the key visuals for Deutsche Telekom's impressive trade show presence at CeBIT. Conceived by q-bus Mediatektur, this year's stand signalled a call for the digitisation of processes. Deutsche Telekom wanted to communicate its leading role in bringing the German economy into the era of digital transformation, and create a motivational environment to demonstrate the advantages. In this way, Industry 4.0 (the computerisation of manufacturing), Machine-2-Machine

(M2M) communication, cloud computing and the telecom network were core topics highlighted in the presentation entitled 'Wirtschaftswunder 4.0 - Digitalization Made In Germany'. Different freestanding showcases were positioned across the whole stand, serving as references for digitisation. Visitors meandered between them in an unstructured way. Oversized white crate-like structures explained digitisation packages for small and medium-sized enterprises. Here content and product presentations were often accompanied by interactive presentation formats, e.g. a robot painted portraits to demonstrate the precision of the technology. Centrally positioned was a long black table that highlighted the Pioneers of Digitisation, industries that have already made the digital transition – this was communicated by choreographed robots, symbolising the convergence of the physical and digital

worlds. Last but not least, a stunning canopy of magenta umbrellas united the presentation, bringing coherence to the individual elements. Certain sections were programmed to move, and some umbrellas were connected to the robots as part of a choreographed performance. Over 1000 umbrellas were used to construct this dramatic roof, a striking symbol for protection and reliability for the digitisation of sensitive production data. ⸺

TRADE FAIR **CeBIT**
WHERE **Hanover, Germany**
WHEN **March 2015**
DESIGNER **q-bus Mediatektur**
STAND CONSTRUCTOR **q-bus Mediatektur**
CLIENT **Deutsche Telekom**
MARKET SECTOR **Telecommunications**
TOTAL FLOOR AREA **5900 m²**
PHOTOGRAPHER **q-bus Mediatektur**

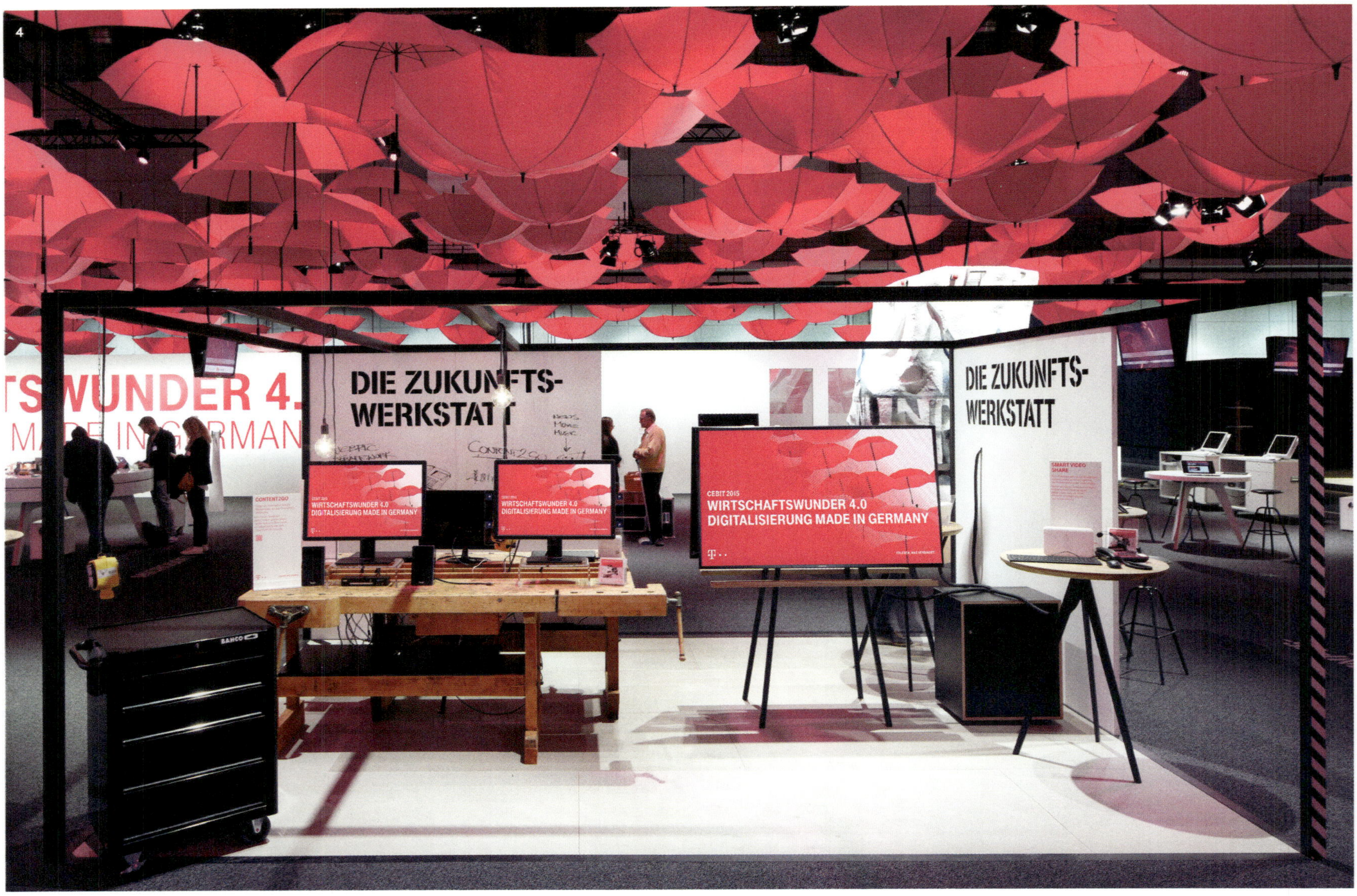

4

DIE ZUKUNFTS-WERKSTATT

DIE ZUKUNFTS-WERKSTATT

WIRTSCHAFTSWUNDER 4.0
DIGITALISIERUNG MADE IN GERMANY

3

4

3   The stand was occupied by freestanding showcases that demonstrated the potential and advantages of digitisation.

4   Situated on the edge of the stand, an enclosed seating area allowed guests and clients to conduct meetings in private.

5   Choreographed industrial robots appeared to be dancing with the canopy of umbrellas as part of the Digitisation Pioneers feature.

6/7 Showcases were designed to encourage maximum visitor participation.

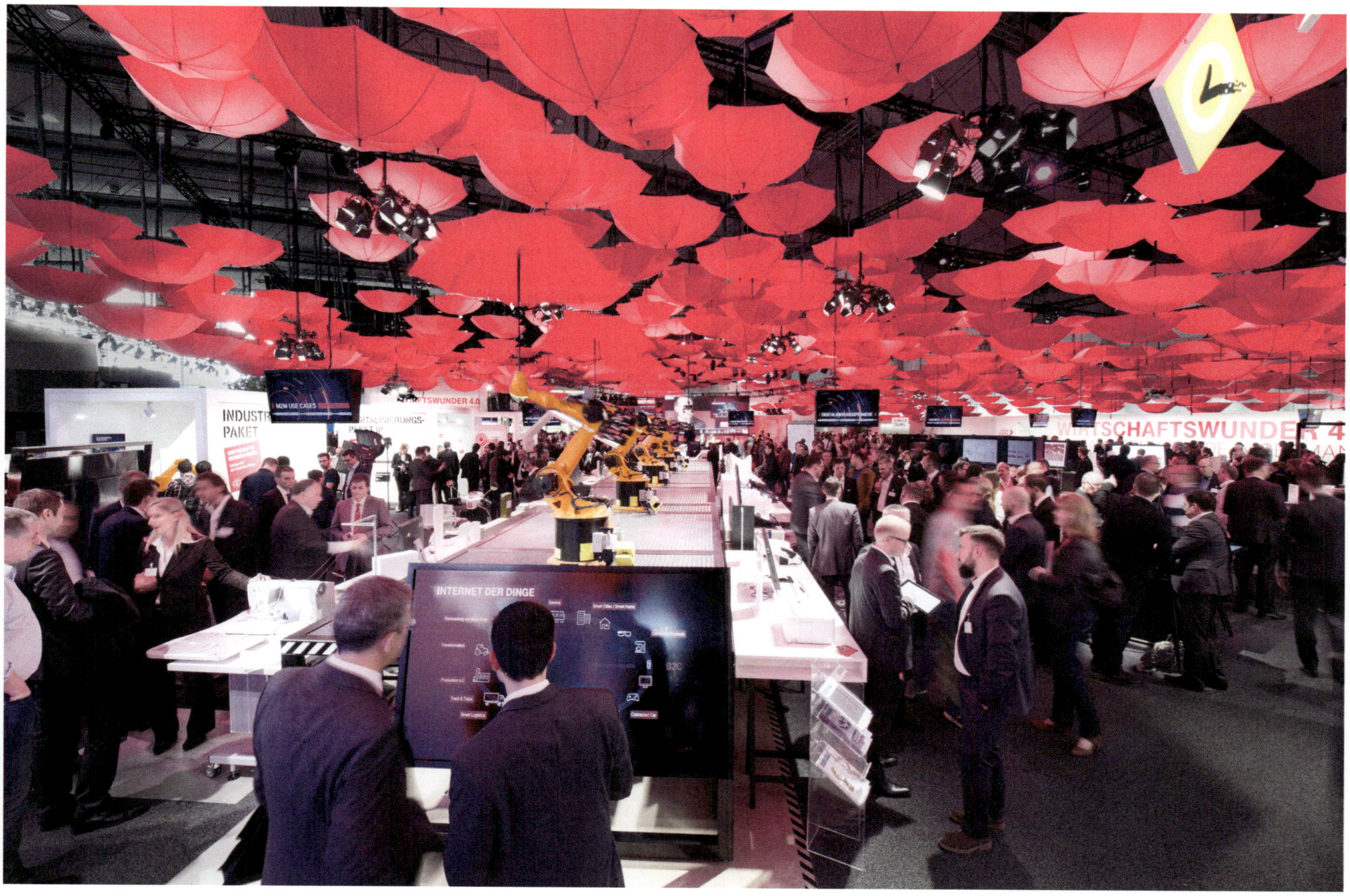

5

THE STAND SIGNALS A CALL FOR DIGITALISATION

6

7

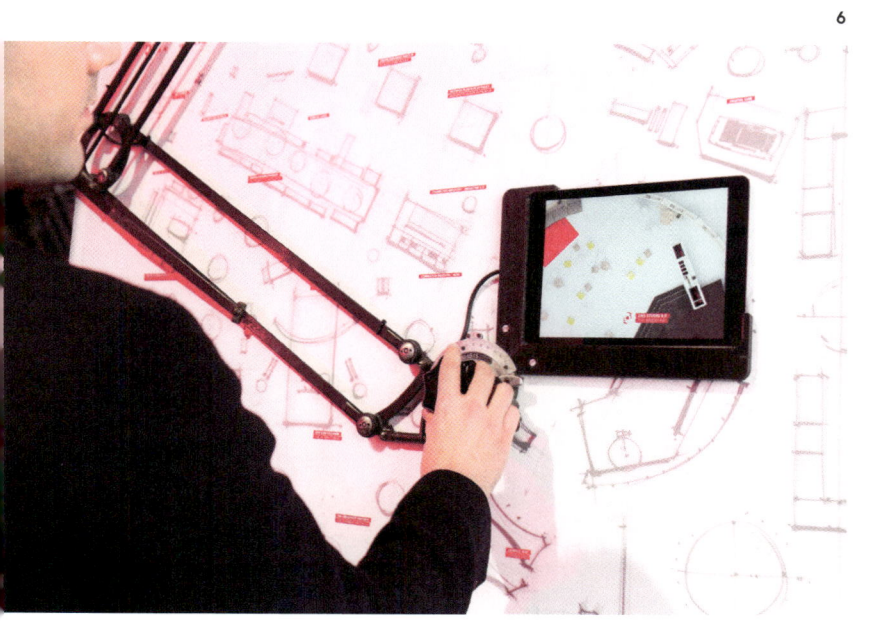

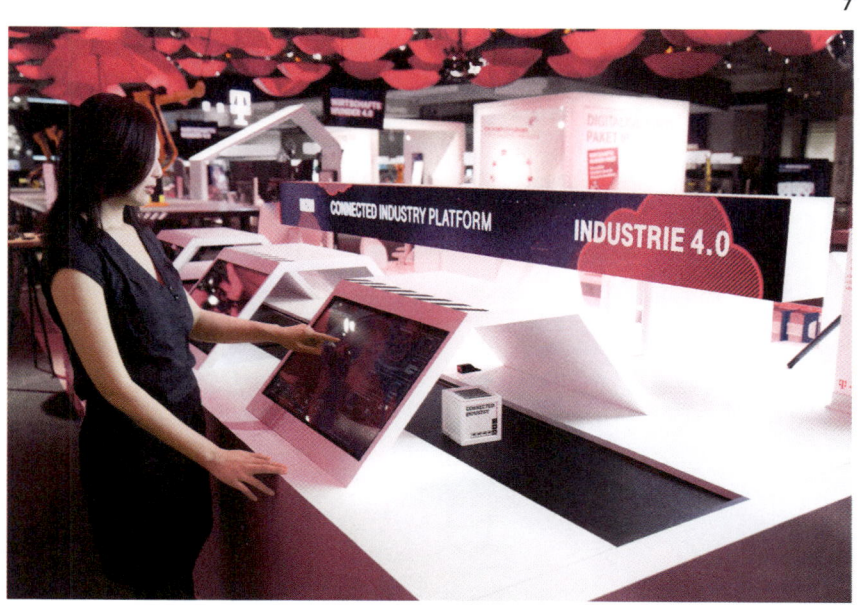

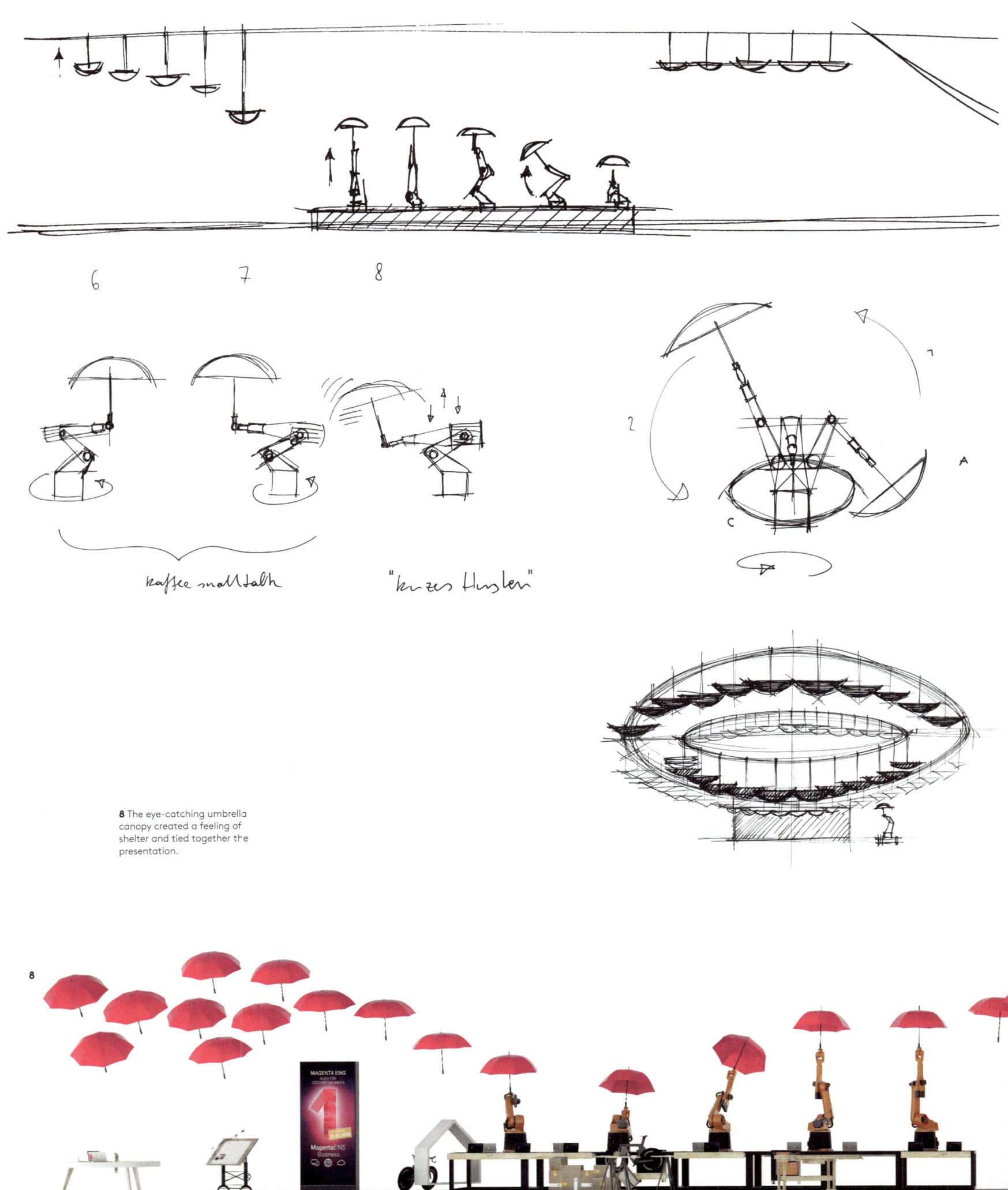

8 The eye-catching umbrella canopy created a feeling of shelter and tied together the presentation.

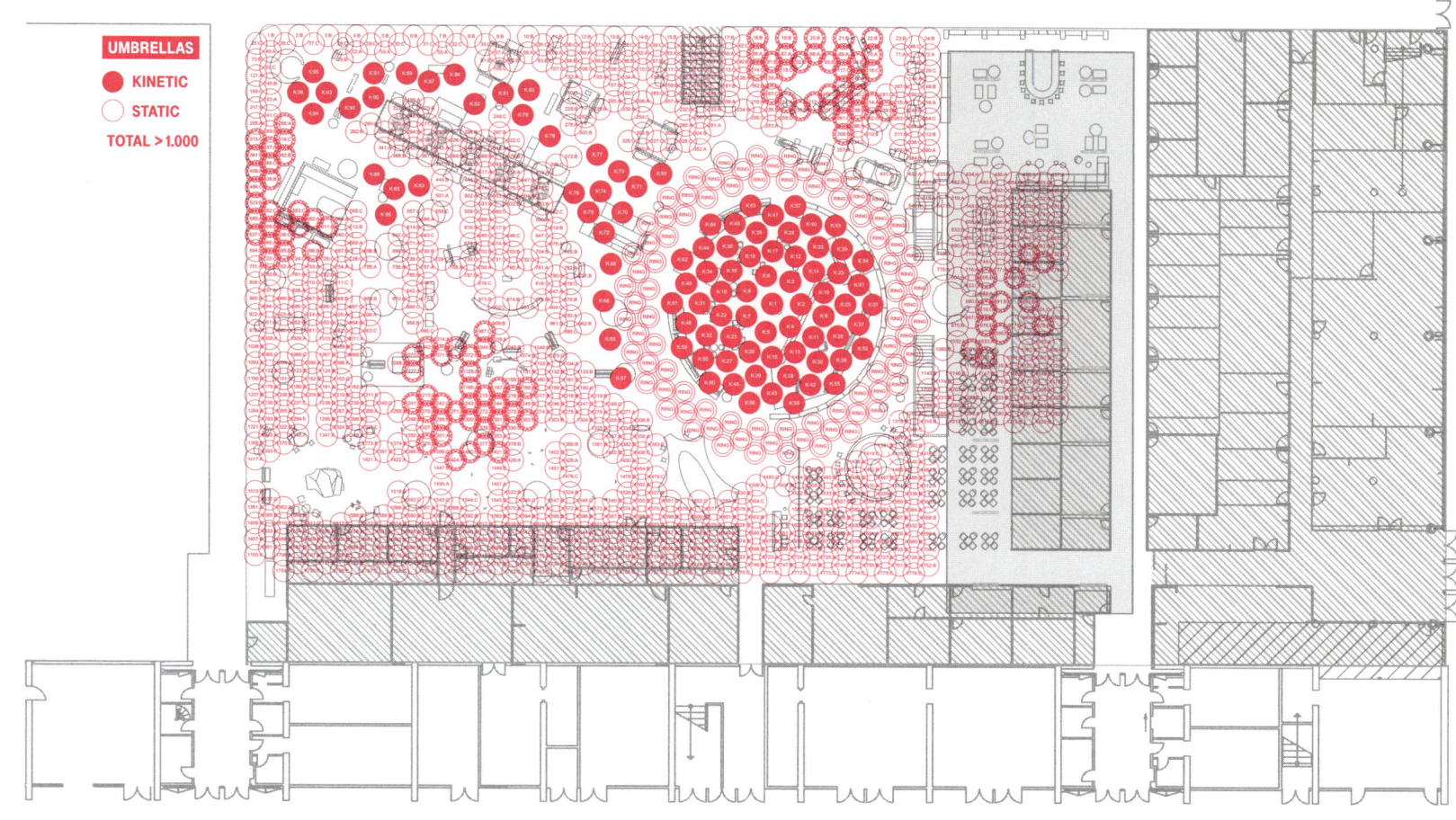

UMBRELLAS
● KINETIC
○ STATIC
TOTAL >1.000

CHOREOGRAPHED INDUSTRIAL ROBOTS APPEAR TO BE DANCING WITH THE CANOPY OF UMBRELLAS

EVERYTHING BECOMES ONE

q-bus Mediatektur

1 The central stage was accompanied by a striking media sculpture as its backdrop.

2 An impressive media forum with a stage and surrounding 3-dimensional projection wall formed the principal element of the stand.

2

'Home and mobile become One. MagentaEins' was the tagline of Deutsche Telekom's lively brand presence at IFA 2014. This theme derived from the presentation's focus that year on the convergence of mobile and fixed networks. To visually communicate this idea, the designers q-bus Mediatektur devised an immersive environment anchored by a vast media forum. A high 130-metre-long U-shaped projection wall wrapped the 3820 m² space, brought to life by 48 high performance projectors. This screen was accompanied by an

angular media sculpture, placed behind the central stage, which was programmed in sequence with the main screen. A dynamic 3D polygonal texture and the number one (representing MagentaEins) formed the main visual elements of the projections, appearing in different configurations and colours. Throughout the day, different themed projections transformed the atmosphere of the space, promoting a sense of excitement. On the trade show floor, the main stage hosted themed discussions as well as music performances for entertainment. With a warm, friendly and inviting feel, the design of the interior was especially suited to the consumer audience. Comfortable furniture, domestic fittings and furnishings and intimate seating areas suggested a familiar home-like environment. Important offers for

customers were highlighted as interactive exhibits across the space. For maximum visibility, these offers were showcased in wooden frames, akin to playful pop-up shops that intuitively drew visitors' attentions. In reference to the theme, the main concept of the design was to make visual melding possible: between analogue and digital, real and virtual, interior and exterior so that everything becomes one. ⇒

TRADE FAIR **IFA**
WHERE **Berlin, Germany**
WHEN **September 2014**
DESIGNER **q-bus Mediatektur**
STAND CONSTRUCTOR **q-bus Mediatektur**
CLIENT **Deutsche Telekom**
MARKET SECTOR **Telecommunications**
TOTAL FLOOR AREA **3820 m²**
PHOTOGRAPHER **q-bus Mediatektur**

3

TELEKOM SHOP
TELEKOM SHOP
TELEKOM SHOP
KASSE

4

ZUHAUSE UND MOBIL WERDEN EINS:
MAGENTA EINS
MAGENTA ENTERTAINMENT
MagentaENTERTAINMENT

6

3/4 Constantly changing
projections on the
screen transformed
the appearance and
atmosphere of the stand
throughout the day.

5 The stand had an
inviting, informal ambience
that suited the consumer
audience.

6 Special offers for
customers were highlighted
in exhibits encased in
white frames so that they
resembled pop-up shops.

7 Different themes
related to the home
structured the main
presentation.

7

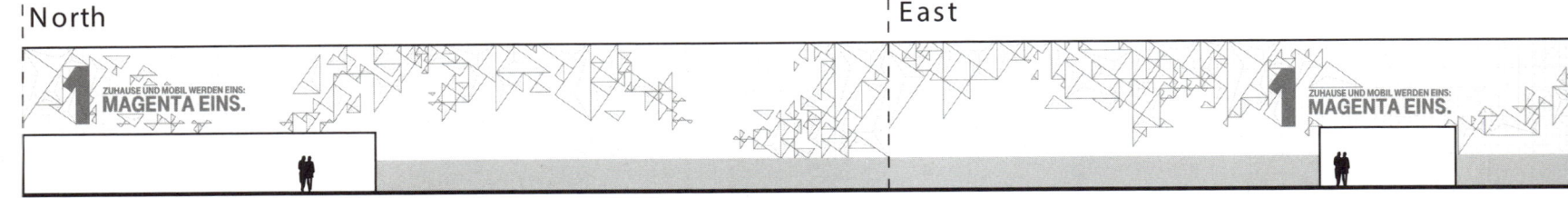

North East

RENDERINGS OF THE VISUAL TEXTURE

8

CLOSE UPS

South

Slogan

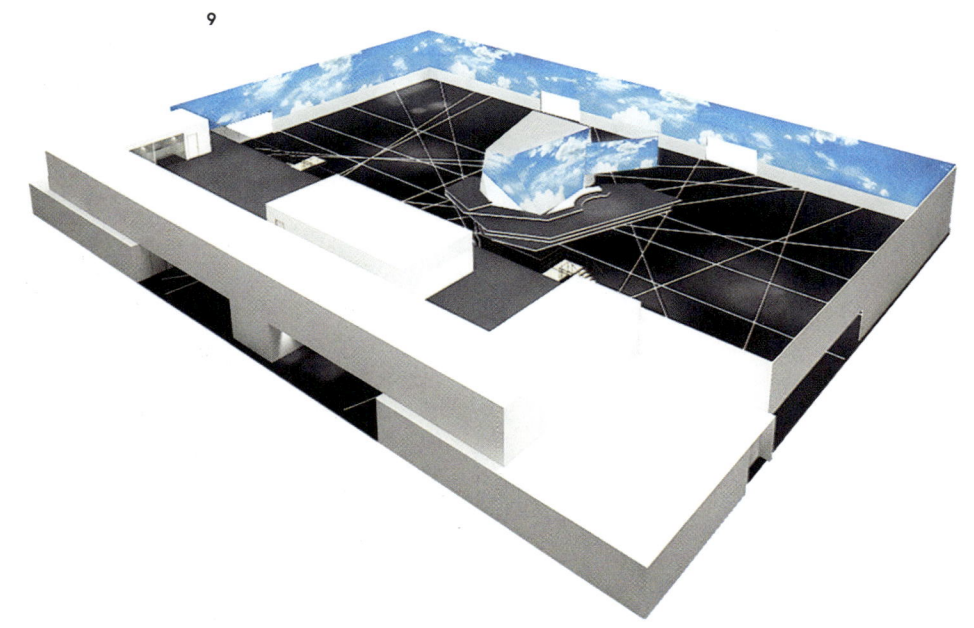

9

8 All furniture was custom-designed and specially developed for the stand.

9 3D rendering showing the interplay between the projection wall and the media sculpture.

FLOOR PLAN

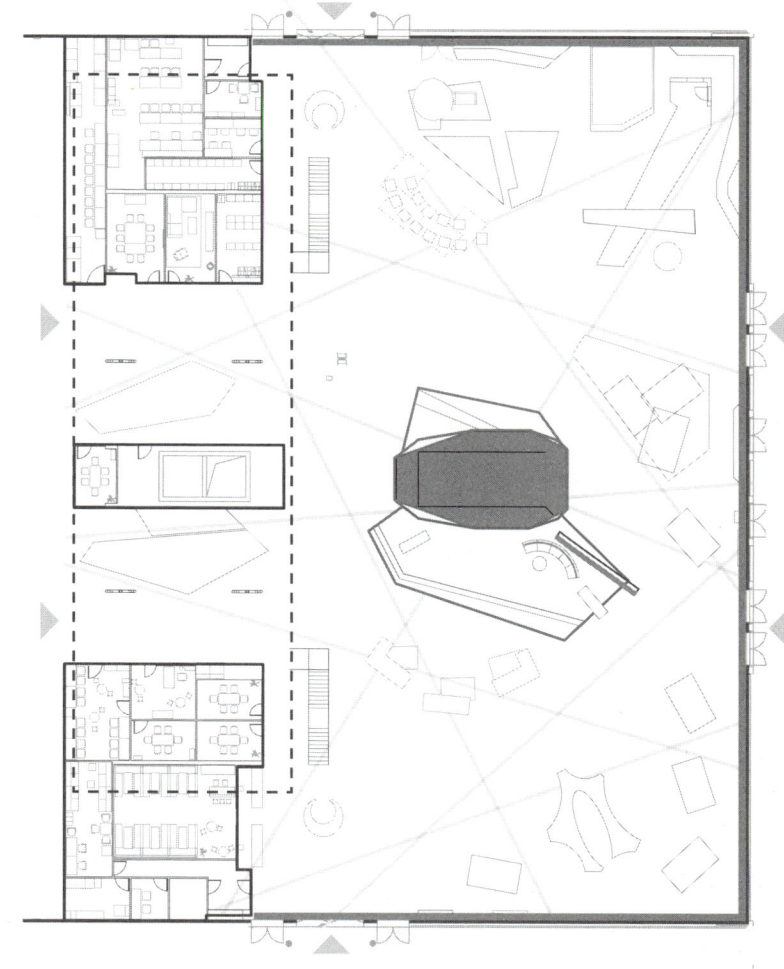

AN IMMERSIVE DIGITAL ENVIRONMENT IS ANCHORED BY A VAST MEDIA STAGE

VODAFONE
Whitevoid

1   The stunning light installation and floor LED strips were programmed in a changing light show.

2   Visual and spatial elements communicated the themes of the Experience Rooms, such as the waiting lounge for the Security theme.

2

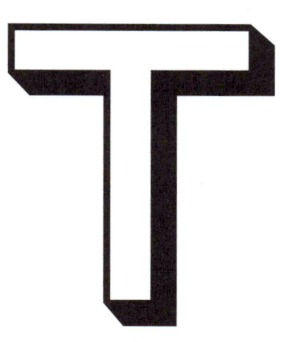

The 'Fast Lane' summed up Vodafone's spectacular presentation at CeBIT in 2015 conceived by Whitevoid. For this edition the client wished to highlight the network and underline its fast speed – the starting point for the 'Fast Lane'. The stand was divided into the indoor stand and outdoor racetrack, which were directly connected through the building entrance that was integrated into the presentation. The idea was to create a feeling of speed, so that visitors not only saw the representation of network speed but could also 'feel' it. Visitors entered through an aerodynamic tunnel punctuated by staggered markings that suggested rapid movement. This track continued inside into the Fast Lane where an illuminated multi-storey presentation unfolded. Recessed LED floor strips on the black floor led to the Porsche Showcase with a race car and sleek black displays that emerged from the track. The perspective continued into the Valley that was flanked on both sides by symmetrical angular structures that contained the Experience rooms. Four major topics were presented here: Cloud and Hosting; Security; Unified Communications; and the Internet of Things. The design of the rooms playfully incorporated key elements from the theme worlds, and glass facades opened the structure to the central area much like spectator grandstands. Hovering over the presentation was an elaborate light installation composed of 600 individually controllable light tubes in a 3D triangular truss. Light animations were programmed into the sculpture, which represented the dynamics of the brand. The Fast Lane seamlessly continued outside, transforming into the Porsche Race Track. Two freestanding Speed Pavilions further presented Vodafone's showcases in the automotive sector. The more restrained choice of materials and colours suited the business environment and focused on the corporate colours of red and tones of grey. Thrill-seeking met telecommunications on Vodafone's stand at CeBIT. ⬅

TRADE FAIR **CeBIT**
WHERE **Hanover, Germany**
WHEN **March 2015**
DESIGNER **Whitevoid**
STAND CONSTRUCTOR **Severich & Partner**
CLIENT **Vodafone**
MARKET SECTOR **Telecommunications**
TOTAL FLOOR AREA **2200 m² (plus racetrack)**
PHOTOGRAPHER **Ralph Larmann**

TELECOM

3 Light animations and compositions, sleek architectural forms and dynamic displays in the Fast Lane conveyed the feeling of speed.

4 Purpose-built outdoor pavilions reflected the dynamic architecture of the stand.

THE 'FAST LANE' UNDERLINES THE FAST SPEED OF VODAFONE'S NETWORKS

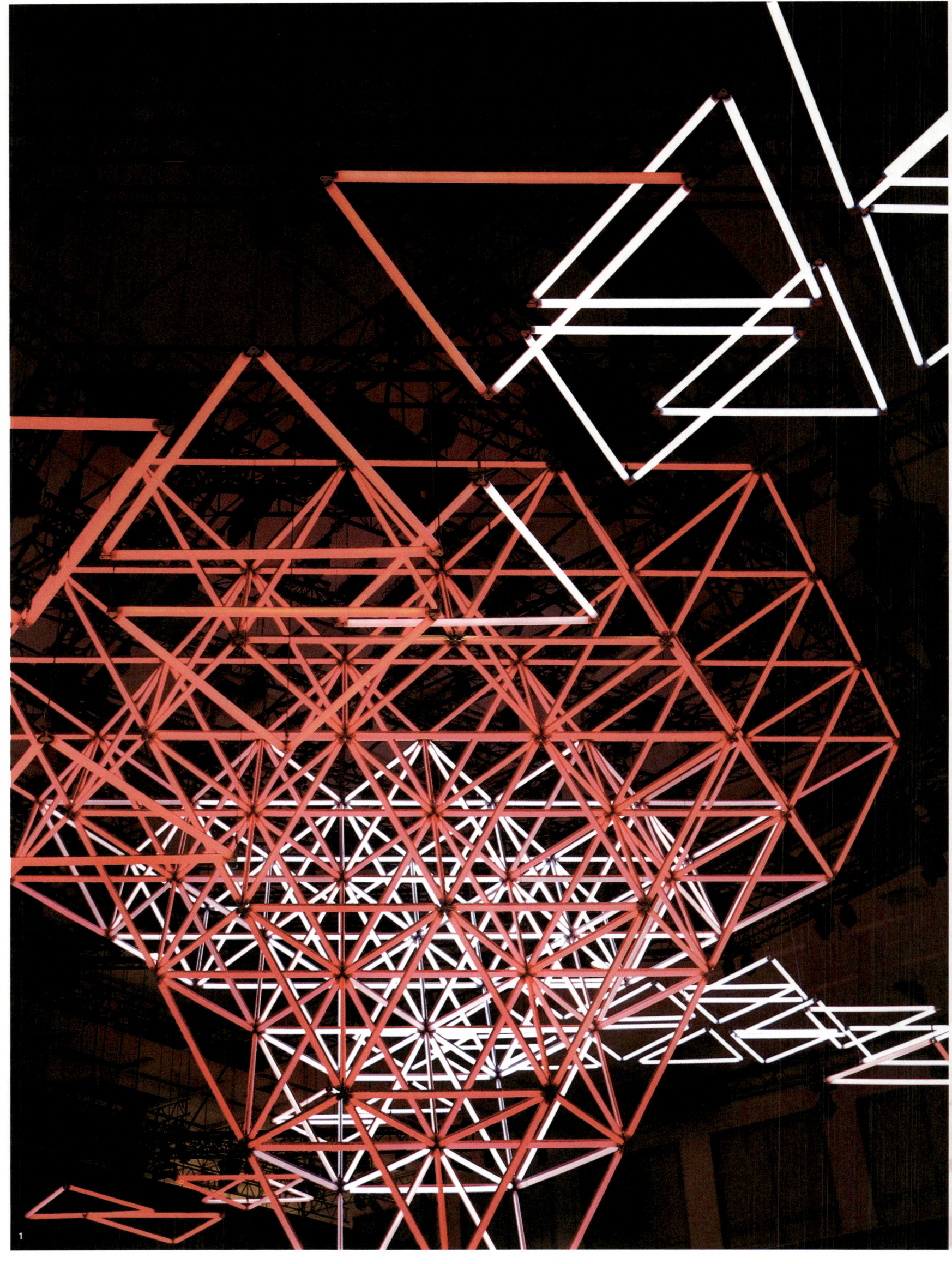

VODAFONE
Whitevoid

1 The network-like light installation was programmed to change appearance according to the relevant stage show.

2 The main island was structured into three zones that showcased the client's key services.

2

The motto 'Experience is the best information' guided Whitevoid's design of the Vodafone stand at the consumer electronics fair IFA in 2014. Considering the event was catered to a consumer audience, the design took a personal approach, aiming to engage visitors through information, entertainment and interactivity. The concept proposed an exciting and detailed multifaceted interior that hosted different worlds and hence different experiences of the brand. A triangular geometry formed the building block of the design. Vodafone's characteristic red featured strongly in combination with other colours and varying materials, resulting in a diverse atmosphere. Dominating the stand was a large island, divided into three sections that highlighted key services provided by the client. Central to this zone was a red stage with a spectacular light installation that symbolised the Vodafone network. Focused on user interaction the stage invited visitors to participate in shows, concerts, games and presentations. Constructed from nearly 1000 kinetic and static LED lights, the stunning installation was meticulously interconnected in a 3D network-like structure. It was programmed with different animations as an integrated part of the stage shows and even featured an interactive applause meter. Opposite the main island were a series of rooms that provided space for the public to test 'real-world' Vodafone products and services. Inspiring and interactive showcases hosted in a cosy café, bustling shop, innovation workshop and modern living room engaged visitors in a personal way. On the mezzanine, a business-like yet relaxed atmosphere pervaded the customer lounge where angular red and white bar and café seating combined with wooden feature walls set the scene. The stand successfully showed visitors the diversity of the products and services on offer through taking them on an engaging and stimulating brand experience. ⇁

TRADE FAIR **IFA**
WHERE **Berlin, Germany**
WHEN **September 2014**
DESIGNER **Whitevoid**
STAND CONSTRUCTOR **Severich & Partner**
CLIENT **Vodafone**
MARKET SECTOR **Telecommunications**
TOTAL FLOOR AREA **1950 m²**
PHOTOGRAPHERS **Christopher Bauder and Nils Hendrik Mueller**

THE MULTIFACETED INTERIOR HOSTS VODAFONE'S DIVERSE WORLDS IN A DYNAMIC, PERSONAL SETTING

3 Materials and colour were strategically utilised to create strong visual impact and convey the atmospheres of different worlds, as seen here in the contemporary lounge.

4/5 With its friendly warm atmosphere, the workshop and its terrace in front were a hit with visitors.

6 Red and white designer furniture combined with feature wood walls created an appealing platform to do business.

5

6

YOTA DEVICES

External Reference Architects

TRADE FAIR **Mobile World Congress**
WHERE **Barcelona, Spain**
WHEN **February 2014**
DESIGNER **External Reference Architects**
STAND CONSTRUCTOR **Craft Art Labor**
CLIENT **Yota Devices**
MARKET SECTOR **Telecommunications**
TOTAL FLOOR AREA **120 m²**
PHOTOGRAPHER **Adrià Goula Sardà**

1   The amorphous white landscape was composed from backlit vertical fins.

2   Light and sound were used dramatically to create a sense of atmosphere and sensuousness.

3   A delicate landscape in itself, the pattern of the exterior skin resembled drops carved on the surface.

2

Y

Yota Devices' stand introduced a contrasting, surreal sense of nature to the digital setting at the 2014 Mobile World Congress. Designed once again by External Reference Architects, the stand appeared as an undulating techno-landscape that took visitors on a deep sensory journey. The idea was to realise a presentation that wowed visitors and ensured the brand maximum visibility without detaching the space from the fair. Taking inspiration from nature the designers devised a natural plaza that immersed visitors in an experience of light, music and projections. A valley and topographic ceiling form the main elements of the space. A mysterious dark perforated skin enveloped the space, parting at the front to reveal the entrance. This twinkling surface gave a teaser of what awaited. Inside a sinuous white landscape unfolded, striated like an eroded canyon. A skeleton of vertical white fins formed the main structure, receding and protruding respectively to incorporate projection screens and displays for the devices. Additionally two meeting rooms and a technical

3

room were sculpted into the structure. Above, the undulating form of the ceiling was derived from the positive volume of the eroded landscape below. Made from 2200 flexible polycarbonate tubes of different lengths, the ceiling had a mesmerizing quality thanks to the glow of the translucent material and changing illumination effects. The ambient lighting program was synchronized with background music while the feature program accompanied projections on the screens in the landscape below. On the exterior, the finely dotted pattern of the skin intensified the ceiling's verticality and complemented the play of lines in the space. Glossy acrylic on the floor suggested a pool of darkness that reflected the light dramatically. Evocative and atmospheric, Yota's stand transported visitors to a whole new digital landscape. ⇒

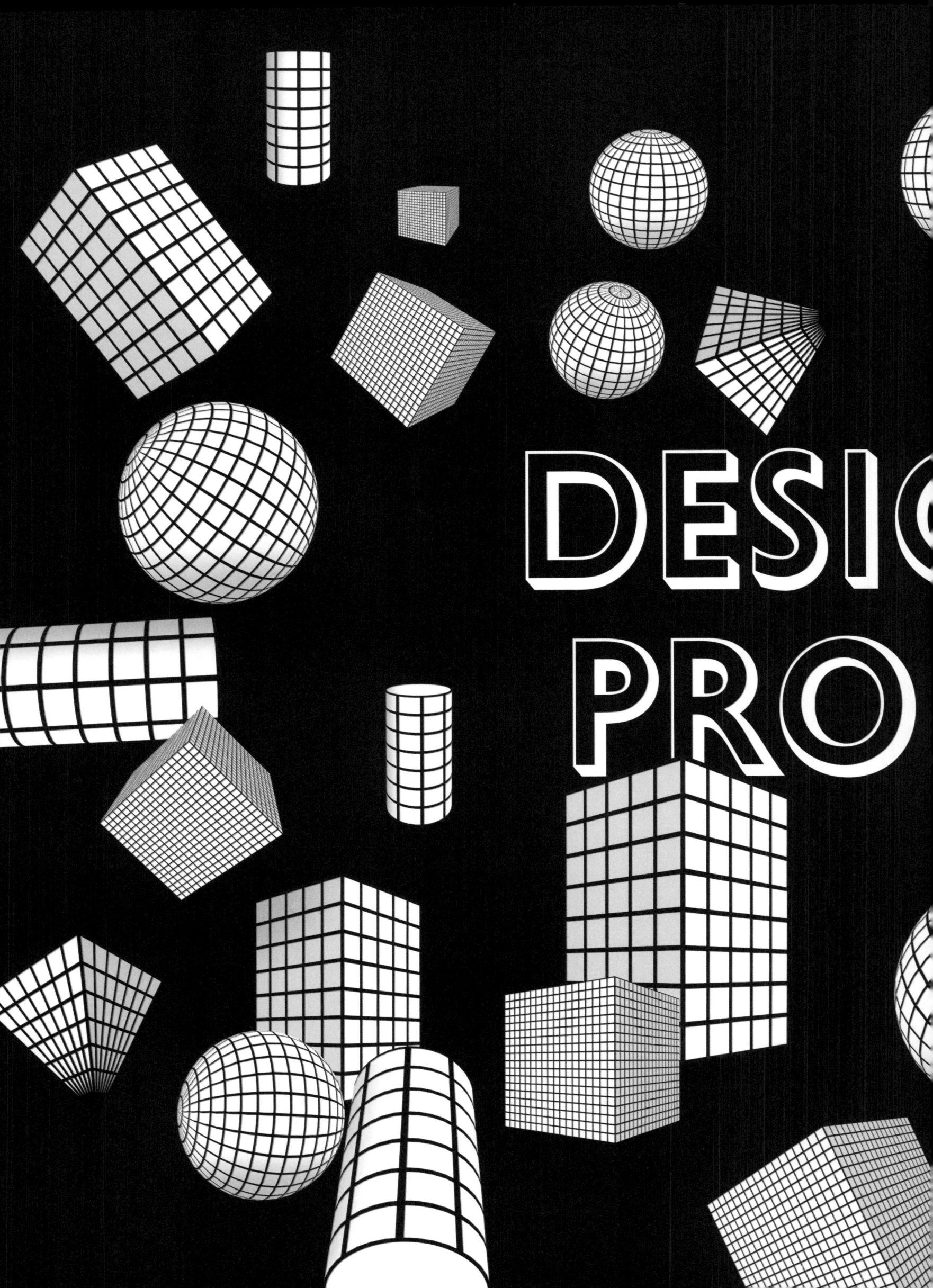

100% INTERIOR
www.100interior.de

Sylvia Leydecker founded her Cologne-based studio 100% interior in 1997. The studio focuses on designing future-oriented corporate interiors, excelling in conceptualising spaces and interiors, with special expertise in healthcare. Sylvia is also the author of three internationally renowned books.

P.140

2LK
www.2LK.com

2LK is an independent, award-winning experiential design consultancy that creates stunning environments and engaging content to deliver unique, effective brand experiences. With expertise, passion and a commitment to intelligent, insight-led design the company combines imaginative architecture, inspiring content and authentic stories to influence understanding, strengthen relationships and forge emotional brand connections. With offices in the UK and UAE, 2LK has a global reach, handling projects for an international client list.

P.108, 330

3DESIGN
www.david-durand.com

Scenographer and ecodesigner David Durand founded 3Design in 2005 in France. His specialisation lies in exhibition spaces, event scenography and trade fair design. Focusing on ecodesign, every project is the result of a challenging creative process that tells a story with materials as well as multi-sensorial spatial experiences. Among his main clients are major event and stand agencies in France, as well as national and international brands.

P.328

A01
www.a01.it

A01 comprises a team of ambitious and enthusiastic architects engaged in designing structures for diverse purposes for residential, commercial and cultural clients, and the creation of modern and functional interiors. The company was found in 2010 and is based in Vilnius. A01 is led by its two partners Zivile Putrimaite and Darius Romanovskij.

P.098

ANIDRIDE DESIGN
www.anidridedesign.com

Venice-based design studio Anidride Design was founded by Nicola De Pellegrini in 2011. Its diverse portfolio spans retail design, branding, packaging, product and web design, advertising and environmental design. Working with originality, enthusiasm and expertise, the studio believes in producing projects that convey emotions but are simultaneously functional. As a growing practice, Anidride Design uses strengthened collaborations with experts from different fields and a global strategy to develop coherent and effective results.

P.342

ARNO DESIGN
www.arno-design.de

Arno Design was established in Munich in 1994. The studio concentrates on the design and realisation of trade fair booths, showrooms and stores. Led by Mirka Nassiri, Peter Haberlander and Claus Neuleib, the design team works with intense creativity, concentration and personal contact to find the best possible solution for every project. Implementing diverse materials guarantees new and unexpected settings, with efficiency and ecology as the keywords that define the studio's design concept.

P.008, 162, 286

ARPALAB
www.arpaindustriale.com

Established in 2010, ArpaLab (Filippo Manetti, Fausto Donato, Sandro Marini) is the ideas laboratory of Arpa Industriale. It was created to engage different and complementary skills within the company. ArpaLab mixes product development, marketing and product innovation, and corporate communication and art direction. The crossover of such specific know-how and experience results in the conception of new ideas for interior design materials that bring together the best aesthetic innovations with technical product development.

P.222

ARQUITECT STUDIO
www.arquitect.eu

Arquitect Studio specialises in the design and realisation of projects for exhibitions, set design, trade fair stands, retail design as well as corporate image management and design consulting. As a full-service partner, the studio is engaged on projects from concept to completion taking care of every step of the design and production process. Arquitect Studio was founded in 2010 by Italian architect Luca Biancoviso, and is based in Vincenza. Its client list counts many companies from the jewellery and watch industry.

P.348

ARTING
www.arting.dk

Arting was founded by Danni P. Nicolaisen in 2002. The studio conceives, designs and builds exhibition solutions that give voice to brand architecture. The company strives for surprising concepts that stretch the boundaries of what's possible while retaining a strong dedication to execution and craftsmanship, and control of the supply chain. A team of 30 experts in design, marketing and production work in its headquarters in Vejle, Denmark as well as the design studio in Copenhagen.

P.176, 198, 296

ASTRID BORNHEIM ARCHITECTURE
www.astridbornheim.de

Astrid Bornheim Architecture was founded in Berlin in 2001 as a multidisciplinary laboratory for architecture. Focusing on the narrative qualities of architecture, the office specialises in museums, exhibition design and corporate design. Astrid Bornheim teaches experimental design at the Technical University of Braunschweig and the Nottingham School of Architecture in London. In cooperation with universities and building material manufacturers she also initiates research and product development.

P.030

ATELIER 522
www.atelier522.com

atelier 522 is an office for strategy and design. Always ready to undertake all possible adventures, atelier 522 loves exploring new territories with its team of interior designers, architects, product designers, graphic and communication designers, communications specialists, business economists, artists and philosophers. It's a place where these interdisciplinary specialists come together to put their energy, knowledge, talent and ideas into designing the things they dream of.

P.044, 054, 180

ATELIER MARKGRAPH
www.markgraph.de

Based in Frankfurt, Atelier Markgraph is an agency that specialises in spatial communication. This interdisciplinary design and planning provider creates tangible experiences for companies and brands for clients all over the world. Using cutting-edge technologies, the studio produces surprising spatial productions at the interface of business, culture and science, from exhibitions and media productions to corporate architecture.

P.260, 272

ATELIER MARKO BRAJOVIC
www.markobrajovic.com

Architect Marko Brajovic founded his atelier in 2008 in São Paulo, and expanded with a second office in Barcelona. The idea of the hybrid, as well as the creation of multi-sensorial and immersive experiences, drives the eclectic works of the multidisciplinary atelier, permeating all areas, formats and aesthetics of his projects. Its portfolio of projects includes scenography, product design, architecture, and creative direction for a diverse global client base.

P.014

ATELIER SEITZ
www.atelierseitz.de

For over 50 years, Atelier Seitz has been designing, creating concepts and constructing exhibition stands, events and showrooms for clients across the globe. Its team of architects develops innovative and custom-made concepts, constantly seeking ways to reduce waste and increase recycling in trade fair projects. Working from a 4000-m² facility with over 40 qualified staff, the studio is a full-service partner for the duration of any project, from the rough sketch to the final touches.

P.068, 230, 356

BACHMANNKERN UND PARTNER
www.bkp-architektur.de

Founded in 2000, architecture and design agency Bachmann.Kern und Partner has its headquarters in the German city of Solingen. The agency focuses on the conceptualisation, mediation and realisation of interior architecture, in particular in the realms of exhibition, retail, event and trade fair design. Creativity, competence and enthusiasm are integral to the agency's operations, along with a network of stand constructors and trade fair-related agencies.

P.026, 208, 212

BARZILAI
www.barzilaidesign.com

Founded in 2000, Barzilai Exhibition Experts is a global, creative powerhouse, dedicated to the design of innovative exhibition spaces. Based in Israel, their seasoned team of 23 creatives and producers bring uncompromising passion for precision and detail to create exceptional spaces where brands come to life. With a global reach exceeding 30 partners, Barzilai provides maximum flexibility and full turn-key solutions to ensure customer success. Together, the practice bridges cultures and business practices to generate innovative spaces that create the right impact.

P.086

BELLPRAT ASSOCIATES
www.bellprat.ch

Bellprat Associates was founded 1981 in Vancouver by Xavier Bellprat. Since 1990 the studio is located in Zurich. Today Bellprat Associates is an international studio for the conception, design, planning and realisation of trade fairs, events, world fair pavilions, brand worlds, theme parks, visitor centres and tourist destinations. Its services include the development of conceptual ideas, creation of a narrative and design of media like architecture, light, graphics and multimedia.

P.278

BRAUNWAGNER
www.braunwagner.de

Braunwagner is a design agency that focuses on environmental, product and communication design, as well as architecture and consulting for strategic brand development. Since its foundation in Aachen 1999, the firm expanded in 2013 with a second office in Berlin. Led by Prof. Manfred Wagner and Marina Franke, the 25-strong creative team emotionalises corporate identities and transforms brand values into spatial communication, with creativity, know-how and enthusiasm.

P.282

BENZ & ZIEGLER
www.b-and-z.com

Benz & Ziegler operates in the fields of architecture, brand architecture and interior design. The practice was established in 2012 by Matthias Benz and Christoph Ziegler. Both founders gained extensive international experience at major architecture practices before setting up Benz & Ziegler in Munich. The practice has a special interest in transitions in architecture, with a focus on closing the missing links between architecture and interior design.

P.110

CON'FETTI
www.confettireclame.nl

Con'fetti is a Rotterdam-based design studio established in 1989 by Monique Morks and Eric Zijffers. The company works on projects in diverse disciplines including interiors, retail and exhibition, as well as product, furniture and graphic design. The Con'fetti team strives to provide inspiring solutions with a young, fresh and innovative approach, and create unique concepts based on an 'atmospheric experience'.

P.338

BLOCHER BLOCHER SHOPS
blocherblocher.com

Blocher Blocher Shops was founded in 2006 in Germany as a subsidiary of Blocher Blocher Partners, the interdisciplinary, international office for architecture and design. Blocher Blocher Shops specialises in the development of monobrand concepts. With strategic storytelling, the office entrenches the brand values of a company to effectively communicate with its target group. Its work translates brand images into the spatial dimension of architecture and design to enable emotional and tangible brand experiences.

P.016, 354

COSTA GROUP
www.costagroup.net

The Costa Group specialises in designing and fitting out hospitality interiors and specialty food and beverage venues. A crafted process that encompasses style, creativity and functionality with careful attention to detail characterises its approach. The company is a full-service partner for any project, with an important service being the total design and realisation of the interior on its premises. The company is wholly owned by brothers Franco and Sandro Costa.

P.304

BONGIANA
www.bongiana.it

Pietro Bongiana founded Bongiana architetture in 1998. Silvia Codato became a partner in 2008. The office mainly operates in the retail design sector in Italy and abroad, and is also engaged in architecture and interior design projects. Its clients span diverse industries including fashion, design, art and hospitality.

P.216

D'ART DESIGN GRUPPE
www.d-art-design.de

Spatial communications firm D'art Design Gruppe was established in 1991. The studio's approach is one in which creative design skills merge with interdisciplinary expertise. Headquartered in Neuss, Germany with a second office in Seoul, the company works in the field of retail and exhibition design for global clients, with a focus on strategic consulting and conceptual development of brand and corporate appearances.

P.048, 104, 308

DORELL.GHOTMEH.TANE/
ARCHITECTS
www.dgtarchitects.com

DGT. (Dorell.Ghotmeh.Tane/ Architects) is an international architecture practice founded in Paris in 2006 and directed by Dan Dorell, Lina Ghotmeh and Tsuyoshi Tane. DGT. gained an international reputation through winning the international competition to design the Estonian National Museum (to be completed in 2016). The work of DGT. aims to reveal high quality, precise and unexpected spaces, be it a museum, dance scenography or art installation.

P.350

DIJON DESIGNS
www.dijondesigns.com

Dijon Designs delivers beautiful exhibition stands and interiors throughout Europe and across the world. Its client list includes leading blue-chip companies from a range of business sectors including information technology, pharmaceutics, travel and finance. The company is based in the beautiful Oxfordshire countryside in the UK and employs 15 full-time staff. Its rural location provides the perfect inspirational backdrop for the company's creative team, which consists of graphic and 3D designers.

P.290

DRÄNDLE 70|30
www.draendle7030.com

Drändle 70|30 is committed to making the brand visible and tangible in a three-dimensional manner. The company's range of services includes consulting, planning and conceiving spatial brand experiences for trade fairs and store branding projects. All solutions are based on the concept of combining brand messages, materials and creative effort into one effective statement.

P.202

DSA
www.dsalive.com

Established in 1995, DSA specialises in developing world-class exhibitions and events for international clients, using the latest knowledge and technology to enhance visitor engagement and deliver outstanding brand experiences. DSA is delighted to work alongside many renowned international brands and global partners. The company works with a UK-based team of 12, led by managing director Emma Lawrence.

P.234

EINSZU33
www.einszu33.com

Established in 1999 einszu33 is an international practice for corporate architecture, brand communication and interior design which develops distinct concepts for interiors and space staging. Co-directors Hendrik Müller and Georg Thiersch lead a team of 10 from its Munich office. Award-winning projects feature the design of showrooms, retail stores, exhibition stands, office environments and concepts for hospitality. einszu33 works for renowned companies in varying sectors with clients including Aesop, Beko, Gaggenau, Kuka and Laurèl.

P.092, 150, 156

EKO DESIGN
www.eko.agency

Founded in 2007 by Nicolas Turpin, eko Design is an agency specialising in ecodesign, particularly for events. The agency endeavours to be as responsible as possible regarding the impact of its events on the environment. Located in Paris, eko Design counts 6 team members working for clients from different sectors (e.g. banking services, media, public institutions) in Paris but also regional areas in France and abroad.

P.328

EXTERNAL REFERENCE
ARCHITECTS
externalreference.com

External reference architects focuses on design and research within the context of interior design and architecture. Founded by Nacho Toribio and Carmelo Zappulla in 2007 the office is based in Barcelona. Its work endeavours to break the boundaries of architecture, visual art and digital tools to generate new spatial experiences. Research through design and collaboration drives the multidisciplinary practice, which draws on the processes of questioning, engaging, speculation and innovation in its work.

P.390

GAMBIT MARKETING AND
COMMUNICATION
www.gambit-do.de

Based in Dortmund, gambit marketing & communication is a B2B communications agency focusing on the building construction and equipment sector. The agency speaks the language of its clients: technical know-how and creativity are bundled together in an interdisciplinary team of marketing and communications professionals, architects and journalists. In the field of fairs and events, gambit develops integrated concepts with the corresponding design of the stands.

P.060

GARP DESIGN
www.garpdesign.no

Based in Haugesund, Norway, Garp is a design agency working within conceptual design and visual communication, the expertise being stand design, trade fairs and exhibitions and interiors. Its name derives from the old Norse word Garpr meaning 'tough or fearless guy'. While the majority of its clients are maritime-based, its portfolio also counts projects for the pharmaceutical, service and retail sectors. Established in 2014 the agency promotes a culture of curiosity, playfulness, pushing boundaries and challenging established truths.

GEORGE P JOHNSON EXPERIENCE MARKETING
www.gpj.com

Nearly 100 years ago, Georgep. Johnson invented experiential marketing. Today, his legacy continues as GPJ helps internationally respected brands attract, engage, and thrill audiences with experiences that drive business results and build lasting consumer relationships. A singular goal drives its approach: to create experiences that change the world and bring brands to life. The company comprises 1300 team members working across 29 offices around the globe.

GIELISSEN
www.gielissen.com

Gielissen has been designing and delivering stands and interior projects since 1937. The firm has 11 offices worldwide, with a global team of 300 professionals who realise around 1500 projects every year and a network of partners that ensures quality throughout. Designing and building award-winning projects, delivering inspiring environments and enabling clients to reach their goals are the company's main driving forces.

GOLD & WIRTSCHAFTSWUNDER
www.gww-design.de

Gold & Wirtschaftswunder is a multidisciplinary design agency based in Stuttgart. Founded by Christian Schiller and Julia Kühne in 2008, the agency comprises a permanent team of 5 employees and cooperates with a wide network of creative partners. Branding and identity, print and editorial, and spatial communication form the agency's main areas of expertise. All its projects are driven by a deep conceptual approach and a transmedia understanding of design.

HEINE/LENZ/ZIZKA
www.hlz.de

Heine/Lenz/Zizka is an agency for visual communication founded in 1989. The agency creates visual identities and brand presences from packaging design and communications to comprehensive corporate design. With offices in Berlin and Frankfurt, the agency has clients from various sectors, serving cultural institutions with the same care and commitment as for small and medium-sized enterprises. Sympathetic understanding, a love of communicating, nonconformism and good common sense are integral tools for the agency's success.

HOLLIN+RADOSKE
www.hollinradoske.de

Bernd Hollin and Alexander Radoske both studied architecture in Darmstadt — Germany. 1997 they founded the architecture and design office Hollin+Radoske in Frankfurt Main. Together with 24 architects and designers the team develops architectural and interior concepts for airline design, hotels, residential architecture and shop design.

HW.DESIGN
www.hwdesign.de

Munich-based hw.design was co-founded by Frank Wagner in 1995 and is an award-winning agency for brand development and communication. Its team of 30 permanent employees manages and realises projects in four core areas of expertise: identity, communication, space and digital. Its portfolio covers an interdisciplinary service spectrum that enables the studio to create contemporary cross-media brand experiences.

IPPOLITO FLEITZ GROUP
ifgroup.org

Ippolito Fleitz Group is a multidisciplinary design studio based in Stuttgart that operates internationally. Founded by Gunter Fleitz and Peter Ippolito, the company currently presents itself as a creative unit of 45 employees, each contributing specific skills to the alternating, project-oriented team formations. Providing creative solutions for its global clients, the studio covers a wide field of design disciplines including interiors, products, graphics and architecture.

JANGLED NERVES
www.janglednerves.com

Jangled nerves comprises an interdisciplinary team based in Stuttgart. Established in 1998 by Prof. Thomas Hundt and Ingo Zirngibl, it specialises in communication through interior design, and merges the sensibilities of a creative agency, planning consultancy and film and media production firm. Its approach considers media and space as inextricably linked, elements that need to be viewed and developed as a whole. Projects include museums, and event and exhibition spaces in the cultural, scientific and industrial realms.

P.258, 272

JÜRGENSARCHITEKTEN
www.juergensarchitekten.de

Based in Munich, jürgensarchitekten is a design studio founded in 2007 by Natalie Jürgens. The practices specialises in trade fair design and corporate interiors. Its clients mainly comprise design-oriented enterprises from the building or sports-related industries. A collaborative process is particularly important to the practice's work and over the years jürgensarchitekten has established a wide network of experts in trade fair design with whom it regularly cooperates.

P.050

KAUFFMANN THEILIG & PARTNER
www.ktp-architekten.de

The office Kauffmann Theilig was established in 1988 and became Kauffmann Theilig & Partner in 1995 with Prof. Andreas Theilig, Dieter Ben Kauffmann and Rainer Lenz as business partners. The office plans and realises variously sized projects for global clients in all fields of building construction, as well as corporate architecture and exhibition design. KTP has cultivated an intensive collaboration between experts and engineers to achieve integrated architectural solutions.

P.260

KEGGENHOFF I PARTNER
www.keggenhoff.de

Keggenhoff I Partner is engaged in the design and implementation of holistic interior architecture and architecture concepts for transformation, modernisation and new building projects. It was founded in 2001 by Sabine Keggenhoff and Michael Than. The practice regards architecture and interior architecture as a cohesive unit that balances atmospheric, emotional, functional requirements, and strives to create valuable, motivating and sensory environments.

P.006

KMS BLACKSPACE
www.kms-blackspace.com

KMS Blackspace creates and designs fascinating brand experiences and their touch points. They focus on activating brands through the disciplines of space, motion design and customer experience design. The results are successful brand experiences, trade shows and events, shops and showrooms, corporate headquarters, exhibitions, museums and crossover activities for companies of any size and sector. Together with KMS Team and KMS Mindshift, KMS Blackspace forms Germany's largest owner-managed branding agency group.

P.116, 248, 252

KOHLHAAS MESSEBAU
www.kohlhaas-messebau.de

Architecture and design for trade fairs form kohlhaas messebau's field of expertise. Its main goal is to create new dimensions in temporary spaces, and bring visitors into tangible brand worlds. Creativity, passion and technical ability ensure a perfect and cost-optimized implementation of 300 projects annually. The company operates with a permanent team of 70 from its offices in Munich and Hannover, and can be counted on as a full-service partner for any project.

P.060

KPLUS CONCEPT
www.kplus-konzept.de

Distinctive store and exhibition designs, multi-sensory brand communication, pioneering worlds of experiences for shopping centres, exciting interiors for healthcare and hospitality - these are the capabilities of kplus concept. Founded in Düsseldorf in 2005 the studio is led by interior designer Bettina Kratz, and communication designer and photographer Markus Kratz. Its team of 20 employees comprises interior, communication, product, 3D and web designers as well as writers and photographers.

P.324

LIGANOVA
www.liganova.com

Liganova.The BrandRetail Company stands for sales-effective, cross-linked brand communication at the cutting edge. Companies are challenged to smooth the boundaries between offline & online and to create seamless brand, product and service experiences. This is where Liganova excels with many years of know-how and expertise. Their areas of competence are networked in a focused manner and 'through-the-line'. Their mission is to close the gap between the physical and digital. They live and breathe the zeitgeist and are moved by aesthetic sensitivity.

P.270

LITTLE
www.little-inc.com

Saori Miwa is an experienced designer based in Japan. After working with Tonerico for more than five years, she established her own interior design studio, Little, in Tokyo in 2010. The studio has already built up a portfolio that includes a range of interior design projects, including restaurants and cafes, offices and exhibition stands, and shops and retail spaces.

MARTIN ET KARCZINSKI
www.martinetkarczinski.de

Established in 2000, Martin et Karczinski builds brands for companies and institutions. Working in the fields of corporate identity, corporate design and corporate branding, the firm combines communication strategies with high-quality design. The company has an international client base, working with such companies as Occhio, Audi and Alape.

MBCO
www.mbco.net

Munich-based studio mbco is dedicated to providing new contexts for personal encounters in the realms of trade show and exhibition design. Since its foundation in 1996, the firm has been demonstrating its comprehensive range of expertise across a broad spectrum of contrasting styles, realising temporary trade fair presentations all over the world. The 17-member team delivers corporate identities with enthusiasm, conceptual clarity and attention to detail, using a flexible approach to create individual solutions with a sustainable edge.

MODE:LINA ARCHITEKCI
www.modelina-architekci.com

mode:lina architekci is an award-winning architecture studio founded by Paweł Garus and Jerzy Woźniak in 2009 in Poznań. Its diverse portfolio of work spans corporate, residential, hospitality, retail and institutional projects for public and private clients. Attention to detail, respect for materials, a strong narrative and playful approach characterise the studio's work.

NEO DESIGN
www.neo.com.tr

Neo Design was founded in Istanbul in 2005 by Cenk Gün and Halise Özel. The studio is active in stand design, the design and implementation of product displays and subsystems, design and realisation of corporate identity at sales outlets, and also works in the field of visual communication and graphic design. Among its clients are VitrA, Villeroy & Boch, E.C.A. – SEREL and Chrysler – Jeep – Dodge.

ONTWERPBUREAU JAN
www.ontwerpbureaujan.be

Ontwerpbureau Jan was founded in 2008 by Jan Hendrix, a young and dynamic designer who gained his Masters in Product Design and Industrial Design at the Media and Design Academy (MAD) in Genk. The studio specialises in the design of interiors, stands and products. By defining the essence of a company and closely engaging the client in the creative process the studio creates unique projects that give clients a competitive edge.

PAOLO CESARETTI
www.paolocesaretti.it

Paolo Cesaretti is a design consultant and art director who explores the concept of designed space as a communication tool. His practice specialises in exhibition and retail design and brand identity, particularly on innovation and research. Clients include companies from diverse fields including manufacturing and trade, mass-market retailing, digital media, finance and communication. Paolo is also a lecturer at the Scuola Politecnica di Design Milano and guest professor at the Domus Academy and Politecnico di Milano.

PLANWERK
www.dargel-planwerk.de

Planwerk was founded by Andreas Dargel, who has been developing concepts for fairs, showrooms and event architecture for more than 20 years. The design office is based in the Ruhr region at a central hub between the large fair sites in Germany. Planwerk is especially active in the automotive sector but also works for clients from diverse industries including banking, construction, healthcare and logistics.

PROJEKTTRIANGLE DESIGN STUDIO
www.projekttriangle.com

Projekttriangle is a design studio for applied and artistic projects from all disciplines of visual, inter-action, information and graphic design. Operating in the crossover zone between design, research and art, the firm executes international projects for corporate clients as well as media installations for industry, research and culture. The studio was founded in 1998 in Stuttgart by Prof. Danijela Djokic, Martin Grothmaak and Prof. Jürgen Späth.

P.146, 240

Q~BUS MEDIATEKTUR
www.q-bus.de

Design agency q~bus Mediatektur is a Berlin-based, owner-managed company, established in 1995. Aiming for the integration of communication, architecture and technology, the firm implements a working method called 'ambient intelligence'. Transcending the boundaries of individual projects, q~bus integrates talents and specialists from different back-grounds such as communication design, architecture, software development and system integration. An Interdisciplinary approach enables the agency to develop and realise pervasive concepts for wide-ranging projects, from brand environments to software solutions.

P.370, 384

QUPIX
www.qupix.nl

Architects Pepijn van de Staak and Jan Doornekamp founded their multidisciplinary design practice Qupix in 2010. Qupix aims to create multi-dimensional spaces across architecture and interiors for fair stands, bespoke events and exhi-bitions. Its concepts connect and engage visitors in the brand experience, trigger surprise and evoke emotion to ensure a lasting impression of the client's brand. Qupix operate as a full-service partner from the first sketch through to final completion.

P.312

RAW EDGES
www.raw-edges.com

Raw-Edges is a London-based design studio founded by Israeli designers Yael Mer and Shay Alkalay. The duo collaborate on ideas and have complementary interests: whereas Yael Mer's primary focus is on turning two-dimensional sheet materials into functional forms, Shay Alkalay is fascinated by how things move, function and react. Their output, which is the product of relentless experimentation, includes unique, limited edition and serially-produced interior objects, and museum and exhibition installations.

P.170

SCHMIDHUBER
www.schmidhuber.de

Established in 1984, Schmidhuber is a Munich-based design studio that specialises in brand-specific architectural solutions. With a team of over 70 architects, interior designers and designers the studio implements visionary concepts and moving brand experiences for trade shows, exhibitions, events, shops and showrooms. Openness, respect and reliability are the main pillars of the studio's successful cooperation with its international client base, fostering a continuous redefinition of and refreshing approach to each new project.

P.116, 120, 124, 166

SIMPLE
www.simple.de

Simple specialises in spatial and media communication. Staged spatial experiences such as exhi-bition booths and showrooms are as an important part of its portfolio as multimedia interactions and virtual spaces. With a core team of 20 and a large network of specialists, simple serves clients from industry, business and the public sector. Felix Hansen and Andreas Salsamendi have been the company's managing partners since the company's foundation in 2000.

P.076

SPACE4
www.space4.de

Space4 operates at the crossovers between architecture, museum design and exhibition planning. For Space4, design is not an end in itself. Instead, it is an ambas-sador – a medium which can be experienced with all the senses, and which connects visitors, space and content. Since its estab-lishment in 2000, the studio, with its specialised team of archi-tects, interior designers and designers, has successfully realised more than 150 projects for public and private clients.

P.034, 334

STUDIO DEGA
www.studiodega.ru

Studio Dega was founded in 2002 by Boris Demin. The studio specialises in designing and constructing exclusive exhibition stands, and also designs and produces the modular exhibition system Infinityconst. Key priorities of the company include creative modern design, construction quality and long-term partnerships with clients.

P.036

STUDIOMFD
www.studiomfd.nl

Studiomfd was founded in 2006 by Martijn Frank Dirks. The 3-member team works in Amsterdam under the motto 'Forms speak louder than words'. Forms and designs reveal the tiniest detail of the character of a company or brand. This way studiomfd puts forward what exactly distinguishes a certain client from others who practice the same profession. Moreover studiomfd designs always boost function and usage. By doing so, the clients customers always know immediately who and what they are dealing with and can be served even better.

P.072

TOKUJIN YOSHIOKA
www.tokujin.com

Tokujin Yoshioka established Tokujin Yoshioka Inc. in 2000. His ethereal works transcend the boundaries of product design, architecture and exhibition design, and are highly evaluated as art. Many of his works are displayed as part of permanent collections in renowned museums including Museum of Modern Art (MoMA), Victoria and Albert Museum, Cooper Hewitt National Design Museum and Vitra Design Museum. He was selected by the Japanese edition of Newsweek as one of the '100 most respected Japanese by the world'.

P.366

UEBERHOLZ
www.ueberholz.de

Established in 1987, Ueberholz is led by architect and communication designer Nico Ueberholz. The firm is fascinated by creating places for encounters, with the aim of establishing and supporting processes of communication. With expertise in the fields of trade fair and exhibition design Ueberholz also develops concepts for event services, retail construction and music architecture.

P.078, 332

UNIPLAN
www.uniplan.com

Uniplan is a leading agency for live communication and creates brand promotions for events, trade fairs, showrooms and road shows. Uniplan's clients include renowned companies and brands such as adidas, Audi, BMW, Daimler, Deutsche Bahn, Deutsche Post DHL, Sony PlayStation, Toshiba and ZDF. The company has a team of 800 employees across its 13 branches worldwide.

P.082, 126, 274

VOIDPLANNING
www.voidplanning.kr

VOIDplanning is a Seoul-based interior design studio. Founded in 1997 by Shinjae Kang and Heeyoung Choi the studio has become renowned for its design approach that integrates Korean traditions in creative ways. Its diverse, award-winning portfolio of work encompasses hospitality, retail, corporate and exhibition design.

P.174

VON M
www.vonm.de

VON M was established in 2004 by Matthias Siegert, who leads the practice together with Myriam Kunz and Dennis Mueller. The studio's expertise spans architecture and communication design, its diverse portfolio of work ranging from construction projects, residential interiors and fair stands to event design and video installations. Characteristic for its work is an open-minded and unbiased approach. The tension and crossover between architecture and interiors and a strong context-based approach drives the practice.

P.240, 300

VPPR ARCHITECTS
www.vppr.co.uk

vPPR Architects is an award-winning practice based in East London that has gained recognition for its striking and theatrical proposals. The practice designs residential, retail and cultural projects in the UK, USA, China and Russia. Its work aims to strengthen communities through the creation of distinctive and beautiful places, and takes inspiration from the crossover between art and architecture. It was founded in 2009 by Tatiana von Preussen, Catherine Pease and Jessica Reynolds.

P.066

WALBERT-SCHMITZ
www.walbert-schmitz.de

Walbert-Schmitz was established in 1966 and is a family-owned company based in Aachen. Specialising in exhibition and stand construction, the firm offers a wide range of expertise in the field of three-dimensional brand communication – strategy, conception, design and architecture – as well as in production, installation and dismantling. The company employs more than 100 members of staff and maintains worldwide partnerships with specialised suppliers.

P. 102, 114, 256, 364

WERKSTATT 65
www.werkstatt65.nl

Alex Sijpesteijn and Bas de Graaf joined forces in 2009 to establish Werkstatt 65. Based in Haarlem, the Netherlands, the studio works mainly in the field of spatial design for lifestyle-based clients. The duo's strength lies in the translation of a brand's DNA into authentic and atmospheric spatial experiences. An independent, nonconformist and playful approach characterises their work.

P.010

WHITEVOID
www.whitevoid.com

Whitevoid operates at the crossovers between art, design, architecture and technology. Founded in 2004 by Christopher Bauder, the multidisciplinary studio realises large-scale art and design pieces and environments. Whitevoid comprises specialists in interaction, media and product design as well as interior architecture and electronic engineering. Its projects focus on the translation of bits and bytes into objects and environments and vice versa. Space, object, sound and interaction form key elements of all works.

P.376, 380

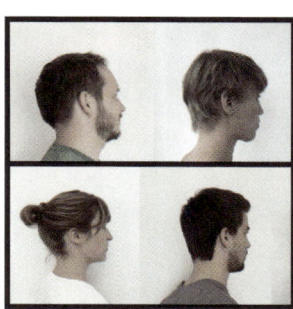

WROOM
www.wroom.co

Wroom was founded in 2012 in Stuttgart. The studio comprises a young team working at the interface between architecture, product design and visual communication. Its aim is to develop individual and unusual solutions through interdisciplinary work and conceptual approaches.

P.226

CREDITS

GRAND STAND 5
Design for Trade Fair Stands

PUBLISHER
Frame Publishers

EDITOR
Sarah de Boer-Schultz

AUTHOR
Jeanne Tan

GRAPHIC DESIGNERS
Barbara Iwanicka (Frame)
Studio Mariëlle van Genderen

PREPRESS
Edward de Nijs

PRINTING
Talleres Gráficos Soler

TRADE DISTRIBUTION USA AND CANADA
Consortium Book Sales & Distribution, LLC.
34 Thirteenth Avenue NE, Suite 101
Minneapolis, MN 55413-1007
T +1 612 746 2600
T +1 800 283 3572 (orders)
F +1 612 746 2606

TRADE DISTRIBUTION BENELUX
Frame Publishers
Laan der Hesperiden 68
1076 DX Amsterdam
the Netherlands
distribution@frameweb.com
frameweb.com

TRADE DISTRIBUTION REST OF WORLD
Thames & Hudson Ltd
181A High Holborn
London WC1V 7QX
United Kingdom
T +44 20 7845 5000
F +44 20 7845 5050

ISBN: 978-94-91727-55-9

The Koninklijke Bibliotheek lists this publication in the Nederlandse Bibliografie: detailed bibliographic information is available on the internet at http://picarta.pica.nl

Printed on acid-free paper produced from chlorine-free pulp. TCF ∞
Printed in Spain

987654321